THE ATLAS OF
Medieval
Man

THE ATLAS OF
Medieval Man
COLIN PLATT

St. Martin's Press
New York

The Atlas of Medieval Man was edited and designed by
Dorling Kindersley Limited

First published in Great Britain in 1979 by
Macmillan London Limited

ISBN 0-312-11549-0

Library of Congress Cataloguing-in-Publication Data available on request

Printed in Hong Kong

ABOVE Self-portrait in sandstone by Nicholas Gerhaert, c.1465
HALF-TITLE PAGE *The Death of Judas* on a capital from Autun Cathedral, France, 12th century
TITLE PAGE French miniature from *Girart de Roussillon*, 1448
FRONT COVER Window in the north triforium at Canterbury Cathedral, England, 13th century
BACK COVER Figures from the south portal of Chartres Cathedral, France, 13th century

Contents

Introduction

Every reader who opens this book will have questions to ask about its plan. What determined originally the overall period, and how can this justly be described as "medieval"? What is the validity of a century-by-century division which employs, even for those areas untouched by Christianity, a Christian dating system? Why compare art over the whole span of the world when certain regions, through all these years, were unaware of each other's existence?

These were the questions we faced ourselves, and the reader may judge, now that the book is before him, how successful we have been with our answers. Nevertheless, it might be useful if I were to say something more here, by way of introduction, about what we have been trying to do. Of course we recognize that the adjective "medieval" is not universally applicable. Nobody could describe Sung China in the eleventh century as "medieval" in the same sense as the word might be used of contemporary societies in the West. But "medieval", for all that, is the term most of us employ to identify this period in our history. We have used it here purely as a period label, implying no judgment on these cultures.

Even as a period, it might still be argued, we have assigned to the Middle Ages a somewhat unorthodox span. We have begun them at the end of the first Christian millennium (rather later than most would have started them), and have cut them off short at 1500 (which is earlier, certainly, than many medievalists would now allow). However, the millennial year has its own clear attractions as a starting-point, not least because contemporaries themselves viewed it so. One of these, Raul Glaber (Rudolf the Bald), a Cluniac monk who died in about 1046, remarked on the great building programmes that were launched in Europe (especially in Italy and France) immediately following AD 1000.

LEFT *Sculptures on the central portal gable, from the west front of Rheims Cathedral, France, c. 1240*

ABOVE *Initial P with* Elijah in the Court of Fire, *from the Winchester Bible, England, 1170-80*

"It was as if", he wrote, "the whole earth, having cast off the old by shaking itself, were clothing itself everywhere in the white robe of the church." Of the new church buildings to which Glaber referred, many are with us still. They make a logical beginning to the discussion of Western European Romanesque.

If there are good reasons for starting at AD 1000, especially in the Christian West, the choice of 1500 as the end of our period is easier still to explain. By convention, the Middle Ages were on the wane in the West during the fifteenth century, if not before. And although this waning was so prolonged that medievalists have since been tempted to claim much of the sixteenth century as their own, the traditional break between medieval and early-modern remains generally acceptable at round about 1500. Later, in our discussion of the Italian Renaissance, of the technological revolution of the fifteenth century, and of the earliest European voyages of discovery, we shall see why this is so. Here it is enough to say that the discovery of the Americas in 1492, closely followed by the first circumnavigation of the globe, challenged so many of man's earlier beliefs that he could never thereafter be the same. If the world remained divided after 1500, it was not (as it had been right through to that point) because half of it had still to be discovered.

It would have been a curious chance if both the beginning and the end of the period we had chosen had worked equally well throughout the world, and, of course, they did not always do so. In India, tantalizingly, the best art belongs either to the centuries before 1000 or to the period of Mughal ascendancy that began with Akbar in 1556. In African art, the year 1000 has no significance, although 1500, with the arrival of the Portuguese on the West African coast, undoubtedly has more meaning. In China, whereas the beginning of our period coincides reasonably happily with the consolidation of the new Sung supremacy, its end merely slices the Ming in two. Nevertheless, for many areas beyond the Catholic West, these five hundred years have a perhaps surprising unity. For Orthodox Russia, they take us from what is often seen as the beginning of Russian art, on the reception of Christianity by Vladimir of Kiev, through to the late-fifteenth-century consolidation of Muscovite power under

LEFT *Detail from tomb of Edward II (d. 1327), in Gloucester Cathedral, England, 1330-5*

ABOVE LEFT *The Angel Choir of Lincoln Cathedral, England, 1256-80*

ABOVE RIGHT *A siege-tower from De Re Militari, a Latin text on military technology printed by Johannes of Verona in 1472*

Ivan III, grand duke of Moscow and the first all-Russian tsar. Islam, in the mid-eleventh century, was brought to life again by the fiercely religious Seljuk Turks, to end our period with the Ottomans triumphantly in the ascendant. For the Americas, the arrival of the Spaniards round about 1500 was as much a new beginning for this undiscovered continent as it was for the old Europe that they left.

There is, then, a clear logic in our selection of these centuries for discussion. But half-a-millennium is a long space of time, and it clearly required subdivision. Over the world as a whole, it hardly needs saying, there is no political, economic, or cultural sequence that is convincingly universal in its application. If there had been, it would have been obviously preferable for chapter divisions to a breakdown by centuries. Yet the conventional century division has, after all, its uses. For one thing, we are all thoroughly familiar with it; it has become part of our culture. For another, this particular dating system has been employed by both cultural and political historians over a very long time, with the result that much that is otherwise very imprecisely dated has been assigned to a century span. There was nothing to be gained by abandoning a system which, with all its faults, was still preferable to any alternative.

Inevitably, the break between centuries has sometimes fallen awkwardly for us, presenting serious problems of assignation. A large building may take decades to complete, and if, like Durham Cathedral, it is begun in one century and finished in the next, there will be difficulties, obviously, in placing it. In the case of Durham, begun in 1093, we have shown the cathedral as an eleventh-century building, for it is to that century, more than to the next, that this great monument of Anglo-Norman architectural ambition undoubtedly belongs in spirit. With similar buildings and other works of art, it has been our usual practice to take the starting date as the determinant of where, on our maps, they should be shown. However, we have been careful not to apply rules of this kind too inflexibly. It is perfectly true, for example, that the magnificent miniatures of Jean de Berry's *Très Riches Heures* belong in date to the early fifteenth century. Yet the buildings they depict are of late-fourteenth-century construction, and it is surely right, for this reason alone, to illustrate these masterpieces of International Gothic in the context to which essentially they relate.

LEFT *Detail of the decoration on the Temple of Heaven, Peking, China, 15th century*

ABOVE LEFT *Figures lining the road leading to the Bayon, Angkor Thom, Cambodia, 12th century*

ABOVE RIGHT *The Monastery Church at Voronet in Rumania, 15th century*

One further subdivision of the text seemed useful. In each of the five century chapters of the book, we have made a distinction between what we have called the "Historical Context", and the "Material Culture" from which we have drawn the bulk of our illustrations. The one is to be seen as the introduction to the next, and some repetition between the two is inevitable. But these repetitions themselves merely serve to underline what I take to be the principal lesson of this book—the near-absolute dependence of art, at least in the Middle Ages, on the patrons and the events that nurtured it. Clearly, a major purpose of a book of this design is quite simply to inform us of what happened concurrently with what else. And for many readers, such will be the chief reason for possessing it. Yet, for myself, what has continued to interest me most have been the links that built up between disparate arts, as politics, religion, or a charismatic individual imposed some new pattern upon them. This, indeed, is my answer to the third of the questions with which I began my introduction. Comparisons do not always work; and why should they? But when they do, they can be the father to significant historical insights.

In writing this book over so generous a field, the problems of selection have proved formidable. And they would have been worse had I not had the benefit of so much specialist opinion, already available in print. Two distinguished authorities upon whom I have found myself to be more than usually dependent have been George Zarnecki (on Western Romanesque) and Cyril Mango (on the architecture of Byzantium). But there have been others, including Laurence Sickman (on Chinese painting), Gordon Willey (on the arts of the Americas), Bernard Lewis (on Islam), Benjamin Rowland and Percy Brown (on the art and architecture of India), and George Heard Hamilton (on Russia), without whose works I would have been lost indeed. To these and many others may I express my gratitude, with the hope that I have interpreted them correctly.

My other great debt is to those on the staff of Dorling Kindersley, who have been the real architects of the volume in the final form in which it is presented to the reader. Any author, in such a work as this, must be continuously dependent on the skill and ingenuity of a team of designers and editors. I have been exceptionally lucky in mine.

Finally, I dedicate this book to my wife, Valerie, and to our children, Emma, Miles, Tabitha, and Theo. They have benefited, as I have, from our confrontation with the arts of the world.

LEFT *Carvings on the temple of Devi Jagadambi, Khajuraho, central India, 11th century*

ABOVE LEFT *Detail of geometric woodwork from the Mosque of Ibn Hulun, Cairo, Egypt, 14th century*

ABOVE RIGHT *Shell gorget engraved with complex religious images, made by the Mississippians of North America, c. 1300–1500*

The Eleventh Century

Map of the world
This 11th-century world map shows how sketchy geographical knowledge then was. Unknown areas are generally presumed to be land rather than sea— a misconception that would persist for another 500 years.

Historical Context

In the year 1000 the world could be said to divide between the ancient continuities of civilizations like China and India, and the profound changes that were beginning to be experienced by, among others, the re-awakening societies of the Christian West. It was not that the old civilizations lacked vigour of their own, or that progress was restricted to the new. On the contrary, China under the Northern Sung had never been more dynamic. But the transmission of cultures across the world was as yet thoroughly imperfect, only religion, as a rare exception, crossing barriers of race. Some of China's technological brilliance would percolate through to the West during the course of the eleventh century. However, the passing-on between seafarers of an idea like the compass was little more than an accident of their profession. The complete failure of the technology of printing to make the same journey underlines the isolation of the world's societies at this time, an isolation which would persist for another five hundred years.

Nowhere was this isolation more complete than in the continents of Africa and America. The territories in North and North-East Africa, known to the Romans and now dominated by Islam, belonged still to an essentially Mediterranean civilization. But south of the Sahara, Arab penetration had only just begun in the eleventh century. Beyond the desert, there flourished empires that had already existed for several centuries—in ancient Ghana, for example, and along the West African coast. On the East Coast, Arab trading stations, with some contacts at least in the interior, were established in the tenth century or earlier. However, the travellers' tales and the geographers' descriptions which, in later Arab literature, become such an important source for the history of Africa before the period of European contact, were still thin or non-existent in the eleventh century, while even archaeology, though the evidence is accumulating, has very little in this century to offer.

As for the Americas, there are stories, hard to confirm, of a Scandinavian presence in North America, with such shadowy figures as the adventurer Leif Ericsson penetrating to Nova Scotia as early as 1003. But the extraordinary and entirely individual cultures of Central and South America remained completely unaware of, and unknown to, Western Europe until the pioneering journeys of Christopher Columbus and his predatory successors, Cortes and Pizarro. For many years even Columbus himself refused to believe that such cultures could exist.

The full flowering of the Mesoamerican civilizations—the so-called ''Classic'' period of the great Mexican cities of Monte Albán and Teotihuacán, and of the more southerly temple culture of the Maya—had in fact occurred as much as a thousand years before the arrival of Columbus. Before the beginning of the eleventh century, these civilizations, together with the related Huari Empire of Peru, one after another had been overthrown. However, the cultures replacing them, although differing in emphasis, continued the now powerful indigenous traditions. The Toltecs of Tula and Chichén Itzá, in Central America, and the Peruvian Chimu of Chanchan both established new traditions in the eleventh century; aristocratic societies, as their predecessors had been, they were dominated and even oppressed by religion. And so strong were the beliefs and the associated religious practices of Classic Mesoamerica that they penetrated far to the north: to the Hohokam of Arizona and the Mississippian of the South Mississippi Valley, as well as less certainly to the Anasazi *pueblo*-builders of Colorado. A centralized, hierarchical organization characterized these societies, separating them very clearly from the migratory hunter-gatherer peoples who inhabited the further north, the south, and the east of the Americas.

In general, civilizations throughout the world had flourished most securely under the stimulus of large-scale and permanent settlement—the bigger, for this purpose, the better. They had been weakest when the units of government were very small. There was nothing small about contemporary China. Under its T'ang emperors from the seventh to the early tenth centuries, China had reached its maximum extent, stretching west across Central Asia and south into present-day Vietnam. Gradually the T'ang had been pushed back, losing Central Asia before the end of the eighth century to the might of Islam, and simultaneously suffering a setback in South-East Asia at the hands of

PREVIOUS PAGE
Dilwara Temple, Mt Abu, India
This Jain temple, built in the late 10th or early 11th century, is one of a complex of sanctuaries on Mt Abu in Rajputana. The lavish white marble interiors, embellished with exotic carvings, make the group of temples one of the architectural marvels of medieval India.

China in the 11th century

Fifty years of anarchy followed the collapse of the T'ang dynasty in the 10th century. By the 11th century China had been stabilized under two rival empires—the Sung, who reunited the central and southern provinces and established a central government at Kaifeng; and the Khitan Liao, who retained their independence in the provinces of the extreme north.

China 960–1127

☐ *Sung Dynasty*   ▨ *Liao Empire*

the Thai kings of Nan-chao. However, the empire that the Sung inherited in the rising of 960, reuniting its provinces after half a century of anarchy (The Five Dynasties and the Ten Kingdoms 907-60), was still immensely large. With its population concentrated in the more fertile regions of South China, in particular the Yangtze valley, and with the development of Sung overseas trade, the empire was also increasingly sophisticated and rich.

One consequence of the T'ang collapse had been to leave North China open to the invasion of barbarian horsemen from the frozen regions of Mongolia and Manchuria, beyond the Great Wall of China. It was these Khitan warriors who established, with the help of their subject Chinese peoples, the rival empire of the Liao (947-1125) in the north. But the continuing force of Chinese leadership over this quarter of the globe meant that the Chinese tradition, both in government and culture, was readily taken over by the Liao. It was just as influential on the Koryo rulers of contemporary Korea and, through the T'ang inheritance, also affected the Fujiwara regents of Japan.

The importance of the Fujiwara family at the Japanese imperial court at Kyoto had begun in the ninth century, and lasted, in one form or another, for over a thousand years. Kyoto itself had been laid out as a new capital, then called Heian, by the Emperor Kammu (781-806). Subsequently the Fujiwara regency coincided almost exactly with the effective survival of Kyoto as capital, from Kammu's move there in 794 until Minamoto no Yoritomo's designation of a fresh capital in 1185 at Kamakura, near the modern metropolis of Tokyo. Japanese culture of this so-called Heian period developed distinctive characteristics of its own, under the enlightened patronage of a wealthy and sophisticated aristocracy. The multiple cultural borrowings from T'ang China were absorbed, assimilated, and transformed into an art and a life-style that were now characteristically Japanese. Nevertheless, Japan remained securely within the Chinese cultural hegemony. The countries of South-East Asia on the other hand, where the T'ang never penetrated, contemporaneously fell under Indian influence. The two spheres touched as a result of sharing a common religion in Buddhism, but rarely in any material sense did they coincide.

In fact, South-East Asia continued to exhibit characteristically hybrid tendencies in religion. Burma and Cambodia, its leading powers from the eleventh to the thirteenth century, were both Hindu and Buddhist. For example, Pagan in Burma was more Buddhist than Hindu, and Angkor in Cambodia, with its celebrated temples, was always more obviously Hindu. For each religion the source was India, and for both countries Indian dominance was further guaranteed by the decline into insignificance of its only possible rival. This was the once great Shrivijaya maritime empire of Sumatra and Java, itself culturally a part of Greater India.

As had been the case with China, India's cultural hegemony was not limited to the period of its greatest political dominance. The Indian subcontinent had long been divided among warring principalities, with empires of comparatively brief duration like those of the Gupta, in the fourth and fifth centuries, and Sri Harsha, over almost the same area of north and central India, in the seventh. But alongside the military competition of successive rulers, and often encouraged by their political ambitions, the trade of Indian merchants had continued to expand, penetrating westwards across the Arabian Sea to Persia and Egypt, as well as eastwards through the whole of South-East Asia. These merchants took their faiths, both Buddhist and Hindu, to all those regions not already under the grip of Islam. To South-East Asia, in particular, they took

Gods and teachers

Islam alone stands out among the world religions as being unwilling to portray its god. For the Christians, although God himself was rarely shown in 11th-century art, Christ was always an acceptable subject, most commonly displayed in poses of dignity and majesty, as in the Christ Pantocrator mosaic at Daphni. Other religions chose to emphasize the qualities particularly revered by their faithful —the serenity of the Hindu Jain teacher (the *Tirthamkara*) of the Mount Abu shrines in India, or the discipline of the Toltec soldier in the great free-standing figures of Tula, in Mexico. There are few sharper contrasts in religious images than that between the solemn and rigid Buddha figure of King Kyanzittha's Ananda Temple at Pagan and the almost grotesque vigour of the Siva Nataraja, the Lord of the Dance, a familiar Hindu image from southern India. Yet Buddhism and Hinduism had originally existed side-by-side on the Indian subcontinent.

Hindu Chola bronze of Siva Nataraja (the Lord of the Dance)

FACING PAGE
One of four Buddhas in the Ananda Temple, Pagan, Burma

Tirthamkara, or Jain teacher, in the Vimala Sha Temple, Mt Abu, India

Mosaic of Christ Pantocrator in the dome of the church at Daphni, Greece

Toltec warrior-god, Tula, Mexico

19

the original fundamentalist Hinayana Buddhism, which before the eleventh century had begun to be replaced in the Indian homeland by the more relaxed Mahayana ("Great Vehicle") Buddhist persuasion of the Amida Buddha, an eclectic cocktail of different beliefs borrowed from many faiths. Hinayana (also known as Theravada) Buddhism became an important instrument in the mid-eleventh-century unification of Burma under its ruler Anoratha (1044-77). It reinforced such trading and cultural links as already existed with the Theravada cult centre in Ceylon.

Buddhism is known to have been favoured by Suryavarman I (1002-50), the rebuilder of Khmer power in Cambodia. But he was not to displace the indigenous cult of the god-king which his great ninth-century predecessor Jayavarman II (802-50) had done so much to build up. Neither did he shake the grip of Hindu Shaivism, the cult of Siva, which, in its principal homeland in southern India, was still the dominant faith. This characteristically Cambodian mingling of the faiths, which took some while yet to yield to the supremacy of Hinayana Buddhism, was no longer the experience of India herself where religion, increasingly, was dictating political alignments. In the southern half of the Indian subcontinent, the Tamil-speaking Chola, devotees of Siva, were building a Hindu

The religions of South-East Asia
In the 11th century the subcontinent of South-East Asia was under the cultural and political influence of India. India's two major religions— Hinduism and Buddhism —were brought to South-East Asia by merchants, and in some countries, such as Burma and Cambodia, they came to exist side by side.

Hinduism and Buddhism in the 11th century

Hinayana Buddhism	*Hindu Shaivism*

empire which brought them into conflict with the Theravada Buddhist rulers of Ceylon. In the north, the exactly contemporary early-eleventh-century Muslim raids of Mahmud of Ghazni, although no more than a series of plundering excursions brought to an end by Mahmud's death in 1030, introduced the rich religious capitals of northern India to the peril of an iconoclastic Islam.

Islam at this time was preoccupied with setting its own house in order. Its great initial period of expansion, which had begun shortly after the Prophet's death in 632, was already long passed by the time the Abbasid caliphs, formerly rulers of a united Islam, were reduced in 936 to a merely nominal suzerainty. In their place, the Samanid rulers of Persia, the Fatimids of Egypt, and the Umayyad caliphs of Spain preserved and even extended an Islamic civilization which, though brilliant still, was now essentially divided. However, in the 1030s a new era was opening in which spiritual regeneration and political conquest went hand in hand, their instruments in the West being the Almoravid reformers of North Africa and Spain, in the East the Seljuk conquerors of Abbasid Baghdad and Byzantine Anatolia, a Turkish steppeland people originating in Central Asia.

The regeneration of Islam posed an immediate and a very disturbing threat to the Christian peoples of the western world. It is to the eleventh century, in particular, that the concept of the "Holy War" belongs, and much of the geography of the Mediterranean world would be rewritten in the name of religion. Before the Council of Clermont and Pope Urban II's preaching of the First Crusade in 1095, other crusading initiatives against Islam in Spain and in Sicily had led to the recovery for the Christian faith of substantial territories formerly part of Christendom. Folk heroes like Rodrigo Diaz de Vivar (El Cid), conqueror of Valencia in 1094, would become part of the legend. But the successes of Christianity in the long-drawn-out *Reconquista* of Spain in the West were matched, and in area greatly exceeded, by Seljuk conquests in the Near East. It was the good fortune of Islam that these Central Asian nomad conquerors should have come to their task already converted to the Muslim faith. Seljuk sultans, captains of the "men of the sword", took the supreme position in a

Council of Clermont, 1095
The recovery of Islam and the threat it posed to Christendom in the Eastern Mediterranean led Pope Urban II to proclaim the First Crusade at the Council of Clermont. Four years later his initiative was rewarded by the capture of Jerusalem.

Alexius I Comnenus
Alexius Comnenus, Byzantine emperor (1081-1118), was successful in his appeal to Pope Urban II for help against the Turks.

Byzantine coin
Known as a numisma, *this gold Byzantine coin was in use between 1042 and 1055.*

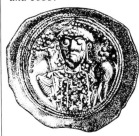

politico-religious order which still found a place for the Abbasid caliphs and which, more importantly, made use of the existing economic infrastructure of the Near Eastern states they dominated. What the Seljuks gave Islam was purpose and a new vitality. What they threatened to snatch from Christendom was Byzantium, still its most glittering jewel.

In 1071, the Seljuk victory over the Byzantines at Manzikert, in Armenia, and their almost simultaneous capture of Jerusalem from the Fatimid caliphs of Egypt, set Christendom by the ears. The consequent loss of the bulk of Byzantine Anatolia to the Seljuks, and the substitution at Jerusalem of a regime less tolerant than the Fatimids to Christian pilgrimage, provided the impulse for the Crusades. And although these were always less important in the general context of Islam than they have seemed to historians of the West, their religious significance, both at that time and later, was undoubtedly very great. For almost two centuries, the Christian principalities of the East Mediterranean coastline were to remain a lance in the side of Islam, being among the chief causes of the growing intolerance displayed by each religion to the other. For Western Europe, moreover, the astonishing success of Pope Urban's initiative, which was crowned by the taking of Jerusalem on 15 July 1099, greatly enhanced the prestige of the papacy at Rome throughout the territories that were traditionally its own, encouraging it further in its private war with the Orthodox patriarchate of Byzantium.

Not so very long before, Orthodox Christianity had achieved one of its most significant coups in the conversion, from the late tenth century, of a still largely pagan Russia. But this should be seen in the context of a long-standing and increasingly bitter division between Catholic and Orthodox which was coming to a head in about the year 1000 over a large part of northern and central Europe. Already, in the second half of the ninth

Mosaics and wall-paintings

The decoration of Christian churches with devotional
paintings and mosaics had become common practice in
both Orthodox and Catholic lands well before the
opening of the 11th century. The most sophisticated
work in this tradition was still being carried out by the
painters and mosaicists of the Byzantine Empire. They
had established a style which reasserted the confidence
of the early years of Christianity, and which was
therefore welcomed as much for its religious
connotations as for its evident technical perfection.
Byzantine influence is clearly visible in the late-11th-
century wall-paintings from the Italian church of
S. Angelo in Formis, and from the Austrian abbey
church at Lambach. Similarly, the mosaics and wall-
paintings of newly Orthodox Kievan Russia were
almost wholly Byzantine in their inspiration, deriving
ultimately from such models as the mosaics in the
important pilgrimage church of Hosios Loukas, in
Greece itself, dating from the first half of the
11th century.

FACING PAGE
Wall-painting of angel,
S. Angelo in Formis, Italy

Adoration of the Magi, *ceiling-painting, Abbey Church, Lambach, Austria*

Apse mosaic of apostle, St Sophia, Kiev, Russia   Daniel in the Lions' Den, *mosaic, Hosios Loukas, Greece*

23

Prince Vladimir of Kiev
Vladimir's adoption of Orthodox Christianity in 988 led to the conversion of his Kievan subjects and, in due course, of all Russia.

century, the Balkans had been won for Orthodoxy. Simultaneously, however, Frankish missionaries had been taking the Catholic persuasion to the Germans, establishing a momentum that would carry them up into Scandinavia by the late tenth century, with Poland accepting Catholicism in 966 and Hungary in 1001.

Just as the Orthodox patriarch of Constantinople achieved new status with the accession of the Balkans and Russia to his faith, so the Catholic bishop, or pope, at Rome gained authority from the leadership he could now claim to exert over his swollen territories in central and eastern Europe. Inevitably, the two jurisdictions met in a conflict which, at Constantinople in 1054, widened into intractable schism. There were many attempts after this date to bring the churches together, not least in the naturally ecumenical setting of the crusader cities of Palestine and Syria. But the fact was that Orthodoxy belonged, in the main, to a declining civilization on the exposed frontier with Islam, whereas Roman Catholicism through these vital centuries had every advantage of growth.

Originally influential in attracting the Russians to Orthodoxy had been the brilliance of imperial Byzantium. Indeed, when Prince Vladimir of Kiev forced through the reception of Christianity in Russia, the Byzantine Empire under Basil II (976-1025) had rarely been greater or more prosperous. But Basil's Byzantine "renewal" was an illusion, and his empire, very soon after his death, suffered a serious eclipse. In this process the Seljuk victory at Manzikert in 1071 was instrumental, followed as it was by the loss to the Byzantine Empire of the Anatolian plateau. This was still by no means the

end of Byzantium. A new period of regeneration began with the Comneni emperors, although even their cunning was not enough to heal the divisions that weakened Byzantine society. Alexius I Comnenus (1081-1118) himself witnessed the permanent settlement of Norman adventurers in the traditional Byzantine territories of southern Italy, and their initial assaults on Greece. The survival of Byzantium had come to be determined by forces beyond its control.

Among these, the Normans were at one and the same time plunderers of the Byzantine empire and some of its most effective mercenaries. And there were few indeed in contemporary Europe who were untouched by these extraordinary adventurers. It had been Vikings in the ninth century who, through the building-up of the principalities of Novgorod, Smolensk and Kiev, and the opening of the trade routes to the South, had begun the awakening of Russia. And the Normans, settled in north-west France from the mid-ninth century and of similar Scandinavian stock, left their mark on the West.

A good part of the success of the Scandinavian settlement can be explained in terms of the quite unusual adaptability of the Vikings and their heirs. It had not been long before the Swedish (Varangian) rulers of Kiev were slavicized. Neither were the Normans, after settlement in Normandy, readily distinguishable from the Franks. Nevertheless, they retained a network of dynastic loyalties that gave their further expansion in eleventh-century Europe exceptional coherence and drive. The Norman magnates who led the invasions of England and Sicily, who fought the Byzantines in southern Italy and Greece, and who took a prominent part in the crusades against Islam, were well known to each other and were often closely related. Everywhere, the states they established continued to exhibit a strong family resemblance, seen especially, perhaps, in the characteristic Norman ability to recognize and preserve what was useful. What the Normans could appropriate of the wool of England, the gold of Africa (just now beginning to be exploited by Arab traders), and the silks and spices of the East, they did. Yet Domesday Book, that unprecedented compilation by which a Norman conqueror sought to determine the resources he could now call his own, was the work very

Christianity in Europe
In the 10th and 11th centuries Catholicism, emanating from Rome, advanced through Germany, Scandinavia and Spain, and Orthodoxy, emanating from Constantinople, spread into Bulgaria and Russia. The two Christian persuasions vied for the allegiance of the Balkans.

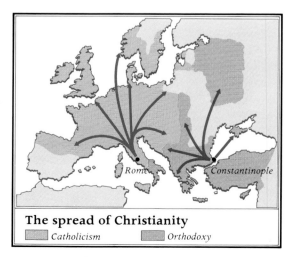

The spread of Christianity
☐ Catholicism   ☐ Orthodoxy

The Norman expansion

The late 11th century was the period of greatest expansion for the Normans. By 1100, they had settled in England, Sicily and southern Italy. These conquests were largely by sea, in vessels such as the one above (from the Bayeux Tapestry). This sea-going tradition was inherited from their Viking ancestors.

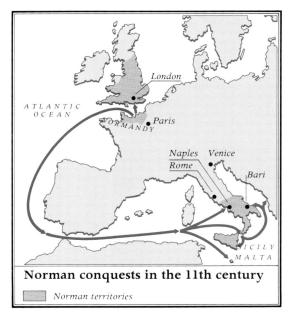

Norman conquests in the 11th century

▨ *Norman territories*

Pope Gregory VII

The Norman presence in southern Italy was influential in the election of the monk Hildebrand to the papacy as Gregory VII in 1073. A reforming pope, he sought to prevent the interference of the State in Church matters.

Domesday Book
Compiled in 1087 at the direction of William the Conqueror, the Domesday Book was a record of land-holding in Anglo-Norman England. It was largely the work of English clerks trained in the Anglo-Saxon tradition.

largely of English clerks trained-up in pre-conquest Anglo-Saxon traditions. In Sicily, Count Roger used a Saracen bureaucracy to help him govern his dominions.

Inevitably, the geographical spread of Norman interests associated their leaders with events in the Church which were happening either within or alongside their dominions. From comparatively early in the eleventh century the Normans were sponsoring ecclesiastical reform in Normandy itself. Shortly after the conquest of England in 1066, they brought reform to the reluctant English with the appointment in 1070 of Lanfranc as archbishop of Canterbury, in place of the discredited Stigand. Three years later, the monk Hildebrand was elected as Pope Gregory VII (1073-85), and the Normans from their vantage point in southern Italy found themselves taking sides in the great struggle between Empire and Papacy (Henry IV of Germany on one side, the newly elected pope on the other). After Henry's short-lived submission at Canossa in 1077 and his return to Rome as conqueror in 1083-4, it was the Norman Robert Guiscard who expelled the Germans in the name of Gregory but who

went on to sack the city. With friends like those, the pope might have asked, what need has a man of enemies?

These were bold times for the Church, and they were far from being altogether destructive. A century and more before Rome itself was sacked, the Church had taken the lead in the promotion of peace movements designed to turn the energies of the feudal classes away from internal rivalries and towards a pagan foe. And great programmes of ecclesiastical building ante-dated the reforms of the 1070s— at the cathedrals of Bamberg, for example, beginning in 1007, of Strasbourg from about 1015, of Basel and Trier from 1019, and at the Abbey of Westminster (Edward the Confessor's extravagant tomb-church and reliquary) from approximately 1050 to 1065.

As the Church advanced on many fronts, wealth and new buildings accumulated along the line of the pilgrimage roads, chief among these the road to the cathedral at Santiago de Compostela, rebuilt at the end of the eleventh century, having been sacked by the Moors in 997. The late-eleventh-century rebuilding of the abbey church at Cluny was financed by Spanish *Reconquista* money, won from Islam in the subjugation of Spain by Alfonso, conqueror of Toledo. And works such as those at Cluny, inspiring emulation in some and a puritanical reaction in others, assisted the birth of the many new monastic orders, the key to which was wealth.

The essential precondition for the generation of wealth was there already in a trans-global population ascent. As true of Sung China as it was of Kievan Russia and of Western Europe in general, the population surge of the new millennium opened fresh markets and restored old trades, being characterized everywhere by land clearance and the building of towns. Satisfactory explanations have yet to be found for both the extent and the nature of this renewal. It had something to do, certainly, with technological advance, with unusually favourable weather conditions (at least in the West), and with the relative insignificance of disease. But however it originated, the overall effect of this population increase was to bring into being a very general revitalization of the economy. To a divided and disordered world, it presented the prospect of a genuine re-birth.

The Normans

The native vigour and military expertise of the Normans recommended them as mercenaries in the many parts of Europe and the Near East which they later took for their own. There were Normans employed in the earlier stages of the Christian reconquest of Spain; they came to England as friends of Edward the Confessor before their invasion of 1066; their annexation of Southern Italy (Apulia and Calabria) and conquest of Muslim Sicily were prepared by long employment in the South; they were known in Norway, being of Scandinavian stock; and they were present again in considerable strength in the armies of the First Crusade. While not obviously creative themselves, they were nevertheless generous patrons of the arts, with a particular enthusiasm for building. Characteristically, they celebrated their achievements in military sculptures, even at ecclesiastical buildings like the English Church of St Mary and St David at Kilpeck, or at Monreale, the greatest of their Sicilian cathedrals. One of their most notable victories, over Harold of England, was the occasion for the commissioning, a decade or so later, of a great commemorative work—the Bayeux Tapestry. A record of the invasion of England, its antecedents and its sequel, this tapestry is both a valuable historical document and an important masterpiece of 11th-century art.

Tapestry, Baldishol stave church, Hedmark, Norway, c. 1180

BELOW *Detail from the Bayeux Tapestry, c. 1080*

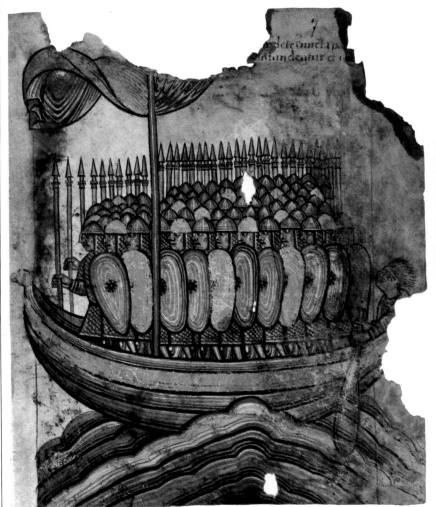

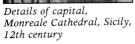

Details of capital,
Monreale Cathedral, Sicily,
12th century

South doorway of church,
Kilpeck, England,
12th century

Manuscript showing Norman soldiers on board ship

Material Culture

Far East

Chinese society was the most sophisticated in the eleventh-century world, just as the Chinese economy was undoubtedly the most highly developed. Chao Kuang-yin, the founder of the Sung dynasty, had come to power in a military coup of 960. And the swollen revenues of the Sung rulers of China introduced an era of cultural brilliance exceptional even in that already advanced civilization. The crowning achievement of the early Sung emperors was to reunify China under a single centralized government with its capital at Kaifeng, the only important exception to this unification being the North Chinese Khitan empire of the Liao. Centralization has its faults, however, and the over-extended civil service of the Sung rulers in due course became notorious for its corruption. Nevertheless, the great armies of the Sung were able to maintain over a century and more a degree of public order such as had not been experienced in China for many generations, this stability being the key to economic progress in the public sector as much as in the private.

Alongside an effective agrarian policy, which extended the existing large-estate system of the late T'ang period and which took the initiative in the reclamation of waste lands, the Sung emperors promoted trading ventures to South-East Asia and beyond. They instituted monopolies, encouraged industrialization, rewarded entrepreneurial initiatives, and imposed systems of selective taxation in keeping with a planned economy unlike anything the world had yet known.

These were the conditions for the development of technology. Sung armies were the first to use gunpowder in warfare, with the earliest known stone-throwing catapults, or trebuchets. Under the Sung, a paper currency was developed; the first navigational compasses were used by Sung ships; printing with movable type immensely increased the circulation of important texts; astronomical instruments were perfected during this period and the first celestial globes were constructed. By 1100, a water-driven mechanical clock had been built at the Liao capital at Peking; the spinning wheel had come into common use in China, and more sophisticated silk-working machinery had been developed.

On that ill-defined frontier between art and craft, pottery technology achieved new perfection under the Northern Sung (as they have come to be called in order to distinguish them from their southern successors after the first Sung collapse of 1126). The classic wares of the Northern Sung were the hard white wares known as Ting and the stonewares called Northern Celadons. In both traditions, the finest specimens were of a quality never later surpassed in Chinese pottery. But what makes these industries of particular interest is the evidence they provide of a highly developed specialization in pottery production, both in the assignment of tasks to individual craftsmen and in the increasing limitation of manufacture to those forms most economically fired and transported, the open and flat wares—bowls, dishes and plates. In due course the introduction of moulding would speed up pottery production even more, allowing the development of a whole new range of shapes, especially for dishes and platters. But as yet this technique was confined to the Liao potters of North China. Early in the twelfth century it would become their most important contribution to the developing pottery technology south of the border with the Sung.

Their taste and achievement in pottery was not the only way in which the Khitan people of the Liao empire demonstrated their artistic independence from their great Chinese neighbour. Devout Buddhists, as the Chinese governing classes increasingly were not, they built their pagodas in a distinctive octagonal shape, further characterized by a sculptural elaboration quite unlike the more severe and restrained work of the Sung. The so-called "Colour of Iron Pagoda" at the

Chinese pottery
Important products of the Northern Sung were the Ting wares, with their fine carved and incised underglaze patterns, and the grey Northern Celadon stonewares, distinguished by their glossy, olive-green glaze.

Northern Celadon wares *Ting ware* *Sung bowl and pot*

**"Colour of Iron Pagoda",
Kaifeng, China**
*This plain stone building,
constructed in the mid-11th
century, is typical of Sung
architecture, which was noted
for its restraint and simplicity,
and its avoidance of sculptural
elaboration.*

Sung capital of Kaifeng contrasts very obviously with the almost contemporary octagonal Liao pagoda at the T'ien-ning temple at Peking. In their use or neglect of sculptural ornamentation, the two belong to entirely separate traditions.

Indeed, the outstanding characteristics of Northern Sung architecture, as of the art of the Sung dynasty in general, were its elegance, its simplicity, and its sophistication, much of which would evaporate in the more baroque taste of twelfth-century China. As was always the case in Chinese art, the sculptors, painters, calligraphers and *literati* of the Sung period looked back to the ancient masters for technique and inspiration, and what they liked in the past was its restraint.

Originality for its own sake was not something that the Chinese painter either sought or admired. The great figure painters had worked under the T'ang in the seventh and eighth centuries, and it was natural enough for the eleventh-century master Li Lung-mien to shape his own style in conscious emulation of theirs. Like the T'ang masters before him, Li Lung-mien frequently chose horses as the subjects for his paintings, although here, as in his other work, he developed a new realism which became in general the hallmark of Northern Sung painting (see pages 30-31). Realism again was the quality sought by Ts'ui Po, the best of the eleventh-century painters of animals, birds and flowers. In landscape painting his contemporary, Kuo Hsi, likewise set up realism as the true ideal, carrying it much further than the great tenth-century landscape painter Li Chêng, on whose style Kuo Hsi had modelled his own.

Such purity of taste and critical understanding were obvious products of a mature society where art could be securely based on the patronage of a discriminating and sophisticated aristocracy. Many of these conditions were similarly present in contemporary Japan during the long supremacy of the Fujiwara regents and the dominance of the great aristocratic families such as their own. Much can be said against such a society. It was introverted, artificial, and given to conspicuous waste. Nevertheless, early in the eleventh century, under Fujiwara Michinaga (966-1027), Japanese culture attained an acknowledged peak. This was the result of ready aristocratic patronage combined with a new emphasis on faith.

Five Horses, *Li Lung-mien*

Clearing Autumn Skies, Mountains and Valleys, *Kuo Hsi*

Chinese painting

Chinese painting in the 11th century was very traditional, looking back for its models to the T'ang period (618-906) when Chinese art had experienced a great flowering. Li Lung-mien's horsemen, for example, have an obvious ancestry in the characteristic T'ang preoccupation with horses. Kuo Hsi's landscapes, on the other hand, belong essentially to a style and class of painting perfected in the 10th century during the troubled period known as the Five Dynasties (906-60). Yet Kuo Hsi's work was also distinguished by a new realism which came to characterize Northern Sung painting. Most obviously, this realism showed itself in paintings of animals, birds and flowers, of which Ts'ui Po's *Hare Scolded by Jays* (dated 1061) is a particularly fine surviving specimen, reducing the towering drama of contemporary landscapes to a more comfortable and comprehensible level of detail.

Chinese calligraphy
This 11th-century writer is approaching his work as if he were painting. The same brush and ink were used in China for both writing and painting—although writing was regarded as the superior art.

RIGHT
Hare Scolded by Jays, *Ts'ui Po*

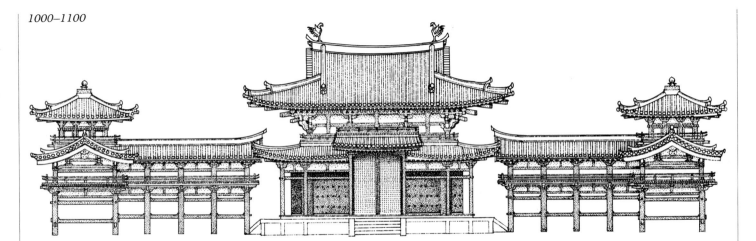

Phoenix Hall, Uji, Japan
A superb example of classical Japanese architecture, this temple, built in 1053, was named the Phoenix Hall, or Hoodo, because its plan was thought to resemble a bird in flight. The hall (now restored) houses the sculpture of the Amida Buddha by Jocho.

Amida Buddha
Jocho's sculpture of the Amida Buddha reflects the forgiving nature of Mahayana Buddhism, which offered the promise of salvation to all its followers. The soft, gentle lines of the sculpture, especially its full, expressive face, convey this characteristic tenderness.

Self-indulgent, worldly, and unwilling to admit a possible end to the society that had rewarded them so well, the Japanese nobility turned to the cult of the Amida Buddha, a merciful deity of the Mahayana Buddhist persuasion who would descend from heaven to receive the departing soul, and transport it thence to paradise. The Phoenix Hall in the Byodoin temple at Uji was dedicated to Amida, and is the most impressive monument of Heian architecture to survive still intact to this day. It was built for Fujiwara Yorimichi, Michinaga's son. In keeping with the principal message of the cult, the great sculptor Jocho's Amida figure, in the central sanctuary of the Phoenix Hall, is represented as a tranquil and forgiving god, very unlike the powerful and austere figures of the past. By the time of the building of the Phoenix Hall in 1053, Japanese religious art everywhere was developing these qualities of tenderness and optimism, a favourite theme being the *Descent of Amida* surrounded by a throng of musicians and other worldly and joyous attendants. This was no ordinary promise of salvation through suffering but the believer's instant passport to paradise.

South-East Asia

There were, of course, harder paths in Buddhism than this. Where Mahayana Buddhism was speculative, mystical and free-thinking, Hinayana Buddhism was fundamentalist, rational and authoritarian. China had chosen to take the softer path of Mahayana Buddhism. In contrast, Burma belonged even more obviously than any of the other South-East Asian kingdoms to an older Indian cultural tradition, and most particularly to Ceylon, headquarters of the Theravada sect of Hinayana Buddhists. And it was certainly appropriate that the unifying drive of Anoratha in Burma (1044-77) should have also been reinforced by a general conversion of the Burmese people to Hinayana Buddhism.

Anoratha's achievement was to bring the kingdom of Pegu, in the south, into union with his own kingdom of Pagan in northern Burma. But his political ambitions were larger than this, causing him to move into the province of Nan-chao in the north, and to open up diplomatic links with the king of Ceylon, who was being threatened at the time by the Hindu Chola kings of southern India. Anoratha's concern in Ceylon was religious rather than military: to assist in the restoration of the Buddhist faith in regions devastated by the Hindu Chola, just then at the high point of their expansion. In return, his monks secured a rich harvest of Buddhist relics, each of which then needed to be appropriately housed in the capital he was rebuilding at Pagan.

Ananda Temple, Pagan, Burma

This white stone temple, with its gilded spires, belongs to the great period of Burmese art. Dedicated in 1090, it was built in the shape of a Greek cross and modelled on an earlier Indian temple at Paharpur. The elaborate stone-carving, however, is characteristically Burmese in style.

Bell-shaped stupa, Pagan, Burma

After Burma was united in the 11th century under the Buddhist ruler Anoratha, a huge number of bell-shaped stupas were constructed in the Burmese capital at Pagan. These shrines to the Buddha consisted of a chamber containing religious relics, surrounded usually by an ambulatory.

With Anoratha's reign, the great period of Burmese art began, to continue through two centuries until the devastations of Kublai Khan. During this period, something like five thousand Buddhist monuments were put up at Pagan alone, from the comparatively modest bell-shaped stupas typical of the Burmese tradition to the great Ananda Temple of King Kyanzittha (1084-1112), dedicated in 1090. The architectural antecedents of the buildings of Kyanzittha's reign have been identified in northern India, and it is probable that the Ananda Temple was modelled on the temple at Paharpur, in Bengal, originally Hindu but subsequently taken over by the Buddhists. As at Paharpur, the plan of the Ananda Temple is a Greek cross, with a great central brick-built mass supporting the sikhara, or spire. In the exuberance of the stone-carving on what is otherwise a strictly symmetrical construction, the Ananda Temple is characteristically Burmese, although both Burma and Ceylon were clearly also affected by the ornate architectural style of the Hindu Cholas.

Part of the Chola expansion in the late tenth and early eleventh centuries had been won at the expense of the weakening Shrivijaya empire of Sumatra, at its greatest two centuries before. One consequence of the further deterioration of Shrivijaya influence was the emergence as a power in South-East Asia of the Khmer kingdom of Cambodia, separated from Burma by the as yet unawakened Siam. Cambodia came into its own especially under Suryavarman I (d. 1050), whose statesmanlike initiatives built up his dynasty to the point where his namesake in the following century would be able to construct such a monument as Angkor Wat. Suryavarman I was probably personally responsible for many of the great hydraulic works which irrigated and enriched his kingdom. But the major building programmes of medieval Cambodia belong rather to the twelfth and early thirteenth centuries. This late development almost certainly explains their comparative freedom from Indian influence.

India

Rajaraja the Great (985-1018) had driven Chola power as far north as the Ganges on the Indian subcontinent, just as his son Rajendra I (1012-42) would later carry the Tamil empire overseas. Characteristically, it was Rajaraja who built the largest temple of its kind, the temple to Siva at Tanjore, in South-East India, in commemoration of his own very considerable achievements. The Rajrajesvara Temple at Tanjore was put up in the first years of the eleventh century, at a great speed and to a massive scale. Yet it is distinguished by its excellent proportions and by a quality of workmanship which makes it one of the

Hindu Chola temples
*Both the Rajrajesvara
and Brihadisvara temples
were built to commemorate
the power and wealth of
the reigning Chola kings.
Although constructed
quickly and on a massive
scale, the buildings are
masterpieces of the Hindu
Renaissance.*

*Rajrajesvara Temple,
Tanjore, India*

*Brihadisvara Temple,
Gangaikondacholapuram,
India*

**Kandariya Mahadeo
Temple, Khajuraho,
India**

*The ascending towers of
the Shaivite temple of
Kandariya Mahadeo were
designed to resemble the
god's mountain dwelling,
while the profusion of
erotic sculptures (right)
that decorated the temple's
exterior symbolized man's
union with the deity.
These figures show Hindu
temple sculpture at
its finest.*

masterpieces of this final major period of so-called "Dravidian" art, also known as the Hindu Renaissance. It is rivalled only by Rajendra's competing temple of Gangaikondacholapuram, near Kumbakonam, completed within a couple of decades of its model.

Both great temples are lavishly decorated with sculptures in the tradition the Cholas had taken over from the Pallavas before them, and which they had continued through the tenth century to perfect. But so rigid were the rules of Hindu iconography that the sculptors were always compelled to work within a language of symbolism which dictated every move and smallest gesture of their subjects, whether they were working in stone or in the bronze for which Chola art is especially well known.

The cult of Siva had long been dominant in southern India, and in bronze one of the more dramatic representations of the god is the Siva Nataraja, Lord of the Dance (see page 19). Already a striking and powerful image, to the Shaivite worshipper the dancing figure spoke of creation and destruction, of energy, disintegration and renewal. It was an icon intended to be read in depth, loaded with significance and meaning.

Symbolism was equally characteristic of central Indian Hindu temple architecture, of which the culmination was surely reached in the great monuments of Khajuraho, dating from the late tenth and

early eleventh centuries. Most imposing of these monuments is the Shaivite temple of Kandariya Mahadeo, an eleventh-century masterpiece which repeats, in the steady ascent of its towers, the image of Siva's mountain residence. At Khajuraho, too, temple sculpture, much of it both voluptuous and erotic, had reached its full maturity. Both on the Kandariya Mahadeo and on the earlier Parshvanatha Temple, the lower panels are filled with deeply-carved groups of deities and posturing, near-naked dancers, competing to show off their charms.

As lavish in their construction, but within a very different tradition, were the Hindu Jain temples of Mount Abu, in Rajputana. An important early example, the Vimala Sha Temple (1032), was built shortly after the lifting of the Muslim threat to northern India on the death of Mahmud of Ghazni in 1030. In this temple, however, as in the similar Dilwara Temple from about the same time (see pages 14-15), the emphasis was not on the exterior appearance of the shrines, but on the exceptionally lavish embellishment of their arcaded and domed white marble interiors, making the Mount Abu sanctuary as a whole one of the principal architectural marvels of medieval India.

At Mount Abu itself, building continued through to the late thirteenth century, when the Muslim rulers of Delhi finally put an end to the rich Solanki Jain dynasty of Gujerat. However, the early-

eleventh-century plundering raids of Mahmud of Ghazni had already introduced the Punjab to Muslim iconoclasm on a massive scale. Although Islam did not return to northern India in any great force until the 1180s and 90s, for those few who would see it, the writing was there on the wall.

Within a decade of Mahmud of Ghazni's death, his Afghan Ghaznavid dynasty was already under attack by the Seljuks, and the rebirth of Islam which was to have such momentous effects in the Mediterranean world had touched India.

Near East

The Seljuks were northern steppe peoples who had been on the move from the tenth century and before. They gained much force by conversion to Islam under the Samanid kings, south-east of the Caspian, and they used that conversion from the middle of the eleventh century to absorb what was left of the Abbasid caliphate. In 1055 the Seljuks became protectors of the caliph; in 1071 they wiped out a Byzantine army at Manzikert, opening Anatolia from then onwards to Islam. By 1078 they had reached Damascus.

The Seljuks came as stampers-out of schism within their demesnes and as wagers of a holy war of conversion outside them. It was what they represented, combined with the loss of Christian Anatolia and the threat to the Holy Places in Palestine, that provoked the First Crusade. But to the Arab world what the Seljuks brought was a precious renewal of the vitality of Islam, with an empire that stretched from their capital at Konia, in Asia Minor, to the central Asian cities of Bukhara, Tashkent and Samarkand, from Armenia in the north southwards to the Persian Gulf.

The restored unity of Islam, and the strength of the faith that lay behind it, manifested itself in a striking uniformity of art, reinforced by the constant movement of traders and other middle-income patrons of the arts from one corner of Islam to the next. It was from the eleventh century, for example, that the cult of the garden—cool, well-watered and essentially formal—took permanent hold on the Muslim world. Simultaneously, rigid orthodoxy exiled figural painting from mosque and home alike, so that Islamic art developed in the Middle Ages along very different lines from the Christian art of the West, expending itself rather on the

The Islamic Near East in the 11th century
In the early part of the 11th century, Mahmud of Ghazni briefly took the Muslim faith to northern India in a series of plundering raids. But the real revitalization of Islam followed the emergence of the Seljuks, a northern steppe people. They invaded Byzantine Anatolia, took over the Abbasid caliphate at Baghdad, and extended their empire to take in Tashkent, Samarkand, Armenia and the Persian Gulf.

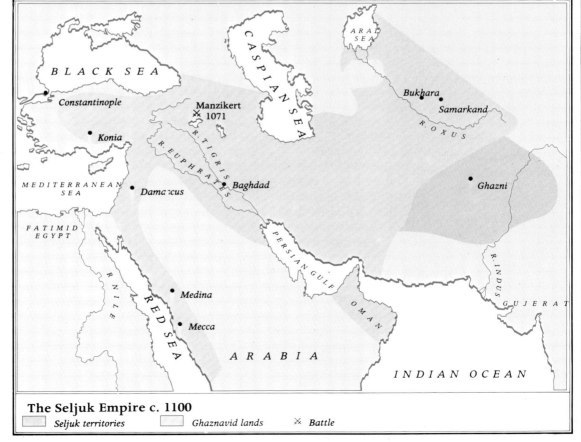

The Seljuk Empire c. 1100

| | Seljuk territories | | Ghaznavid lands | ✕ Battle |

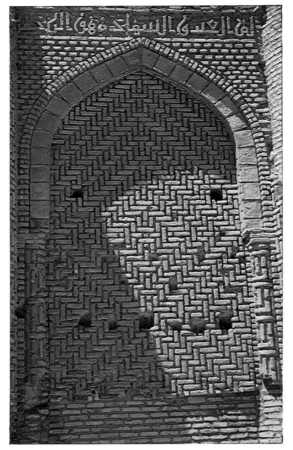

Seljuk tomb, Qarraqan, Persia
The doorway of this 11th-century Seljuk tomb is a fine early example of the patterned brickwork which became a distinctive feature of Islamic decoration, as one consequence of the banning of figural representation by the Muslim faith.

Celestial globe
This early Arab celestial globe was made by a servant for the investiture of his master as vizier in Valencia c. 1081.

decorative arts, on the infinitely repeating geometric and vegetal patterns it had practised originally in textiles.

If the representation of the human figure had any place at all, it was in the illustration of the medical and other scientific texts of the time, in the compilation of which the Arabs were still far in advance of any culture other than the Chinese. Arab science progressed in bursts with little evident continuity. However, to the eleventh century belong the great medical encyclopedias of Avicenna and Ibn Sina, codifying the learning of both the Greek and the Arab worlds; during the first half of the century Ibn al-Haytham completed his pioneering work on optics, or the theory of vision; during this century again Arab mathematicians furthered their understanding of Hindu algebra and arithmetic, to begin its transmission to the West in the next century. Having the resources of Greek scientific thinking to draw on, the Arabs were perhaps less original than the Chinese. But although much of their creative energy was taken up in the translation of Greek texts and in commentary upon them, there were nevertheless areas such as the development of

more refined observing instruments in astronomy where the Arabs made genuine progress. It was these instruments that made possible the compilation of improved astrological and navigational tables, among them the eleventh-century *Toledan Tables* of al-Zarqali, which remained unreplaced for another two centuries.

When Toledo fell to the Christians in 1085, another victim of the civil wars that had followed the collapse of the Umayyad caliphate in Spain, the community that had nurtured al-Zarqali went with it. But tragic though the calamity of Toledo was for the society of Muslim Spain, cut off at the height of its promise, it was as nothing compared with what was happening contemporaneously at the far end of the Mediterranean, where Byzantine Anatolia was falling to the Seljuks. In the second and third quarters of the eleventh century Byzantine architecture experienced a phase of innovation and renewal, which was the product of unusual prosperity. The defeat at Manzikert in 1071, immediately followed by the Seljuk occupation of the rich Byzantine provinces in Asia Minor, brought this prosperity to an abrupt and a brutal end.

Less than two generations earlier, towards the end of the long reign of Basil II (976-1025), the Byzantine empire had rarely been richer, more extensive, or more powerful. Although Basil himself, preoccupied with his conquests, had been no great builder, just the opposite was the case with his successors. By an accident of survival, the great majority of the remaining monuments dating from the half-century after Basil's death are to be found either on mainland Greece or on its islands. They include the church of St Mary of the Coppersmiths (Panagia tôn Chalkeôn) at Thessalonica (1028), Constantine IX's lavish and influential New Monastery (Nea Moni) on Chios (1045), and the important pilgrimage church of Hosios Loukas, also in Greece and again datable to within the first half of the eleventh century.

What these and contemporary buildings shared was an experimentalism in architecture, appropriate to a period of self-confidence and optimism, that disappeared after the Anatolian collapse. One of the expressions of this new experimentalism was greater emphasis on the decorative exterior treatment of church façades. Another was a willingness to use Islamic styles, whether in the glazed tiles

St Mary of the Coppersmiths, Thessalonica, Greece
One of the Byzantine churches to be built in the optimistic aftermath of Basil II's reign, St Mary of the Coppersmiths (1028) makes use of Islamic motifs in the patterned brickwork of its exterior.

with Kufic lettering under the cornice at the Panagia tôn Chalkeôn, Thessalonica, or in the employment of decorative patterned brickwork, with its origins in textile design, in the characteristically Arabic manner.

This openness to exotic influences spread through every branch of Byzantine art, from the fine silk fabrics for which the capital was famous to the many exquisite objects in ivory and precious metals for which models have been found in Arab, in Persian, and even in Chinese art. Yet the crafts of Constantinople were less a phenomenon of eleventh-century eclecticism than the product of a continuing tradition, going back through almost two centuries of enduring Macedonian rule. Under the Macedonians Byzantine civilization had reached new heights, and its exchanges with the Islamic world had enlarged and enriched them both. The stamp of the Macedonians, brilliant but stern, is still to be seen beyond the end of their era upon the mosaics, for example, of the church at Daphni, near Athens, where the Christ Pantocrator, in the crown of the dome speaks of judgment, reproach, and command (see page 19).

Constantinople in the days of the Macedonians had indeed been an impressive capital. Those who were privileged to see it when its glory was greatest could not easily have forgotten its many marvels. One visitor was the Grand Duchess Olga, whose state visit from Kiev to Constantinople in 957 was stage-managed with every pomp of which the imperial court was capable, complete with baptism in Justinian's cathedral under the supervision of both the patriarch and the emperor.

Eastern Europe

The conversion and baptism of Olga's grandson, Prince Vladimir of Kiev (d. 1015), in the late tenth century had been followed by the reception into Greek-Orthodoxy of the people he ruled and the conversion in due course of all Russia. Vladimir's bride, in a match of both religious and political significance, was a Byzantine princess, sister of the emperor Basil II. The conversion to Christianity of the Russian peoples had many important consequences. Literacy, for example, was much advanced by the adoption of the Bulgarian Slavonic alphabet of St Cyril and St Methodius. Byzantine law and Christian practice smoothed off the rough edges of a society torn by blood feuds and gripped by its ancient superstitions. In architecture and the arts the change was especially momentous. Massive popular conversions required the provision in a short space of time of buildings adequate to house the new congregations.

Something is known of Vladimir's initial building programme, with the recovery by excavation of the foundations of his Cathedral of the Dormition of the Virgin, founded at Kiev in 989. Certainly we have it on the authority of Thietmar of Merseburg, a German chronicler, who travelled to Kiev in 1018, that the churches of the capital were numbered already in their hundreds. But the most important surviving buildings of the early conversion period belong to the reign of Yaroslav the Wise (1019-54), Vladimir's son, being the cathedrals of St Sophia (Hagia Sophia) at both Kiev and Novgorod.

In Yaroslav's reign, as in that of his father, the architects and artists of Kievan Russia still worked within the Byzantine

Basil II and his Byzantine dominions
During the reign of Basil II (976-1025), the Byzantine Empire had reached its furthest limits, extending to southern Italy in the west and eastwards towards Persia. Before the end of the 11th century this territorial sovereignty had been conceded to the Seljuk Turks and to the Normans.

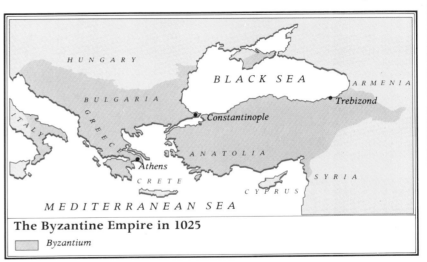

The Byzantine Empire in 1025
☐ *Byzantium*

St Sophia, Novgorod, Russia
Built between 1045 and 1062, St Sophia is a good example of the Byzantine style as it had to be adapted to meet the needs of northern Russia. Windows were small to keep out the cold, the whole emphasis of the building being vertical rather than horizontal.

St Sophia, Kiev, Russia (plan)
Probably constructed between 1018 and 1037, this was one of the first great churches to be built in Russia. The basic Byzantine plan was expanded at Kiev to accommodate the huge Russian congregations.

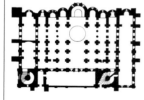

tradition. It is not yet very useful to attempt to identify a specifically Russian contribution to art forms that were clearly imported. Nevertheless, the particular conditions of Russian society brought pressures to bear on the builders of the two cathedrals. Meeting the need to accommodate a large congregation, the architect of St Sophia at Kiev expanded his basic cross-in-square plan (the three-aisled and five-domed church of his Byzantine model) to comprize what was eventually a nine-aisled structure, spectacularly crowned by no fewer than thirteen cupolas. In the north, it may have been the same architect again who put up the cathedral of St Sophia at Novgorod, completed between 1045 and 1062 to the direction of Prince Vladimir, Yaroslav's son. Not as large as and much plainer than St Sophia at Kiev, the Novgorod cathedral had distinctively northern features in its height and in the small size and number of its windows.

Indeed, these characteristics, unknown in Constantinople, are enough to indicate that the art of Byzantium did not simply imprint itself on the *tabula rasa* of Russia, as if nothing had ever preceded it. Even

before the conversion to Orthodoxy, there had been Christian communities in southern Russia, with churches of their own, as far back as the late ninth century. And although there is no doubt that imported Byzantine paintings, mosaics, and stone-carvings added much to the indigenous eleventh-century tradition, transforming it in many particulars, the high-quality metalwork of Yaroslav's Kiev, with its sophisticated cloisonné enamels, goes back essentially much earlier.

In just the same way, it would be a mistake to see Vladimir's conversion as the snatching of Russia from the jaws of barbarism, wedding it indissolubly to Byzantium. Some of the characteristics of St Sophia at Novgorod have been attributed to contact, however indirect, with the Romanesque of central and northern France. Neither is this as unlikely as it might at first appear, for Novgorod's trade with the western world was already well-established by the eleventh century, while Yaroslav's wife was a Swedish princess and his daughters Anastasia, Elizabeth and Anna eventually became the queens of Hungary, of Norway and of France, respectively.

Pilgrimage routes and churches
Pilgrimages were one manifestation of the 11th-century revival of popular faith. The cult of saints led to the foundation of churches built to house relics. Constructed to a similar pattern, these churches then became centres on the pilgrimage roads, the most important of which converged on Santiago de Compostela.

Pilgrimage routes

- Pyrenees
- Centre
- Church

St-Denis · Paris · St-Martin, Tours · Poitiers · Ste-Madeleine, Vézelay · Autun · Lyons · Limoges · Le Puy · Santiago de Compostela · Bordeaux · Roncevaux · St-Pierre, Moissac · Ste-Foy, Conques · Leon · Burgos · St-Sernin, Toulouse · St-Gilles-du-Gard · Arles · S. Domingo de Silos · Puente la Reina

ATLANTIC OCEAN · FRANCE · SPAIN · MEDITERRANEAN SEA

Santiago de Compostela, Spain (façade restored)

St-Sernin, Toulouse, France

St-Martin, Tours, France (plan)
The plan of St-Martin recommended itself to the builders of pilgrimage churches elsewhere.

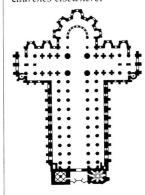

Western Europe

There was certainly nothing exclusive about the developing art of the West. Romanesque architecture, during the eleventh century, advanced most significantly in France, in particular in Burgundy and the valley of the Loire. But the inspiration for this progress was frequently derived· from elsewhere, and every achievement had its follow-up in imitations. At the late-eleventh-century monastic church of Cluny, one of the most influential buildings of all time, the pointed arches of the nave arcades were probably derived from Montecassino, in central Italy, and would lead the way into the development of French Gothic; in the same arcades, the fluted pilasters were purely Roman in inspiration; the wall-paintings, if the early-twelfth-century ones at the neighbouring Berzé-la-Ville are indeed a true guide, had Byzantine models perhaps taken from manuscripts preserved in the abbey library; for such few sculptures as survive, one possible source is Germany.

Cluny, sadly, is gone. But the abbey— the so-called Cluny III of Abbot Hugh (1049-1109)—was always more than a building, for it stood at the heart of a religious revival of unprecedented interest and importance. Alfonso of Spain, the conqueror of Toledo, provided the initial funds for the rebuilding of the abbey church, on which work began in 1088. And Abbot Hugh, during the long span of his government at Cluny, took a leading role in the reform of the papacy (the so-called Hildebrandine or Gregorian Reform). He also witnessed the beginnings of the great new monastic orders (the Cistercians, the Carthusians, the Augustinians and their imitators), and the apparent miracle of the First Crusade.

One of the earliest expressions of a less intransigent religion was the cult of the saints and the habit of pilgrimage which was growing around their relics. In favourite cult centres, large numbers of pilgrims needed to be accommodated; it was both the necessity for space and the wealth the pilgrims brought which promoted the building of the great pilgrimage churches—St-Martin at Tours, St-Sernin at Toulouse, and that focus of pilgrimage, second only to Jerusalem, Santiago de Compostela, in Spain.

At St-Martin at Tours, the ambulatory at the east end of the church, an aisled chevet with five radiating chapels, was carried round for the first time into the transepts, aisled and galleried on three sides. Bringing room for movement round the relics and greatly increased accommodation for worshippers in the transepts, this plan was followed almost identically at St-Sernin, in Toulouse, and with minor modifications only at Santiago.

Apostle in Niche
*St-Sernin, Toulouse,
France*

St Durandus
St-Pierre, Moissac, France

A further link between St-Sernin and Santiago is the exceptional quality of the sculpture, in both cases very likely the work of Bernardus Gilduinus, who had perfected his art at Toulouse. At Santiago, Gilduinus, or a sculptor trained in his workshop, was employed on the ornate twin portals of the transepts. But his finest work is preserved at Toulouse in a set of seven marble slabs. It is these reliefs, probably modelled on ivory originals of a Carolingian or Ottonian source, that Professor Zarnecki has judged to be ''the first truly monumental works of French Romanesque sculpture'' (*Art of the Medieval World*, Abrams).

At Moissac, a Cluniac house near Montauban north-west of Toulouse, the dramatic sculptures on the cloister piers, dating from the late eleventh century, are closely related in technique and style to the work of Gilduinus at St-Sernin. They are paralleled again, as Zarnecki points out, at the Spanish abbey of S. Domingo de Silos, near Burgos, where there is also work of Arab derivation in the capitals of the fine double cloister. This is indeed the ''art of the pilgrimage roads'', with the achievement of one sculptor echoed by another, both sharing and transmitting their inspirations.

If the cult of relics and the constant exchanges of the great pilgrimage roads helped to push out the frontiers of Romanesque art, another agent at least as powerful was the political drive of the Normans. In their own Norman homeland, since the first years of the eleventh century, they had been active in monastic reform. And when they broke out to take their part in the reconquest of Spain, to invade England, and to occupy southern Italy and Sicily, they took their devotion with them, building with as much single-minded purpose in the lands they subjected as they had been doing back in Normandy itself.

In post-Conquest England, Bishop Gundulf of Rochester, in addition to rebuilding his own cathedral, became known as the greatest castle-builder of his generation, the architect of London's mighty White Tower. Among his contemporaries, Lanfranc of Canterbury achieved reconciliation with his rebellious Anglo-Saxon monks at least in part by remodelling their cathedral priory on a new and magnificent scale. The first thought of Bishop Herbert Losinga, on the removal of his see from Thetford to Norwich in the 1090s, was to start a new cathedral in the grand French manner, which he lived to see at least partially completed.

Some of the building conventions for this post-Conquest work in England had already been arrived at in Normandy under its reforming dukes. The abbey church at Jumièges, with the two western towers that were to become one of the principal hallmarks of Norman religious building, is thought to have been the model for Edward the Confessor's Westminster Abbey even before the Conquest. But since Norman political interests were wide and their tastes catholic, building in England over the next generations was to draw inspiration from as diverse parts as Venice, southern Italy and Byzantium, from Alsace and Aquitaine. Indeed, so invigorating was the climate of reform and reconstruction in Anglo-Norman England that one of its products before the end of the eleventh century was that unexcelled masterpiece of Romanesque architecture, the cathedral at Durham, begun in 1093. Perhaps the earliest example of successful rib-vaulting, gracefully completing the complex arcading of the choir, Durham stands at the peak of an architectural tradition which had already made such progress on English soil that in less than a generation a distinctive Anglo-Norman style had evolved.

Other elements of this style, prominent again at Durham, included the use of chevron ornament, locally developed perhaps from a Near Eastern model. And this same adaptability among Norman patrons of the arts showed itself in the continuing strong tradition of Anglo-Saxon manuscript painting, as in such cooperative works as the Bayeux Tapestry (see pages 26-27), where the narrative style of the pre-Conquest Winchester and Canterbury schools was adapted to French Romanesque.

To the entirely different environment of southern Italy and Sicily, the Normans were equally responsive. From the mid-eleventh century, their role as mercenaries to the Italian princes had changed to that of conquerors. Under their count, Robert Guiscard, they first expelled the remaining Byzantine governors of Italy south of Rome, and then took the guise of Christian crusaders in driving the Arabs from Sicily. By 1091 the Norman conquest of Sicily, begun with the capture of Messina exactly thirty years before, was at

Durham Cathedral, England
Begun in 1093, only 27 years after the Conquest, Durham Cathedral, with its massive grandeur, is the supreme example of Anglo-Norman Romanesque.

Abbey Church, Jumièges, France
This building, begun in 1037, was influential in England even before the Norman Conquest; Edward the Confessor took it as the model for Westminster Abbey. Its system of alternating compound and cylindrical piers was later followed at Durham.

last complete. But by then Norman settlement in Apulia and Calabria was already old. It had a cultural impact on those neglected and backward provinces very similar to the experience of England.

In a move of great political and artistic importance, the Normans had early given their support to Abbot Desiderius, later Pope Victor III, in the rebuilding of Montecassino. And they followed Desiderius in a deliberate return to the art of the Early Christian period, to which they added both Byzantine and purely classical influences. Of course, they did not altogether abandon the architecture of their homeland, Robert Guiscard's tomb-church at Venosa being a Romanesque building conceived in the typical French manner. In the course of the next century, they would wed Northern Romanesque in astonishing harmony with the Greek, Arab, and classical traditions at the Sicilian cathedrals of Monreale and Cefalù. But even more significant of the competing pressures caused by the early Norman presence in Apulia is that curious hybrid, the church of S. Nicola at Bari, a former Byzantine possession, where so much is a

return to the Late Roman basilica and where there is so little to recall the developing Romanesque tradition, at least as it was understood in the North. From a Byzantine source, too, is the architectural sculpture that enriches S. Nicola, the work of the sculptor Ursus. Like the other Byzantine-influenced sculpture of southern Italy, for which there is no parallel in the north, it makes much use of animal figures, one of them being the ubiquitous lion which from that time on would support such a number of Italian columns.

Borrowings from Byzantium were not confined to the arts alone. It was in the eleventh century that the fore-and-aft lateen sail, enabling beating into the wind, was passed on to the West by the Greeks. In the 1070s, Constantine the African brought Greek medicine to the western world. Earlier than that it was probably through Byzantium that important astronomic instruments like the astrolabe reached Europe, with the new technology that permitted, for example, the building of tidal mills as a power source on the Venetian lagoon. Indeed, it was in the exploitation of water-power, above all, that western technology during the eleventh century made its most significant progress. In France, before the end of the century, water-power had been used to drive hemp-mills and fulling-mills, and to lift other water for irrigation. In England, the Domesday record of 1087 lists the stamping-mills and hammer-mills of an increasingly mechanized iron industry, as well as the almost six thousand water-mills which by then were in use for the grinding of corn.

This growing interest in the application of water-power is an important pointer to the direction in which western society, by the late eleventh century, was going. The classic military feudalism of the North French world had been comparatively short-lived. It had developed towards the middle of the tenth century and was exhibiting strain scarcely more than a hundred years later. The recovery of trade was beginning to encourage the emergence of a monied middle-class, urban-based and distinct in its interests from the military aristocracy by which it continued to be ruled. Conflict in the eleventh century was avoided. But the sources of friction are easy to recognize. Stoked by tension, the European economy had significantly changed its course.

Serpent Wall, Tula, Mexico
The theme of the frieze on both sides of the free-standing Serpent Wall—rattlesnakes devouring warriors—reflects the Toltec preoccupation with war and death.

Toltec temples
The massive Toltec temples at Tula and at Chichén Itzá belong to an architectural tradition established much earlier during the Classic Period of Mesoamerica in the 5th and 6th centuries AD.

Temple of the Warriors, Chichén Itzá, Mexico

Toltec temple, Tula, Mexico

The diffusion of Mesoamerican influence
During the 11th century there is some evidence that the strong religious and cultural traditions of the Toltecs and their predecessors in Central America reached as far north as the Hohokam of Arizona, the Mississippian of the South Mississippi Valley, and, to a lesser extent, the Anasazi cliff-dwellers of Colorado.

The Americas

In a different society, totally uninfluenced by any other, the opposite way had been chosen. Coincidentally, the millennium had proved to be a turning-point in the Americas, just as it had in Europe. The opening of the so-called Late Intermediate Period in South America, around the year 1000, saw the beginnings of the Chimu empire of Peru which later would result in the astonishing monuments of Chanchan. In the North American Southwest, a distinctive agricultural society was at last emerging, with an apartment-house architecture of its own. But most striking were the changes in Mesoamerica, where the early tenth century had witnessed the final collapse of the great Classic civilizations, and their subsequent replacement by the Toltecs of Tula. Once this invading tribe from the northwestern frontier had settled at Tula, before the end of that century, the main emphasis of Meso-american society was radically altered. The priest had been the hero and cult figure of Classic Mesoamerica. In the Post-classic Period, that role fell to the warrior.

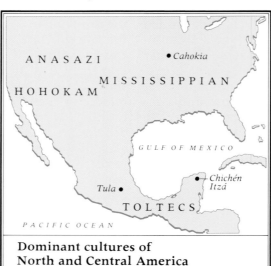

Dominant cultures of North and Central America

One of the principal monuments of the Toltec capital at Tula is the *coatepantli*, or "serpent wall", so-named from the theme of the frieze it carries, showing rattle-snakes and their warrior victims. It was this continual stress on war, on death, and on the ferocity of beast and man, which characterized the art of the warrior aristocracies by this time dominant in Mesoamerica. Toltecs, or a military people very much influenced by them, penetrated Yucatán, setting themselves up in a former Mayan city which they renamed Chichén Itzá. It is not yet entirely clear whether the Toltec aristocracy established itself first at Chichén Itzá or at Tula. However, the parallels between the art and religious beliefs of the two cities are too close to be anything but deliberate. To both, Toltec rule throughout the eleventh century brought a sculptural florescence of a vigorous but characteristically brutal inspiration, manifesting itself in such spectacular works as the free-standing Atlantean stone warriors of Tula (see page 19) and the recumbent stone figures, called Chacmool, for which the two centres are equally well known.

Chichén Itzá had been an important Mayan city before the Toltec ascendancy, and Mayan architecture survived there intact throughout the period of Toltec rule. Similarly, at Tula itself the architectural inspiration is essentially that of the Classic Period of Mesoamerica, of the vanished civilization of Teotihuacán. Although there had been a check and even a drift backwards in the years round about the millennium, the cultural tradition of Mesoamerica proved in most of its particulars continuous, with powerful influence both to the south and to the north in the sculptures and ceramics, for example, of Pacific Nicaragua, as in the platform mounds and plazas of the Mississippi.

Mississippian art
These two Mississippian shell artefacts suggest that the cult of the dead had already spread north from Mesoamerica. Both objects portray human heads, and were probably religious symbols.

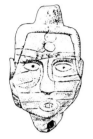

Hohokam pottery
This pottery dish is in the characteristic Hohokam monochrome style. Strong pattern, rather than colour, is the dominant feature.

In part, of course, the diffusion of Meso-american religious practices and other cultural traits was itself the product of the breakdown of the Classic Period civilizations which had nurtured them. There is no reason to hypothesize a mass migration of peoples northwards in the decades that followed the mid-seventh-century collapse. But occasional emigrations there must certainly have been, with trading and other contacts. As a result, the three major cultures of the North American South—the Hohokam of Arizona, the Mississippian of the Mississippi Valley, and the Anasazi of Colorado—all exhibit Mesoamerican influence in one form or another, but more especially the first and the second.

In both the Hohokam and the Mississippian traditions, for example, platform mounds in the Mesoamerican style are common. The great Mississippian site of Cahokia, in southern Illinois, has over a hundred of them. The Hohokam, too, played a distinctive ball game, using a rubber ball in an elaborately constructed ball court that was clearly modelled on Central American prototypes. Through the Sedentary Period art of the Hohokam (*c.* 900-1200) and the Southern Cult art of the Mississippian tradition (after *c.* 1000), there runs a thread, recognizable enough, of consistent Mexican inspiration, whether in pottery vessel forms, in figurines, or in the many other decorative artefacts in stone or in shell for which both cultures are celebrated. The weaving of cotton textiles, practised by the Hohokam in the eleventh century or even earlier, must also have originated in Mexico.

As stable agricultural peoples, settled in dry and inhospitable places, the Hohokam and the Anasazi each developed elaborate irrigation systems, canal-fed, which remain to this day some of the more striking residues of their cultures. For the Hohokam, this was an ancient and continuous tradition, going back to the middle of the first millennium AD and reaching its peak, very probably, in the so-called Classic Period of the Hohokam (1200-1400). The Anasazi came to this also in due course. Their most important canal projects belonged, it is thought, to the Pueblo III Period (*c.* 1050-1300), and coincided with the flowering of an urban-based society with its characteristic apartment-type villages and towns.

The dry desert-canyon conditions which had made irrigation so essential to the Anasazi were also those which have preserved their towns to this day as monuments of unusual social interest. In the Chaco Canyon, the largest of these monuments is Pueblo Bonito, built between 919 and 1067 in a complex beehive of over eight hundred rooms, frequently piled on top of each other in a great D-shaped enclosure of approximately three acres in extent. Pueblo Bonito, like the very different Cliff Palace built under the overhang of a great sandstone cliff in Mesa Verde, Colorado, was clearly a local organizational centre of some importance. Both sites are characterized by an exceptional number of the circular sunken rooms, known as *kivas*, in which the Anasazi conducted their religious rites and other communal business. In both sites, again, the community's resources had evidently been mobilized in well-directed programmes of construction and fortification. They belonged, it is plain, to a hierarchical society which yet could accommodate consultation and cohabitation of an order still exceptional today.

Pueblo Bonito (plan) and Mesa Verde, Colorado
Pueblo Bonito (below) was built as a fortified enclosure packed with rectangular "apartment houses". The circular kivas *were communal areas. The Cliff Palace at Mesa Verde (right) was a sophisticated complex built under the overhang of a cliff as protection against attack.*

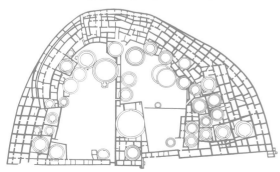

World Architecture

The survival rate of religious buildings is much higher than that of their secular equivalents. Almost all the monuments of eleventh-century civilization had a religious function of some kind, only the remarkable apartment-house towns of the Anasazi of Colorado, in North America, remaining to suggest some of the complexities of what was already, at sites like Pueblo Bonito and Mesa Verde, a highly developed social order.

Elsewhere, different religions evoked very contrary architectural responses. Buddhism in Japan and in China was the inspiration of buildings of notable quality and restraint, among the best of these being the Phoenix Hall at Uji in Japan and the "Colour of Iron Pagoda" at Kaifeng, the capital of the Chinese Sung. But Buddhism was also the source for a more elaborate temple architecture both in North China, under the Liao, and in such monumental Burmese works as the great Ananda Temple at Pagan, itself based on a much earlier Indian model.

In India itself, the highly decorative quality of Hindu architecture, placing great emphasis on the elaboration of sculptural ornament, was exhibited in the great temple-building enterprises of the Chola rulers of the South. First Rajaraja built the Rajrajesvara Temple at Tanjore, and then Rajendra rivalled his father with the temple of Gangaikondacholapuram, near Kumbakonam. Simultaneously in central India, the great monuments of Khajuraho, while also making much of sculptural elaboration, rose to the sky in a series of gracefully ascending towers.

Far removed was the severe monumentality of Toltec temple-building at the Mesoamerican religious capitals of Tula and Chichén Itzá, while almost as different again were the works of the Christian church-builders of Byzantium and of the newly-converted Russia. In both Byzantium and Russia religious architecture was experiencing a notable flowering, the first under its cultivated Macedonian rulers, the second under the princes of Novgorod and Kiev, who were newly converted to Orthodoxy.

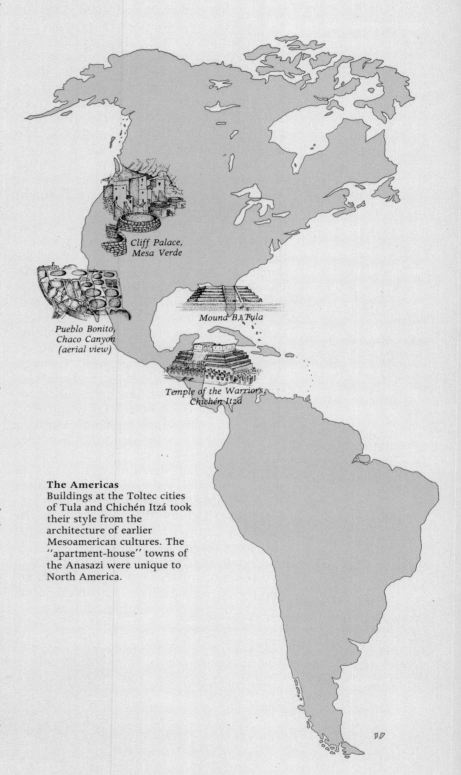

Cliff Palace, Mesa Verde

Pueblo Bonito, Chaco Canyon (aerial view)

Mound B, Tula

Temple of the Warriors, Chichén Itzá

The Americas
Buildings at the Toltec cities of Tula and Chichén Itzá took their style from the architecture of earlier Mesoamerican cultures. The "apartment-house" towns of the Anasazi were unique to North America.

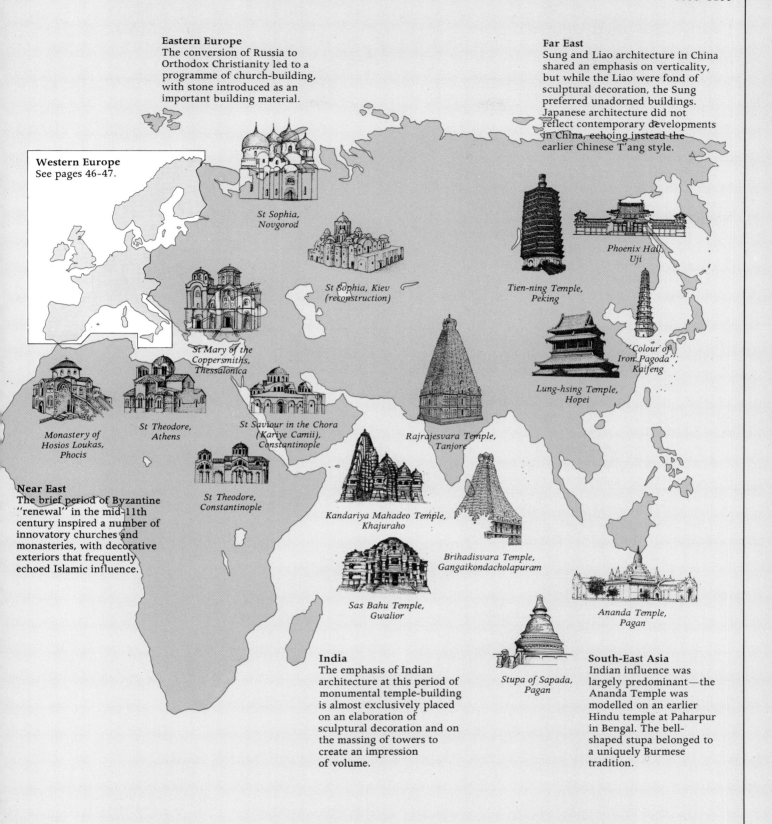

Eastern Europe
The conversion of Russia to Orthodox Christianity led to a programme of church-building, with stone introduced as an important building material.

St Sophia, Novgorod

St Sophia, Kiev (reconstruction)

Western Europe
See pages 46-47.

St Mary of the Coppersmiths, Thessalonica

Monastery of Hosios Loukas, Phocis

St Theodore, Athens

St Saviour in the Chora (Kariye Camii), Constantinople

St Theodore, Constantinople

Near East
The brief period of Byzantine "renewal" in the mid-11th century inspired a number of innovatory churches and monasteries, with decorative exteriors that frequently echoed Islamic influence.

Far East
Sung and Liao architecture in China shared an emphasis on verticality, but while the Liao were fond of sculptural decoration, the Sung preferred unadorned buildings. Japanese architecture did not reflect contemporary developments in China, echoing instead the earlier Chinese T'ang style.

Phoenix Hall, Uji

Tien-ning Temple, Peking

"Colour of Iron Pagoda", Kaifeng

Lung-hsing Temple, Hopei

Rajrajesvara Temple, Tanjore

Kandariya Mahadeo Temple, Khajuraho

Brihadisvara Temple, Gangaikondacholapuram

Sas Bahu Temple, Gwalior

Ananda Temple, Pagan

Stupa of Sapada, Pagan

India
The emphasis of Indian architecture at this period of monumental temple-building is almost exclusively placed on an elaboration of sculptural decoration and on the massing of towers to create an impression of volume.

South-East Asia
Indian influence was largely predominant—the Ananda Temple was modelled on an earlier Hindu temple at Paharpur in Bengal. The bell-shaped stupa belonged to a uniquely Burmese tradition.

Western European Architecture

Both politics and religion in eleventh-century Europe combined to create a new architecture. The Norman conquerors of Anglo-Saxon England brought with them the tradition of wholesale rebuilding developed already in their homeland.

One great monument of Norman energy in England is the massive rectangular stone keep at the White Tower, London. Norman zeal for new works, financed by the profits of the invasion of 1066, was still more obvious in the rebuilt cathedrals, among them the fine new cathedral of Archbishop Lanfranc's Canterbury (of which only the crypt now survives) and the great cathedral at Durham, begun in the late eleventh century.

It was the Normans again, after their conquest of southern Italy, who helped finance the rebuilding of Abbot Desiderius' Montecassino and who encouraged a revival of classical traditions seen most clearly in a church like S. Nicola at Bari but detectable too even in Burgundian Cluny. The reconstruction of Cluny inspired imitations throughout the Catholic West. Among monuments of a similar scale were the great pilgrimage churches of Tours (St-Martin) and Toulouse (St-Sernin), while work began on the major cathedral at Santiago de Compostela, in north-west Spain.

Spain
Santiago was the focal point of the European pilgrimage routes. The cathedral of Santiago de Compostela was constructed to a pattern similar to the French churches which grew up along these routes.

Britain
Greenstead Church was built in the old Anglo-Saxon timber tradition, but most important buildings of this period were commissioned by the Normans after the Conquest—among them the cathedrals at Canterbury, Winchester and Durham, which is one of the great surviving Romanesque masterpieces.

France
The seminal building of the period was the rebuilt Cluny III, widely copied inside and outside France. The religious revival which also spread from Cluny resulted in the spate of building by the Normans and along the pilgrimage routes.

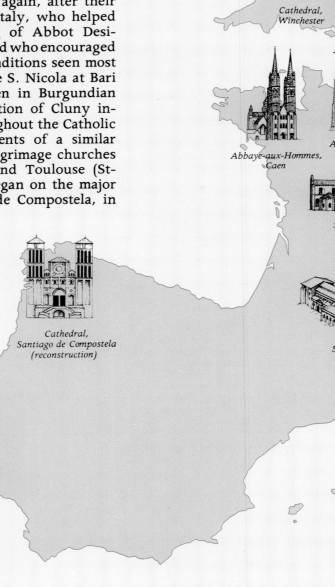

Cathedral, Durham

Greenstead Church, Essex

Cathedral, Winchester

White Tower, London

Abbaye-aux-Hommes, Caen

Abbaye-aux-Dames, Caen

Abbey Church, Jumièges

St-Hilaire, Poitiers

Abbey Church, Cluny III

Ste-Foy, Conques

St-Sernin, Toulouse

Cathedral, Santiago de Compostela (reconstruction)

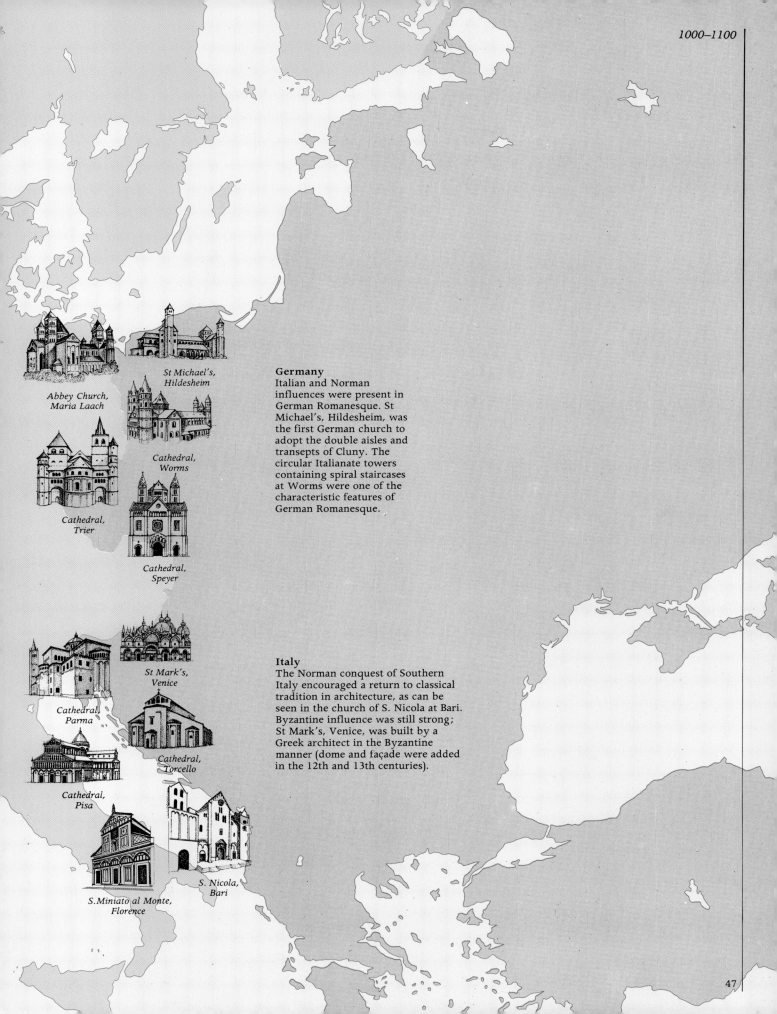

Abbey Church,
Maria Laach

St Michael's,
Hildesheim

Cathedral,
Worms

Cathedral,
Trier

Cathedral,
Speyer

St Mark's,
Venice

Cathedral,
Parma

Cathedral,
Torcello

Cathedral,
Pisa

S.Miniato al Monte,
Florence

S. Nicola,
Bari

Germany
Italian and Norman
influences were present in
German Romanesque. St
Michael's, Hildesheim, was
the first German church to
adopt the double aisles and
transepts of Cluny. The
circular Italianate towers
containing spiral staircases
at Worms were one of the
characteristic features of
German Romanesque.

Italy
The Norman conquest of Southern
Italy encouraged a return to classical
tradition in architecture, as can be
seen in the church of S. Nicola at Bari.
Byzantine influence was still strong;
St Mark's, Venice, was built by a
Greek architect in the Byzantine
manner (dome and façade were added
in the 12th and 13th centuries).

World Art

The finest art of the eleventh-century world undoubtedly came from Sung China, whether in the new realism of its painting or in the exceptionally fine hard white pottery known as Ting. But the knowledge and influence of Chinese art were essentially confined to the regions of East Asia that accepted Chinese hegemony. One of these was Fujiwara Japan, where the cult of the Amida Buddha, imported from China, inspired a sophisticated, relaxed and optimistic art both in scroll-painting and in the wood-carvings of the great sculptor Jocho and his school.

The restraint and self-discipline of Chinese art had few contemporary parallels. It was matched, perhaps, by the Byzantine mosaics of a church like Daphni, in southern Greece near Athens. But here again it was the product of a long-established, very old and very sophisticated society, threatened by change but not yet entirely engulfed by it.

Other world societies, even very ancient ones, completely failed to achieve this calm. Although clearly under the influence of Byzantium, Russian art of the eleventh century, most especially in its characteristic cloisonné enamels, remained essentially barbaric. The vividly expressionistic sculptural traditions of the antique cultures of India and Indian-influenced South-East Asia were meanwhile notable for their freedom from restraint. Indian temple sculpture reached a high point of elaboration in the lavish figure-carving of the temples at Khajuraho (Central India), emphasizing the voluptuous charms of the temple dancers in work of plainly erotic intention.

In a very different tradition, Toltec stone-carvers in eleventh-century Mexico were also concerned to cover their surfaces with figural and abstract ornament. It was an ancient art, centuries old already. And its influence was felt up and down the American continent, to appear just as clearly in the decorative painted pottery, the textiles and the figurines of a North American culture like the Mississippian.

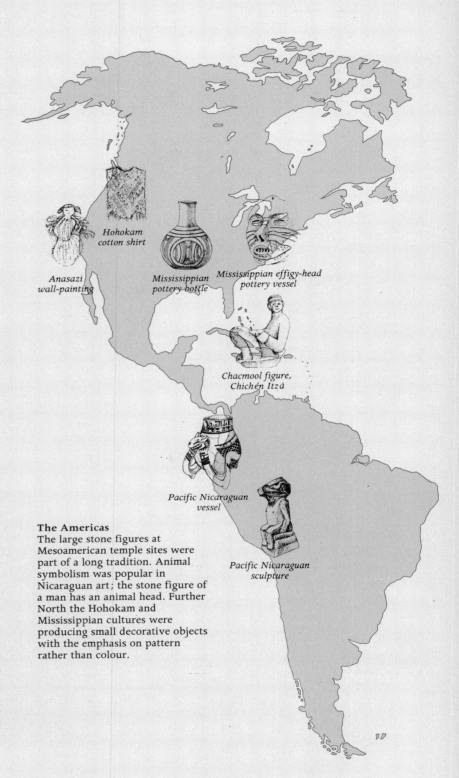

Anasazi wall-painting

Hohokam cotton shirt

Mississippian pottery bottle

Mississippian effigy-head pottery vessel

Chacmool figure, Chichén Itzá

Pacific Nicaraguan vessel

Pacific Nicaraguan sculpture

The Americas
The large stone figures at Mesoamerican temple sites were part of a long tradition. Animal symbolism was popular in Nicaraguan art; the stone figure of a man has an animal head. Further North the Hohokam and Mississippian cultures were producing small decorative objects with the emphasis on pattern rather than colour.

Eastern Europe
Enamelwork belonged to an indigenous Russian tradition; the mosaics and frescoes followed the conversion to Orthodoxy and show Byzantine influence.

Far East
Chinese ceramics of this period were glazed with a single colour over incized decoration. The use of ink was in vogue among the realist painters of China, such as Li Lung-mien, famous for his paintings of horses. The Japanese statue of the Amida Buddha inspired many other gilded wood images.

Western Europe
See pages 50-51.

Russian cloisonné enamel pendant

Mosaic, St Sophia, Kiev

Fresco, detail, St Sophia, Kiev

Japanese Amida Buddha by Jocho

Byzantine silk

Byzantine gold and enamel chalice

Liao stone effigy of Buddha

Ting bottle

"The Parinirvana" Japanese scroll, detail

Near East
Byzantine art, which abounded with figural images, continued to flourish even though a revived Islam was simultaneously producing stylized abstract patterns to the exclusion of figural representation.

Seljuk patterned brickwork

Mosaic, Daphni church

Byzantine ivory panel

Chinese painting, detail, by Li Lung-mien

Northern Celadon bowl

Hindu carving, Kandariya Mahadeo, Khajuraho

Fresco, detail, Ananda Temple, Pagan

Chola bronze of Siva Nataraja

Chola carving of Siva, Gangaikondacholapuram

Jain carving, Mt Abu

Ceylonese bronze Tara

South-East Asia
Indian influence was strongly reflected in South-East Asian art of this period.

India
Sculpture in India was closely associated with architecture; the carvings shown here belong to larger designs that cover temple surfaces. Many beautiful bronzes of Siva, the Lord of the Dance, were produced in Southern India.

Western European Art

In eleventh-century European art, the work of the individual creative artist can at last be traced to source. In south-west France and northern Spain, we know of one sculptor, Bernardus Gilduinus, trained in Toulouse, who was likely to have worked also on the portals of the transepts at Santiago. The sculptured figures attributed to Gilduinus at the great pilgrimage church of St-Sernin at Toulouse, and at the contemporary monastic cloisters at Moissac and S. Domingo de Silos, may be stiff and formal in their postures. Yet, for all that, nobody could deny their rare dramatic power.

Another individual artist, the sculptor Ursus, is known to have been employed on the Byzantine-influenced architectural sculptures of the Norman church of S. Nicola at Bari, in southern Italy. The largely Byzantine inspiration of the sculptures at Bari is not untypical of an art in the West that was still finding a style of its own; and Byzantine and classical models continued to be experimented with through much of the twelfth century.

One still flourishing native tradition was the narrative art of Anglo-Saxon England, coming under the influence of a Norman tradition from the conquest of 1066. Certainly the best known product of the resulting Anglo-Norman style was the Bayeux Tapestry.

Spain
The art of Christian Spain was influenced by both East and West in this period. Islamic inspiration is evident in the Christian illuminations of Beatus of Liébana, while the French Romanesque style of sculpture can be found in the major churches of the pilgrimage routes.

Britain
The rich, decorative style of the Winchester School of manuscript illumination was at its height, and its influence spread into other art forms, including carvings in ivory, metal and stone.

Anglo-Saxon manuscript illumination, Winchester School

Christ in Majesty, walrus-tusk carving, Winchester School style

Gold enamelled Towneley brooch

Christ in Majesty, manuscript illumination, Stavelot Bible

Bayeux Tapestry, detail

King David, portal sculpture, Santiago de Compostela

Doubting Thomas, detail of marble carving, S. Domingo de Silos

Manuscript illumination of Beatus of Liébana

Christ in Majesty, marble relief by Gilduinus, St-Sernin, Toulouse

St-Durandus, marble relief, St-Pierre, Moissac

Carving on capital, Cluny III

France
The early Romanesque sculptural style of Toulouse spread along the pilgrimage routes; this style, like that of the illuminated manuscripts, was still comparatively stylized and formal. In the Bayeux Tapestry can be seen a mingling of Norman influence and Anglo-Saxon art.

Byzantine orb

Panel from bronze doors made for St Michael's, Hildesheim

Germany

The great bronze doors commissioned by Bishop Bernward for St. Michael's, Hildesheim, created a style that was imitated throughout Europe. The emerging German empire also retained artistic links with the older empire of Byzantium; the Holy Roman Emperor's majestic orb was copied from a Byzantine model.

Bronze Islamic griffin, Pisa

Detail of Apostles, apse mosaic, Torcello Cathedral

Italy

The abbey of Montecassino, rebuilt by Abbot Desiderius in the 11th century, was highly influential in the spread of Byzantine-inspired painting and sculpture through Italy. Apart from the occasional object imported from Islam, most mosaics and sculptures of this period can be seen to show Byzantine derivation.

Desiderius offering the Church, wall-painting, S. Angelo in Formis

Throne of Archbishop Elia, S. Nicola, Bari

St Benedict Drawing up his Rule, manuscript illumination, Montecassino

"Lion Door" by Ursus, S. Nicola, Bari

	Events and developments	People	Technology
Western Europe	Norman capture of England (1066), southern Italy (from 1057), Sicily (1091). Christian *Reconquista* of Spain begun. Increase in papal power; start of "Investiture" dispute with Empire. 1st Crusade proclaimed by Urban II (1095). Rapid increase in population. Old towns expanded, new ones founded. Definite trade routes evolved.	Henry IV, Holy Roman Emperor 1056-1106. Robert Guiscard, Norman Count of Apulia 1057-85. William I, King of England 1066-87. Lanfranc, Archbishop of Canterbury 1070-89. Pope Gregory VII 1073-85.	Arrival from Byzantium of Greek medicine, fore-and-aft lateen sail, astrolabe, and other astronomic instruments. Exploitation of water-power eg. tidal-mills on lagoon at Venice; stamping-mills and hammer-mills in England.
Far East	Great prosperity enjoyed by China under Northern Sung dynasty (founded 960). Large increase in China's population. Monetary tribute paid as a peace-keeping measure to Khitan Liao by Sung; tributes also paid to Tibetan state of Hsi Hsia. Rice introduced by Sung from Champa. Growth of distinctive Japanese culture, at its height under Fujiwara regents.	Fujiwara Michinaga, Japanese regent, (d. 1027). Murasaki Shikibu, Japanese novelist, (978-?1031). Ts'ui Po, Li Lung-mien and Kuo Hsi, Chinese painters, (fl. 1020-1100).	In China, gunpowder first used in warfare; printing with movable type developed; paper currency created; first compasses used; astronomical instruments perfected. Water-driven mechanical clock at Peking; spinning wheel in common use.
South-East Asia	Dynasty of Anoratha founded at Pagan (1044). Kingdom of Pegu joined with Pagan; Anoratha first king of united Burma. Rise of Khmer kingdom of Cambodia, to become dominant power in South-East Asia under Suryavarman I. Malay empire destroyed by Cholas (1025).	Anoratha, King of Burma 1044-77. Suryavarman I, King of Cambodia 1002-50.	Great hydraulic works (for land irrigation) in Cambodia.
India	North-west India invaded by Mahmud of Ghazni, a zealous Muslim; Punjab annexed to his central Asian empire. Zenith of Chola power in southern India and Ceylon, under King Rajaraja the Great and his son Rajendra I.	Rajaraja, King of the Cholas 985-1014. Rajendra I, King of the Cholas 1014-44. King Bhoja of Malwa, scholar and writer (d. 1060).	
Near East	Lands previously lost to Arabs by Byzantine empire recovered under Basil II. Territorial decline after Basil's death (1025). Defeat of Byzantines by Seljuks at Manzikert (1071); most of Byzantine Anatolia overrun by Seljuks. Capture of Jerusalem by knights of 1st Crusade (1099). Decline of Fatimid dynasty of Egypt.	Mahmud of Ghazni 971-1030. Basil II, Emperor of Byzantium 976-1025. Avicenna, Arab philosopher and physician, (980-1037). Omar Khayyam, Arab poet, (?1050-?1123). Alexius I, Comneni Emperor of Byzantium 1081-1118.	Development of more refined astronomical instruments by Arabs; improved navigational tables.
Eastern Europe	Death of Vladimir I of Russia (1015); succession of Yaroslav, his son (1019). Kingdom of Hungary founded under Stephen I (1000). Political and ecclesiastical independence achieved by Poland with crowning of Boleslav I (1000).	Vladimir I of Russia (d. 1015). Yaroslav I (the Wise) of Russia 1019-54. Boleslav I, King of Poland 1000-25. Stephen I, King of Hungary 1000-38 (later saint).	
Africa	Rise of Almoravid (Berber) empire in North Africa. Morocco conquered by Berbers and city of Marrakesh founded. Overthrow of negro empire of Ghana by Almoravids (1076).		
The Americas	Beginnings of Chimu empire in Peru. Rise of Toltecs of Tula in Mesoamerica; continuation of Maya culture centred in northern Yucatán. Three major cultures in North America: Hohokam (Arizona), Mississippian (Mississippi Valley), Anasazi (Colorado). Nova Scotia reached by Scandinavian seaman Leif Ericsson (?1003).		Elaborate, canal-fed irrigation systems built by Hohokam and Anasazi.

Religion	Architecture	Art and music	Literature and learning
Spiritual authority of Papacy over Christendom extended. Heretics burnt at Orleans. Election of popes confined to cardinals. Celibacy imposed on clergy. Church dominated by Cluniac reformers. Pilgrimage routes established. Split between Roman and Greek Churches. Carthusian Order founded (1084), Cistercian Order founded (1098).	Abbey Church, Jumièges; St-Sernin, Toulouse; Cluny III. Santiago de Compostela. Durham Cathedral; Westminster Abbey; White Tower, London. St Mark's, Venice; Pisa Cathedral; S. Nicola, Bari.	Bayeux Tapestry. Sculptures of Bernardus Gilduinus. Bronze doors, St Michael's, Hildesheim. Systematic study and practice of sight-singing begun by Guido d'Arezzo.	Many new cathedral schools founded – some forerunners of universities. *Chanson de Roland*, national epic of France, composed (*c.* 1098).
Confucian revival in China, decline of Buddhism among governing classes. Cult of Amida Buddha adopted by Japanese nobility. Buddhism re-established in Tibet.	Phoenix Hall in Byodoin temple, Uji, Japan. "Colour of Iron Pagoda", Kaifeng, Sung China. T'ien-ning temple, Peking, Liao China.	Period of unsurpassed excellence in Chinese ceramics and painting. Realism in Sung painting exemplified by painters Kuo Hsi and Ts'ui Po. Amida Buddha figure by Japanese sculptor, Jocho.	Seishonagon's *The Pillow Book*. Murasaki Shikibu's novel, *Tale of Genji*. Chen Kuo's encyclopedic survey of Chinese technical knowledge.
Hinayana Buddhism established as official religion of Burma by Anoratha. Buddhism favoured by Suryavarman in Cambodia, but indigenous cult of god-king and also Hindu Shaivism tolerated.	Buddhist monuments at Pagan, Burma: Ananda Temple of Kyanzittha (dedicated 1090), Nan Paya and Manuha temples.	Stone-carving, Ananda Temple, Pagan.	
Hindu cult of Siva dominant faith in southern India. Original authoritarian form of Buddhism (Hinayana or Theravada Buddhism) superseded by more relaxed form— Mahayana Buddhism. Invasions of Mahmud of Ghazni paved way for establishment of Islam in north-west India.	Temple to Siva, Tanjore; Brihadisvara Temple, Gangaikondacholapuram, southern India. Shaivite temple of Kandariya Mahadeo, Khajuraho, central India. Jain temples at Mount Abu, Rajputana, central India.	Chola temple sculptures at Tanjore and Gangaikonda-cholapuram. Erotic sculptures at Khajuraho. Jain sculptural decorations, Mount Abu temples.	Writings on astronomy, poetry and architecture by King Bhoja of Malwa, scholar and patron of the arts. Kashmir centre of thought, literature and Buddhist studies. Sanskrit herbal composed by Suresvara.
Schism between Byzantine Orthodox and Roman Churches (1054). Revitalization of Islam brought about by emergence of Seljuks.	Nea Moni, Chios; Hosios Loukas, Greece. Tower of Victory, Ghazni, Afghanistan. Tomb-Mosque of al-Juyushi, Cairo, Egypt.	Mosaics at Nea Moni and at Daphni, Greece. Constantinople famed for silks and ivories. Seljuk patterned brickwork.	Avicenna's *Canon of Medicine*. Stephen Asolik's universal history. Firdausi's history, *Book of Kings*. Michael Psellus' *The Chronography, 976-1078*. University of Constantinople re-founded (1045).
Christianity accepted in Russia under Vladimir, and in Hungary under Stephen I. Personal appointment of first archbishop to Gniezno by Boleslav I (1000) to demonstrate his independence of the Pope.	St Sophia, Kiev. St Sophia, Novgorod.	Apse mosaics, St Sophia, Kiev.	*Law of Russia* revised by Yaroslav the Wise.
Conversion of parts of West Africa to Islam begun with invasion of Muslim Almoravids.			
Penetration of Mesoamerican religious beliefs to Mississippians of North America evident in platform mounds and plazas in Mississippi Valley.	"Apartment-house" architecture in North American Southwest. Pueblo Bonito, Chaco Canyon, and Mesa Verde, Colorado. Toltec temples at Tula and at Chichén Itzá.	Toltec stone figures, Tula. "Serpent wall" frieze, Tula. Anasazi and Hohokam pottery.	Mathematics and astronomy highly developed in Mesoamerica; various calendars in use.

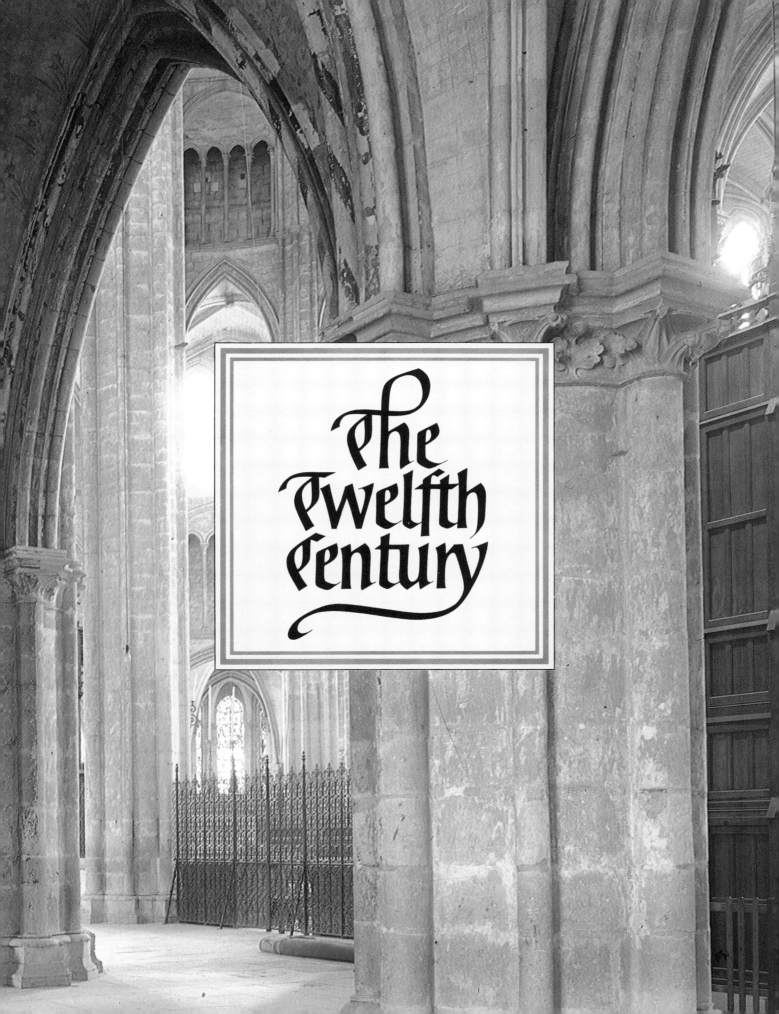

The Twelfth Century

PREVIOUS PAGE
Bourges Cathedral, France
Started in the late 12th century, and completed by 1275, Bourges Cathedral combines a profusion of flying buttresses with the absence of transepts to give an impression of massive volume.

Frederick Barbarossa
Frederick I (1155 - 90), who died in Turkish Anatolia on crusade, did much to unify Germany under the imperial crown.

Henry II and Eleanor of Aquitaine

Henry II of England's marriage to Eleanor of Aquitaine in 1152 was one of a series of alliances which brought him control of Central and Western France at the expense of the French Kings.

Historical Context

There are no world events in the twelfth century to compare with the Seljuk assumption of military leadership in eleventh-century Islam, or with the all but global impact of the Mongol expansion out of thirteenth-century Central Asia. It was not that the century lacked drama. In the Holy Land, Richard the Lion Heart, king of England (1189-99), confronted his rival Saladin, sultan of Egypt and Syria (1175-93). In Japan, after much bloodshed, the military government of the Kamakura shogunate took the place of the long-established and now decadent Fujiwara. In China, the Jürched Tartars overran both the Northern Sung and the Khitan Empire of the Liao. But serious though these upsets were, they lacked a more general significance. Broadly speaking, there was a climate of political stability and economic expansion over a large part of the twelfth-century globe.

In the West, certainly, the growing wealth and increasing sophistication of twelfth-century society facilitated the emergence of political institutions of the very greatest importance—the first of the national monarchies. And it was these, above all, that shifted the cultural focus of Europe away from its pre-eleventh-century centres in Rhineland Germany to the new pastures of England and France. Here the light of kingship shone brightest. Germany, even under the leadership of Frederick Barbarossa (1155-90), was torn and divided, on the rack of its contest with the popes in Rome and by the jealousies of its quarrelsome aristocracy. In contrast, England had enjoyed the benefits of a strong royal government from the mid-eleventh century and before, while the French kings of the Capetian line, although overshadowed for many generations by their greater nobility, were on the ascendant in the last decades of the twelfth century; they were soon to achieve new dominance under Philip II Augustus (1180-1223), Richard of England's contemporary and rival.

Indeed, the rivalry between the Capetian kings of France and their over-powerful vassals, the Angevin kings of England, became an important stimulus to economic advance in both dominions. Under Henry II of England (1154-89), a series of dynastic alliances had brought much of Central and Western France

France in 1189

▢ English possessions	▢ English dependencies
▢ French possessions	▢ French dependencies

The Angevin Empire
Under Henry II of England (d. 1189) the English possessions and dependencies in France—known as the Angevin Empire—reached their furthest extent.

under the control of those who had once been counts of Anjou and who were now kings of England as well. So long as Henry II remained alive, the French kings could make little impression on what came to be called the Angevin Empire, much enlarged in 1152 by Henry's astute marriage to Eleanor, the rejected queen of Louis VII and heiress to Aquitaine. But new opportunities for the French arose on the death of Henry in 1189 and on the accession of Richard and then John, his sons. Richard's preoccupations in the Holy Land, followed by his capture and long imprisonment first in Austria and then in Germany on the way home, left his kingdom open to the joint intrigues of John, his brother, and of the French king Philip Augustus. When John himself succeeded to the throne in 1199, he found it still more difficult to hold the Angevin Empire together. His misdemeanours, whether real or imaginary, gave the pretext for war between the kingdoms, and, in a series of campaigns initiated by Philip, the bulk of his French dominions were overrun. The collapse of the Angevin Empire in 1203-4 was the making of the kingdom of France.

Throughout this contest, the armies that both Capetian and Angevin were able to field were financed out of rapidly expanding royal revenues. The growth of towns and the expansion of trade in Western Europe had persisted since the eleventh century, showing no signs as yet of pause. The great centres of industry and finance continued to be Flanders and Northern Italy, with the meeting-points of international trade at the fairs of Champagne and of Brie. However, the prosperity of these trades and the contemporary boost given to agriculture by the new markets were felt over a very much wider area. Amongst the aristocracy, wealth began to show itself in the building of castles and in the cultivation of a life-style increasingly dependent on the purchase of luxury goods. In the towns, the suppliers of these goods grew wealthy in their turn, built themselves fine houses, and protected their communities with walls. In the Church, a revived popular piety beneficially combined with a surplus of property among its patrons, resulting in unprecedented endowments.

In particular, the new riches of the Church, making it everywhere a landowner without equal, proceeded from the climate of monastic revival and reform which had been launched some years before the end of the eleventh century. The mood for this reform had been initiated by the papacy itself, and expressed in the Hildebrandine reforming programme of the 1070s. But the dry arguments over papal power and the proper form for the investiture of bishops were quickly translated into a more popular enthusiasm, fed by the success against paganism of the First Crusade and by the cults of saints and their relics, of Christ and the Virgin Mary.

The monastic revival found its strongest support in France. Chief among the new monastic orders were the Cistercians, and it was from a base in France that the Cistercians expanded, taking their austere fundamentalist code from Burgundy to Spain, Britain, Scandinavia, Germany and Italy. Alongside the Cistercians, and frequently in direct competition with them for money and lands, grew other orders—the Carthusians and the Premonstratensians, the Augustinians, the Gilbertines (of England), and the Victorines (principally of France). Not all of these were equally successful. However, they illustrate the great variety that existed in the Church, ranging from a major Cistercian community like Fountains Abbey in Yorkshire to the diminutive houses of Augustinian canons, which everywhere sprang up as landowners disposed of their parish churches, formerly held as private property, on suitably qualified recipients.

Officially, although not in practice, the troubles within the Church that later became known as the Investiture Contest were brought to an end with the Concordat at Worms of 1122. Agreement was there reached between Pope Calixtus II and Henry V of Germany on the outstanding issues of the election and investiture (with ring, staff and lands) of bishops. It was conceded that the priority in the appointment of these princes of the

The Cistercian order
This new monastic order, promoted by the genius of St Bernard of Clairvaux, was at the forefront of a great period of monastic revival. From their centres in France—Clairvaux, Cîteaux and Morimond—the Cistercians carried their beliefs across much of Western Europe. Although they are known for the austerity of their discipline and the plainness of their buildings, the Cistercians were also renowned for the decorative splendour of their illuminated manuscripts, which were not always severe in tone.

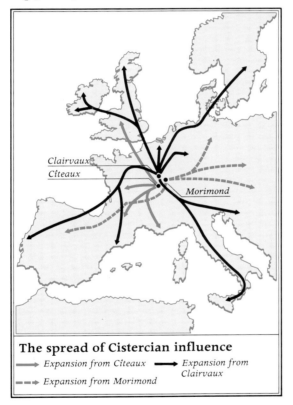

The spread of Cistercian influence
→ *Expansion from Cîteaux*   → *Expansion from Clairvaux*
--→ *Expansion from Morimond*

Initial letter, St Gregory's Moralia in Job, *Cîteaux, France*

Chertsey tile of Richard I with Saladin, Chertsey Abbey, England, 13th century

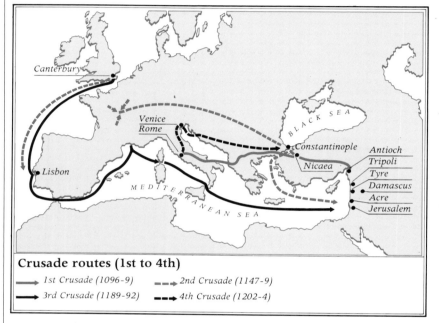

Crusade routes (1st to 4th)

→ 1st Crusade (1096-9) →→ 2nd Crusade (1147-9)

→ 3rd Crusade (1189-92) ▪▪→ 4th Crusade (1202-4)

The Crusades
The Crusades marked the expansion and establishment of Latin Christendom. The First Crusade was initiated by Pope Urban II in 1095 to counter the threat of resurgent Islam; Muslim counter-attacks were answered by the unsuccessful Second Crusade (1147-49), and the Third Crusade (1189-92) ended with a truce between the two great rivals, Richard I of England and Saladin, Sultan of Egypt and Syria. The Crusaders turned against Orthodoxy in 1204, when the Fourth Crusade, originally recruited to attack Egypt, was diverted into sacking Constantinople.

Church should now lie with the papacy. But the Contest itself had generated much intellectual opposition to Rome, chiefly in the great law schools of Pavia and of Bologna (granted a university charter by Frederick Barbarossa in 1158), and in the North European cathedral schools and their kindred institutions (many of them later universities) at Utrecht and Oxford, Paris and Chartres, Rheims, Orleans and Tours. Abelard, one of the most noted of the scholars of Paris, saw his theological teachings condemned at the Council of Soissons in 1211. Other theologians, like the Victorines later in the century, avoided the conflict by escaping into mysticism. A few, like Thomas Becket of Canterbury, embarrassed the papacy in quite another way by an absolute insistence on the property rights of the Church, when the Pope himself had wanted to arrive at a more amiable compromise with the State.

Before the end of the twelfth century, the western Church had discovered heresy even within its own dominions. The initial movement against the Albigensians of Toulouse, also known as the Cathars, was authorized by Pope Alexander III at the Lateran Council of 1179. And just fifty years later the Church would give birth to its most infamous creature, the Inquisition. But these were also the years of further attempts to reconcile Catholic and Orthodox, and although the sack of Constantinople in 1204 put paid to this reconciliation for centuries, not every omen for Christendom in general was unfavourable. The Second Crusade, even if turned back at Damascus in 1148, had usefully assisted Alfonso of Portugal the year before in the capture of Lisbon from the Arabs. And through the century as a whole, the losses of Christendom in the Eastern Mediterranean were made up by its triumphs in the West.

In fact, Islam had troubles of its own. A growing introversion had spread through the Muslim world with the popularity of Sufi mysticism, especially as taught by the great Persian philosopher Al-Ghazzali (d. 1111). The Seljuk sultans were afflicted with pagan invasions from Central Asia. And Saladin's successes against the Christian Franks of Palestine were put continually at risk by the murderous activities of the notorious Assassins, a schismatic sect of his own religion.

Those who gained by the stalemate were the Latin cities of the East Mediterranean, principally Antioch, Acre and Tripoli, left to themselves while their enemies quarrelled. For the same reason, another clear beneficiary of the politico-religious divisions of Islam was the now permanently weakened Byzantine empire of the Comneni. Byzantine civilization, as restored by the Comneni emperors after the disaster of Manzikert, preserved through most of the twelfth century its characteristic brilliance, even if culturally it had become somewhat backward-looking. Only in the last quarter of the twelfth century did the erosion of its lands begin again, both from the West and from the East, culminating in the sack of Constantinople in 1204.

North of Byzantium and north-eastwards into Russia, the pressures were more intense. By the end of the twelfth century, many Balkan peoples had escaped the suzerainty of Constantinople: they

Pope Alexander III
*Pope Alexander (1159-81)
authorized a movement
against the heretical
Albigensians of Toulouse
at the Lateran Council of
1179. This papal
antagonism to heresy led
directly to the Inquisition
in the next century.*

**Russia in the 12th
century**
*By 1200 the 11th-century
state of Kiev had
diminished in power and
size in the face of civil
wars and nomad assaults,
and its former territories
had been broken up into
independent principalities.
Predominant among these
were Vladimir-Suzdal and
the growing Novgorod
state which both
benefited from a
northward drift of
population.*

had fallen to an expanding Catholic Hungary, had come under Hungarian suzerainty of some kind, or had won a precarious independence of their own. In effect, Latin Christianity was spreading southwards through former Orthodox territories, while also pushing vigorously eastwards across Central Europe, taken there by German settlers who, displaced by growing population pressure at home, were now clearing and developing the lands of the western Slavs. In the far north, along the Baltic coastline, the fierce crusading order of the Teutonic knights drove Catholic lordship as far ultimately as Livonia, on the very boundaries of Orthodox Novgorod.

Russia itself, despite its own internal divisions and its growing freedom from Byzantine influence, remained obstinately Orthodox. The state of Kiev which, from the late tenth century, had brought Russia closest to Constantinople, had not survived the civil wars and southern nomad assaults of the eleventh century. But the movement of Russian settlement northwards on the decline of Kiev had assisted the development of the northern principalities, in particular Vladimir-Suzdal at the head of the Volga River, and the expanding trading empire of commercial Novgorod. Both of these states benefited from an increasing population; indeed the population increase in medieval Russia, before the thirteenth-century devastations of the Mongols, was one of the

Russian principalities c.1200

▢ *Extent of principalities*

— *Kievan Russia in 1054*

steepest in Europe. However, what gave these two states their advantage over the other principalities into which Russia continued to be divided was most particularly their predominance in trade. Novgorod's rich fur trade kept it in close contact with the growing commercial centres of northern Europe, while Suzdalia's situation on the navigable Volga gave it access to the markets of the Black Sea. Both showed the strength of their trading alliances in distinctive characteristics of their cultures.

Under the Seljuks in the eleventh century, the Islamic trading network, which touched Russian Suzdalia in the twelfth century, had spread through much of East-Central Asia. Increasingly, it was opening new doors into Africa. Arab interest in West Africa was chiefly mercantile, being attracted there by gold, ivory, and slaves. However, a direct consequence of this interest was to bring wealth to the regions where gold originated, or through which such trade had to pass. This in turn fostered the growth of indigenous empires. Comparatively little is known still of these, for they left no independent record. However, in Nigeria, at least, the roots of African civilization go back into the pre-Christian era, while even those undocumented empires of the Sudanic belt, straddling the principal Arab trade routes to the South, must have originated in the tenth century or earlier.

In East Africa, the Arabs continued to colonize the lowland coastal plain, as well as off-shore islands like Zanzibar. But this was only part of the intensifying drive of Arab traders to make first the Arabian Sea, and later the entire Indian Ocean, a further extension of Islam. For at least two centuries before Islam's successful political establishment in India, Arab commerce had been bringing prosperity to parts of western India, in particular to Gujerat in the north-west, which provided suitable bases for such trade. However, the political divisions of late-twelfth-century India now provided quite a different sort of opportunity for Islam. Both politically and religiously at loggerheads with each other, India's warring rulers were no more able to meet the challenge of Muhammad Ghuri's invasion of the North than they had been prepared, 150 years earlier, to face up to Mahmud of Ghazni. The taking of Delhi in 1192, and the establishment there within a generation of a long-

Parakrama Bahu I
This colossal stone figure, presumed to be of the Singhalese ruler Parakrama Bahu I (1153-86), was carved from the rock at his capital of Polonnaruwa. Parakrama initiated a great temple-building programme to reaffirm Theravada Buddhism in Ceylon after the retreat of the Hindu Cholas.

lived Islamic regime, opened a new era of Muslim domination in India which persisted thereafter for centuries.

The whole of India did not fall to Islam at once. It took a century and a half of aggression and retreat for the Muslim regime, usually known as the Delhi Sultanate, to reach its maximum extent, after which it again suffered some serious reverses. Nevertheless, the placing of the greater part of India under the control of an image-despising Muslim aristocracy exposed it to an iconoclasm which, at least for the time being, more fortunate regions, to the south and the east of the Indian subcontinent, were lucky enough to avoid. In the late twelfth century, just when Muhammad Ghuri was absorbing northern India for Islam, the Singhalese rulers Parakrama Bahu I and Nissanka Malla were re-establishing Theravada Buddhism as the principal religion of Ceylon, following the retreat of the Hindu Cholas. And although in time Islam would spread into South-East Asia, to Malaya principally but also to parts of both Java and Sumatra, it was this Ceylon-inspired Theravada Buddhism that continued to exert a principal influence over the South-East Asian land mass as a whole.

Buddhism, however, had little of the proselytizing intolerance of Islam. It was thus entirely in keeping with the relative religious freedom of the subcontinent that the civilization of Cambodia, South-East Asia's greatest power in this century, should have continued to combine elements of the Hindu Shaivism traditional in its culture with the Buddhism now favoured by its rulers. Towards the end of the twelfth century the most powerful of these rulers, Jayavarman VII (1181-c. 1220), himself became a convert to Mahayana (Theravada) Buddhism, the religion of the easier road. His personal switch to this essentially Chinese version of the faith underlines the influence that China retained even beyond the territorial limits of its accepted cultural predominance.

Chinese influence in any event was on the increase during the four decades of Jayavarman's reign. Weakened by differences of opinion in the leadership between reformers and traditionalists, and by a succession of peasant revolts, North China had fallen to the Jürched Tartars in 1126-7. And humiliating though this was for the surviving Southern Sung dynasty, one important consequence of the loss of great territories in the North, including the former imperial capital at Kaifeng, was to concentrate resources in the South. To maintain themselves and to keep out their enemies, the Sung emperors encouraged the further urbanization of South China, on the model of their new capital at Hangchow. During their time, Hangchow became one of the greatest cities that the world has ever known. The emperors also fostered the development of a powerful mercantile class, and deliberately promoted initiatives in overseas trade. It was the fleets of the Southern Sung that brought Chinese exports to South-East Asia. Furthermore, the manifest superiority of Chinese culture at this time, on display throughout the Far East, left its mark on every nation to which Chinese traders came.

The cultural hegemony of the Chinese was all the more remarkable for its persistence even among peoples who reacted adversely to the political intervention of outsiders. Thus the literary language of Korea remained Chinese although China's suzerainty over Korea in the twelfth century was scarcely more than nominal. And the intensely nationalistic Kamakura shoguns of Japan, who ousted the Fujiwara towards the end of the twelfth century and who, a century later, would successfully defend their country against the fleets of Kublai Khan, were nevertheless more evidently the inheritors of a Chinese cultural tradition than their aristocratic predecessors had ever been.

Over the world as a whole, by the late twelfth century, the major alignments had shaped themselves, to remain stable until the coming of the Mongols. Coincidentally, in the Americas also the century's last decades would seem to have evolved into a period of relative stability. In Central America, the collapse of the Toltecs in the mid-twelfth century had removed the last imperial power before Aztec expansion three centuries later. In the South, there was little to disturb the apparent continuity of cultures while the Peruvian Chimu consolidated a strictly regional control. Nor was this a period of upheaval in the North, as the Hohokam, the Anasazi and the Mississippian cultures continued to experience profound calm. Ultimately, it was just this continuity, reaching back into the immemorial past, that made the disturbance of the early-modern Americas seem so very much more shocking.

Material Culture

Western Europe

Whereas the civilizations of the East stood out in the eleventh-century world, those of the West take priority in the twelfth. In several important particulars, as we have seen, the way for this had been laid down and prepared already. In technology, the continuing evolution of the earlier water-mill led naturally to the windmill of twelfth-century Europe; in the economy, the success of the towns before 1100 was emulated by the many new foundations of the following decades; in the arts, the architect-mason who could study the achievement of the builders of St-Martin at Tours, St-Sernin at Toulouse, or the Anglo-Norman cathedral priory at Durham, stood already on the shoulders of giants. Nevertheless, the surge of creativity after 1100 was surely more than mere evolution. It had all the drama of exceptional change.

Appropriately enough, the beginning of the century was heralded by an event of rare dramatic power. When Pope Urban II proclaimed the First Crusade at the Council of Clermont in November 1095, he can have had little expectation of its success. Yet he touched a chord in the public imagination that led to scenes of unprecedented enthusiasm. And less than four years later, on 15 July 1099, the Crusaders entered Jerusalem.

In a God-fearing society, those who witnessed such events could not remain unmoved, even if they personally took little part in them. To many, the apparent miracle of the First Crusade assumed the force of a personal revelation of God, confirming the authority of his instrument, the pope. But important though this aspect of the crusading movement was, fuelling a veritable explosion of popular faith, the consequences of the First Crusade were felt as much outside religion as in it. The confidence that Christian arms had won first in Spain, then in Sicily, and now in the Holy Land as well, was sure to rub off on the traders who followed in the wake of the Knights. And business confidence, above all, was what was most required for expansion.

The great international trading fairs, at Bar-sur-Aube and at Troyes in Champagne, are first heard of early in the twelfth century. It was also in the twelfth century that the population pressures throughout Western Europe drove out the frontiers of rural settlement and caused the multiple foundation of new towns. In naval technology, the stern-post rudder, in place of the simple steering oar, became known to northern seafarers; the lateen sail spread from the Mediterranean to the North. Land transport, likewise, was experiencing its own revolution. The padded horse-collar, replacing the earlier breast-band harness, multiplied the tractive power of a horse by a factor of as much as five. The St Gothard Pass was opened, and another public work of major importance, the "Naviglio Grande", irrigating thousands of rich acres in Lombardy, was begun. There are records of an artesian well in twelfth-century Europe, of the first movable lock-gate on the canal linking Bruges to the sea, and of the spread of the fulling-mill through the cloth-producing centres, as well as that of the water-powered stamping-mill in metallurgy. The manufacture of silk in mid-twelfth-century Sicily began with the abduction of Greek weavers. In just the same way the Arabs, having originally snatched the secret of paper-making from the Chinese, proceeded to set up an industry of their own in twelfth-century Spain and perhaps also in Norman Sicily.

Paper, in due course, would transform book-making, and it is one of the coincidences of history that the earliest western experiments in printing on parchment should also have occurred in mid-twelfth-century Europe, with the use of woodcuts for the initial letters of manuscripts, first seen at the monastery of Engelberg, in Switzerland. In the event, another three centuries had still to pass before Gutenburg's development of a movable metal type opened the floodgates to mass-production. But the dissemination of knowledge through the medium of the Church had long been familiar in the West, and it was in the course of the twelfth century that the groundwork was laid for the major intellectual advances of the thirteenth.

Essentially, this meant a change in direction from the liberal arts (the poetry and history) of the cathedral schools to the philosophy and science of the universities. There were those, such as the theologian John of Salisbury, who would lament this. But equally the new movement generated an excitement of its own as the translators of Toledo, gathered

Stone head of a Crusader
This sculptural decoration from the Frankish castle of Belvoir in the Holy Land was broken off from its original position when the castle was captured by the Saracens.

**Sculptures from Autun
and Vézelay**
*The work of Gislebertus
and the Master of Vézelay
marked a growing
maturity in Romanesque
sculpture. In their hands
the stiff, formal style of
early Romanesque gave
way to more naturalistic,
expressive figures. One of
the supreme examples of
this new style is
Gislebertus' vision of the
Last Judgment on the
tympanum at Autun.*

*Mystic mill of St Paul,
capital, Vézelay, France*

*West tympanum, by
Gislebertus, Autun, France*

there by Archbishop Raymond in the wake of retreating Islam, opened up new vistas by at last making available to their contemporaries in the Latin-speaking West the scientific achievements of the Greeks and of their successors, the Arabs.

Given the preoccupations of the day, it is in no way surprising that so much effort was spent, both at Toledo and at Palermo in Sicily (the other centre of translation), on rendering into Latin works on astrology, alchemy and magic. However, with these came Euclid's *Elements*, translated at Palermo by Adelard of Bath. Eugenius of Palermo gave Ptolemy's *Optica* to the West. And the many translations of the prolific Gerard of Cremona, from his base at Toledo, included works of the Arabs Alkindi, Rhazes, Alfarabi and Avicenna, of the Greeks Hippocrates and Archimedes, Diocles, Galen and Alexander of Aphrodisias, Ptolemy (the *Almagest*) and, most influential of all, the great Greek philosopher Aristotle.

One of the chief agents in the early dissemination of Aristotle's works was the so-called "School of Chartres", an intellectual centre to the south-west of Paris that flourished especially during the first half of the twelfth century under the brothers Bernard and Thierry of Chartres. Characteristic of the scholars of the Chartres school was their openness to

new influences, their freedom from dogma, and their desire, as individuals, to participate in the entirety of knowledge. The individual thinker and independent artist were both achieving an identity in this century. Neither is it a long step, in such a society, from the scholars of the Chartres school to the confident assertiveness of Gislebertus, the sculptor of Autun, who signed his masterpiece, the tympanum at Autun, with the words "Gislebertus the Master made this".

Gislebertus and the anonymous Master of Vézelay, both of them working in the third and early fourth decades of the twelfth century, almost certainly received their first training at Cluny. And it was from Cluny that the elaborate and expressive sculptures that decorate the doorways at Autun and Vézelay further pointed the way to the influential mid-century work at St-Denis and Chartres, and ultimately, in the next century, to those crowning glories of High Gothic sculpture, the western portals at Rheims. However, alongside the extravagance of the traditional Church there also flourished a puritan reaction. St Bernard (1092–1153), the dominant voice in the Cistercian order and the greatest religious figure of his time, castigated the Cluniacs and their imitators for the "ridiculous monsters", the "unclean apes", and the "monstrous

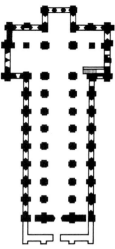

Abbey Church, Fontenay, France (plan)
The simple cruciform plan on which all Cistercian churches were built was laid down by the order's early legislators.

South porch (detail), Moissac, France
This carving of the head of the Prophet Jeremiah, by an unknown Master, has an expressive gentleness which is characteristic of the sculptures of Moissac.

Eagle flagon, St-Denis, France
This gold and porphyry flagon was part of Abbot Suger's assembled treasures, at St-Denis.

centaurs'' with which they decorated their churches. "For God's sake," he asked, "if men are not ashamed of these follies, why at least do they not shrink from the expense?" Indeed, the architecture of St Bernard's own prescription, at least for as long as the saint still lived, was itself forbiddingly austere.

St Bernard was not critical of all art. His own Cistercian order, despite the starkness of its church interiors and dull uniformity of their plans, became known for the quality of its manuscript illumination (see page 65). And on occasion even the Cluniacs, his accustomed target, were capable of notable restraint. It is unlikely that the saint himself could have found much to criticize in the work, for example, on the south porch of Moissac, where the dignified sculptures of the tympanum, the lintel, and the central supporting mullion stand out as perhaps the greatest achievement of the Romanesque tradition of Toulouse. And inevitably, an order that built as extensively as the Cistercians, with well over three hundred houses established before St Bernard's death, could not fail to be touched itself by the contemporary revolution in architectural methods, a revolution which it helped indeed to promote.

Although this revolution was anticipated elsewhere in many of its details, it is generally thought to have reached its first fruition at St-Denis, immediately north of Paris. Under the direction of Abbot Suger, and with the support of successive kings of France at exactly the period when the Capetian line had succeeded in establishing its authority, the abbey at St-Denis acquired the first great church in the Gothic manner, a model to a legion of imitators. What the new style depended on, and what so clearly distinguished it from the old, was the pointed arch, opening the way to an unprecedented verticality in building. In part a triumph of architectural engineering, but at least as much a product of aesthetics, the abbey church or cathedral of northern France was to become an area for experiment, as well as increasingly for competition. What was being sought was a building always higher, lighter, and more graceful than the last, with the form eventually reaching its climax in the thirteenth-century cathedral of Beauvais.

Whereas the Romanesque semi-circular arch had been relatively inelastic, its

Church of St-Denis, France
St-Denis, built 1137-44, was the first great Gothic church; its pointed arches were fundamental to the Gothic style, liberating builders from the limitations of the semi-circular arch.

height having to equal half its span, the new Gothic pointed arches, varying in angle, could spring from a single column, giving opportunities for intricacies in vaulting that would tempt the virtuosity of any architect. Similarly provoking were the problems of how to counteract the lateral thrust of a vault. In due course it was these that led to the development of the flying buttress and to its use with spectacular effect in such turn-of-the-century works as the great cathedrals at Chartres and Bourges.

Moreover, the enthusiasm of contemporary builders and their patrons was not limited to the stonework of their churches. Chartres is well known for the quality of its surviving stained glass, much of it dating from the early thirteenth century. And although there are now few survivals of the church furnishings of St-Denis, collected and described so lovingly by Abbot Suger, we know that they included work of the goldsmiths and enamellers of the Mosan region and Liège, already famous for a century or more.

Also influential in contemporary church-building were the traditions of Byzantium and the Islamic Near East. They

Eastern influences on architecture
Partly as a result of the Crusades, Eastern Mediterranean influences touched Western Europe in the 12th century. In the church of St-Front, Perigueux (1120), the domes are Byzantine in style, and at the cathedral of Monreale in Sicily (1174-82) Romanesque capitals and eastern mosaic-decorated columns are used together in the cloister. Castle architecture also changed dramatically. The keep declined in importance, and a new tradition of multiple defensive rings and fortified gate-towers grew up. Krak des Chevaliers in the East and Château Gaillard in the West were two notable examples of the new style.

Church of St-Front, Perigueux, France

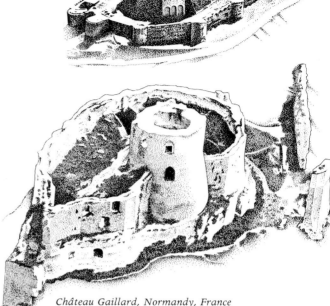

Krak des Chevaliers, Syria

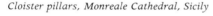

Cloister pillars, Monreale Cathedral, Sicily

Château Gaillard, Normandy, France

FACING PAGE
Cistercian art
An Englishman, Stephen Harding, ruled the abbey of Cîteaux between 1109 and 1133. Under his influence, Cistercian art adopted the lively and inventive English tinted drawing style, very different in character from the order's contemporary austerity in architecture.

are to be detected in the five domes of St-Front at Perigueux and more obviously still in the cathedrals of Sicily, that hybrid Norman and Saracen kingdom. Indeed, the cathedral of Monreale near Palermo, begun in 1174, produced its own miraculous amalgam of the competing cultures of East and West. But while in ecclesiastical building local traditions reasserted themselves comparatively quickly in the North, the growing sophistication there of military architecture was the result of quite another creative interaction, its forcing-house being the disputed coastal lands of the Eastern Mediterranean.

The eleventh-century castle-palaces of William the Conqueror, at London and again at Colchester, had belonged to an antique tradition, with roots in the architecture of the Carolingians. In contrast, the castle-builders of twelfth-century Europe looked outwards to a world they had only recently encountered in the Crusader States. So rapid, indeed, was the development of castle architecture in twelfth-century Europe that the great stone keep of Dover Castle was already something of an anachronism even at the time of its construction. The keep at Dover was built by Henry II on the model of the keeps that Henry I, his grandfather, had had constructed at Norwich and elsewhere. Scarcely more than a generation

later, the entire castle had to be replanned with multiple rings of concentric defences, entered through a sophisticated, strongly-fortified gate-tower. This concentric layout had been the lesson learned from the Holy Land, where the experience of the Byzantine, the Arab, and the western ''Frank'' had been brought together in the rebuilt former Arab fortress at Krak des Chevaliers or the once Byzantine castle at Saone.

In Normandy, Château Gaillard, as a purpose-built, one-period castle put up for Richard I in 1196-8 under the king's personal and very active supervision, demonstrates what the castle had become. Richard, it is thought, never visited Krak des Chevaliers, though he certainly knew of the work in process of completion there in the earlier 1190s while he himself was in the Holy Land on crusade. He had become experienced himself in a castle warfare which had quickly developed great sophistication, following from the perennial shortage of men in the East and the consequent reluctance to expose them to pitched battles. No expense was spared at Château Gaillard in the extraordinarily rapid completion of Richard's ''Fair Castle of the Rock''. He equipped it, on the outer curtain wall, with cylindrical towers in the up-to-date manner, and with machicolations in the style that his fellow crusaders

EVE
RENTIS
SIMO
ET SCISSIMO
FRI LEANDRO
CO EPO
GREGORI

SERVVS

SERVORV DI;

Capital, Church of the Annunciation, Nazareth, Israel
The Crusades carried both Western and Byzantine styles to the Holy Land. This Romanesque capital, by the Master of Plaimpied, was one of many works of art commissioned for the new churches of the Christian holy places.

had borrowed from their opponents, the Arabs. He supplied it with a deep-set, easily defended gate-house, and lavished much attention on the cylindrical keep, experimental in form like many of the near-contemporary tower keeps of the West, among them the English Orford and Conisborough.

The cross-fertilization of cultures, already evident enough at Richard's great fortress at Château Gaillard, was naturally still more obvious in the Holy Land. During the course of the twelfth century, the aristocracy of Christian Jerusalem developed a life-style which was truly oriental in its magnificence, crossing traditional cultural barriers. Thus, by the mid-century, they were ready to take their church plans from Burgundy and the Auvergne, even while developing in the circular or polygonal churches of the Knights Templar a distinctive plan of their own, based on the Church of the Holy Sepulchre, Jerusalem. They might tempt over a great sculptor from the West, as they did the anonymous Master of Plaimpied, near Bourges, and then set him to work on the capitals of the Church of the Annunciation at Nazareth, while the ecumenical spirit of the Christian Holy Places allowed them to draw on the whole company of saints and martyrs—Eastern and Western, ancient and modern—to provide subjects for the wall-paintings that decorated the columns at the Church of the Nativity, Bethlehem.

The style of these paintings and their whole conception clearly originated in Byzantium. And certainly the tradition of Byzantium—in wall-paintings, in mosaics, and in the indigenous "Franco-Byzantine" architectural style—would continue dominant in the Holy Land. Not surprisingly, the high quality of the Byzantine achievement inspired many imitations in the Mediterranean world, penetrating even to the North. Many Greek mosaicists worked in Sicily on the Palatine Chapel and on the cathedrals of Monreale and Cefalù. They were employed again at St Mark's, in Venice, and at various dates, both in the eleventh and twelfth centuries, at the nearby cathedral of Torcello. In English wall-paintings of the later twelfth century, Byzantine influence is well-marked.

Some part of the popularity of Byzantine art in the West may have had to do with a sharing of religious preoccupations. For Byzantium, it is true, the defeat at Manzikert and the loss of Anatolia had been followed by a reaction against all earlier artistic experiments. At Constantinople, there was now a return in architectural practice to tenth-century norms, to be seen in a building as important as the monastery of the Pantocrator, tomb-church of the Comneni, completed before 1136. Simultaneously, at least one movement in the arts favoured a markedly linear style, picking out the highlights both in mosaics and in enamels in such a way as to enhance the formality of the subject. But alongside this essentially traditional fashion there had grown another of a very much wider appeal. The cult of the Virgin, developing contemporaneously in the West, was accompanied by a novel emphasis on the humanity of Christ and on the intercessionary role of the saints. In twelfth-century art, both in Byzantium and (only slightly later) in Western Europe, the consequences of this new attitude brought about a transformation in style which demonstrated vividly the shifting foundations of belief (see pages 68-9).

In both East and West, up to this point, Christian art had chosen to lay stress on the majesty of God, on the dignity of Christ, and on the authority of the fathers of the Church. Christ is triumphant in a Romanesque crucifixion scene; even as a child, he sits equipped with the symbols of his majesty, enthroned on his mother's knee. The contrast with the developing sensitivity of the twelfth-century portrait could scarcely be more marked. Passion, tenderness and suffering return to religious art in the twelfth century. And although all extremes of emotion were not recaptured at once, this was certainly the way towards the new realism, later more fully developed in the West.

Eastern Europe

One of the earliest of the Byzantine masterpieces in the new tradition became, because of its subsequent history, a work of exceptional artistic importance. The icon now known as the *Virgin of Vladimir* is thought to have been painted in Constantinople in about 1125. As was the case with many other icons of the then flourishing Byzantine school, it was brought to Russia within a few years of its completion, probably between 1132 and 1136, to find its first Russian home at Kiev. The *Virgin of Vladimir* is an icon

Russian church architecture

In the 12th century Russian church architecture began to develop an indigenous style, characterized by a modest plan and a compact, cubical appearance. Elaborate decoration was also avoided, except in Vladimir-Suzdalia.

The Pokrov, Suzdalia, Russia

Cathedral of the Dormition, Vladimir, Russia

St Dmitry, Vladimir, Russia

St George in the Yuriev Monastery, Novgorod, Russia

Carving, St Dmitry, Vladimir, Russia

Elaborate external carvings became a distinctive feature of Suzdalian church architecture. Those shown below, which cover the drum and side-walls at St Dmitry, exhibit both Byzantine and Middle Eastern influence.

infused with a melancholy tenderness which, among the artists and worshippers of medieval Russia, established an instant rapport. Yet at least part of its influence must have been owed to its continued presence at the heart of artistic innovation in Russia. It was subsequently taken from Kiev to Vladimir by Andrey Bogoliubsky, prince of Vladimir-Suzdal, and it later continued to follow the fortunes of the Russian state, coming to Moscow in 1395 where it has since remained, the most sacred of Russian icons and an object of veneration to every Christian of the surviving Orthodox persuasion (see page 69).

The principality of Vladimir-Suzdal, deep in central Russia towards the head of the Volga River, had risen on the weakness of the Kievan state, by then isolated from Byzantium and under continued nomad attack. And although its own period of independent prosperity was to be even shorter than that of Kiev, being brought to an end before the mid-thirteenth century by the Mongols, Suzdalia was able to develop during the century of its dominance an art that at last was distinctively Russian. The roots of Suzdalian architecture are identifiably Kievan, going back beyond that to original models in Byzantium. Yet the very first surviving stone churches of Suzdalia, dating to the 1150s, already exhibit the most obvious characteristics of the developing Vladimir-Suzdalian style: a cube-shaped elevation, a tall drum tower supporting the central dome, and at least some of the decorative external panelling which quickly became such a feature of mature Suzdalian church architecture.

Some of these characteristics, in particular the cubical appearance and the restricted simplified plan, can be found repeated in the architecture of contemporary Novgorod, to become a part of the essential Russian tradition. But unique to Suzdalia was the remarkable architectural sculpture that developed in this region, first seen at Andrey Bogoliubsky's Church of the Protection and Intercession of the Virgin (1166), known as the Pokrov.

Andrey, it is known, was fond of decoration. His palace and church at Bogoliubovo, completed just before the building of the Pokrov, are said to have been especially ornate, it being, in the words of a contemporary, "hard to look at all the gold". Nevertheless, the tradition he established lasted for as long as the independence, admittedly brief, of the Vladimir-Suzdalian principality. Vsevolod III, Andrey's brother and successor, rebuilt his Cathedral of the Dormition at Vladimir, after the fire of 1183, in a style still more splendid than before. And Vsevolod's second church, the Church of St Dmitry (1194-7), again at Vladimir, is the most complete illustration, in the low-relief carvings which cover the drum and the side-walls above the colonnettes, of

The Ascension, stained-glass window, Le Mans Cathedral, France

The cult of the Virgin

One of the most obvious expressions of a new humanity in religion was the 12th-century cult of the Virgin. A great number of churches were dedicated to Mary in this century, and representations of the Virgin were often central to the art of the period. Characteristic of the cult was an increasing emphasis on the tenderness of Christ's mother, and on her role as an understanding and forgiving intercessor between the supplicant Christian and his God. Accordingly, while the Virgin may still be shown in 12th-century art in the stiff and formal poses of the earlier tradition, the most influential renderings of the Mother and Child theme were already those which dwelt on the Virgin's essential compassion. Of unexampled importance to Orthodox Christianity in Russia was that great icon, the *Virgin of Vladimir*. Painted in Constantinople in about 1125, it was one of the earliest examples of the new tradition in art which emphasized the motherhood of Mary in place of her more formidable regality.

FACING PAGE Virgin of Vladimir, *icon*

ABOVE *Annunciation (detail) on cloister capital, Monreale Cathedral, Sicily*

Cistercian manuscript illumination, Cîteaux, France

Mural (detail), Eski Gumus, Turkey

Apse mosaic, Torcello Cathedral, Italy

Stave church, Borgund, Norway
This 12th-century building is typical of the wooden churches which proliferated in Norway, but of which only a few survive today.

Giralda tower, Seville Cathedral, Spain
A minaret for a mosque until the surrender at Seville in 1248, the body of the Giralda tower retains its original 12th-century Islamic decoration.

the skill and originality of the sculptors of the developed Suzdalian School.

St Dmitry, in its plan, is an almost exact copy of the Pokrov. And the same inclination to repeat a plan once successfully developed and refined occurred again more influentially still at that real cradle of Russian architecture, the principality of Novgorod the Great. Here it was that churches like the Cathedral of St George in the Yuriev Monastery, built by Master Peter, a Russian architect, in the third decade of the twelfth century, established the main principles of Russian ecclesiastical architecture, becoming in due course a fixed and immutable model. In sharp contrast to the great eleventh-century cathedrals of St Sophia at Kiev and at Novgorod itself, the Church of St George was a simple building, vertical rather than horizontal in its emphasis, compact and comparatively austere. And in general Russian church architecture was moving in a different direction from that contemporaneously being taken both in Byzantium and the West. Except in Vladimir-Suzdalia, it eschewed elaborate external decoration, achieving its effects by the massing of domes, usually assymmetrically disposed, or else by a roof-line, simply but strikingly gabled.

Such particular emphasis on the decorative possibilities of the roof undoubtedly stemmed from the native building instinct of what was still (as it would long continue to be) a "carpentry culture". The Norwegian stave church, of which there are some remarkable twelfth-century survivals, is an example of just such another equally vigorous tradition in the North. Obviously, the climate had much to do with gables angled to get rid of the snow, just as it had with that characteristically Russian onion dome, the antecedents of which are recognizable already in early-twelfth-century Novgorod.

Similar domes are to be seen throughout the Middle East, and would be taken by Islam into India. But the Russian dome, originating in the far North at least a century before the arrival of the Mongols, must surely be an indigenous development. Indeed, if we are to look for oriental influence on the ripening art of Russia, we are more likely to find it in sculpture. Here the Vladimir-Suzdalian carved reliefs are again of the greatest importance, for the animal and floral motifs certainly derive from the East.

Historically, this is reasonable enough, for Andrey Bogoliubsky's fashionable "zeal for the Virgin" is said to have attracted to him "architects of all countries . . . brought to him by God". However, even without the intervention of the deity, Suzdalia's situation at the source of the mighty navigable Volga River had made it an obvious point of exchange for the cultures of East and West. And there are clear parallels between the crowded overall decoration of the Christian Suzdalian church façade and that same striving after a closely patterned effect on the walls of an Islamic Seljuk mosque.

Near East

Over the whole Islamic world, dominated in the twelfth century by the Seljuks, the arts were taking refuge in the abstract patterns and mannered calligraphy still permitted by the renewed religion. Seljuk architecture, characteristically, set the plain wall surfaces of the body of a building against the elaborate brickwork, the stone-carving and the faience tile-mosaics of its gate or minaret. Contemporaneously, the first attempts were made in Persia at the complete covering of a dome or a large wall surface with glazed tiles. Syrian glass and Persian pottery are at their finest in this period, with inlaid brass throughout the Middle East achieving an exceptional perfection.

Rather apart from this was Muslim Spain, certainly less influenced in its relative isolation by some of the more showy manifestations of the current Islamic revival. Architecturally, this was the period of the superb Giralda Tower at Seville Cathedral, formerly a minaret of the Almohad mosque there and decorated up to the level of its sixteenth-century belfry with the characteristic broad-mesh stone-carving of that tradition. But above all it was as an intellectual centre that Muslim Spain was still distinguished in the twelfth century, the more so because of the contemporary reaction against the study of science and philosophy by now gripping Middle Eastern Islam.

The revival of learning in Arab Spain had begun as early as the mid-eleventh century, following the collapse of the Umayyad Caliphate (1031). However, not until the twelfth century, and particularly after the establishment of the Almohad dynasty in 1140, did science and philosophy in Muslim Spain achieve their

Map from atlas of al-Idrisi
This map, completed in 1154, reflects Arab knowledge of the Mediterranean, Africa and Asia, acquired through their travel and trade.

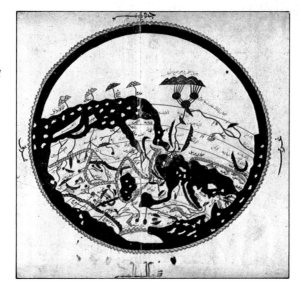

Persian tankard
This Lugor tankard has the characteristic Kufic inscriptions of Seljuk-dominated Islamic art.

Terracotta head, Ife, Africa
One of the many found at Ife, this sculpture has the characteristic naturalism of Ife's "classical" period.

most notable flowering, with Averroës (d. 1198), the learned and influential Arab commentator on the works of Aristotle, Ibn al-'Arabi (d. 1240), the famous mystical philosopher, Ibn al-Baytar (d. 1248), the botanist, and Abu Marwan ibn Zuhr (d. 1161), physician and co-author with Averroës of a medical encyclopedia.

Averroës, in particular, became well-known to Latin scholarship, his commentaries being translated and made available to the West by Michael Scot, working in early-thirteenth-century Christian Toledo. Moreover, this tradition of contact between East and West, long established already in Toledo, was equally important in the conveying of practical skills, such as the learning of Arab geographers.

Arab travellers, from the ninth century onwards, had built up an impressive knowledge of distant lands. And it was accumulated expertise that made possible the work of such celebrated cartographers as al-Idrisi (d. 1162) of Palermo, whose *Geography* (the so-called *Book of Roger* named after its Sicilian Norman patron) placed him first among the great Arab geographical compilers of his time. Al-Idrisi's atlas, researched, he tells us, over a period of fifteen years, was completed in 1154. And it shows us his already sound understanding of the Mediterranean world, of Western Europe, and of central and southern Asia, all of these being the familiar territories of the Arab traveller and merchant. Less well known, but still an area long penetrated and exploited by the Arabs, was the African continent with its ivory and gold on the East African coast, and with its slaves.

Africa

We have no means of telling when the Arabs first opened the way to Nigeria, though they were there certainly by the eleventh century and may have traded there occasionally much earlier. Al-Idrisi himself knew West and Central Africa to a point not far beyond the southern limits of the Sahara, with a better knowledge of the East African coast, beyond Zanzibar to Madagascar. Iron, he informs us, was the chief commodity sought by the Arabs in East Africa, but there were important trades also in ivory and gold, with slaves both from East Africa and from West.

Very probably, it was the slave trade which brought wealth to the kings of Ife, near the point where rain forest and savanna meet in what is now modern Nigeria. And certainly wealth was what was needed to generate the kind of art we associate with Ife's "classical" period. Difficult to date, as all African art has tended to be at least until the recent revolution in scientific dating methods, there is nevertheless good reason to suppose that the terracotta sculptures of Ife and just a few of the bronzes date from the twelfth century, though the tradition then persisted for some centuries.

It is still debatable where Ife art originated. In some respects, it seems related to the very much earlier Nok tradition of central Nigeria, and there are parallels too with the remarkable art of

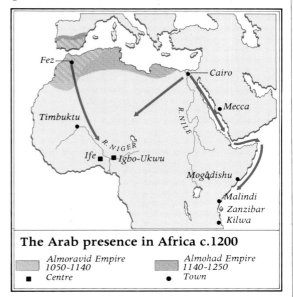

The Arab presence in Africa c.1200

Almoravid Empire 1050-1140	Almohad Empire 1140-1250
■ Centre	● Town

The Arabs in Africa
Arab trade in Africa flourished under the Muslim Almoravids and their successors, the Almohads. The East African coast, a source of iron, ivory and gold, was exploited and Arab settlements established. On the West coast, Arab slave trade brought wealth to Ife.

Mosan art

Taking its name from the Meuse River and centred at Liège, in modern Belgium, Mosan painting, metalwork and ivory-carving was highly regarded in 12th-century Europe. Abbot Suger of St-Denis, one of the century's most ambitious and discerning patrons, was among the many who employed Mosan craftsmen, clearly attracted (as others were) by the range and ingenuity of their talent. The inspiration for this art was partly classical and partly Byzantine, although a good number of these elements were picked up locally from surviving work of the Carolingian Renaissance, going back to the 9th century, or of the 10th-century Ottonian revival. However, in metalwork, with the development of the champlevé enamelling technique, Mosan craftsmen stand out as innovators in their own right.

RIGHT *English champlevé enamel plaque*

BELOW *German reliquary in the shape of a church*

ABOVE *Head reliquary of Pope St Alexander*
BELOW *German reliquary executed by Nicholas of Verdun*

RIGHT *One of four champlevé enamel plaques from a French coffer*

BELOW *French champlevé enamel plaque*

BELOW *Four champlevé enamel plaques from the Klosterneuburg Altarpiece, by Nicholas of Verdun*

Qutb Minar, Delhi, India
The Qutb Minar, the minaret of the Qutb mosque, was begun in 1199, soon after the Muslim capture of Delhi. The new Muslim presence is apparent in the Koranic inscriptions which band the minaret; all other decoration belongs to the Indian tradition.

nearby Igbo-Ukwu, which may itself date back as far as the ninth century. But wherever it came from, we find it virtually fully formed in the important collection of terracottas and bronzes from the shrine at Ita Yemoo, in Ife, radiocarbon-dated to the twelfth century. Exhibited there is the idealized naturalism that would continue to be the principal characteristic of Ife art throughout the classical period. It is a sophisticated art requiring not merely modelling skill but also a considerable degree of technical expertise, most particularly in the casting of the bronzes. And it flourished in an aristocratic society which has left other twelfth-century cultural relics, such as the handsome soapstone human figures still worshipped in the sacred grove at Esie, north-east of Ife, or the distinctive potsherd pavements, early examples of which are the pavements at Ita Yemoo and Lafogido. At Lafogido, pottery vessels, some retaining their original animal-head lids, were found in association with the pavement.

There is nothing at all comparable to the Ife modelled figures along the East African coastal belt. However, the Arabs had been at Zanzibar since the ninth century, and as they took in further trading bases like Mogadishu, Malindi and Kilwa, they established a permanent presence on the coast that would result in its thirteenth-century engrossment by Islam. East Africa in these years took its place in the Muslim trading system, while the great Islamic powers made themselves masters of the Indian Ocean and of every territory that adjoined it. And inevitably, wherever the Muslims penetrated, a climate spread that was distinctly unfavourable to native art.

India

Muslim power had its most disastrous effect on India, which had already been the victim of Muslim religious vandalism during the early-eleventh-century raids of Mahmud of Ghazni. Now, in the late twelfth century, India was again exposed to Islamic puritanism with the conquest and settlement of Muhammad Ghuri and the long line of his Muslim successors. Entering India from Afghanistan, as Mahmud of Ghazni had done before him, Muhammad Ghuri took Sind by 1182, Lahore by 1185, and Delhi by 1192. And everywhere the Muslim went, the exotic art of Hindu and Buddhist India provoked

his deliberate iconoclasm. Characteristically, the courtyard of the Qutb, or "Might of Islam", Mosque at Delhi was supplied on three sides with a stone arcade supported on columns looted from Hindu temples. The mosque's dominant feature is the formidable Qutb Minar, a great minaret begun in 1199 and conceived as a Tower of Victory. It was a small triumph for Indian art that whereas the inscriptions that banded the Qutb Minar were taken from the conquerors' Koran, such other decoration as was permitted on the tower was very plainly of traditional Indian inspiration.

At the Qutb Mosque, for the first time, there are indications of what an Indo-Islamic culture could produce. However, the flowering of that culture had to await the Mughal empire of Akbar four centuries later. In the intervening period, more interest attaches to the unbroken art tradition of Hindu southern India, especially in the thirteenth century, and to the twelfth-century Buddhist renaissance of Ceylon.

Much of the inspiration of Buddhist architecture in Ceylon in the twelfth century remained with the Hindu Cholas. But the expulsion of the Cholas from Ceylon had begun in the late eleventh century, and the power of the Singhalese kings grew steadily through the next decades as the threat of the Cholas diminished. In the event, the Singhalese ruler who, by invading the mainland, actually took the war into the enemy's camp, would also become known as one of Ceylon's most notable builders. Parakrama Bahu I, succeeded by his nephew Nissanka Malla, ruled Ceylon throughout the second half of the twelfth century, creating between them a great walled capital at Polonnaruwa, in the north-eastern part of the island.

In a cultural renaissance which included the revival of crafts such as metalwork and ivory carving, both ancient Singhalese skills, the patronage of Parakrama the Great promoted also an unprecedented building programme. Of the many impressive survivals from this programme, the Thuparama Temple at Polonnaruwa has clear antecedents in the many Shaivite temples of the eleventh-century Chola rulers of Ceylon. Yet it is constructed entirely of brick and stucco in the native Singhalese manner, as is that Buddhist shrine, the Lankatilaka Temple, with its exterior influenced by Chola architecture but built for a colossal Buddha figure.

Other monumental Buddha figures, together with a sculpture of a Singhalese king—possibly Parakrama Bahu himself—are carved from the living rock at Polonnaruwa, being among the more remarkable sculptural achievements to have survived from the twelfth-century world (see page 60). And the central role of Ceylon as a Buddhist headquarters, guardian of a uniquely important tooth relic, is commemorated again in two adjoining temples, the Hata-da-ge and the Wata-da-ge, both in the Great Quadrangle at Polonnaruwa.

The Wata-da-ge, with its distinctive and unusual circular plan, is thought to have been built by Parakrama Bahu, and ranks as the principal architectural masterpiece of his reign. But most of the shrines in the Great Quadrangle complex are more clearly associated with Nissanka Malla, and they include a building of particular interest, the Sat Mahal Pasada, a terraced stupa of pyramidal form. What is especially intriguing about this temple is that its origins seem not to lie in Ceylon itself but in the Khmer architecture of Cambodia and of the adjoining Khmer-dominated Siam. Whether or not the Sat Mahal Pasada was built, as has been suggested, for Cambodian mercenaries in the employ of the Singhalese kings, its presence at Polonnaruwa is important evidence of the continuing influence of Singhalese Buddhism on the countries of South-East Asia. Most obviously it was present in Burma. But it touched even a kingdom like Cambodia which had taken another religious road.

South-East Asia

Earlier in the century, Cambodian civilization had reached a peak of artistic creativity never afterwards regained, under Suryavarman II (1112-52), builder of Angkor Wat. It was not exclusively a Buddhist civilization, and Angkor Wat was dedicated at first to Vishnu, a Hindu deity. But in any event Cambodian Buddhism was to remain generous and loosely defined. The conversion of Jayavarman VII (1181-*c.* 1220) to Mahayana Buddhism proved of immense importance to the cultural tradition of his period. His choice of the mystical, free-thinking road of the followers of Mahayana was indeed a fortunate one, enriching the art of contemporary Cambodia where a more rigid fundamentalism might otherwise seriously have distorted it.

The Cambodian kingdom, although beset from the East by the Chams of Champa who were later absorbed by Vietnam, nevertheless experienced considerable periods of prosperity under Suryavarman II, through the first half of the century, and then again under Jayavarman VII, during its final decades. Both kings were patrons of the arts on a munificent scale, the builders of monuments at Angkor Wat (pre-1150) and Angkor Thom (post-1150) which have never ceased to astound the spectator.

No doubt, a fair part of the impact of the Angkor ruins today may be explained by the way that they were subsequently overtaken by the jungle. Yet even without this additional dramatization, the temples of twelfth-century Cambodia can stand on their own as architectural conceptions

Buddhist temples, Polonnaruwa, Ceylon

The circular Wata-da-ge temple (right) was built by Parakrama Bahu I. The Sat Mahal Pasada (above) was built by Nissanka Malla, and is reminiscent of Cambodian architecture.

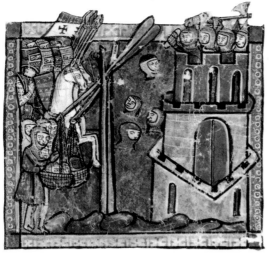

Crusaders bombing Nicosia with their captives' heads,
Les Histoires d'Outremer, 13th century

RIGHT *Knights on horseback,*
Froissart Chronicles, 15th century

The Crusades

The taking of Antioch in 1098 and the successful siege and storming of Jerusalem a year later remained stories frequently re-told and illustrated in the literature and art of the medieval Christian West. But such exploits were rarely repeated. Jerusalem was lost to Saladin, Sultan of Egypt and Syria, in 1187, and although Richard of England, during the Third Crusade, twice more got within reach of the city in 1192, he never succeeded in retaking it. The Fourth Crusade, far from building on the Third, was misguidedly directed against Orthodox Byzantium. The sack of Constantinople in 1204, resulting in the dispersal of rich art collections, has since been recognized as one of the greatest artistic disasters of all time. In the Holy Land itself, Antioch fell to the Egyptians in 1268, amid scenes of unbridled carnage.

The siege of Antioch, Les Histoires d'Outremer, 13th century

Tomb-effigy of a Crusader,
Dorchester Abbey, England, c. 1270

Jerusalem in the Crusades, Joinville, 14th century

The siege of Jerusalem by the Crusaders, manuscript illumination, 15th century

Angkor Wat, Cambodia
The huge temple of Angkor Wat consists of several sanctuaries, on a central platform over 3,000 feet square, linked by a series of connecting galleries. Magnificent sculptures, such as The Churning of the Sea of Milk *(above right), adorn the walls of these galleries. At the centre of the temple are five towers; the highest of these towers tops the central shrine.*

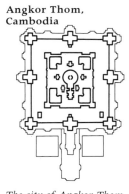

Angkor Thom, Cambodia

The city of Angkor Thom has at its centre the great temple-mountain of the Bayon. Its many towers each display four carved faces, in all probability Jayavarman VII.

where the imaginative genius of the patron and designer has been fully matched by the quality of the craftsman. Not only did the buildings of Angkor Wat constitute the full flowering of the Cambodian architectural tradition, but the same peak was reached by the sculptors, to show especially in the finely-executed relief carvings of the famous cloister frieze.

Later in the century, in the grandiose works of Jayavarman VII at Angkor Thom, some of the delicacy of the early carvings was lost in mass-production, all but submerged in that profusion of detail which has labelled the style ''Flamboyant''. But where Jayavarman's buildings lose in quality, they gain in monumentality, especially in that centre and focus of the king's new capital, the great temple-mountain of the Bayon.

Suryavarman's Angkor Wat had been a funerary temple, both memorial to the king and monument to death itself. To the Buddhist Jayavarman, seeing himself as a true *bodhisattva* setting his people on the road to salvation, the Bayon was something more. The consistent central characteristic of the multiple towers of the Bayon is the gigantic carved face of the Bodhisattva Avalotikeshvara, looking out in every direction and probably to be identified with none other than Jayavarman VII himself. The gesture is political as much as religious, the king's divinity reaffirming his secular authority.

Jayavarman's kingdom, even before his death, had been strained financially by his over-ambitious architectural enterprises. Early in the thirteenth century, while work on the Bayon was still continuing, the Chams were again on the move, with little in the field to oppose them. Moreover, within a few decades, a more serious threat would arise as the Thais came south out of their Yunnan homeland. Throughout Asia generally, such pressures from the North were to prove a continual threat. And nowhere were the pickings as rich as in the vast Chinese empire of the Sung.

China after 1127

Jürched China

Sung China

...... Border of Sung China before 1127

The Jürched invasion of North China
In 1114, the Tartar Jürcheds rose against the empire of the Liao; by 1127 they had captured Kaifeng, the capital in North China of the Sung. The survivors were forced southwards, and had to establish a new capital at Hangchow.

Far East

A Tungusic people, known as the Jürched Tartars, broke into China in the second decade of the twelfth century, rolling up the empires first of the Liao and then of the Northern Sung. Their task was made easy by the political troubles besetting the empires they took over—the long-standing struggle between reformers and traditionalists and the growing discontents of the peasants. But just as had been the case with the Khitan Liao in the previous century and would come to be true of the Mongols in the next, the success of the Tartars was at least partly owed to what the Chinese themselves had taught them. In 1115, only a year after their first uprising against the Liao, the Jürched rulers adopted for themselves the Chinese dynastic name of Chin. It was as Chin Tartars in 1126 that they besieged the Sung capital of Kaifeng, using every device known to Chinese military technology, including gunpowder, in the course of the struggle.

One of the tragedies of the siege and sack of Kaifeng was the dispersal of the great art collection of the Emperor Hui-tsung, both a connoisseur and a painter of distinction in his own right. Another unwelcome cultural consequence of the Sung collapse was an immediate halt in the production of Ju-yao ware, a highly-fired earthenware of unusual distinction which had flourished under imperial patronage only in the last generation of Northern Sung rule. As a result of the invasion, high achievement in art now moved to South China, to thrive under the protection of the Southern Sung emperors now established at their new capital at Hangchow. However, even the Chin, although lacking the refined taste of the Sung they displaced, were not inclined to meddle with whatever survived their invasion. Ting ware, unlike Ju-yao, continued to be manufactured in North China, developing the new moulding techniques introduced under the Sung at the beginning of the twelfth century, and showing no reduction in quality. It was only in the following century, under the Mongols, that the Ting kilns went into an obvious decline.

Cultural continuity was only the more obvious for being consciously sought after by the first Sung emperor based in Southern China, Kao-tsung (1127-62), as a buttress and justification of his dynasty. The art of Chang Tse-tuan and the other genre painters of the early twelfth century seems, it is true, to have died with the Northern Sung. There would never again be such precious historical documents as Chang Tse-tuan's great scroll, *The Ch'ing-ming Festival on the River* which, quite apart from its obvious pictorial merits, tells us so much about contemporary Chinese society. However, the revival under imperial patronage of the Academy of Painting at Hangchow, including among its members many of those who had worked for the Emperor Hui-tsung at Kaifeng, made sure that little else was lost to Chinese painting in the debacle. The greatest achievements of the Hang-chow Academy had to await the beginning of the thirteenth century with the work of Hsia Kuei and Ma Yüan. But the transition to them from the Northern Sung academicians is foreshadowed in the landscape paintings of Li T'ang, the most

Chinese scroll by Chang Tse-tuan (detail)
This great Sung scroll, The Ch'ing-ming Festival on the River, *was produced in Kaifeng by the painter Chang Tse-tuan in the early years of the 12th century. The painting is a valuable historical document as well as a work of art since it shows many details of the sophisticated society that characterized China at the time.*

Japanese art

The 12th century saw the refinement of narrative painting on the horizontal hand-scroll, and the emergence of a school of portraiture in the strikingly realistic art of Fujiwara Takanobu (1142-1205). One of the best-known of the earlier hand-scrolls is the romantic *Tale of Genji*, the narrative continuing through many scenes of which only one is shown here. In contrast, Takanobu's portraits are immobile but very powerful, their realism picked up by contemporary sculpture where a complicated idea like the incarnation of a deity can be shown on a figure which is otherwise true to life.

ABOVE The Tale of Genji *(detail of scroll)*
LEFT Portrait of Minamoto no Yoritomo *by Fujiwara Takanobu*
BELOW *Heian carving of the priest Hochi*

Chinese pottery

The pottery industry of South China flourished in the 12th century under the patronage of the Southern Sung. Among its products were the jade-coloured Lung-ch'üan celadons and the high-quality Kuan ware, initially developed for the imperial court as a substitute for the lost Ju-yao wares of Kaifeng. Both were widely exported. However, in Japan the Chinese were particularly successful with their dark brown Chien ware, a functional ware used only for teabowls.

Lung-ch'üan covered vase, Southern China

Lu incense burner, Kuan ware, Southern China

Chien teabowl, China

respected of the first masters of the Hangchow Academy. While Li T'ang looked back into the past for the restraint and self-discipline of the earlier landscapists, he offered some suggestion too of the bolder techniques of the future.

Perhaps inevitably, the minor art of the Southern Sung was both escapist and backward-looking, dwelling on the luxuries of contemporary palace life and on the historical triumphs of the past. It was to be a long time before the Sung emperors would acknowledge the permanence of their defeat. But the enforced migration of the imperial court to the South was not without its advantages. Already under the Sung of Kaifeng the wealth of China had shifted appreciably southwards, to become located especially in the fertile lands and multiplying cities of the Lower Yangtze valley. Now Hangchow itself became a rich and populous city. And it was the commercial development of South China during this period, bringing to the surface, as it did, a new source of patronage in the emergent mercantile class, that did most to transform the art and architecture of the embattled Southern Sung. Once austere, aristocratic, pure and conservative, it was now very much broader based.

A good part of this growth was no doubt owed to simple demographic factors: to an expanding population and to the widening markets and developing agricultural technology that came with it. But some was the result of deliberate government policy, as evidenced, for example, by the organization of a state medical service during the first half of the twelfth century, and most particularly by the fostering of trade. One of the industries most directly affected by the Southern Sung search for new revenues was that of the potters, neglected in the South before the twelfth century for want of discerning and sophisticated patronage, but now experiencing an unlooked-for boom. In addition to a flourishing home market, fine Chinese porcelains were much in demand in every area to which Chinese trade, under active government sponsorship, now penetrated—in South-East Asia, in Korea and Japan, in India, Central Asia, East Africa, and throughout the Middle East. Probably the best known of these wares, which reached their fullest development in the thirteenth century although already important in the twelfth, were the Lung-ch'üan celadons and the

"Waterfall of Kotoin" by Li T'ang
The vertical emphasis of the soaring cliffs in this landscape painting echoes the old style of Kaifeng. Yet in his treatment of the trees and rocks, Li T'ang was a forerunner of the new, direct style that would become predominant at the Academy of Hangchow.

related Kuan ware, thought to have been made initially for the imperial court as a substitute for the lost Ju-yao wares of Kaifeng. Also in demand overseas were the Chi-chou wares, the Chien, and the *ch'ing-pai* of Jao-chou.

An important rival of the export wares of China was the distinctive inlaid celadon which was perhaps the finest individual product of the Korean pottery industry. Much admired by the Chinese themselves, and later very influential in Japan, these Korean celadons were entirely characteristic of a society which, while still overshadowed by its Chinese suzerains, had yet achieved considerable political as well

Korean stoneware
*The black Koryo celadons
of Korea were very
popular with the Japanese,
even rivalling the Chinese
porcelains exported
to Japan.*

**Great South Gate,
Todaiji, Japan**
*The shogun Yoritomo
rebuilt the religious centre
of Todaiji in the late 12th
century. Since very little
12th-century Southern
Sung architecture survives
in China, this building,
with its decorative
multiple brackets,
demonstrates how ornate
Chinese architecture was
itself becoming.*

as artistic independence under its Koryo dynasty. One Koryo ruler, the hedonistic King Uijong (1146-70), earned the title "Lord of Tranquillity and Literature Appreciation". And although Korean society through most of the twelfth century was in fact very far from tranquil, being troubled by repeated military coups and by risings of peasants and slaves, the high civilization of its aristocracy and the sophistication of its intellectual élite are indisputable. Remarkable in world historical scholarship still is the mid-century *Samguk sagi*, or *History of the Three Kingdoms*, compiled by Kim Pu-sik. Significantly, it reflects the persisting duality of Korean culture, for it was itself based on a model from China and it was even written in Chinese.

The pervasive influence of Sung China, diffused throughout East Asia, is especially detectable in Japan. From the ninth century, under the patronage of the Fujiwara regents, Japan had been shaping a culture of its own. Yet behind the considerable achievements of Japanese art through the Fujiwara (or Middle and Late Heian) Period there remained a Chinese presence, which intensified rather than weakened under the military governors of late-medieval Japan.

Before the end of the twelfth century, these military rulers took over, and the Kamakura period began. However, some of the new vigour and realism that we associate with their dominance had begun to show itself rather earlier. In particular this is so in Japanese painting and in that parallel development of the romantic and the popular narrative styles on the horizontal hand-scrolls of the Late Heian Period—on the one hand, the sophisticated and lyrical romanticism of the early-twelfth-century scrolls of the *Tale of Genji* (see page 80); on the other, the restless movement and racy characterization of the *Scroll of the Flying Storehouse*, not more than half a century later.

In China, where it had originated, the horizontal scroll had developed as a medium for landscape painting. And although, as we have seen, there were examples in the Northern Sung of genre painting in this tradition, it was the painters of Japan who used such scrolls for the fast-moving narrative art that they were to make especially their own. In portraiture too, starting with the art of Fujiwara Takanobu (1142-1205) and continuing through the long line of his pupils and successors, the Japanese were to make a significant individual contribution to the art of the medieval world. Fujiwara Takanobu's realistic portraits of the courtiers of his day contrast very strikingly with the benign effeminacy of contemporary religious art, whether in the carved *bodhisattva* images of Shansi in North China, or in those other essentially decorative Buddhist paintings characteristic of Late Heian Japan.

Takanobu painted his imperial courtiers only a decade before Minamoto no Yoritomo, one of his sitters (see page 80), triumphed over the rival Taira clan in 1185. After his victory, Yoritomo settled on Kamakura, near Tokyo, for his new capital, and it was from this that the military dictators of thirteenth-century Japan took their generic name. Properly speaking, the principal artistic achievements of the Kamakura Period also belong to the thirteenth century. However, Yoritomo's immediate rebuilding of Todaiji, a religious centre that had been devastated in the recently concluded civil wars, had already made important progress before the end of the twelfth century, being one of the first manifestations of the resurgence of Chinese Buddhist influence that later characterized the Kamakura dictatorship.

The most striking survival of the Todaiji rebuilding is the remarkable *nandaimon*, or Great South Gate. Interestingly, its inspiration is almost entirely Chinese, coming as a Buddhist import from Southern Sung China in the style misleadingly called "Indian" (*Tenjikuyo*). Very little of Southern Sung architecture survives in China itself, the best examples being the provincial exports to Korea and Kamakura Japan. However, we know that during

the later twelfth and thirteenth centuries Southern Sung architecture was experiencing a phase of progressive elaboration, eventually taken to extreme and unnecessary lengths. Something of this is visible at the Todaiji gate in the multiple brackets, bracing the deep overhang of the eaves. A clear Sung import, these were already more decorative than functional although modest still beside the tiresomely ornate bracketing of the *Karayo* (or ''Chinese'') style, introduced to Japan by Zen Buddhist missionaries during the course of the following century.

Such a fully developed polity as Southern Sung China was in danger of stifling that very creativity on which initially it had thrived. The architecture that the Zen monks imported to Japan, faithfully copying it in an effort to re-create the unique ambience of the Chinese houses they had left, was already degenerate. It lacked the graceful simplicity of earlier Sung architecture, and marked a step backward in building practice even in Japan itself.

Contemporaneously, in South-East Asia, there are clear parallels with what was happening in both China and Japan in the elaboration and coarsening of the art of Cambodia, its choice motifs multiplied to the point of monotony at Jayavarman's Angkor Thom. While across the Pacific at just this time, identical symptoms of a retreat in art, fallen a victim of political efficiency and an all-embracing state, are to be found again in the sophisticated empire of the northern Peruvian Chimu.

The Americas

There is another close parallel between twelfth-century Cambodia and the Chimu Empire in the independent development at each of these of the so-called ''urban élite centre''. Both were city-dominated societies, and both grouped the priests and the aristocracy together, to the exclusion of the less fortunate masses. But more important than this to the history of art was a populous urbanism (which they shared, for example, with Southern Sung China)—the obvious environment for mass-production. Chimu potters, while remaining dependent on Mochica prototypes, lost the skill of their ancestors as they met the demands of an enlarged urban market. Individual artistry in the painting and modelling of Chimu pots disappeared in commercial production.

Chimu civilization, as indeed had been the case with Mochica before it, persisted a very long time. Emerging perhaps as early as the eleventh century in Peru, it was still in a formative stage throughout the twelfth century, to last intact well into the fifteenth century and the conquest of Chanchan by the Incas. For just this reason, it is impossible to take the impressive ruins of Chanchan, the Chimu capital, where one building plainly overlies another, as the product of any one century, while the same difficulties attach to the precise dating of the roads and canal systems which the Chimu established or maintained. Yet unquestionably Chimu power expanded during the twelfth century, resulting in impressive public works. And it was probably the increasing sophistication of Chimu government that did most to protect it from the assaults and commotions that contemporaneously were rending the Mesoamerican Toltecs. By about 1160, the Toltecs' Mexican empire had been swamped. After barely two centuries, they had fallen a victim to fierce northern frontiersmen of an origin very similar to their own.

The troubles of Mesoamerica, scarcely penetrating the South, were equally unknown in the North. The Anasazi of Colorado, in their Pueblo III Period (*c.* 1050-*c.*1300), experienced a phase of ambitious building, most evident in their spectacular stone towns. Like their contemporaries the Hohokam of Arizona, still in their Sedentary Period (900-1200), the Anasazi were talented potters, employing a wide range of forms and a variety of painting techniques. They were makers of cotton-cloth, which they got from the Hohokam, and skilled workers in turquoise and other stones. Cloth-making techniques, originally at least, had come north out of Mesoamerica. Other Mesoamerican influences continued to be important throughout the twelfth century in the more developed North American cultures. To the Hohokam especially, on the northern borders of Mexico, and to the Mississippian, on the North American south coast, Mesoamerican civilization, in religion and art, remained a vital cultural inspiration. It contributed to the tradition that marked them off, as sedentary settlement-builders and agriculturalists, from the more primitive societies of huntsmen and herdsmen who ranged the grassy prairies further north.

World Architecture

It is to the twelfth century that the Cambodian temple cities of Angkor Wat and Angkor Thom belong, together constituting an architectural achievement on a scale that has found few parallels. To this day, the sheer monumentality of Jayavarman VII's mighty temple-mountain of the Bayon, at the focal point of his new capital at Angkor Thom, has rarely been equalled. From its towers, Jayavarman's face stares in all directions.

This bringing together, in a single architectural frame, of religious and political authority is a characteristic of the twelfth century at similar "urban élite centres" as far apart as the Singhalese walled city of Polonnaruwa, the creation of the Buddhist rulers Parakrama the Great and Nissanka Malla, and the still developing Peruvian Chimu capital at Chanchan. Elsewhere, urbanization on a considerable scale was an obvious consequence of population expansion and of the rising tide of wealth. From the continuing tradition of Anasazi stone-built apartment-house towns in Colorado, to such burgeoning cities, largely of timber, as Vladimir and Novgorod in north-west Russia, men came together in new urban concentrations which thrived on economic growth. Particularly this was so in Southern Sung China, where the loss of the North to Jürched invaders had led to the development of a new capital at Hangchow and to the multiplication of characteristically populous walled towns. Sadly, few of these monuments remain, and it is to Japan that we must look for the prevailing Chinese style.

The Seljuk restoration of the economic unity of Islam was always distinguished by a religious preference for abstract decoration, whether in brickwork, in stone-carving, or in the patterning of rich tile-mosaics. Fruitful though this may have been for the Middle East, the renewal of Islam had less happy consequences when expansion began into India. The first major Islamic monument in northern India is the Qutb Minar at Delhi, built at the very end of the twelfth century. Constructed in part out of the looted fragments of destroyed Hindu temples, it commemorated one of the first campaigns in the long-lasting struggle for survival of Hindu art when confronted by Muslim iconoclasm.

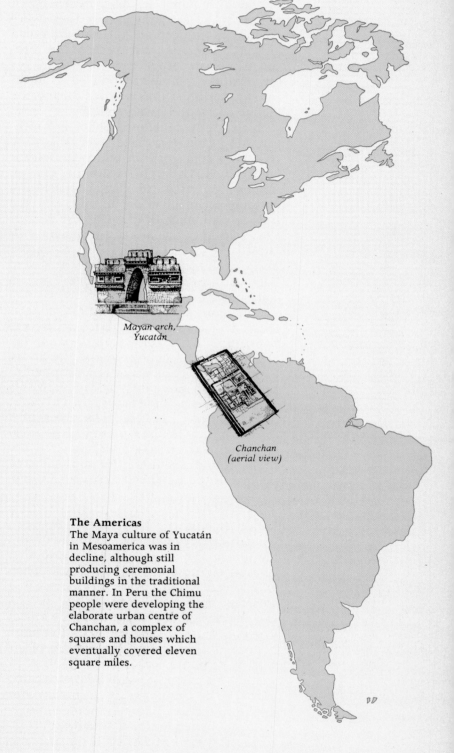

Mayan arch, Yucatán

Chanchan (aerial view)

The Americas
The Maya culture of Yucatán in Mesoamerica was in decline, although still producing ceremonial buildings in the traditional manner. In Peru the Chimu people were developing the elaborate urban centre of Chanchan, a complex of squares and houses which eventually covered eleven square miles.

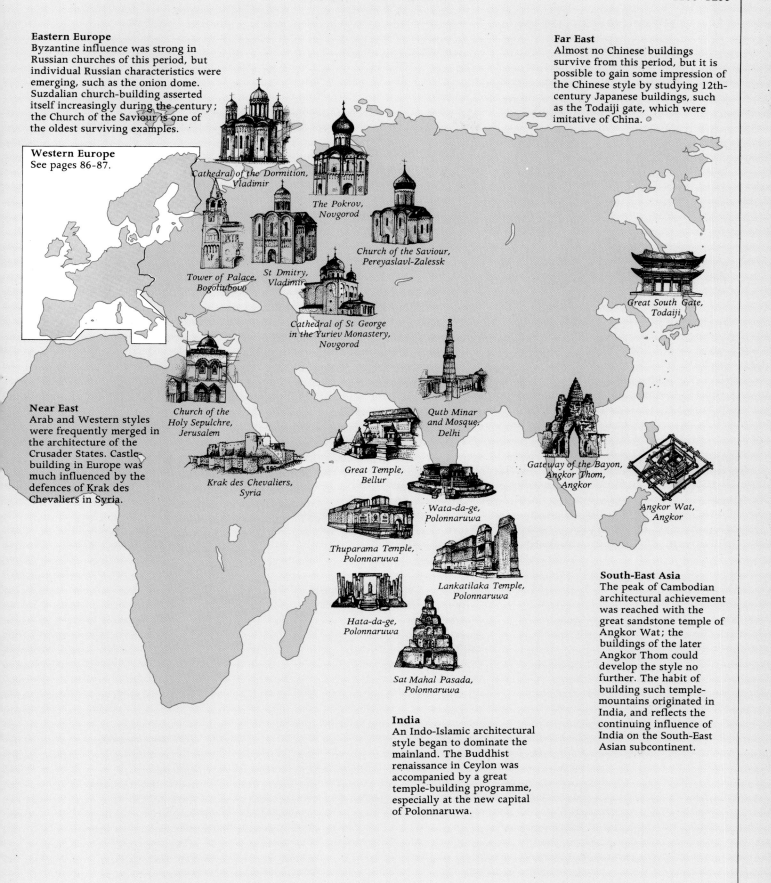

Eastern Europe
Byzantine influence was strong in
Russian churches of this period, but
individual Russian characteristics were
emerging, such as the onion dome.
Suzdalian church-building asserted
itself increasingly during the century;
the Church of the Saviour is one of
the oldest surviving examples.

Western Europe
See pages 86-87.

*Cathedral of the Dormition,
Vladimir*

*The Pokrov,
Novgorod*

*Church of the Saviour,
Pereyaslavl-Zalessk*

*Tower of Palace,
Bogoliubovo*

*St Dmitry,
Vladimir*

*Cathedral of St George
in the Yuriev Monastery,
Novgorod*

Far East
Almost no Chinese buildings
survive from this period, but it is
possible to gain some impression of
the Chinese style by studying 12th-
century Japanese buildings, such
as the Todaiji gate, which were
imitative of China.

*Great South Gate,
Todaiji*

Near East
Arab and Western styles
were frequently merged in
the architecture of the
Crusader States. Castle-
building in Europe was
much influenced by the
defences of Krak des
Chevaliers in Syria.

*Church of the
Holy Sepulchre,
Jerusalem*

*Krak des Chevaliers,
Syria*

*Qutb Minar
and Mosque,
Delhi*

*Great Temple,
Bellur*

*Wata-da-ge,
Polonnaruwa*

*Thuparama Temple,
Polonnaruwa*

*Lankatilaka Temple,
Polonnaruwa*

*Hata-da-ge,
Polonnaruwa*

*Gateway of the Bayon,
Angkor Thom,
Angkor*

*Angkor Wat,
Angkor*

*Sat Mahal Pasada,
Polonnaruwa*

South-East Asia
The peak of Cambodian
architectural achievement
was reached with the
great sandstone temple of
Angkor Wat; the
buildings of the later
Angkor Thom could
develop the style no
further. The habit of
building such temple-
mountains originated in
India, and reflects the
continuing influence of
India on the South-East
Asian subcontinent.

India
An Indo-Islamic architectural
style began to dominate the
mainland. The Buddhist
renaissance in Ceylon was
accompanied by a great
temple-building programme,
especially at the new capital
of Polonnaruwa.

Western European Architecture

Twelfth-century Europe experienced a massive expansion in building patronage both in lay and in ecclesiastical circles. The restoration of a thriving international trade brought new wealth to the towns and to their rulers. The shaping of nations under powerful kings resulted in the building of great palaces and castles. Many towns acquired their first walls in the twelfth century, assisting also in the rebuilding of the major cathedrals.

To the twelfth century belong such innovatory masterpieces as the choir of the abbey church of St-Denis, near Paris, and the west front of the great cathedral at Chartres. Both St-Denis and Chartres are Gothic in style, marking important stages in the evolution of an architectural convention which would last at least another three centuries in the North. However, in Italy the continuing southern resistance to Gothic is exemplified by such buildings as the largely classical, or Romanesque, campanile of Pisa Cathedral, built in 1174 and now known as the "Leaning Tower". And in keeping with Norman artistic eclecticism generally, the cathedrals of their Sicilian kingdom at Monreale and Cefalù brought together elements of three styles at least—North European, Byzantine, and Arab.

Spain
Built in the 12th century as the minaret of the Great Mosque in Seville, the fate of the Giralda Tower reflects the fate of Muslim Spain. The Christian *Reconquista* led to the building of a cathedral on the site of the Great Mosque in the 15th century, with the minaret as its tower. A lantern and belfry were added by the Christians in the 16th century.

Giralda Tower, Seville

Britain
Cistercian influence is visible at Fountains Abbey in Yorkshire and Romanesque in the Benedictine foundation at Peterborough. Castle architecture was changing fast. Experimental keeps were fast obsolete: the concentric defences were added to Dover in the 13th century.

Fountains Abbey, Yorkshire

Conisborough Castle

Cathedral, Peterborough

Dover Castle

Château Gaillard, Normandy

Cathedral, Chartres

St-Denis, Paris

Cathedral, Laon

Cathedral, Angoulême

Cathedral, Bourges

St-Front, Périgueux

St-Gilles-du-Gard, near Arles

France
The Romanesque style was perfected in this century; and by 1200 the great Gothic cathedrals of Chartres and Bourges had been begun, as had the "proto-Renaissance" abbey of St-Gilles-du-Gard, with its strong Roman and Byzantine influences. Byzantine and Near Eastern influence is visible in the fortress of Château Gaillard, and in the church at Périgueux.

Stave Church,
Borgund

Cathedral,
Lund

Scandinavia
The most significant independent contribution
of Scandinavia to the architecture of the
Middle Ages was the stave church. Most
common in Norway, the church at Borgund is
the most celebrated surviving example. Such
stone buildings as there were betray Norman
influence—Lund Cathedral in Sweden, although
reflecting Nordic inspiration, was designed by
a Lombard architect.

St Martin,
Cologne

St Gereon,
Cologne

Abbey Church,
Murbach

Germany
The Holy Roman Empire,
continuing—if precariously—in
the 12th century, led to a spate
of building in the German
Romanesque style. Italian
influence was not truly affecting
what was essentially still a
Carolingian method.

Church of the Apostles,
Cologne

Baptistery,
Cremona

S. Zeno Maggiore,
Verona

Campanile,
Pisa

Baptistery,
Pisa

Italy
The persisting classical traditions of
northern Italy meant that austere
façades and Romanesque baptisteries
predominated at the expense of the
Gothic tradition. The Norman
kingdom in southern Italy was
producing quite different buildings—
their geographical position meant that
the Sicilian cathedrals were receptive
to diverse influences.

Cathedral,
Monreale

Cathedral,
Cefalù

World Art

One of the most significant historical developments in twelfth-century culture was the emergence in late Fujiwara Japan of the horizontal narrative scroll. Doubtless, as was so often the case with Japanese culture, the origins of the tradition were Chinese. Nevertheless, Japanese handscrolls of the twelfth and subsequent centuries, beginning with such works as the urgent and racy *Scroll of the Flying Storehouse*, have an immediacy about them which is truly original to Japan. In China itself, one of the last examples of the genre was Chang Tse-tuan's early-twelfth-century narrative scroll, *The Ch'ing-ming Festival on the River*, (see page 79). Unfortunately, following the sack of Kaifeng by the Chin Tartars the narrative scroll found no place among the painters of the Southern Sung Academy at the new capital of Hangchow.

The Chin Tartars were not universally destructive. Under them, the Ting kilns continued to produce pottery of high quality. But Ting pottery only played one part in a century everywhere notable for the importance of its ceramics. Beginning in the twelfth century, the Lung-ch'üan celadons and Kuan wares of South China attained particular perfection; in Korea, this was the century of the far-famed inlaid celadons; in Persia, there were the fine incised and painted wares of Rayy and Kashan; in West Africa, the first securely datable terracotta sculptures belong to the twelfth century, as do some of the most remarkable products of the North American Hohokam potters.

Among stone-carvers, too, the twelfth century had its own notable triumphs. Cambodian temple-sculpture reached its peak on the monuments of Suryavarman II's Angkor Wat, but began to experience a decline before the end of the century at Jayavarman VII's over-ambitious Bayon. The great rock-cut statues of the Singhalese capital at Polonnaruwa date from the late twelfth century. This was also the period of the first highly distinctive, low-relief sculptures that decorated the exteriors of the Orthodox churches of Vladimir-Suzdal, in Russia. The Suzdalian sculptures, without any doubt, united elements of both Eastern and Western art, demonstrating that characteristic ambiguity of medieval Russian society, neither of nor outside Christian Europe.

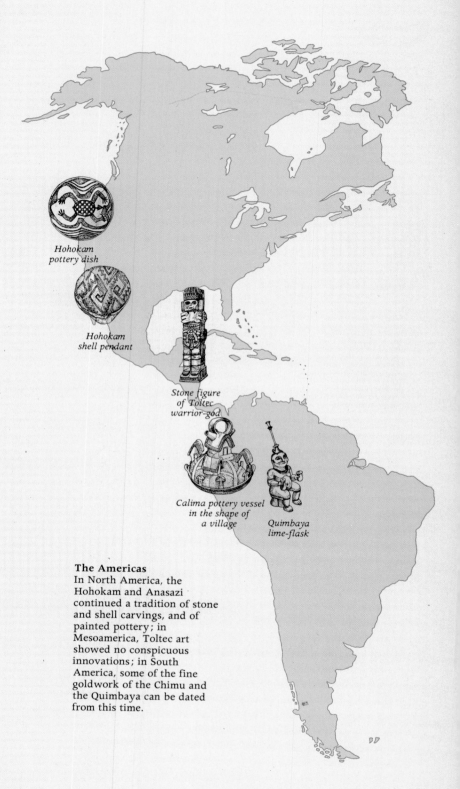

Hohokam pottery dish

Hohokam shell pendant

Stone figure of Toltec warrior-god

Calima pottery vessel in the shape of a village

Quimbaya lime-flask

The Americas
In North America, the Hohokam and Anasazi continued a tradition of stone and shell carvings, and of painted pottery; in Mesoamerica, Toltec art showed no conspicuous innovations; in South America, some of the fine goldwork of the Chimu and the Quimbaya can be dated from this time.

Eastern Europe
In Suzdalia, the low-relief carvings combine both Romanesque and Islamic influences. In the Byzantine tradition, icon-painting flourished, with the "Virgin of Vladimir" dictating the style of Russian icons for centuries.

Far East
In China under the Southern Sung, high-quality pottery continued to be produced, and the Academy of Painting at Hangchow was revived. In portraiture and in the art of the hand-scroll, Japan began to shape a culture of its own.

Western Europe
See pages 90-91.

Near East
In Islam, Persian pottery and Syrian glassware were at their finest. The tradition of Byzantine ivories was strong.

India
Indian erotic art suffered under the puritanism of invading Islam with the first indications of an Indo-Islamic culture visible in the inscriptions of the Qutb Minar. Under the patronage of Parakrama the Great, Ceylon was experiencing an artistic renaissance; the great figures carved from the rock at Polonnaruwa date from this time.

South-East Asia
In the finely executed relief carvings at Angkor Wat and in the monumental sculptures at Angkor Thom, Cambodian art reached its peak under the two great patrons Suryavarman II and Jayavarman VII.

Africa
In West Africa, the soapstone figures of Esie, the terracotta sculptures and some bronzes of Ife, can be dated to the 12th century.

Relief carving, St Dmitry, Vladimir

Virgin of Vladimir, icon

St George, detail of fresco, Church of St George, Staraya Ladoga

Silver bangle, Kiev

Byzantine ivory casket

Kashan lustreware ewer

Tibetan bronze of Manjusri

Copper figure of devotee of Kali

Nepalese gilt bronze of Tara

Lung-ch'üan vase

Ju ware bowl

Ch'ing-pai vase

Korean inlaid celadon

The Flying Storehouse, detail

Portrait of Minamoto no Yoritomo by Fujiwara Takanobu

Byzantine ivory statuette of Madonna and Child

Persian plate from Rhages

Islamic bronze bucket

Koranic inscriptions, Qutb Minar, Delhi

Reclining figure of Buddha, Polonnaruwa

Carved giant, The Bayon, Angkor Thom

Khmer sandstone head of Buddha

Cloister relief of apsara, Angkor Wat

Terracotta pot-lid of animal head, Ife

Brass head, Ife

Soapstone head, Esie

Western European Art

A new self-confidence in Western European art becomes apparent during the course of the twelfth century. Quite early in the century, the great Last Judgment tympanum over the west doors of the new cathedral at Autun was signed with the proud words "Gislebertus the Master made this"; nor was this claim to recognition unfounded. The building boom in late-eleventh- and twelfth-century Europe provided sculptors of the calibre of Gislebertus and his contemporary, the anonymous Master of Vézelay, with what was truly an exceptional opportunity. They had been trained themselves in the stone-carving tradition of Cluny, and they stood in a line of progressive development from Cluny itself to the High Gothic sculptures of mid-thirteenth-century Rheims. Within the twelfth century, Vézelay and Autun were followed by the influential churches of St-Denis and Chartres, richly decorated with architectural sculptures.

Byzantine influence was still very strong in western art: visible, for example, in English wall-paintings of the later twelfth century, despite the vigour of the native painting schools. In the South, still more obviously, it was Greek mosaicists who were employed, in preference to local craftsmen, on the decoration of such major twelfth-century cathedrals as Cefalù and Monreale, in Norman Sicily.

Spain
The silks of Arab Spain were in their design uncompromisingly Islamic. But despite the strength of Arab influence in northern Spain, Christian art was on the ascendant.

Britain
While sculpture was in general much affected by the trends current in France, Kilpeck Church displays an independent Anglo-Saxon style. Influences from abroad affected several different art forms: Byzantine influence shows in many Bibles and Psalters; it is visible again in the exceptional Gloucester candlestick.

France
Architectural sculpture blossomed, at its most exquisite in the work of Gislebertus and the Master of Vézelay. Mosan art also flourished, at its height in the goldwork of Nicholas of Verdun and in the bronzes of Rainier of Huy. The austere Cistercian abbey of Cîteaux was a centre for highly decorative manuscript illumination.

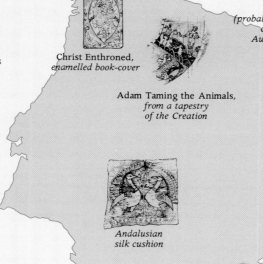

Virgin and Child, Shaftesbury Psalter

Gloucester candlestick

Black marble font, Winchester Cathedral

South doorway, Kilpeck Church

Capital in crypt, Canterbury Cathedral

Bronze baptismal font by Rainier of Huy, Liège

Sardonyx chalice, St-Denis

Cistercian manuscript illumination

The Annunciation, stained-glass window, Chartres Cathedral

Prophet Joel, from the workshop of Nicholas of Verdun

Eve (probably by Gislebertus), carving from Autun Cathedral

Figure of Christ, tympanum at St-Pierre, Vézelay

Carved figure from the tympanum, St-Pierre, Moissac

Christ Enthroned, enamelled book-cover

Adam Taming the Animals, from a tapestry of the Creation

Andalusian silk cushion

*Detail from a tapestry
of the Seasons*

Scandinavia
Partly as a result of the
Viking exodus, medieval
art in Scandinavia was
somewhat impoverished.

Prophet Daniel,
*stained-glass window,
Augsburg Cathedral*

Germany
The oldest complete stained-
glass windows in the world,
showing five prophets, are to
be found in Augsburg
Cathedral. The heavily
stylized design of the figures
is repeated in Rhenish works
of art, such as the several
outstanding reliquaries of
the period.

Eltenberg reliquary

Italy
Byzantine influence can be traced
throughout Italy. In the South it was
sometimes combined with Islamic
motifs, as in the mosaics of the
Sicilian cathedrals. Similarly, although
the manufacture of European silks
began in Norman Sicily, their design
remained fundamentally Islamic.

The Last Supper,
*detail of mosaic,
St Mark's, Venice*

*Panel from bronze doors,
S. Zeno, Verona*

Christ with Adam, *mosaic,
Palatine Chapel,
Palermo*

Isaac and Esau,
*detail of mosaic,
Monreale Cathedral, Sicily*

Sicilian silk

Apse mosaic of Christ,
*Cefalù Cathedral,
Sicily*

	Events and developments	People	Technology
Western Europe	Concordat of Worms (1122): official end to "Investiture" dispute. Conflict between Thomas Becket and Henry II resulted in Becket's murder (1170). Strong centralized government under monarchs, notably in England and France. Christian conquest of Muslim Lisbon (1147). Increase in population; large-scale cultivation of new land.	Pierre Abelard, French theologian (1079-1142). St Bernard, Abbot of Clairvaux (1091-1153). Frederick Barbarossa, Holy Roman Emperor 1155-90. Thomas Becket, Archbishop of Canterbury 1162-70.	The "Naviglio Grande" (irrigation canal), Lombardy, begun (1179). Increasing use of windmill. Simple steering oar replaced by stern-post rudder. Manufacture of silk, Sicily. Paper-making introduced. Woodcuts used for initial letters.
Far East	Overthrow of Khitan Liao and conquest of northern China by Jürched (1126–7). Chin empire of Jürched established. Retreat of Sung to south; new capital created at Hangchow. Tribute paid to Chin by Sung. Japanese Fujiwara ousted by Minamoto. New ruler Yoritomo; start of Kamakura shogunate. Degree of independence in Korea under Koryo.	Hui-tsung, Sung Emperor 1082-1135. Yoritomo, Kamakura shogun 1147–99. Li T'ang, Master of painting at Hangchow.	Public medical service organized in China. First recorded use of gunpowder.
South-East Asia	Peace and prosperity in Cambodia. Period of anarchy and disorder in Burma from 1130 onwards.	Suryavarman II, ruler of Cambodia 1112–52. Jayavarman VII, Buddhist sovereign of Cambodia 1181–c.1220.	
India	Northern India split into small, warring principalities, whose divisions facilitated Muslim conquest. Defeat of Delhi rajah (1192) by Muhammad Ghuri followed by Delhi Sultanate. Decline of Chola dynasty (southern India).	Parakrama Bahu I, ruler of Ceylon 1153–86. Muhammad Ghuri, founder of Muslim power in India, (d. 1206).	
Near East	Economic and political decline of Byzantium. Trade lost to Venice and Genoa; frequent military defeats and consequent reduction of territory. Establishment of Crusader states. 2nd Crusade caused by fall of Edessa (1144). Jerusalem destroyed by Saladin (1187). 3rd Crusade concluded by truce between Richard I and Saladin.	Al-Ghazzali, Persian teacher of Sufism (1058-1111). Saladin, Sultan of Egypt and Syria 1175-93. Manuel I, Byzantine Comneni Emperor 1143-80.	First arrival of Chinese porcelains in the Middle East.
Eastern Europe	Revolt by Byzantine-ruled Bulgars (1185). 2nd Bulgarian Empire founded (1186). Growth of Russian culture, influenced by priests, teachers, artists and architects from Byzantium. By 1200 most cities Byzantine in character; law based on Byzantine; marriages between Russian rulers and Byzantine royal house. Kiev replaced by Vladimir-Suzdal as main state.	Andrey Bogoliubsky, Prince of Vladimir-Suzdal 1157-74.	
Africa	Rise of Berber Almohads in North Africa; Morocco, Algeria, Tunisia and southern Spain under their control. Trade in iron, gold, ivory and slaves by Arabs in West, Central and East Africa, resulting in new wealth and consequent growth of indigenous states, such as Ife (Nigeria).	Ibn Tumart, founder of Almohad empire (d. 1130). 'Abd al-Mu'min, Almohad Caliph 1130–?	Bronze casting at Ife.
The Americas	Toltec capital of Tula destroyed by Chicimecs (c. 1160). Migration of Toltecs to new settlement at Xicalango. Chimu civilization of Peru in a formative stage; expansion of Chimu power.		

Religion	Architecture	Art and music	Literature and learning
Success of Cistercian order; abbeys built all over Europe. 2nd (1147) and 3rd (1189–92) Crusades directed against the Muslims. Abelard persecuted as a heretic for publicly questioning Church doctrine.	Church of St-Denis; Chartres Cathedral; Château Gaillard, France. Cathedrals of Monreale and Cefalù, Sicily. Giralda Tower, Seville. Wells and Lincoln Cathedrals; Dover castle keep.	Sculptures by Gislebertus, Autun Cathedral, France. Mosaics at Monreale and Cefalù cathedrals, Sicily. Music in two to four parts developed at Notre Dame, Paris. Composer Maître Léonin active at Notre Dame c. 1160–80.	Chrétien de Troyes' Arthurian romances. Geoffrey of Monmouth's *History of English Kings*. Toledo, Spain, centre for translations of ancient texts. Universities growing at Paris and Oxford; law schools at Pavia and Bologna.
Taoism and Buddhism popular in China. Neo-Confucianism formulated by philosopher Chu Hsi (1130–1200). Belief in road to salvation through Amida Buddha taught by Japanese monk, Honen (1133–1212).	Religious centre of Todaiji rebuilt by Yoritomo. Elaborate Southern Sung architectural style exported to Korea and Japan.	Chang Tse-tuan's scroll, *The Ch'ing-ming Festival on the River*, Kaifeng. New Sung Academy of Painting, Hangchow. Ju-yao ware, south China. *Tale of Genji* scroll; portraits by Fujiwara Takanobu, Japan.	Chu Hsi's philosophical work, *Reflections on Things at Hand*. Korean *History of the Three Kingdoms*, compiled by Kim Pu-sik.
Jayavarman VII converted to Mahayana Buddhism.	Temple buildings and monuments at Angkor Wat and Angkor Thom, Cambodia.	Relief carvings by Angkor Wat sculptors; carvings at temple-mountain of Bayon (Angkor Thom), Cambodia.	
Islam dominant in northern India. Indian religious life influenced for centuries by Ramanuja's teachings, based on a belief in Vishnu. Jainism strong in Gujerat.	Qutb Minar and Mosque, Delhi. Temples at Polonnaruwa, Ceylon, notably the Wata-da-ge and Hata-da-ge.	Buddha figures carved from rock at Polonnaruwa, Ceylon.	Bilhana's Kasmiri love song, *Chauraspanchasika*. Jayadeva's *Song of Songs*, a Hindu work. Ramanuja's commentaries on *The Upanishads*. Hemachandra's philosophical works on Sanskrit grammar, logic and poetics.
Christian orders of knighthood (eg. Knights Templar, Jerusalem) developed from Crusades. Sufi mysticism popular in Muslim world. Formation of Sufi fraternities. Emergence of Assassins, a fanatical Muslim sect.	Krak des Chevaliers, Syria. Church of the Holy Sepulchre, Jerusalem. Mosque of al-Aqmar, Cairo. Monastery of Pantocrator, Constantinople.	Sculptures by Master of Plaimpied, Church of the Annunciation, Nazareth. Byzantine style wall-paintings, Church of the Nativity, Bethlehem. Syrian glass and Persian pottery at their finest.	Anna Comnena's *Alexiad*, life of her father, Emperor Alexius I. Maimonides' *Guide for the Perplexed*. Omar Khayyam's *Rubaiyat*.
Spread of Latin Christianity in Eastern Europe with decline of Byzantine Empire; Russia firmly Orthodox in religion, with metropolitans (archbishops) frequently appointed from Constantinople.	Stone churches, Suzdalia. Andrey Bogoliubsky's palace and church, Bogoliubovo. The Pokrov, Bogoliubovo. Cathedral of the Dormition, Vladimir. St Dmitry, Vladimir. Cathedral of St George, Novgorod.	*Virgin of Vladimir* icon a strong influence on Russian painting after its arrival in Kiev from Constantinople. Carved reliefs by sculptors of Suzdalian School.	Birth of Russian literature marked by *The Campaign of Igor*, an epic prose poem. *Chronicle of Kiev*, Russian historical work.
Sufi mysticism used by Ibn Tumart in Almohad campaign against Almoravids. Sufi mysticism rejected by 'Abd al-Mu'min once in power.		Terracotta sculptures of Ife.	
	Stone towns of Anasazi, Colorado. Impressive public works carried out by Chimu.	Atlantean figures, Tula.	

The Thirteenth Century

A Mongol horseman
*This portrait of a Mongol
and his horse is a Persian
copy of a Chinese original.*

**The achievement of
Genghis Khan**
*In the first decades of the
13th century the Mongol
horsemen, united by
Genghis Khan in 1206,
conquered the empire of the
Chin Tartars to the south
of their homelands, and
advanced west through
Muslim Asia as far as the
Caucasus, thus creating
the nucleus of an empire
that would become, under
Kublai Khan, larger than
any the world had seen.*

Historical Context

There has been the merest handful of men, through the recorded ages, upon whom history itself seems to pivot. One of these was Genghis Khan, the first "Great Khan" of the Mongols. When Genghis Khan died in 1227, he had both conquered and occupied more territories already than any man before him, and the forces he had set in motion were unchecked.

Of course, there were important regions of the thirteenth-century world that never saw nor even heard of the Mongols. In some areas to which they did penetrate, the reality of Mongol power was to prove in the event short-lived. Nevertheless, for China, Burma, Central Asia, Russia, Iran and the Middle East, and briefly but traumatically for Eastern Europe as well, the Mongol armies took on the aspect of a terrible but inescapable scourge. Like the Black Death in the following century, there were few remedies available to meet it other than a retreat to prayer, while even in a nation such as Japan which by good fortune escaped the Mongol invasion, the mere threat of their coming was enough, it appears, to freeze civilization over the course of a couple of decades.

Genghis Khan's power was built initially on the unification under his leadership of the many separate Mongolian-speaking tribes then living the nomadic life of herdsmen on the open steppes between North China and the southern reaches of the Siberian forest. Having been confirmed

as "Universal Ruler" at a meeting of the tribes in 1206, Genghis Khan had already the previous year begun the attack on the Hsi Hsia of Inner Mongolia which would lead him into inevitable confrontation with the neighbouring Chin rulers of North China, originally steppe people themselves. Within four years, between 1211 and 1215, he had destroyed these in their turn, and was then ready to move westwards through Central Asia to the sacking of the great trading cities of Bukhara and Samarkand and to his first major confrontation with Islam.

The death of the conqueror was far from the end of Mongol expansion. Persia was overrun by 1231; southern Russia destroyed in 1236-8; Poland, Silesia and Hungary ravaged in 1241, that being the year too when, at the far end of the empire, the conquest of North China became complete. Only the death in the same year of the Great Khan Ogodai, son and successor of Genghis Khan, spared Western Europe the Mongol onslaught. Batu, conqueror of the Hungarians, was required to return home and assist in the election of a new Great Khan. He never revived his European ambitions.

Elsewhere, Mongol triumphs continued. The Seljuks of Anatolia collapsed before the Mongol armies. In 1258 Baghdad was seized and the Abbasid caliphate foundered. That same year, Korean resistance to the Mongols ended, while already before this the long assault on Southern China had begun. It was Kublai

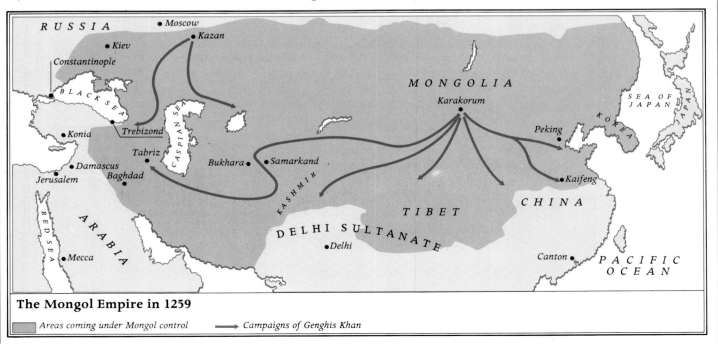

The Mongol Empire in 1259

▨ *Areas coming under Mongol control* ⟶ *Campaigns of Genghis Khan*

Marco Polo

Marco Polo (1254-1324) was not the first European traveller to reach China; his father and uncle, Nicolo and Maffio Polo, both Venetian merchants, had already spent some years there before setting out again in 1271, accompanied on their second journey by the young Marco. However, it was Marco Polo's *Travels to Tartary and China*, dictated to a fellow-prisoner in a Genoese jail after their capture at the sea battle of Curzola in 1298, that for the first time alerted a wide audience in the West to the extraordinary civilization of China.

ABOVE *Marco Polo arriving at Kublai Khan's court*

Marco Polo

Marco Polo leaving Venice on his way to China

The Great Khans
Genghis Khan, and his grandson Kublai Khan, first and last of the Mongol Great Khans, had a simple philosophy of empire, summed up in Genghis' own words: "A man's greatest pleasure is to defeat his enemies, to see those whom they cherish in tears, to hold their wives and daughters in his arms."

Genghis Khan

Kublai Khan

The Mongols defeated by the Mamelukes
The battle of Ain Jalut, where the Mamelukes under Baybars defeated the Ilkhan Hulegu in 1260, marks the end of the westward expansion of the Mongols. Hulegu withdrew to the Khanate of Persia; the Mamelukes were free to consolidate their hold on Syria, and to begin their final attack on the Christian coastal cities.

Khan, grandson of Genghis and himself last in the line of Great Khans, who completed the subjection of the Southern Sung in a long series of bitterly contested campaigns that ended in 1279. And it was Kublai Khan again who launched the two unsuccessful Mongol invasions of Japan in 1274 and 1281, his armies moving into Vietnam in the 1280s and bringing about in 1287 the utter collapse of Burma.

Genghis Khan had been a pagan, tolerant of other religions. And in countries like China where belief was already relaxed, the religious eclecticism and willingness to learn of the Mongols were important constituents of their success. But in the case of Islam, there was no room for a similar compromise. Arab commentators, more than any others, bewailed the onslaughts of the Mongols. With some justification they saw them as a watershed in Islamic history—the first time that the lands of the Prophet Muhammad had become subject to non-Muslim rule. They felt this as a humiliation not just to an existing polity but to the religion and the philosophy that, over long centuries, had given the polity its meaning.

Not even the powerful Mongol dynasty was immune from problems of succession. Just as the Catholic West was saved from the Mongols by the death of Ogodai in 1241, so the Mameluke rulers of Egypt were given an opportunity to fight back for Islam when Ogodai's nephew, the Great Khan Mongke, died in 1259 and the empire, effectively, came to be divided among his brothers. The battle of Ain Jalut on 3 September 1260, fought by the

Mamelukes against a much reduced Mongol army, brought to an end the advance into Syria and Palestine of the forces of the Ilkhan Hulegu (d. 1265), younger brother of Mongke and conqueror himself of the Abbasid caliphs of Baghdad. Hulegu thereafter brought into existence the independent Khanate of Persia. But while Baghdad remained a part of his dominions, Syria was restored to what was left of the original Muslim heartland, now under the hegemony of the Mameluke sultans of Egypt, standard-bearers of a united and newly-confident Islam.

To the Christians of Palestine, who had hoped to benefit from the continuing Mongol confrontation with Islam, this re-apportionment of lands promised nothing so much as disaster. The battle of Ain Jalut had set, at last, a limit to Mongol conquests in the Near East. And the Mamelukes, now fully in control of the lands they had held only since 2 May 1250, when a palace rebellion had extinguished the Ayyubid Sultanate, were able to profit from Mongol retrenchment to reassert the local dominance of Islam. In due course the Mameluke rulers came to claim for themselves the title of "Sultan of Islam and the Moslems". And Christian Palestine, very early in their advance, became both an obvious and an attainable target. Within two years of the coming to power of Sultan Baybars (1261-77), he had carried the holy war on to the Palestinian coastal plain with the first attack on Acre. In 1265 Caesarea fell; in 1268 Jaffa was taken and Antioch brutally destroyed. For more than two decades the kingdom of Acre survived. But Acre too was stormed and sacked in the spring of 1291, and the Christian presence in the Holy Land, after almost two centuries of endurance, was at last decisively at an end.

The Christians had better fortune elsewhere. In Muslim Spain, the battle of Las Navas de Tolosa in 1212 broke the power of the Almohad dynasty, leading directly to the progressive Christian reoccupation of all except the diminutive Moorish kingdom of Granada, in the extreme southeast corner of the peninsula. Cordoba fell to Ferdinand of Castile in 1236; Valencia to James of Aragon in 1238; Seville to Ferdinand in 1248, and the kingdom of Murcia in 1266 to Alfonso, Ferdinand's son. These were very real compensations for the succession of disasters met by Christianity in the East.

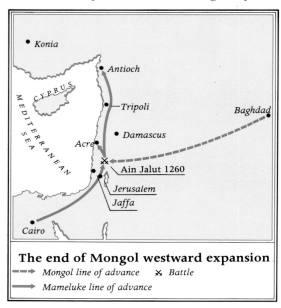

The end of Mongol westward expansion
- - - → *Mongol line of advance* ✕ *Battle*
——→ *Mameluke line of advance*

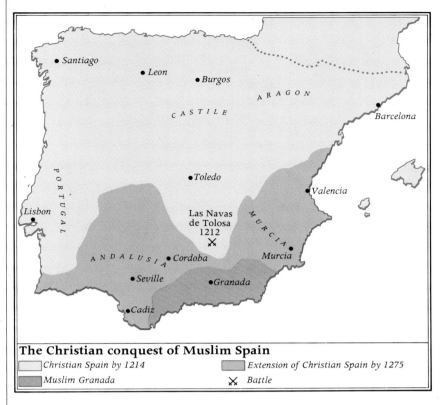

The Christian conquest of Muslim Spain

☐ *Christian Spain by 1214*	▨ *Extension of Christian Spain by 1275*
▨ *Muslim Granada*	✕ *Battle*

The "Reconquista"
The Christian reconquest of Muslim Spain in the 13th century began with the battle of Las Navas de Tolosa in 1212, after which Cordoba, Valencia, Seville, Murcia, Lisbon and Cadiz fell in turn. By 1275 the Kingdom of Granada was the only remaining Moorish possession in the Iberian peninsula: it held off the Christians for another two centuries.

More traumatic even than the expulsion of the crusaders from Palestine, although perhaps less strongly felt in the Catholic West, was the Mongol assault on Orthodox Russia. The destruction of Vladimir in 1238, and the fall of Kiev to the Mongols two years later, exposed southern Russia for two centuries and more to the brutal and oppressive Golden Horde. Neither Kiev nor Vladimir ever resumed their leadership of Russia, and, as the Golden Horde weakened, it would be from the North that first Novgorod and then Moscow would initiate the eventual recovery of the principalities.

Not everything the Mongols did was as savage and unproductive as their rape of Orthodox Russia. With an empire that spread from Persia in the West over the roof of the world to China, they brought into being a unique community of interests which promoted trading contacts across great distances and which encouraged, if only for the period of their rule, a valuable cross-fertilization of cultures. However, for a civilization like China's, where the benefits of such cross-fertilization are most obvious, the price was certainly too high. Kublai Khan's final victory of 1279 over the Sung emperor of South China was followed, it is true, by the establishment of a Mongol (Yüan) regime in these provinces which

was not unlike the indigenous empire it replaced. And this was the extraordinary civilization recorded for the West in the last decades of the century by Marco Polo, the Venetian traveller and merchant. But the Mongol campaign in China had met long and determined resistance, in particular from China's many walled towns, and the conquest was only achieved, in the final event, by the practice of unprecedented brutality. It has been estimated that China's population, over these years, may have been reduced by as much as a third. Brought down again in the following century by the heavy mortalities of the Black Death, it would not recover its pre-Mongol total until well into the sixteenth century.

Whether as a result of full-scale invasion or as a consequence of Mongol movements elsewhere, there was scarcely any region over the whole of the Far East that remained uninfluenced by Mongol imperialism. Korea, in 1258, was one of the earlier victims of this aggression. And it was not until much later in the thirteenth century that Japan, paralyzed for the best part of a generation by continual threats of Mongol invasion, was spared the prospect of further assault by Kublai Khan's expanding preoccupations in South-East Asia. In 1287, Burma disintegrated before the Great Khan's armies, to be left helpless in later years before the warlike ambitions of the Thais, themselves already threatening Khmer Cambodia and displaced from a more northerly homeland by the southward advance of the Mongols. Early in the 1290s, it was Java's turn to face up to a Mongol fleet. In that same decade, another Mongol host burst through the defences of Muslim Northern India, opening a further episode of characteristic violence in the long-lasting Mongol feud with Islam. There were few regions, indeed, of the civilized world that had failed to feel Mongol pressure before the century reached its end.

Untouched by these events, although troubled by warfare of their own, the island peoples of Pacific Polynesia had by the thirteenth century developed the hierarchical societies which could engage in relatively elaborate programmes of common defence, and in religious and public works. Something of the nature of this isolated civilization can be established from its surviving artefacts. Yet the historical sequence in Oceania, with little

Trade and travel

One of the happier consequences of Mongol expansion was the reorganization of the Central Asian trade routes and the bringing together, under Mongol lordship, of commercial systems as distinct as those of Persia and China. But trade, both by land and sea, had long been active, before the coming of the Mongols, throughout the more populated world. Men travelled familiarly, whether as pilgrims or as merchants, over what are still considered to be difficult routes even in the better conditions of today. By the 13th century, Arab shipping had made the Indian Ocean a particular Muslim preserve, while the commercial revival of the Christian West, in this century more than any other, had brought unprecedented prosperity to many great ports as well as to the inland trade-fair towns which studded the traditional roads to the North.

FACING PAGE
Muslim pilgrims on their way to Mecca, from a Persian manuscript

ABOVE *Commerce in the Gulf of Cambaye, scene from a 15th-century French manuscript*

ABOVE *A Mongol horseman plaiting the tail of his horse*

ABOVE *Detail of* Good Government, *a 14th-century fresco by Ambrogio Lorenzetti*

ABOVE *The Bishop of Paris blessing Lendit Fair, from a 14th-century French miniature*

ABOVE *Carpenters at work, detail from the Noah window in Chartres Cathedral, France*

The friars
The two great orders of friars, Franciscan and Dominican, were founded in the first decades of the 13th century as a reaction against the decline in strict observance and the wealth of the older monastic orders. Initially based on poverty and preaching, both orders of friars turned their attention increasingly to scholarship.

Dominican friars

Franciscan friars

save a fragmentary oral tradition to illuminate it, continues to appear forbiddingly obscure.

Hardly less so is the story of the contemporary Americas, of which only tantalizing glimpses have been granted to us. It is now evident that some of the legends of a fabulous El Dorado had their origin in an exotic gold-using society based in what is today the republic of Colombia, and that this society flourished during the thirteenth century, as indeed it did until the arrival there much later of the Spaniards. Meanwhile, the Peruvian empire that had been established well before 1200 by the Chimu people of Chanchan continued to develop until swallowed in its turn during the fifteenth century by the fast-growing Inca state. In Central America, the Toltec Maya entered into a period of manifest, sometimes violent, decline, while for the North one obvious consequence of these Mesoamerican disturbances was to drive still more Mexican peoples northwards. It was these emigrants who carried with them further elements of a powerful culture which, well before the thirteenth century, had already touched the more advanced societies of the Mississippi valley and of the North American Southwest.

On another continent, that of Africa, the same mixture of archaeology and legend has at least the support of recorded history in the tales of Arab travellers. It was in the thirteenth century, especially, that Muslim traders began the systematic exploitation of the east coast of Africa, making it, from this time on, an important element in the mercantile economy of Greater Islam. As a consequence of this, a good deal has been recorded of such major Muslim trading cities as Mogadishu and Kilwa on this coast, while practically nothing of the history of the African interior has survived, even in legends. The gold of Zimbabwe, without any question, lay already at the root of the Arab trade. Yet it came from an unknown society, as little understood, even by the Arabs, as their other gold source in West Africa.

In effect, the wealth and hence the political dispositions of black Africa were already being determined by an insatiable demand for the products of the continent, arising beyond its shores. Zimbabwe in the east, Ife in the west, and the legendary empires of the southern Sahara (the most important of which was Mali), all belonged, even if indirectly, to a trading

system that fed the economies of the northern world with the gold essential for their working. In this particular, Catholic Europe was as much in need of African gold as were the Islamic states that had first organized the trade to the South. And there was to be no sign of the demand slackening, either in the thirteenth century or later.

What with the steady growth of European population and the increasingly effective organization of government under the now established western monarchies, economic prospects in the West had never looked brighter than they did during the thirteenth century. In 1259, the great quarrel between the French and the English kings was resolved at the Treaty of Paris in a settlement which, although acceptable to neither in the long term, at least put a damper on the most controversial issues for well over a hundred years. The major industrial centres of Flanders and northern Italy, if not without their difficulties, flourished as never before. In the Church, Pope Innocent III (1198-1216) presided over a great assembly in 1215—the Fourth Lateran Council—which seemed to many who took part in it to be the opening of an especially hopeful new era. The assembly concerned itself with problems of diocesan reorganization and discipline, it defined doctrine and came to grips with heresy, and it accepted the Dominicans (Friars Preacher) and the Franciscans (Friars Minor) in their role as teachers and confessors in the towns.

For the time being, under firm papal leadership, the Church was indeed set on a new and more promising course. But its administrative structure, although increasingly efficient, had become both insensitive and remote. On a popular level, heresy continued, fought by the friars but not uncommonly preserved even within their ranks. At the summit, political divisions between Empire and Papacy continued to widen. It was Pope Innocent IV (1243-54) who, through his repeated campaigns against Frederick II, did most to bring the Hohenstaufen dynasty down.

Frederick II, as king of the Romans (1196), king of Sicily (1198) and Holy Roman Emperor (1220) as well, had been for some decades already without peer in Western Europe. His wealth derived principally from his Italian dominions, but this was precisely where his empire

Pope Boniface VIII
Elected in 1294, Boniface VIII brought the papacy into a conflict with France which, after his death in 1303, culminated in the "captivity" of the papacy at Avignon.

was most vulnerable to expanding papal ambitions. Frederick's death on 13 December 1250, after half a century of suzerainty over most of Italy, as well as the best part of Central Europe, gave Innocent IV the opportunity he had long been awaiting to drive the Hohenstaufens from the South. This papal campaign was not immediately successful, and Innocent IV did not live long enough himself to see the Germans evicted. But the Hohenstaufens experienced increasing difficulties in the control of the northern Italian cities over which they still had claim as suzerains. As for Sicily and the other German dominions in the south, Charles of Anjou's defeat of the Hohenstaufen Manfred at Benevento in 1266 established the French in southern Italy with an interest they lost no time in developing. It was only a matter of decades before Pope Boniface VIII's ill-judged claim to political supremacy in the West led him into direct confrontation with France, to humiliation and death in 1303, and to a French-controlled papacy which, from 1309, began the agony of its "captivity" at Avignon.

The papacy's victory over the Holy Roman Empire, closely followed by its own collapse before France, must take its place in a pattern of events which, through the thirteenth century, had brought about an increasingly westward shift in leadership. Charles of Anjou, who remained king of Sicily until his death in 1285, was the brother of Louis IX (1226-70), the saintly ruler whose lengthy reign, followed by official canonization in 1297, marked the apogee of kingship both in France and throughout the medieval West. Further, it is not without significance that Henry III of England (1216-72) was himself related by marriage to Louis IX—they were married to sisters—as he was also to the German Frederick II. In this close-knit society of matrimonial and other family alliances, France was able to profit from the weakness of its competitors to rise to a position of indisputable superiority in the West. French expansion eastwards at the expense of Germany began well before the end of the thirteenth century, while the English presence in France itself, although still significant, was at least contained within the south-west region defined at the Treaty of Paris.

Of course, the cultural dominance of France had already begun well before the years of its political supremacy. In

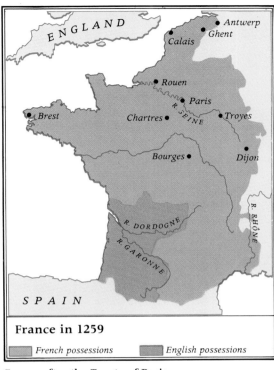

France in 1259

French possessions   English possessions

France after the Treaty of Paris
The loss of Normandy by England in 1204, and half a century of intermittent fighting, ended in 1259 with the Treaty of Paris, by which English possessions in France were limited to Aquitaine and Gascony. Under Louis IX and Philip IV the French crown became stronger and more cohesive, and Paris became, for the first time, a real capital city.

England, such cathedrals as Canterbury in the 1170s, Lincoln in the 1190s, and Salisbury from the 1220s, owed almost everything to French inspiration. Nevertheless, Louis IX's influential reign undoubtedly set its seal on this achievement. It was under St Louis and his son and successor, Philip the Bold (1270-85), that High Gothic reached its peak in architecture and sculpture and that the "court style" developed in painting. More significantly still, French involvement in the affairs of Italy became one of the chief elements in the cross-fertilization of cultures that resulted in the innovatory work of a painter like Giotto (*c.* 1265-1337), acknowledged father of the Italian Renaissance. Intellectually in the writings of the great philosopher and humanist Thomas Aquinas (d. 1274), established at the emergent University of Paris, artistically in the sculptures of the Joseph Master, working in the mid-century on the west façade of the royal cathedral and tombhouse at Rheims, and politically in the great pre-eminence of St Louis, the thirteenth century in the western world belongs undeniably to France.

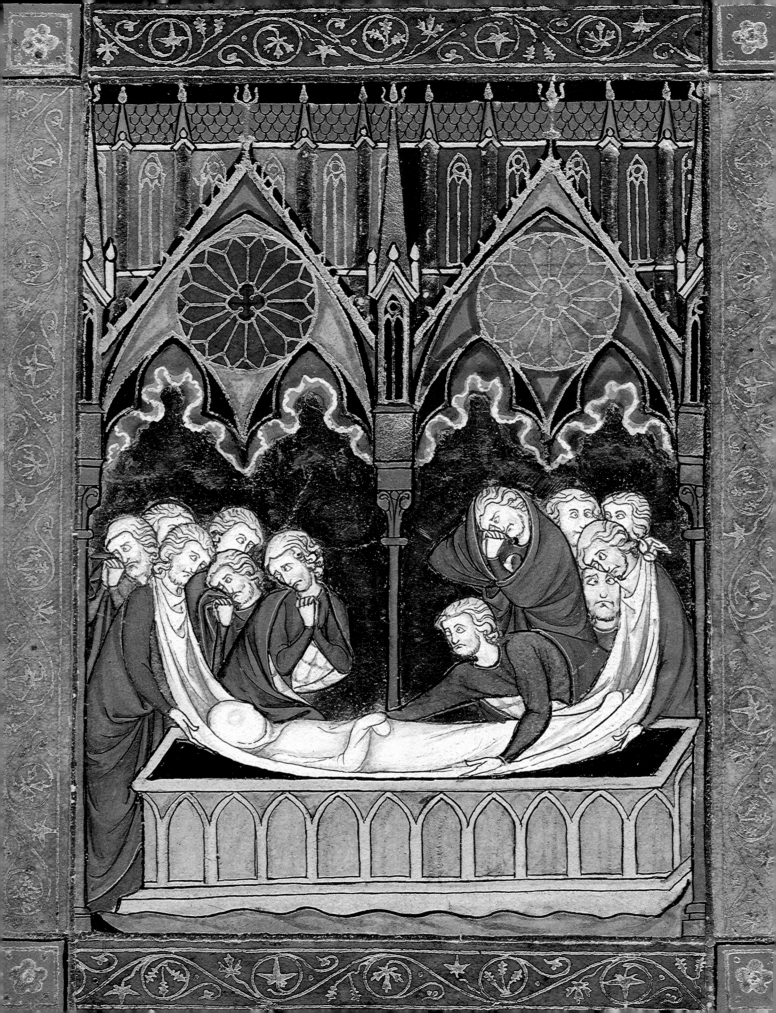

Western art

Continuing economic expansion in the 13th-century West brought into being a period of rare artistic brilliance. Undoubtedly, the best of this art is to be seen in such refined court products as the *Psalter of St Louis*, painted for Louis IX of France within a few years of 1250. But its consistently high standards are to be seen again in the much less spectacular but still remarkable work of the tilers of Chertsey Abbey, in England, representing a high point in the tile-making craft. In Northern Europe, this was the century for the full flowering of Gothic, whether in France, in England, or in Germany. However, in Italy it took the mastery of a sculptor like Nicola Pisano to reconcile High Gothic naturalistic traditions, borrowed from the best work in France, with the native Roman inheritance. In its use of both elements in such evident harmony, Nicola Pisano's carved pulpit at Pisa (1259-60) anticipates the Italian Early Renaissance.

FACING PAGE
Page from the Psalter of St Louis

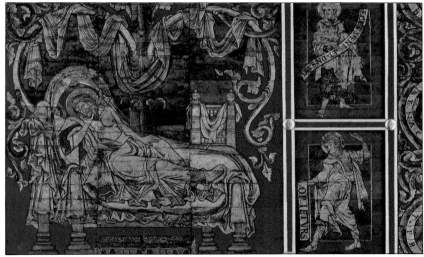

ABOVE Jesse Asleep, *ceiling-painting, St Michael's, Hildesheim, Germany*

LEFT *Pulpit by Nicola Pisano in the Baptistery, Pisa, Italy*

ABOVE *Scene from* Historia Major, *an English manuscript, illuminated by Matthew Paris*

RIGHT *Chertsey tiles showing a queen, from Chertsey Abbey, England*

BELOW *Altarpiece of Trinity with St Mary and St John, Soest, Germany*

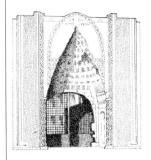

Sultan Han, Turkey
The hans *were caravanserais providing stopping-places on the roads of Seljuk Turkey: the greatest were endowed and built by the Sultan. This Sultan Han, on the road between Konia and Aksaray, has a façade that is highly decorated, with rich contrasts of texture.*

Metalwork of Mosul
Dated 1232, this brass ewer, inlaid in copper and silver with scenes of "courtly" life, is a fine example of the work produced by the craftsmen of 13th-century Mosul.

FACING PAGE
Ince Minare Medrese, Konia, Turkey
The entrance façade of the Ince Medrese, one of the theological colleges of Konia, shows Seljuk decorative art at its most sophisticated, with its floral motifs and its complex, knotted bands of calligraphy.

Material Culture

The Islamic Near East

No civilization exposed to the Mongols came through their assault unscathed, least of all the fundamentalist Islam. Through much of the twelfth century, internal divisions had weakened the Muslim world. Yet a recovery had begun before the end of the century, and when the Mongols struck, shortly afterwards, it was at a society of re-burnished brilliance.

Some part of this brilliance was preserved in Seljuk Anatolia, the architecture of which reached a notable peak in the great religious and other charitable buildings of the early-thirteenth-century sultans. Among these were the *medreses*, or schools of theology, at the Seljuk capital at Konia, one of which, the Sircali Medrese, was an early example of the successful use of brilliantly coloured faience tiles in the external cladding of the building. But more immediately impressive are the fortified caravanserais, the Seljuk *hans*, built as stations for the refreshment (both physical and religious) of travellers between the major Anatolian cities. In the decoration and further endowment of these, the sultans spared little expense. The Sultan Han, built between 1229 and 1236 on the road between Konia and Aksaray, although now no more than a dramatic ruin, still preserves something of the

scale of these great lodging-hospital-mosque complexes. As at the *medreses* of Konia, the fantastically carved stonework of the gates of the Sultan Han is typical of Seljuk artistic achievement at its highest; the architectural equivalent of the contemporary fine metalwork of Mosul, in Mesopotamia, or the brilliantly painted pottery of twelfth- and early-thirteenth-century Iran (see page 108).

Into this culture the Mongols broke. In Anatolia, it is claimed, the deterioration of sculpture can be dated from the beginning of Mongol dominance. And certainly in Persia one result of the invasion of 1231 was to cause the flight of skilled metalworkers on such a scale as to depress their craft over a couple of centuries. Yet it was Persia that, in other ways, gained most from its Mongol Khanate—in politics through the recovery of an effective identity long lost under the rule of the Abbasid caliphs of Baghdad; in art through such innovations as the introduction of Chinese techniques both in painting and the manufacture of pottery.

One effect of the bruising of Islam by the Mongols was to turn it, vengefully, on the surviving Christian communities of the Holy Land. Another was to increase an existing tendency towards isolationism in the Muslim faith, promoted by its defeats in the West. The decisive battle of Las Navas de Tolosa in 1212, with its sequel in the Christian reconquest of Spain, had forced a great exodus of scholars and of mystics, bringing back to the most sensitive centres of Islam (embattled Egypt and Syria) the resentments of religious refugees. Of course, to an appreciable extent, the sophisticated civilization of Muslim Spain continued under its Christian conquerors. It was at the court of Alfonso the Wise (1252-84), conqueror of Murcia, that the work of Archbishop Raymond's Toledan school of twelfth-century translators was revived and brought to a new flowering, with important consequences to the intellectual life of the West. However, to the Arabs in Spain the advance of the Christians was a tragic and an irreversible catastrophe, eloquently lamented by Abu l-Baqa' ibn Sharif (d. 1285), one of their most notable poets. It can have made little difference to the victims of these oppressions that the Christians themselves, in far-off Russia, were contemporaneously experiencing a still more unhappy reversal.

Islamic decorative art

The distinguishing characteristic of Islamic art was its emphasis, religiously inspired, on abstract decoration, frequently combined with calligraphy. Men and animals may occasionally be shown, but they are rare. In their place, Muslim artists developed a complexity of design entirely unmatched in the art of the Christian West, where portraiture, even in religious art, was always acceptable to the Church. The concentration on shape and pattern, to the virtual exclusion of a narrative or portrait art, resulted inevitably in a loss of dramatic power. But where the Islamic artist made up for this loss was in the intricate ingenuity of his flowing designs, as much a feature of ceramics and metalwork as of larger projects like the Friday Mosque at Isfahan.

BELOW *Scene in a pharmacy, from* Materia Medica, *Baghdad, Persia*

ABOVE *Pottery goblet, Persia*

ABOVE *Ceramic vase, Damascus, Syria*

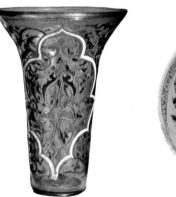

ABOVE *Glass vase, Syria*

ABOVE *Mina'i bowl, Rayy or Kashan, Persia*

ABOVE *Kasman wall tiles from a mosque at Meshhed, Persia*

FACING PAGE *Seljuk glazed tilework, Friday Mosque, Isfahan, Persia*

St George, Yuriev-Polsky, Russia

Cathedral, Suzdal, Russia

Eastern Europe

The Mongol assault on Russia in the late 1230s came at a particularly unfortunate moment for the arts. Just a few decades before, the architecture of Suzdalia had begun to develop a distinctive style of its own, at last independent of those Byzantine influences that continued to permeate the arts of the more westerly Kiev. Already before the end of the twelfth century, at the Church of St Dmitry at Vladimir, a new sculptural tradition had evolved. And this was further developed in the first decades of the thirteenth century, to yield such remarkable relief sculptures as those that still survive on the lower parts of the walls of Suzdal Cathedral (1222-5) and at the Church of St George (1229-34) at Yuriev-Polsky. Two years after the completion of the latter, Batu and his Mongol army were on the lower Volga and had occupied Georgia. They were threatening Suzdalia the next year, and the sack and destruction of Vladimir on 8 February 1238 was closely followed by that of a number of other central Russian cities, including the still insignificant Moscow. Novgorod held out, forcing the retreat southwards of the Mongols. But Kiev fell before the end of 1240, and with the collapse of the Russian principalities came the demise of the art they had fostered. At a stroke, the Vladimir-Suzdalian architectural tradition disappeared, for although it was used much later by the Muscovite princes as a model for their own considerable building enterprises, it had no direct successor. Even at Novgorod, drained of its profits by the annual tribute demanded by the Mongols of the South, patronage of the arts for the rest of the century suffered a serious relapse. It was not until the fourteenth century that returning prosperity again brought with it the recovery of building in the principalities.

Byzantium

Byzantium, the cradle of Orthodox Russian culture, had suffered its own catastrophe in 1204 at the hands not of the pagan Mongols but of the Venetians and other fellow Christians in the misdirected fury of the Fourth Crusade. But while it subsequently escaped the worst of the Mongol onslaught and indeed eventually made useful allies of the ilkhans of Persia, it never, even after the return of Byzantine rulers to Constantinople itself in 1261, recovered much more than the shreds of its past wealth. Associated with the return, there was to be a final phase of Byzantine culture before the Ottoman conquest of 1453—the so-called Palaeologue Revival. And although its best work belongs to the fourteenth century, some characteristics of the new humanity and realism it manifested were already visible in the sophisticated wall-paintings at the Serbian Church of the Trinity at Sopocani, dating from about 1265. Moreover, the roots of the revival are also to be seen in contemporary work of the Byzantines in exile, for example in the extraordinary vivid wall-paintings of *c.* 1260 at the Church of St Sophia at Trebizond.

In architecture certainly, Palaeologue Byzantium, without the resources for such major building programmes as had characterized earlier and more prosperous reigns, had by this time descended into no more than the second rank. From the West, Byzantine architects, during the long period of Latin dominance after the Fourth Crusade, borrowed the belfry and the elongated ground-plan of their churches, developing further such features as the pointed "Gothic" window and the architectural engineering of the vault. Yet for reasons as much political as practical, the true sophistication of contemporary western European architectural practice effectively passed them by.

Indeed, the Byzantine reaction against Frankish influence, following the recovery of Constantinople in 1261, had had the effect of halting experiments with western techniques, even of the more fruitful kind, substituting for these a dogmatic return to the past. Still, in the Balkans and in the Greek principalities, the cross-fertilization of Latin and Greek cultures could yield such interesting hybrid buildings as the church of the Parigoritissa at Arta, in Epirus, built towards the end of the thirteenth century for princes whose family alliances were as much with the West as with Byzantium. But in Constantinople itself, the exactly contemporary extension and rebuilding of the monastery church of Lips was a conservative work, distinguished externally from the adjoining tenth-century church by little more than the decorative patterned brickwork which was one of the identifiable characteristics of the later Byzantine style.

Wall-painting, Trebizond, Turkey
The murals in the church of St Sophia at Trebizond were painted in about 1260. Their vivid colours and dynamic, realistic characterization were an important source for the art of the Palaeologue Revival, which began after the return of Constantinople to Byzantium in 1261. Here the Christ Child teaches in the temple.

Western Europe

It is to the West that we must look for one of the most extraordinary architectural flowerings the world has ever experienced—long-lived with its roots in the eleventh century and a trail at least as late as the sixteenth, but at its peak in the thirteenth century and in the culminating triumph of pure Gothic.

Although in due course High Gothic became dominated by the French example, in particular by the court style of Paris, it was not accepted simultaneously in all parts of thirteenth-century Europe, nor would it ever be without its distinctive local variants. Its penetration of Italy was negligible, Italian architects preferring to find their models in the Romanesque tradition, or even further back in the monuments of ancient Rome. Intriguingly, too, its reception in the North was preceded by a Transitional phase (also known as Early Gothic) during which Byzantine and antique Roman influences became especially strong. In Provence, there were the so-called "proto-Renaissance" churches like that of the abbey of St-Gilles-du-Gard, dating to the same late-twelfth-century decades as the Early Gothic buildings of the North. And although Roman influence was rarely as powerful elsewhere as in those regions of south-eastern France where there were many imperial monuments to reinforce it, it reappeared quite clearly in the drapery style of the Mosan metalworker, Nicholas of Verdun, at the turn of the twelfth and thirteenth centuries, being detectable also in the over-emphasized drapery folds of the sculptured figures on the north transept portal at Chartres Cathedral (shortly after 1205) and in the work of the Master of the Antique Figures at Rheims (c. 1230).

These works at Chartres and at Rheims, with the still more immediate example of the Mosan school of Nicholas of Verdun (see page 73), were the obvious inspiration of the contemporary sculptures on the south transept at Strasbourg Cathedral, also dating from c. 1230. What the Strasbourg figures show us is a typically German emotion-charged style, exemplifying those significant localized developments in the arts, which characterized the first decades of the thirteenth century before the later dominance of the French. Thus in England there was a tendency towards ornateness in architecture, visible in such

Figure on south portal, Chartres Cathedral, France

Visitation figure, Rheims Cathedral, France

Synagoga figure, Strasbourg Cathedral, Germany

Sculptural style
The early 13th century saw a "Transitional" style in northern European sculpture, notable for its softening of lines and growing naturalism. The figures on the south portal at Chartres, carved after 1205, show the classical deep folding of the drapery that is characteristic of this style. It becomes more marked in the Strasbourg "Synagoga" figure (c. 1230), and almost dominates the Rheims "Visitation" figure of about the same date.

FACING PAGE
Sainte Chapelle, France
Louis IX's Sainte Chapelle at Paris, one of the most influential buildings in the rayonnant *style, was built between 1243 and 1248. The great areas of window, made possible by structural innovations, fill the interior with coloured light, and every available wall surface is decorated with blind tracery in the style of the windows.*

major turn-of-the-century buildings as Lincoln Cathedral, which was quite as distinctively English as the colour-tinted outline drawings of the Matthew Paris St Albans School, dating from the mid-thirteenth century and after (see page 105). And even in France itself, a building like Bourges Cathedral, conceived on a massive scale, could represent a significant independent departure from the more usual model of the cathedrals at Chartres, Rheims and Amiens, with its soaring ground arcade in an extreme extension of the new High Gothic tradition, and with its external profusion of flying buttresses (see pages 54-5).

The progressive enlargement of the nave arcade, disposing of the gallery and tucking the triforium up under the windows of the clerestory, had begun at Chartres. And at Chartres again the transition from Early to High Gothic was most clearly demonstrated in the difference between the formal Romanesque statuary of the great west portal, which survived the fire of 1194, and the much rounder, softer, gothicized figures on the early-thirteenth-century portals of the rebuilt transepts. Equally important, and only a few decades later, was the change observable in the

sculptural tradition of the two royal cathedrals at Rheims and at Notre Dame in Paris. In practice the classicizing tendencies of the Transitional Period were abandoned at these buildings well before the mid-century. In their place, sculpture developed a new naturalism and a delicacy verging on daintiness, close to the contemporary court tradition in painting and other decorative arts, and itself the fount of a whole movement in European taste. One of the manifestations of French High Gothic sculpture, widely copied elsewhere, was the capital carved with naturalistic foliage, imitated at Naumburg in Germany before 1250, in Spain on buildings of the second half of the thirteenth century, and in England most subtly at Southwell Minster, in the famous set of chapter-house capitals datable to *c.* 1295.

Such ornamental capitals belonged to a long tradition, at its liveliest in Cluniac Romanesque. Yet they stood outside the mainstream of architectural development, in which the parts, increasingly, had come to be submerged in the whole. The new mid-century *rayonnant* architecture of Paris had several distinguishing characteristics. Prominent among these was the use of blind tracery to decorate wall surfaces, while the dominant emphasis was now on the height of buildings and on their lighting by the great new windows permitted by recent advances in vaulting and buttressing techniques. Most famous of the buildings in this new court style, influential in contemporary building projects in England and in Germany too, was Louis IX's Sainte Chapelle, in Paris, an elaborate reliquary in stone built to house the precious devotional objects, including fragments of the Crown of Thorns, which the king had lately purchased.

Work on the Sainte Chapelle began in 1243, and the three other most important buildings in the *rayonnant* tradition were all launched within that decade: Westminster Abbey in 1245 and the cathedrals at Beauvais and at Cologne in 1247 and 1248 respectively. Beauvais demonstrated some of the faults of an architecture still in its formative stage. Its over-ambitious choir vault, pushed to a height of 158 feet (never afterwards exceeded in medieval Europe), collapsed in 1284. But the more successful buildings of the Sainte Chapelle, Westminster and Cologne demonstrated all the main principles of the *rayonnant*

Henry III of England
Henry III (1216–72) was an extravagant patron of the arts. His expensive building projects included the rebuilding of Westminster Abbey between 1245 and his death, in the Gothic rayonnant style.

Orvieto Cathedral, Italy

At Orvieto Cathedral, begun in 1290, the Gothic details are secondary to a fundamentally Romanesque conception. The façade, as it was built (right), is an Italian confection of mosaic work and sculptural detail, chosen in preference to a more daring Gothic design.

designers—their stress on the totality of the decorative programme in which no surface was left unadorned. Significantly, only the Sainte Chapelle was completed in good time, within the space of just five years. Westminster, despite Henry III's personal concern, remained half-finished at its patron's death and took another two centuries to complete, whereas the final work on Cologne Cathedral had to wait till the nineteenth century. Nevertheless, the extravagance and complexity of the new French style were to capture the imagination of contemporary architects, among their more celebrated works being the cathedrals in Spain at Leon and Toledo, with the incomplete western façade of Strasbourg Cathedral, and the incomparable Angel Choir at Lincoln Cathedral, begun as early as 1256.

The design for Louis IX's Sainte Chapelle is thought to have been based on the elaborate metalwork reliquaries of the period. Indeed, the particularly striking characteristic of the French court style in general was this close intermeshing of contemporary artistic media. Not only was the cheerful delicacy of the sculptured figures of the Rheims Joseph Master picked up by German stoneworkers on the west portals of the cathedral at Strasbourg, but the contemporary interest in architectural embellishment, shown by great patrons of the arts like the English Henry III and like Louis IX (St Louis) himself, was very exactly reflected in manuscript illumination, an exceptionally

fine example of which is the mid-century Psalter of St Louis (see page 104). The same preoccupations persisted through the rest of the century, to emerge in such works as the Westminster Retable and, down the scale, in the charming and unusually sophisticated products of the tile-makers of Chertsey Abbey (see page 105), both from the late thirteenth century.

Further developments of great significance also emerged before the end of the century, one of these being the refinement of a genuine portrait sculpture in the sepulchral effigies of the period, another the first suggestion in Parisian court painting of the currents by now flowing in Italy. In both of these, the fullest expression was not to be found before the art of the early fourteenth century. Nevertheless, the elaboration of tombs, frequently under spectacular architectural canopies, had begun quite early in the thirteenth century. And although the influence of Italy on the paintings of the North before 1300 remained still of the subtlest, it was already quite clear by the late thirteenth century that there had come into being a vigorous traffic of ideas.

Italy had hitherto stood outside the Gothic tradition, beating a path of its own in architecture which, while it took in selected elements of Gothic, reverted more commonly to Antique and Byzantine models within a matrix that stayed obstinately Romanesque. Right at the end of the thirteenth century, the nave of a major new building like Orvieto Cathedral, begun as late as 1290, could still be constructed in a Romanesque manner which would have excited derision in the North. And when, early in the next century, a western façade in the French *rayonnant* manner was projected for Orvieto, the Italians themselves would show their contempt for the northern style by discarding this plan in favour of a more traditional hybrid confection of their own.

Even in Italy, however, well before 1300 the traffic in ideas had begun to take effect. In the work of the sculptor and architect Nicola Pisano (fl. 1259–78), the best of the Gothic sculptural tradition penetrated the South. The roots of Nicola's art are obscure. Yet it emerged fully formed in the pulpit of 1259–60, carved for the Baptistry at Pisa (see page 105), where the sophisticated relief carving and sharp drapery folds of the Joseph Master of Rheims were combined with a strong

element of antique Roman portraiture which, in this context, is wholly Nicola's own. This Roman influence was seemingly as necessary a transitional element in Nicola's work as it had been in that of the Early Gothic masters of the North; in due course it disappeared. Nicola's Siena pulpit of 1265-8 was very much in the softer French manner, while his son Giovanni later developed a dramatic, agitated technique more reminiscent of the style of the stone-carvers of Strasbourg. Arnolfo di Cambio, another of Nicola Pisano's apprentices, carried the French tradition of sepulchral sculpture to Rome, employing the art of the indigenous *Cosmati* marble mosaicists in the decoration of a series of monumental tombs. The effigies on these tombs, like their northern originals, suggest realistic portraiture.

Earlier in the century, the rather mechanical art of the Roman *Cosmati* marblers had attracted northern patrons, who found a place for their mosaics in the works, for example, at Westminster. But a more important southern influence soon manifested itself in painting. It developed first in the manuscript illuminations of the Parisian court painter Maître Honoré towards the end of the thirteenth century, and became especially significant from the early fourteenth century in the work

of another royal painter, Jean Pucelle, a contemporary and follower of Duccio. Maître Honoré's manuscripts show several innovations, including the abandonment of the architectural settings favoured by earlier court-style illuminators, the proliferation of marginal illustrations in the contemporary English manner, and the beginnings of that naturalistic ivy-leaf decoration that became so familiar in fourteenth-century manuscript illumination. But it is his use of light and shade, picked out especially in the folds of garments and giving the illusion of depth, that betrays Italian influences.

It was Italian innovations on just these lines, showing in the late-thirteenth-century work of the Isaac Master of Assisi and in the frescoes and mosaics of the Roman Pietro Cavallini, that prepared the way into the Early Renaissance and the revolutionary art of Giotto. What interested the Italians, and what had already preoccupied the Byzantine masters by whom they were still deeply influenced, was the science of perspective, the practice and rules of which Giotto seems to have been teaching himself even as he worked down the walls of his celebrated Arena Chapel (see page 150). With the wall surfaces of their many new churches uncluttered by tracery ornament, the Italians

Technical innovations in Italian painting

In the late 13th century, Italian painting began to combine a more careful use of light and shade with an interest in perspective that came largely from Byzantium. The work of Pietro Cavallini and the Isaac Master of Assisi pointed the way forward to the major artistic innovations of Giotto. Italian influence is also clearly visible in the work of the French court manuscript illuminator Maître Honoré, who experimented with light and shade in his modelling, as well as drawing on the English tradition for his lively marginal sketches.

BELOW
Adoration of the Magi
by Pietro Cavallini,
S. Maria in Trastevere,
Rome, Italy

ABOVE Humility, Pride, the Sinner and the Hypocrite, *from* La Somme le Roy *by Maître Honoré*

ABOVE Isaac and Esau *by the Isaac Master, S. Francesco, Assisi, Italy*

Technological advances
Among the technological innovations of the 13th century were the cog, a broad-beamed cargo ship; the windmill and refinements on the water-mill, between them making possible considerable mechanization; and spectacles, deriving from the work on optics being done at the universities of Europe.

Hanseatic cog

Water-mill

Spectacle-vendor

were uniquely able to develop fresco-painting on an unprecedentedly generous scale. One of the most important of these opportunities occurred at the newly-built church of St Francis at Assisi where the Isaac Master, with other major painters employed on the overall decorative scheme at the basilica, was able to perfect his art. Yet patronage and opportunity by themselves would not be enough to explain the astonishing technical advances of Italian painting in the years round about 1300, for these have their place in a wider movement of technological expansion and experiment.

The movement took many forms. At sea, this was the period of the introduction of the cog, which was a sturdy, high-sided, broad-beamed cargo vessel well suited to northern waters; charts were developed and compasses mounted more efficiently. In the building industry, new skills in carpentry cleared the floor of cumbrous aisles and permitted the spanning of much wider structures with roofs in the new hammer-beam, tie-beam, and base-cruck traditions, all of which would continue to be refined and perfected. Mechanization on a large scale is first found in the water-powered silk-throwing mills of thirteenth-century Italy, where a mere handful of operatives could do the work formerly requiring hundreds. And water-power again was made to drive saw-mills and paper-mills, serving the iron industry also for stamping and grinding, and operating hydraulic bellows.

In almost every field, innovations were striking and continuous, so that a man of the late thirteenth century might feel, much as we do today, the bewilderment of runaway progress. Through the century, windmills spread throughout northern Europe, harnessing an important new power source. Before 1300, the spinning-wheel had been introduced for the manufacture of yarn, the weight-driven clock had made an appearance, the wheelbarrow had been invented, and we have our first record of spectacles in common and familiar use.

Spectacles, of course, had their importance in preparing the way for the later revolution of reading habits, towards which block printing, introduced at Ravenna before the end of the thirteenth century, contributed another major advance. Optics, indeed, were a continuing preoccupation of much thirteenth-century

experimental science, both Bishop Grosseteste of Lincoln and the Franciscan scientist Roger Bacon, two of the most original minds of their day, being aware by the mid-century of the magnifying properties of lenses, which they recommended as a corrective for weak eyesight. Each of these men worked within a context of high creativity where science and philosophy merged in the reception of Aristotle (as useful to the natural scientist as to the theologian), and in the commentaries of Aristotelians like Alexander of Hales and the great Thomas Aquinas.

The common characteristic shown by all was an eagerness to experiment, advance and instruct. At the very beginning of the century, in 1202, the publication of Leonardo of Pisa's *Liber Abaci* introduced the West to Arabic numerals, with important applications, later developed, to commercial arithmetic and banking. And what the towns were learning in business expertise was matched in the countryside by the growing body of agricultural lore, diffused through the medium of popular treatises like the mid-century *Hosebondrie* of Walter of Henley and the rather later *Ruralia Commoda* (*c.* 1306) of the Bolognese landowner Crescenzi. In medicine, there were human dissections before the end of the century, the first reference to these being published in 1275 in the *Chirurgia* of William of Saliceto. In practical chemistry, the most important advance was in the refinement and application of distilling apparatus, used in the manufacture of alcohol and in the preparation of the commoner acids.

A number of these currents, both technological and artistic, merged in the thirteenth-century castle architecture of the West. Thus Frederick II's symmetrical castle-plans at Catania and Syracuse in Sicily, and at his exquisite octagonal Castel del Monte in Apulia, showed a mathematical precision new to European fortress design. At one and the same time, they met the demands of military science in their regularly-placed mural towers providing flanking fire, while also containing domestic accommodation of a very sophisticated standard. Frederick II was himself a connoisseur of architecture, like his direct contemporaries Henry III of England and Louis IX of France. Castel del Monte, built as a hunting-lodge rather than a fortress, clearly reflected his personal tastes. Completed in about 1240, it

Castel del Monte, Italy
An octagonal fortress built in Apulia for the Emperor Frederick II in about 1240, Castel del Monte was really a luxurious hunting residence rather than a military strongpoint, but it shows the uniform mural towers that were becoming common in 13th-century castles, as well as a clear classical influence in its fine pedimented portico.

English castle-building
Castle-building as a defensive science reached its peak in the 13th century, with the multiple curtain walls built by Henry III at Dover, and with Edward I's great chain of fortresses in North Wales. All virtually impregnable, and often associated with fortified towns, Edward's castles show the development of the concentric plan, of which Beaumaris — although never completed — is the perfect example.

had a pedimented portico in the classical Roman manner, surmounted by a purely Gothic window. In its interior, the accommodation was planned to a standard of luxury, even in its plumbing, more at home in the crusader castles of Outremer than in the Latin West. The fine vaulting and other architectural details of the domestic quarters were Gothic in the best French tradition.

Castel del Monte, at a crossroad of cultures in Hohenstaufen southern Italy, was a more exotic building than most of the castles of its day. But the projecting mural towers that are such a prominent feature of its external design were becoming common at this time in castle architecture throughout the wealthier nations of western Europe, as was the greatly increased luxury of its accommodation. Pre-dating Castel del Monte, the huge private fortress of Coucy in France, built in 1225-30, was already regularly-planned, with great drum towers at the angles of its curtain wall, and a massive cylindrical keep. And there is no example more striking of the curtain wall and cylindrical mural tower tradition than Louis IX's impressive fortress at Angers, on a tributary of the Loire, begun during his minority in 1228 and completed some ten years later.

Castles on the whole grow slowly, reflecting many influences in their plans.

Certainly, this was the case in the multiple baronial fortresses of medieval Germany, as it was again in an important royal castle like Dover in England, where the sophisticated curtain-wall defences of Henry III left the anachronistic stone keep of his grandfather, Henry II, stranded like a whale in the middle. Yet there was one group of castles that, because of the concentrated period of its building, stood out as a uniquely important example of a unified strategy and design. Towards the end of the thirteenth century, starting in 1277, Edward I carried out a programme of castle-building in Wales which ended with the re-modelling or construction from new of no fewer than eight great castles—Aberystwyth, Builth, Flint, Rhuddlan, Harlech, Conway, Caernarvon, and Beaumaris—five of which, moreover, carried with them the building of an associated fortified town. With the contemporary baronial fortress of the Clare lords of Glamorgan at Caerphilly, these Edwardian castles stand at the peak of a castle-building tradition which, on account of its enormous expense, had by now very clearly outpriced itself.

Significantly, Beaumaris, the last and most refined of Edward's castles, was never completed. It may well be that the sophistication of military science in the hands of men like Edward's Savoyard architect, Master James of St George, had

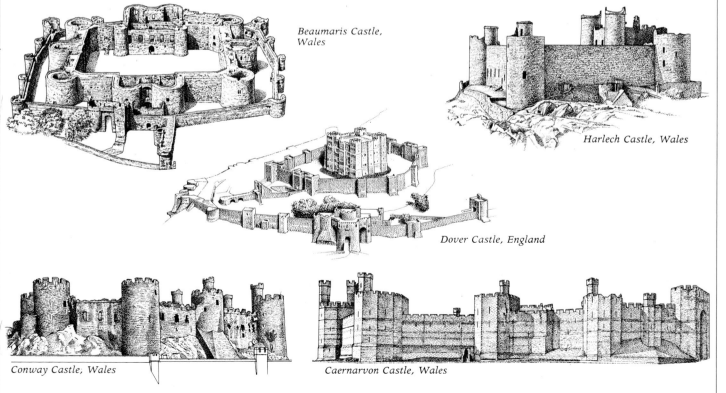

Beaumaris Castle, Wales

Harlech Castle, Wales

Dover Castle, England

Conway Castle, Wales

Caernarvon Castle, Wales

Great Mosque, Kilwa, Africa (plan)
The Great Mosque at Kilwa was massively rebuilt in the 13th century, when Kilwa became the foremost Arab settlement in East Africa and a centre for the trade of the Indian Ocean.

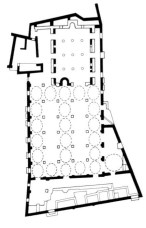

Arab East Africa
Arab traders followed the monsoon winds south, establishing a chain of settlements along the East African coast. Mogadishu and Kilwa were centres for the Indian and Chinese trade, and Sofala, far to the south, for the gold trade with Zimbabwe in the interior.

Arab trade routes in East Africa

⬜ *Muslim areas*

outstripped the resources even of the wealthiest and most determined patrons. When another English king, Henry VIII, similarly interested himself in a programme of massive refortification, he too would come close to bankruptcy. And there are other parallels between the two monarchs in the ages of discovery during which both lived, and in the readiness of both to look overseas for the technical accomplishments not immediately available at home.

It is now generally accepted that the model for Edward I's Caernarvon was the great Theodosian city wall of Constantinople. The German emperor, Frederick II, found inspiration for his works at Castel del Monte in the East as well as in the West, and threw in Classical Antiquity for good measure. This readiness to welcome alien precedents was in every way characteristic of the century. For a long time already, European interest in a remote world beyond the known Mediterranean lands had been stirred by tales of the legendary Prester John, a monarch supposedly Christian in his sympathies, who at one time, bizarrely, had been identified with Genghis Khan himself. And it was the years of Mongol supremacy in particular which opened the doors of Central Asia and China to the first inquisitive travellers and missionaries from the West, protected by Mongol religious indifference.

Before the Polos, Maffio and Nicolo, reached China in 1262, Franciscan friars had already been received at the court of the Mongol Great Khans. The Polos were back in Rome by 1269 with a message to the pope from Kublai Khan, and set off again two years later with Marco Polo, Nicolo's more celebrated son. In the late 1280s, when Marco Polo was in the service of Kublai Khan, Rabban Sauna, a Nestorian Christian monk of Peking, crossed Central Asia to the Mongol court in Persia, subsequently travelling to Rome and northern Europe as an emissary from China, seeking allies against Islam. The tolerant reception he was accorded in Rome, where he expounded his Nestorian beliefs, was fully matched in Mongol China where an Italian Franciscan, John of Montecorvino, was encouraged to set up a Christian mission at Peking. There he experienced some considerable success, allegedly baptizing some six thousand converts within a decade of his coming.

Africa

When Marco Polo came back from China, and when John of Montecorvino went out there, they both made much of the journey along the southern sea routes via India and South-East Asia. Traditionally, these were the routes of both Arab and Chinese traders, and the Arabs, despite their reverses in Central Asia, were still very much in control of them. One of the more recent initiatives of the Arab merchants, dating from about 1200 or not very much before, was to carry their trade southwards down the length of the East African coast, as far as the monsoon winds would take them. With Mogadishu flourishing especially during the thirteenth century as their first major port-of-call south of Aden, the gold trade through Sofala to the interior was opened up by Arab traders, who were responsible too for the commercial development of Muslim Kilwa as another important staging-post on the way.

Kilwa would reach its economic peak in the early fourteenth century. However, already before this, it had supplanted Mogadishu as the most important Muslim city on the coast; it had a bronze coinage of its own, with many stone buildings including the surviving Great Mosque, and much evidence of a flourishing overseas trade. No attempt seems to have been made by the Arabs to carry this exclusively coastal civilization into the uplands of what are now Kenya and Tanzania. The traditional Arab trade along the coast was always narrowly based, concentrating especially on high-value commodities like ivory and gold for which the market in the Mediterranean was continually expanding, and focusing at its northern end on the long-established entrepôt cities of the Persian Gulf. Nevertheless, the penetration to Kilwa of Chinese porcelains, present there already in the thirteenth century and the dominant ceramic import by the fourteenth, is a significant pointer to the role of the East African coast in a wider trading system, spanning the Indian Ocean and extending beyond Sumatra to the Far East. It was stage-by-stage along this ancient commercial trail, taking in India on the way, that Marco Polo returned to Venice in 1295, by sea from Hangchow in China to Ormuz on the Persian Gulf, in an adventurous journey, prolonged by detentions, which took almost three years to complete.

Kesava Temple, Somnathpur, India
The Kesava Temple at Somnathpur, founded in 1268, is typical of Hoysala sacred architecture, with its three star-shaped sanctuaries clustered around a pillared hall. Its wealth of intricately executed sculpture (top) covers the entire surface, even the grill-windows having a sculptured complexity of their own.

FACING PAGE
Hoysala sculpture, Mysore, India
This sculpture of Ganesha, the elephant-headed god of prudence and sagacity, is rich in symbolic detail, and has all the delicacy and almost rococo elaboration of the best Hoysala work.

India

Comparatively little of the India that Marco Polo visited, and in which he, his father and his uncle were detained, had remained untouched by the Islamic puritanism of Muhammad Ghuri and his iconoclastic successors in the Delhi Sultanate. Nevertheless, the Delhi sultans were to have little to do with southern India before the fourteenth century, leaving the former Tamil empire of the Hindu Cholas, already bereft of Ceylon, to be partitioned between its more powerful feudatories: the Pandyas of Madurai to the south and, to the west, the Hoysalas of Mysore. And it was the wealth of the Pandyan kingdom, rich in lands and trade, that chiefly impressed Marco Polo.

One of the characteristics of post-Chola architecture in the South was its rococo richness of detail, where the art of the sculptor replaced in emphasis the skills of the architect and mason. Very obviously, this southern Indian concentration on sculptural detail is visible in such well-known Hoysala works as the Kesava

Temple at Somnathpur, built in 1268 as a trio of star-shaped sanctuaries set about a central pillared hall, the whole surrounded by a cloister. Yet there is little that is monumental in this Hoysala temple. Indeed, it is squat in form and comparatively modest in scale. However, what distinguished both this work and Hoysala sculpture in general was the rich intricacy of the stone-carving, a characteristic shared by the contemporary art of surviving non-Muslim northern India.

It was not until 1298 that a fresh drive of conquest from Delhi absorbed Gujerat and west Rajasthan, bringing the Jain architecture of Mount Abu to an end. In the meantime the Jain tradition had produced at the temple of Tejpala, built in the early 1230s, one of its outstanding monuments, very similar in conception and even in detail to the neighbouring eleventh-century Vimala Sha and Dilwara Temples, yet at the peak of this long-lived architectural tradition in which ornamental sculpture had maintained its predominant and spectacular role.

Certainly, wherever the Muslims penetrated in thirteenth-century India, the old Hindu and Buddhist artistic traditions experienced a serious decline. And nothing was more likely to excite the fury of the Muslim image-breakers than the erotic art associated with Hindu Tantrism, where the sex act might be part of the temple ritual. It is therefore especially fortunate that the great Surya Temple at Konarak, in the Mahanadi delta southwest of Calcutta, escaped their attention. Apart from its great size, emphasized by its isolated position on the coast, the distinguishing characteristic of this temple of the sun is its representation in stone of

Surya Temple, Konarak, India

The temple of the sun-god Surya at Konarak (right), largely built during the reign of Narasimhadeva (1238-64), but never completed, is in the form of the sun-god's chariot. The whole temple appears to rest on twelve great wheels (bottom), and to be pulled by seven horses (above). The greatest work of the Orissan temple-builders, it is famous for its erotic carvings, of a quality never again matched in Indian sculpture.

the chariot of the sun-god, Surya. With the seven sculptured horses of the sun-god myth to draw it, the body of the temple was carried at its base on twelve great wheels, finely carved in the stone-work of the plinth, while above and around these were the erotic paired-off sculptures which have made the Surya Temple notorious. Although largely constructed in the mid-century during the reign of Narasimhadeva (1238-64), it is unlikely that the temple was ever fully completed, for its builders ran into problems of subsidence in the sand which stopped them capping the main structure. Yet this extraordinary allegory in stone can still be seen as the culminating achievement of the Orissan temple builders, bringing to a close a temple-building tradition with its roots at least as far back as the eighth century. Moreover, in the quality of its sculpture it preserved a standard not afterwards surpassed or even equalled in India. As much a piece with its tradition as the contemporary Jain temple of Tejpala on Mount Abu at the opposite corner of India, it stood at the end of an even longer road.

Mahabodhi Temple, Pagan, Burma
The Mahabodhi Temple at Pagan, dedicated in 1215, was copied directly from the famous shrine at Bodh Gaya, in India, which was built and rebuilt from the 2nd century onwards, and enclosed the Buddha's bodhi tree. The Pagan temple differs, however, in rising to a much finer point, and it is crowned by a quite different finial.

Mingalazedi stupa, Pagan, Burma
The Mingalazedi stupa, begun in 1274, illustrates the indigenous Burmese style in shrine-building that had developed at Pagan by that date: in particular, the flights of steps at the four points of the compass are a typically Burmese feature.

South-East Asia

Before the end of the thirteenth century, Burma saw also both the culmination and the end of a tradition. Since the days of Anoratha, their great eleventh-century ruler, Burmese architects and patrons had persisted in finding their inspiration in the buildings of the Buddhist heartland in northern India. The great Mahabodhi Temple at the Burmese capital at Pagan, dedicated in 1215, was deliberately modelled on its still more famous namesake at Bodh Gaya, in North India, where the Buddha had meditated under the bodhi tree. However, although the imitation of Indian models continued to be common in thirteenth-century Burma right through till the collapse of the kingdom in 1287, the Burmese themselves independently developed stylistic features very much their own in the stupa architecture of Pagan, one of the last and finest examples of which was the Mingalazedi stupa of 1274. Characteristically Burmese were the external stairs on the four sides of the Mingalazedi stupa, its bell-shaped drum and conical spire, and the emphasis on verticality carried through every detail of the monument. And yet scarcely more than a decade after the completion of this temple, Pagan was sacked by the Mongols, leaving Burma itself to Thai domination and its art from then on to the folk.

To some extent the Thais themselves continued the Burmese tradition. The brick-built Wat Chet Yot, in northern Siam near Chiengmai, was in fact a late-thirteenth-century imitation of the Mahabodhi Temple at Pagan and thus of its original northern Indian prototype. But the Khmer art of Cambodia was equally important in this initial birth phase of Thai power in Siam, a genuine national tradition emerging only on the ruins of the great civilizations of Burma and Cambodia. The Thais had originally been driven from their own homeland in Yunnan in South China under the pressure of Mongol expansion, to occupy new territories in Burma and Cambodia which, although threatened by the armies of Kublai Khan, were never permanently settled by them. Thus Mongol power, directly in Burma with the sack of Pagan in 1287 and indirectly in Cambodia via the Thai, was characteristically destructive in mainland South-East Asia, being only less so in contemporary Java because of the impossible distances that had to be covered by the invasion fleet of 1292-3.

Java from the mid-thirteenth century had begun to experience a renaissance of the arts which, while it owed little to the traditions of the golden age of seventh- and eighth-century Middle Java, yet developed considerable quality of its own. Especially this was the case under the Majapahit dynasty of East Java in the fourteenth and fifteenth centuries. But already under Singhasari rule in the period 1250-92, there was a resurrection of temple-building in the Jago (1268), for example, or at the slightly earlier Kidal (1250). These were buildings on a comparatively small scale, with nothing of the monumentality of the original temples of Middle Java. However, what chiefly distinguishes them is their manifest display of an independent development of the arts in Java, free from the influence of Greater India which was still such a potent force in Burma and northern Siam. Characteristically Javanese were the grotesque masks over the doorways of monuments, a reflection perhaps of the taste for drama in which so much of the vigour of Indonesian folk art is still expressed today.

Easter Island statuary
There are some 600 half-length statues on Easter Island, dating from the later centuries of the "Middle Period" of the island's culture (c. 1100-1680). Their exact significance is still open to conjecture.

Early Oceanic settlement
By the 13th century the migration of Polynesian peoples was virtually complete. Starting from Indonesia or the Philippines, the colonists had reached Fiji by 1300 BC, and a further eastward migration led to the Marquesas Islands, which were the centre for expansion throughout Polynesia, including Tahiti and Easter Island, as far as Hawaii in the north, and New Zealand to the south-west.

Oceania

In still greater isolation, east of Java and barely touching the coast of New Guinea, Melanesian and Polynesian peoples had settled the islands of the South Pacific and had developed a culture of their own. The origins of the Polynesians are obscure. However, it seems likely that they derived originally from Indonesia or the Philippines, migrating eastwards to Fiji by about 1300 BC, and thence by stages into Polynesia itself by way of Tonga and Samoa. Crucial to the spread of Polynesian culture, which remained isolated and dispersed until the arrival centuries later of the Europeans, was the occupation by about AD 300 of the Marquesas Islands in eastern Polynesia. From there, during the next five hundred years, settlement extended north to the Hawaiian Islands, south-east to Easter Island, and in a general south-westerly direction to Tahiti and through the Society and Southern Cook Islands to New Zealand.

Very little is known of the details of these movements, and a firm relative chronology has yet to be established by the archaeologists. However, it would appear that, by the beginning of the thirteenth century and probably earlier, clearly stratified societies had been established on islands as far apart as Tonga, Easter Island and Hawaii, whereas over eastern Polynesia as a whole population growth was everywhere promoting many new social initiatives. The colossal stone statuary of Easter Island, still insufficiently understood, belongs largely to what, in western terms, might be called the later Middle Ages. On Tongatapu, the Tui Tonga dynasty is thought to have been responsible for the setting up in about 1200 of the coral trilithon known as the Ha'amonga-a-Maui. And the religious platforms characteristic of Polynesian society, although later developed on a more impressive scale, undoubtedly first appeared in this period.

One of the better studied regions of Polynesian settlement is New Zealand, reached by the Maoris in about AD 850 with a first concentration on the coastal plains, especially those of the South Island. Although culturally akin to the Polynesians of the Marquesas heartland from which originally they had come, the Maoris developed a hunter-gatherer society of their own, forced on them by the harsher climate of the South. Not surprisingly, the rock-art of the South Island, generally datable before 1500, reflected the hunting and fishing preoccupations of Archaic Maori society. Ornaments attributable to the pre-Classic period include simple whale- or shark-tooth pendants, with the more spectacular carved whale-ivory amulets especially common in the South Island.

In what was never much more than a subsistence economy, population was held back to a modest growth, and innovations, whether in hunting techniques

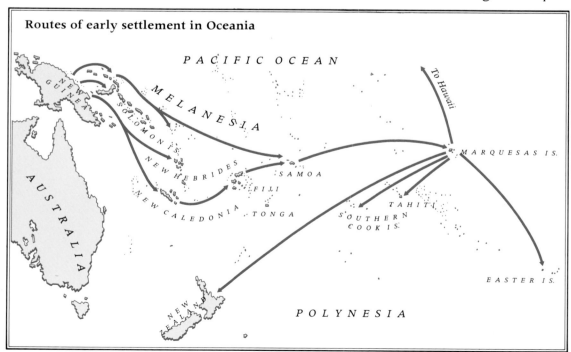

Routes of early settlement in Oceania

PACIFIC OCEAN

MELANESIA

GUINEA

SOLOMON IS.

NEW HEBRIDES

NEW CALEDONIA

SAMOA

FIJI

TONGA

To Hawaii

MARQUESAS IS.

TAHITI

SOUTHERN COOK IS.

EASTER IS.

AUSTRALIA

NEW ZEALAND

POLYNESIA

Chinese pottery
In the 13th century, the Lung-ch'üan celadons of southern China flourished, their monochrome greens in studied imitation of jade. The imperial Kuan ware developed the deep-stained crackle with which Lung-ch'üan potters experimented. Kuan wares were highly prized by the Sung court for which they were first made, and continued so under the Mongol Yüan dynasty.

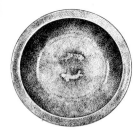

Kuan bowl

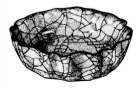

Lung-ch'üan plate

The Mongol conquest of China
The Mongols conquered first the Chin Empire of the Jürched Tartars, and then the Sung, which finally fell in 1279. Establishing his capital at Peking, Kublai Khan adopted the Chinese dynastic title Yüan, setting the tone for a China dominated, but not fundamentally altered, by the Mongols.

or in agriculture, were few in New Zealand before the arrival and settlement of the Europeans. Throughout the Middle Ages and substantially through the Early Modern period as well, Polynesia as a whole remained in deep isolation, even its parts being ignorant of one another. The contrast with the more northerly lands of the West Pacific was complete.

Far East

Southern Sung China was still in the thirteenth century the most splendid and the most sophisticated civilization that the world had ever known. Even through the Mongol conquests of the second half of the century, Sung China preserved its cultural dominance in East Asia. And if there were signs towards the end of the period, in architecture as in ceramics, of a retreat from the high points reached at its beginning, these were as yet insignificant dents in the total profile of a society unquestionably without peer. Certainly we may see in the decline of the Southern Sung the weariness of a dynasty that had outlived its usefulness and the bankruptcy of a stale overly-conservative culture. Yet it took Kublai Khan a full two decades to bring down the military might of the Southern Sung. With victory secured in 1279, it was legitimate succession that Kublai Khan chose to emphasize, his dynasty Sinicized under the title Yüan and the institutions of Chinese civilization protected under Mongol lordship.

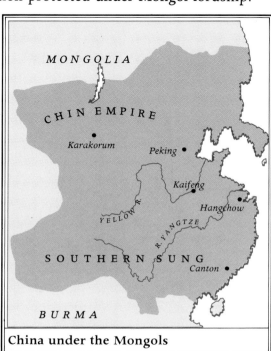

China under the Mongols

In some areas Mongol patronage was not enough to keep in existence what may already have been fading traditions. Chinese medicine, in which the most important advances were made in the twelfth and early thirteenth centuries, produced little that was new after Sung Tz'u, in 1247-8, published his *Hsi-yuan lu* (*Instructions to Coroners*), a study of forensic medicine extending to nine volumes in all. A similar halt was brought to Chinese mathematics, following the work of the three great Sung mathematicians, Ch'in Chiu-Shao, Li Yeh and Yang Hui, and their early Mongol successor, Chu Shih-chieh. In the pottery industry, again, the Mongol conquest of Chin North China in 1241 was closely followed by a decline in the quality of the famous Ting wares, kept in production by the Jürched conquerors of the Northern Sung but now suffering a diminution in standards, to be succeeded by the closing of the kilns. Yet despite the upheavals of the Mongol invasions, and the inevitable extinction of some interests as a result, the usual instinct of the Mongol Yüan emperors was to preserve rather than to destroy. This was as clearly the case in the pottery industry as, for example, in the higher art of painting.

Unquestionably, there was much of value to protect. In an effort to raise revenues for the defence of their empire, the Southern Sung had encouraged the potters to professionalize their industry. And it is to the thirteenth century that the great multiple kilns of the Lung-ch'üan, or southern, celadons belong, some of which had a capacity of up to 25,000 pieces. Most of this production went into bowls, or into the basins and plates particularly in demand for export. However, it also included vases modelled with deliberate antiquarian intent on the fine bronze vessels of prehistoric China, as well as on individual Yüan importations, among them the distinctive long-spouted ewers from those Middle Eastern markets into which Chinese products now had so much easier an entry.

In the "official" Kuan wares, with their characteristic crackled glaze, the imitation of antique bronze models is still more obvious. And there is an interesting link between the backward-looking taste of the Southern Sung courtiers, who were the principal patrons of these kilns, and a similar conservatism present in Chinese painting, which became increasingly

Chinese painting

During the 13th century Southern Sung painting developed two distinct styles, the "Lyrical" and the "Spontaneous". Ma Yüan and Hsia Kuei were the greatest "Lyrical" painters, moving away from symmetrical composition with their rapid, calligraphic brush strokes, often in monochrome ink, and their large areas of empty silk. The "Spontaneous" style took this abbreviated but highly controlled brushwork further, under the influence of Zen Buddhism: Mu-ch'i's Six Persimmons *is the style's most extreme, bold, and enigmatic expression.*

ABOVE Fisherman in his Barque *by Ma Yüan*

ABOVE River Scenes *by Hsia Kuei*

BELOW Six Persimmons *by Mu-ch'i*

Solitary Man under a Broken Pine *by Ma Yüan*

introverted, refined and specialized as "literary men" of the old tradition withdrew to the isolation of their country estates in reaction against the court of the Mongols. Inspired by them, and directly reflecting the despair they felt about their own times, Chinese painting in the early fourteenth century paradoxically entered upon one of its most fruitful periods. However, already through the length of the thirteenth century, the landscape painter and the Zen monk between them had explored some entirely new areas.

In the first quarter of the thirteenth century in particular, the Southern Sung Academy at Hangchow yielded work of great distinction in the landscape paintings of its most original members, Ma Yüan, Hsia Kuei and Liu Sung-nien. These painters combined a new sense of the quality of space with an angularity which deliberately heightened the drama of even the most tranquil scene. At their fullest development, painters of the so-called Ma-Hsia School achieved their effects by a deliberate simplification. They placed great emphasis on the techniques of brushwork and on the subtle grading of inks, and cut down where they could on the number of strokes needed to depict their subject. For them, this was the logical

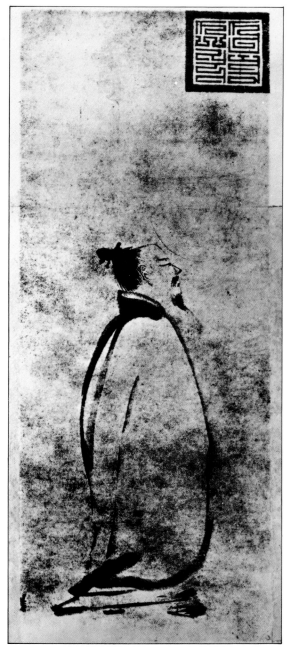

''Portrait of the Poet Li Po'' by Liang K'ai
Liang K'ai was both a notable landscape painter and a master of the ''Spontaneous'' school of Sung painting. He used a very broad range of textures in his brush strokes, which he might apply, as in this portrait, to the representations of the sage traditional among all Zen painters.

vision are the rewards of Zen contemplation, so the Ch'an painter of the early thirteenth century strove to capture his ecstasy in the few brush-strokes that the length of his inspiration allowed him. There is an immediacy about Mu-ch'i's art, particularly obvious in his impressionistic *Six Persimmons*, that marks him out as one of the greatest practitioners of Zen painting. Yet he lived alongside the more traditionalist artists of the Hangchow Academy, and it is a tribute to the cultural eclecticism of Southern Sung society that Liang K'ai, one of the most widely respected landscape painters of that same academy, should also have practised Zen art. Besides representations of nature, a typically Zen subject was the portrait of the master and the sage. Liang K'ai's *Portrait of the Poet Li Po* exactly captured what was best in the Zen tradition, freezing with exceptional clarity and economy the inspiration of both the painter himself and his subject.

Cultural eclecticism can show itself in many ways. One consequence of Mongol religious toleration in China was the penetration of the Chinese court by Arab architectural influences; another, the introduction of the Tibetan style of Lamaistic Buddhism to Peking, as seen, for example, in the Miao-ying-ssu pagoda (1271), which is a heavy bottle-shaped building, graceless and forbiddingly austere. However, the cultural cross-currents of thirteenth-century East Asia were best illustrated in contemporary Japan, where the Southern Sung taste of the Buddhist missionaries, in all its ornate sophistication, met up with the vigour and realism of Kamakura warrior art, the latter originating from a truly Japanese source.

The hereditary military dictatorship of the Kamakura shogunate had begun effectively in 1185 with the sea battle of Dan-no-ura and the final destruction of the rival Taira clan. And while civil government had been preserved around a puppet emperor in the old imperial capital of Kyoto, the real power in Japanese society now resided indisputably with the military Kamakura regime. In terms of the cultural development of a people, there have been few political changes of equivalent importance. Although showing some signs, in portraiture and the narrative hand-scroll, of the new directions to be taken in the thirteenth century, the court art of Fujiwara Japan

progression from the heroic tradition of Chinese landscape painting in the tenth and eleventh centuries. And they carried it about as far as it would go. However, in the contemporary art of the Zen Buddhist monk there would be a further reduction to essentials. From the abbreviated landscapes of the court painter Hsia Kuei, the next leap forward was to the supreme austerity of Mu-ch'i's *Six Persimmons*.

Mu-ch'i was a Ch'an, or Zen, Buddhist priest, a member of a sect that was attracting much interest and support in the society of the Southern Sung capital, where he lived. And just as intuitive understanding and the instant flash of

Burning of the Sanjo Palace (detail)
This scroll, illustrating episodes from the Heiji war of 1159, shows the narrative scroll-painting of the Kamakura period at its best. Action and characterization combine with masterly composition to produce a detailed and very immediate treatment of historical events.

Amida Buddha statue, Kamakura, Japan
By 1252, when this great statue of the Amida Buddha was cast, Kamakura sculpture was past its peak. Here, despite the grandeur of the Buddha, a new formality is visible.

had become effeminate, overly concerned with the details of life in an aristocratic society and with a soft, worldly religion. What the Kamakura shoguns introduced in its place was a fresh vigour both in sculpture and in painting, characterized especially by realism. They favoured the treatment of military themes, glorying in nationalism and in the legends of folk heroes of the past. In religion, they proceeded to encourage reform.

In every way the most significant cultural achievement of the Kamakura period, and unquestionably Japan's principal contribution to the art of the medieval world, was the horizontal narrative scroll. It was brought to perfection in the well-known *Burning of the Sanjo Palace*, one of a set of three surviving scrolls, dating from the second half of the thirteenth century, which tell the story of the Heiji Insurrection of 1159. The significance of the Heiji Insurrection was that it began the military rivalry of the Minamoto and Taira families which ended only with Minamoto no Yoritomo's victory in 1185 and with the establishment of the Kamakura shogunate. And the famous story of the sacking of the imperial palace by Minamoto warriors during the night of 9 December 1159 seems to have acted as a special spur to the creative imagination of the anonymous painter. What above

all distinguished the scroll was its vivid movement, an exceptional confidence in the placing of figures, and strikingly well-conceived decorative effects. But this was not an exclusively impressionistic art, for its detail, especially in the careful depiction of the armour and other military hardware of the warriors, was notably meticulous and exact.

A very similar emphasis on realism in art, encouraging the precise representation of the things of this world, accompanied the Kamakura popularization of religion. It is true that the great bronze Amida statue at Kamakura itself, a mid-thirteenth-century work, is a conventionally bland and idealized portrait of the Buddha. However, the money to erect it was raised in 1252 not by taxes but by popular subscription, while in smaller temple projects throughout Japan—both Buddhist and Shinto—the taste of the worshippers showed itself in an uncompromising depiction of reality very different from that benign effeminacy thought appropriate to religious subjects in the days of the Fujiwara regents. Among the best-known products of the new tradition was the early-thirteenth-century carved wood figure of the priest Kuya by Kosho, one of the sons of the great sculptor Unkei whose own works decorate the approaches to the temple of Todaiji, rebuilt after the

"Kuya" by Kosho
The sculptural realism of the early Kamakura period reached its peak in the wooden figure of the priest Kuya, by Kosho. Kuya is shown dressed as a traveller, with gong and staff; from his mouth issues a string of little Buddhas, representing the name of Amida.

Part of the process of instruction in religion was the re-creation, as nearly as possible, of the original environment in which the Zen Buddhist missionaries had found their own inspiration. Zen Buddhism was brought to Japan in the mid-thirteenth century by Tao-lung, a Chinese missionary and master of Zen from one of the Ch'an monasteries of Hangchow. He himself is said to have built his new monastery at Kamakura as an exact imitation of one of the Ch'an houses he had left, and this faithful copying of Southern Sung models remained characteristic of Zen architecture in Japan, the genesis of the *Karayo*, or "Chinese", style.

Following the Chinese fashion, the Zen meditative ideal eventually altered the emphasis in temple architecture, replacing the pagoda of the ancient tradition with the garden and hall of meditation of the new. Already from the late thirteenth century we have an example of one of these halls in the surviving relic hall, or *shariden*, of Engakuji at Kamakura, which is as precious for the architectural history of Southern Sung China (of which so little else has been preserved), as it is for that of Japan. The Engakuji hall has been supplied at a later date with a roof of steeply-pitched thatch. However, it is still possible to reconstruct the form of the original thirteenth-century building with a fair degree of certainty, while much of the distinctive and characteristically elaborate *Karayo* timber bracketing has remained perfectly intact.

Of course, the greater part of Japanese temple building in this period, uninfluenced by Zen, remained securely within the old tradition so fruitfully developed during the long Fujiwara supremacy. But despite the nationalism of the Kamakura shoguns, Chinese influence was on the increase again in late-thirteenth-century Japan, assisted by the moratorium in Japanese art seemingly brought on by persisting Mongol threats of invasion. Japanese culture was still too fragile to live through these crises unchanged.

The Americas
There was still one substantial area, the Americas, which continued to pursue a path of its own, untouched by such world events. It was not that the thirteenth century was necessarily tranquil in the Americas. Prior to the Inca expansion of the fifteenth century, we know rather

twelfth-century civil wars. The Kuya figure, in portraiture as in the exact representation of its drapery folds, was a work of outstanding realism. And this was the most obvious quality also of what became almost a cartoon art in the religious scrolls of the period. These, of which the Shinto *Life of Sugawara Michizane* (a ninth-century statesman and poet) is perhaps the most important survival, were the religious equivalent of such military scrolls as the *Burning of the Sanjo Palace*. Like them, the intention of the painter was to entertain but also to instruct.

little of the sequence of events in the South. The Peruvian Chimu empire continued its course, with the further growth of its extraordinary capital at Chanchan. In Colombia, a radiocarbon date of AD 1250 on the Calima sites at least gives us one fixed point in the long cultural sequence that yielded the splendid goldwork in the Calima and Quimbaya styles which so attracted the Spaniards. However, the apparently undisturbed continuities of the southern civilizations were not obviously matched in Central America or in the North. The great Toltec Maya city of Chichén Itzá went into a decline in the thirteenth century, to be replaced by a new more westerly capital at Mayapán. Moreover, what was especially significant about this change was that it showed the arrival of an entirely new emphasis in the culture of Late Postclassic Yucatán. Chichén Itzá had been above all a ceremonial centre, with functions in religion and government, and with a great cluster of temples, platforms and other monuments to meet those particular needs. In contrast, Mayapán was both ceremonial centre and urban place, being a large walled enclosure sheltering the houses and temples of a town-dwelling population perhaps as many as 12,000 strong.

Culturally, too, there is evidence at Mayapán of a very pronounced decline. The so-called "Castillo" of Mayapán, probably from the late thirteenth century, although a straight imitation of its Chichén Itzá equivalent, was only half its size. In building generally, standards were abandoned, with cheaper materials like stucco coming into common use for ornament. Most significantly, the defences at Mayapán, as at other Mayan Late Postclassic settlements both in the Yucatán Peninsula and on the Guatemalan Highlands, are evidence of a society under threat. Eventually, after somewhat over two centuries of dominance, Mayapán would itself fall a victim to the civil wars that afflicted the mid-fifteenth century, leaving the Maya lowlands exposed to the Spaniards without benefit of central rule.

The ripples of these Mesoamerican political disturbances, from as far back as the tenth century and before, spread steadily outwards. One of their more obvious consequences was the fertilization of alien cultures in those regions especially well adapted to receive them— the larger central islands of what are now the West Indies and, in North America, the great zone of the southern Mississippi. In both of these areas, the thirteenth century witnessed a cultural climax which outlived the century itself. The long-living Chicoid culture of the Greater Antilles centred on Hispaniola. In the Mississippian, the Temple Mound II Period was distinguished by such monuments as the Cahokia temple mound in the Central Mississippi Valley and by those other important sites at Etowah (Georgia) and Moundville (Alabama).

There is really no need to explain this Mesoamerican cultural spread in terms of folk migrations. It could have been advanced as easily by trade, by minor population dispersals, or even by the widespread sharing of a common religion. In any event, what it promoted in the areas it touched was a vigorous pottery and sculptural tradition, with a ceremonial architecture which included the stone-lined plazas, or "ball courts", of the Greater Antilles and the impressive rectangular platform mounds of the North American Southeast.

In the Southwest too, the Hohokam culture, with its own painted pottery, its ball courts, and its elaborate canal systems, entered its Classic Period in about 1200. This almost exactly coincided with the innovatory Temple Mound II Period of the Mississippian of the Southeast, and lasted similarly through the length of the thirteenth and the fourteenth centuries. It is thought that this new phase may well have resulted from the arrival in eastern Arizona of the Salado, an Anasazi group with its own architectural tradition to import. Whether driven from their territories by aggressive invasions, of which there is certainly some evidence, or by the onset of a devastating succession of droughts, it is a fact that the Anasazi had embarked by the late thirteenth century on a deliberate re-grouping of settlement, concentrating in the south of their original cultural homeland and abandoning the arid plateau country of the north. In about 1300 the Anasazi thus entered the final era of their pre-European-contact cultural history, the so-called Pueblo IV Period, which would carry them through to the sixteenth century and to the first sight by astonished Spaniards of the distinctive multi-storied apartment-house settlements in which some of their descendants may still be found residing to this day.

South American metalwork

The Chimu empire of the Peruvian coastal plains succeeded the earlier Mochica culture, and later provided many cultural themes for its own Inca successors. At the huge mud-brick capital, Chanchan, Chimu goldsmiths produced exquisite work: one of their most common themes is the winged moon-god, seen here as a turquoise-inlaid knife-handle (bottom left). Other artefacts included funerary masks, plates, and pectoral ornaments, as well as the magnificent stone and mother-of-pearl inlay-work they inherited from their Mochica predecessors (right). Further north, in the Colombian highlands, where platinum was common enough to be used for fish-hooks, the Quimbayas too excelled in fine metalwork, and perfected methods of casting in *tumbaga*, an alloy of gold and copper.

ABOVE *Chimu gourd inlaid with mother-of-pearl*

ABOVE *Chimu gold funerary mask*

Chimu gold ceremonial knife

Chimu gold ceremonial dove-shaped vessel

Chimu gold funerary mask

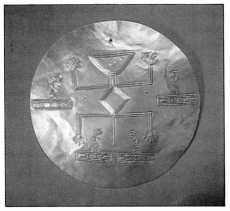

Quimbaya tumbaga *disc*

Chimu gold plate

World Architecture

Even while under the threat of the expansion of Islam and of the imperialism of the Delhi Sultanate, Indian temple architecture in the thirteenth century was experiencing a final great flowering. Characteristically ornate, its best products included the southern Indian Kesava Temple at Somnathpur, symmetrically-planned in a great colonnaded cloister, and the extraordinary chariot temple of the sun-god Surya at Konarak.

On a very much smaller scale, Javanese temple-building had entered a renaissance of its own with the Singhasari rulers of the second half of the thirteenth century, commemorated in such buildings as the Kidal. Uniquely, the Singhasari kings had brought together in thirteenth-century Java the Buddhist and Hindu religions, and it was this fusion of the faiths that both informed and inspired their architecture. Further to the north, the religious eclecticism of the new Mongol rulers of China was contemporaneously leading to the toleration in Yüan court circles under Kublai Khan of a wide variety of beliefs.

Another sect, the Zen Buddhists, had become well established, before the arrival of the Mongols, at the Southern Sung capital at Hangchow. Within the century, they had spread to Kamakura Japan, and it was there, rather than in China itself, that they consolidated and preserved their influence. An early Zen monument, surviving in Japan where its Chinese equivalents have long since vanished, is the relic hall (*shariden*) of Engakuji at Kamakura. In its elaborate timber bracketing, it betrays its origin in Southern Sung building practice.

In the Near East, piety also is the explanation for the architectural patronage of the Seljuk sultans whose great *hans* (hospices) and decoratively-fronted *medreses* (schools of theology) were established as memorials to their faith. Although experiencing a profound setback under the Mongols, Islam was to continue through the thirteenth century as a major proselytizing religion. Before the end of the century it had finally swamped the remaining Christian outposts in Palestine and Syria, the legacy of the First Crusade. On the East African coast it was completely triumphant in such trading cities as Kilwa, now in Tanzania, equipped in the thirteenth century with its Great Mosque.

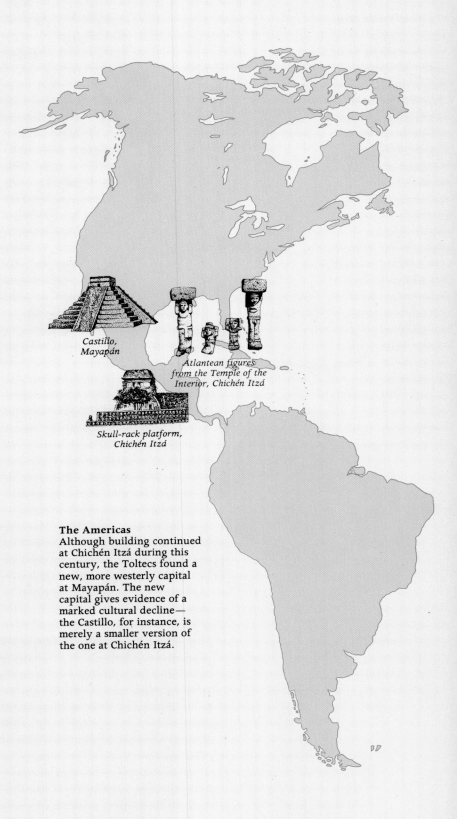

*Castillo,
Mayapán*

*Atlantean figures
from the Temple of the
Interior, Chichén Itzá*

*Skull-rack platform,
Chichén Itzá*

The Americas
Although building continued at Chichén Itzá during this century, the Toltecs found a new, more westerly capital at Mayapán. The new capital gives evidence of a marked cultural decline— the Castillo, for instance, is merely a smaller version of the one at Chichén Itzá.

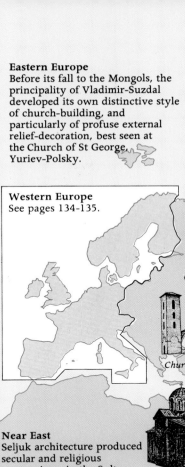

Eastern Europe
Before its fall to the Mongols, the principality of Vladimir-Suzdal developed its own distinctive style of church-building, and particularly of profuse external relief-decoration, best seen at the Church of St George, Yuriev-Polsky.

St George, Yuriev-Polsky

Pjatnica Church, Chernigov

Far East
Zen Buddhist influence from China brought to Japan the *Karayo* style, a conscious imitation of Sung architecture, of which the Engakuji relic hall at Kamakura is typical.

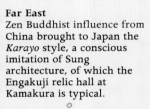

Engakuji relic hall, Kamakura

Western Europe
See pages 134-135.

Church of the Parigoritissa, Arta, Epirus

Church of the Trinity, Sopocani

Lips Church, Constantinople

Ince Minare Medrese, Konia

Mahabodhi Temple, Pagan

Near East
Seljuk architecture produced secular and religious masterpieces in the Sultan Hans of Anatolia, and the *medreses* of Konia. Meanwhile Byzantium, after 1261, looked to the past.

Little Metropole Cathedral, Athens

Sultan Han, Konia

Kesava Temple, Somnathpur

Stupa of Mingalazedi, Pagan

Wat Chet Yot, Chiengmai

Candi Kidal, Malang

Lalibela Church, Ethiopia

Surya Temple, Konarak

Great Mosque, Kilwa

India
Despite the iconoclasm of the Muslim Sultanate of Delhi, this century produced two of the greatest examples of Hindu temple architecture—the Surya Temple at Konarak and the intricate Hoysala Temple of Kesava at Somnathpur.

South-East Asia
The Mahabodhi Temple at Pagan, modelled on an earlier Indian building, itself provided a model for Wat Chet Yot in Siam. The indigenous Burmese style can be seen in stupas such as the Mingalazedi at Pagan, and an individual Javanese style is visible at Candi Kidal.

Africa
While Arab settlers were bringing new Islamic influences to East Africa, and building mosques like that at Kilwa, the isolated empire of Ethiopia created Christian monuments such as the Church of St George at Lalibela, a cruciform building cut from rock.

Oceania
The unique and enigmatic coral trilithon on the Tongan island of Tongatapu, called the Ha'amonga-a-Maui, is said to represent the two sons of a Tongan king, and may also have some astronomical significance.

Coral trilithon, Tongatapu

Western European Architecture

In thirteenth-century Europe, it was the cathedral-builders above all who placed their mark on the contemporary landscape. The most sustained building campaigns at the French cathedrals of Bourges, Chartres and Soissons had just started in the late 1190s; at Rheims work began in 1210-11, at Amiens in 1220, at Beauvais after the fire of 1225.

High Gothic peaked in the elaborate *rayonnant* architecture of mid-thirteenth-century Paris, its conventions spreading from Louis IX's Sainte Chapelle, in that city, to the German cathedral of Strasbourg, and to Leon Cathedral in Spain.

Building on this scale would not have been possible had there not been considerable resources to back it. It was Louis IX, builder of Sainte Chapelle, who financed the building of the mighty fortress at Angers, begun in 1228.

Other kings, both contemporaries and successors, built on a similar scale. Frederick II of Germany, also known as "Stupor Mundi", deployed his wealth in the building of many castles, some of the finest of which, like Castel del Monte in Apulia, guarded his Italian inheritance. And one of the more lasting achievements of Edward I of England was to plan and largely to complete an expensive chain of fortresses, eight in all.

Spain
Leon Cathedral is a rare case of a Spanish architect closely studying the examples provided by contemporary French architecture to produce a *rayonnant* building.

Britain
The Welsh castles erected by Edward I are almost uniform in their design. Built during a concentrated period towards the end of the century, they stand at the peak of the castle-building tradition. English Gothic was also advanced, reaching a high point in the façade of Wells Cathedral.

France
The 13th century saw the summit of Gothic: Amiens, Rheims, Notre Dame, with Sainte Chapelle as the perfect example of the *rayonnant* style. It was also the age of military technology and the fortified town: even the cathedral at Albi resembles a fortress rather than a church.

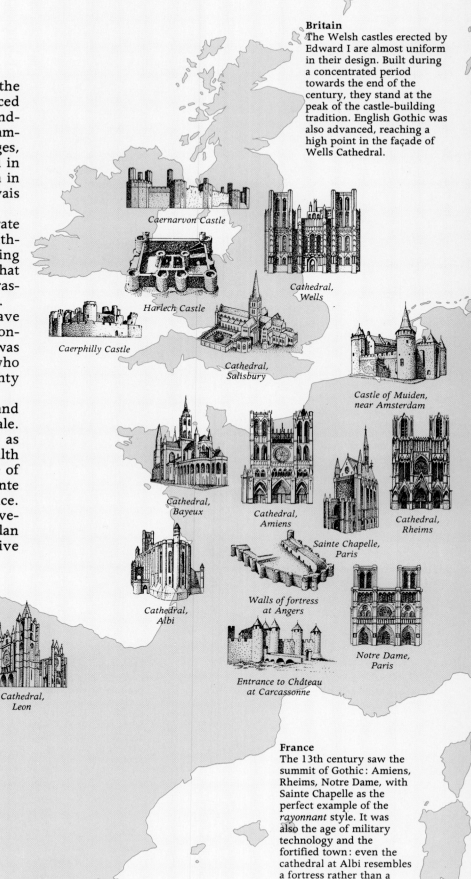

Caernarvon Castle

Harlech Castle

Caerphilly Castle

Cathedral, Wells

Cathedral, Salisbury

Castle of Muiden, near Amsterdam

Cathedral, Bayeux

Cathedral, Amiens

Cathedral, Rheims

Sainte Chapelle, Paris

Cathedral, Albi

Walls of fortress at Angers

Notre Dame, Paris

Entrance to Château at Carcassonne

Cathedral, Leon

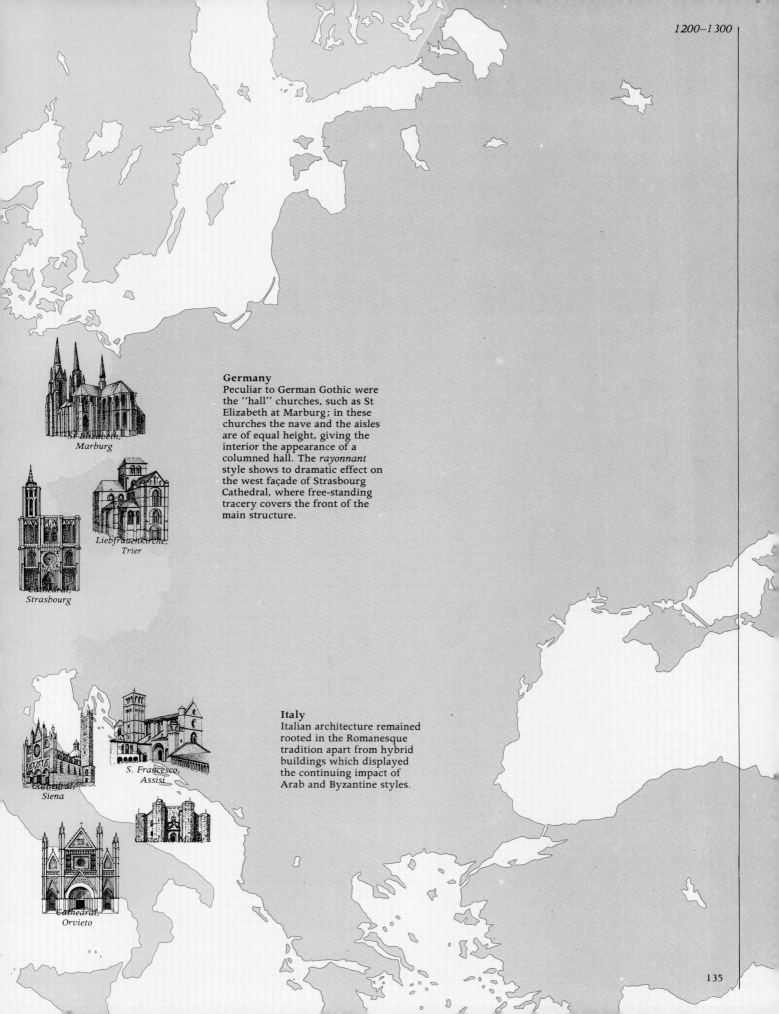

Germany
Peculiar to German Gothic were the "hall" churches, such as St Elizabeth at Marburg; in these churches the nave and the aisles are of equal height, giving the interior the appearance of a columned hall. The *rayonnant* style shows to dramatic effect on the west façade of Strasbourg Cathedral, where free-standing tracery covers the front of the main structure.

St Elizabeth, Marburg

Liebfrauenkirche, Trier

Cathedral, Strasbourg

Italy
Italian architecture remained rooted in the Romanesque tradition apart from hybrid buildings which displayed the continuing impact of Arab and Byzantine styles.

S. Francesco, Assisi

Cathedral, Siena

Castel del Monte

Cathedral, Orvieto

World Art

Supreme achievement in art, as the Chinese well understood, can result from great economy in technique. Chinese landscape painting of the early thirteenth century, in the hands of such distinguished court painters as Ma Yüan and Hsia Kuei, became abbreviated and free of impediment, content with the individual dramatic effect. Contemporaneously, a new religious art developed at Hangchow. Mu-ch'i, one of the first of the Zen artists of Hangchow, has remained to this day the unchallenged master of Zen Buddhist painting. In his best-known painting, the marvellous *Six Persimmons*, he at once created a cult.

The art of Mu-ch'i, although influential in China, found its real home in Japan. Zen missionaries from Hangchow were welcomed by the newly-established Kamakura shoguns, the austerity of their beliefs appealing very strongly to the military leadership of Japan. In Japanese painting, the best Zen art belongs to the fourteenth and fifteenth centuries. Nevertheless, some of the qualities the Kamakura shoguns sought in Zen were to be found also in the indigenous art of Japan itself, whether in the dramatic immediacy of a narrative scroll or in the naturalism of Japanese wood-carving.

Beyond the limits of Chinese cultural hegemony, the arts were developing in quite different directions. From Polynesian-settled New Zealand, we have the first datable examples within the thirteenth century of a whale-ivory and wood-carving art that would ultimately achieve great distinction. Some of the best of the elaborate Calima and Quimbaya goldwork of Colombia belongs to this century, while the stone-carvers of India demonstrated great virtuosity, if less taste, in the incredible wealth of sculptured ornament on such monuments as the Surya Temple at Konarak.

More real distinction in architectural ornament was attained during the first decades of the century in the flowering of abstract and calligraphic decorative sculpture under the patronage of the Seljuk sultans. Displayed at its best on the imposing main entrances of the *medreses* at their capital of Konia, in Anatolia, Seljuk stone-carving seems quickly to have lost its original inspiration once Konia submitted to the Mongols.

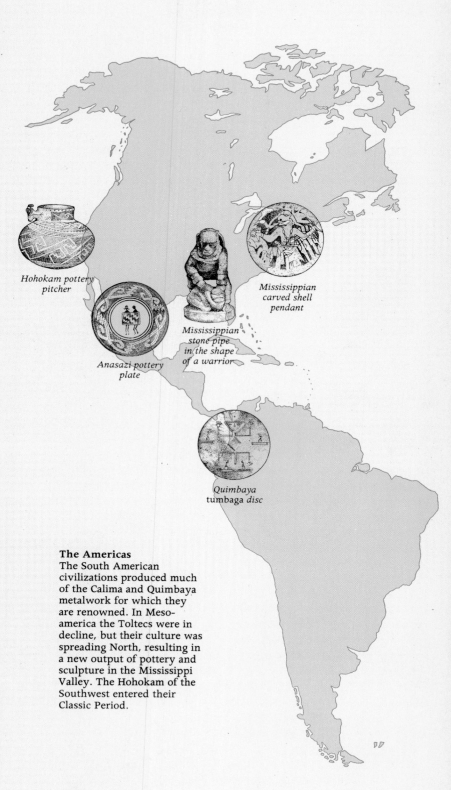

Hohokam pottery pitcher

Anasazi pottery plate

Mississippian stone pipe in the shape of a warrior

Mississippian carved shell pendant

Quimbaya tumbaga disc

The Americas
The South American civilizations produced much of the Calima and Quimbaya metalwork for which they are renowned. In Mesoamerica the Toltecs were in decline, but their culture was spreading North, resulting in a new output of pottery and sculpture in the Mississippi Valley. The Hohokam of the Southwest entered their Classic Period.

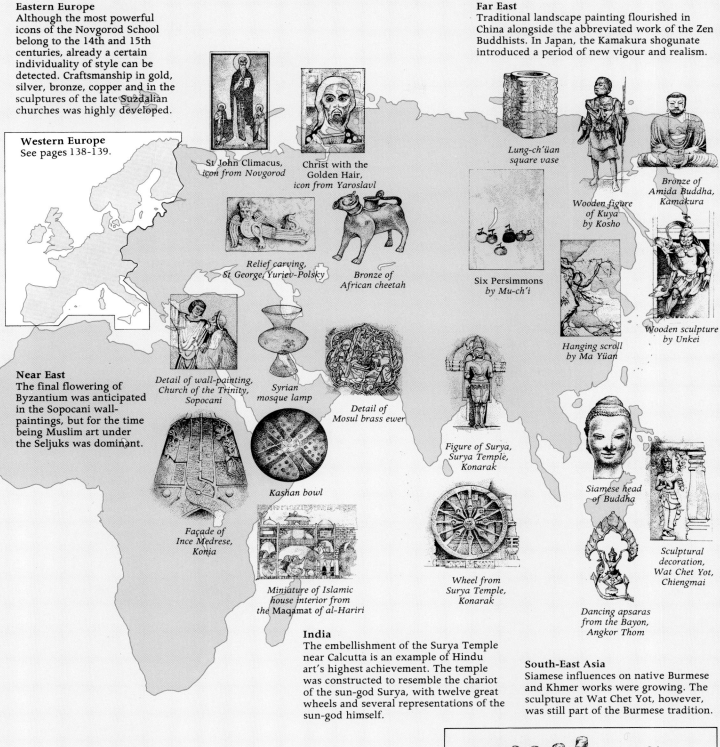

Eastern Europe
Although the most powerful icons of the Novgorod School belong to the 14th and 15th centuries, already a certain individuality of style can be detected. Craftsmanship in gold, silver, bronze, copper and in the sculptures of the late Suzdalian churches was highly developed.

Western Europe
See pages 138-139.

Near East
The final flowering of Byzantium was anticipated in the Sopocani wall-paintings, but for the time being Muslim art under the Seljuks was dominant.

Far East
Traditional landscape painting flourished in China alongside the abbreviated work of the Zen Buddhists. In Japan, the Kamakura shogunate introduced a period of new vigour and realism.

St John Climacus, icon from Novgorod

Christ with the Golden Hair, icon from Yaroslavl

Lung-ch'üan square vase

Wooden figure of Kuya by Kosho

Bronze of Amida Buddha, Kamakura

Relief carving, St George, Yuriev-Polsky

Bronze of African cheetah

Six Persimmons by Mu-ch'i

Hanging scroll by Ma Yüan

Wooden sculpture by Unkei

Detail of wall-painting, Church of the Trinity, Sopocani

Syrian mosque lamp

Detail of Mosul brass ewer

Façade of Ince Medrese, Konia

Kashan bowl

Figure of Surya, Surya Temple, Konarak

Siamese head of Buddha

Sculptural decoration, Wat Chet Yot, Chiengmai

Miniature of Islamic house interior from the Maqamat of al-Hariri

Wheel from Surya Temple, Konarak

Dancing apsaras from the Bayon, Angkor Thom

India
The embellishment of the Surya Temple near Calcutta is an example of Hindu art's highest achievement. The temple was constructed to resemble the chariot of the sun-god Surya, with twelve great wheels and several representations of the sun-god himself.

South-East Asia
Siamese influences on native Burmese and Khmer works were growing. The sculpture at Wat Chet Yot, however, was still part of the Burmese tradition.

Stone statues, Easter Island

Whale-ivory amulets, New Zealand

Oceania
The earliest examples of Easter Island's colossal stone statuary date from this century, as do many ornaments from the Maori pre-Classic period.

Western European Art

Early in the thirteenth century, national predilections in sculpture made themselves evident in the contrast between the emotion-charged work of the German sculptors of Strasbourg and the almost painful sentimentalism of the influential French school of the only slightly later Joseph Master of Rheims. But these characteristics, although never lost altogether in the art of medieval Northern Europe, assumed less importance later in the century. Through court art generally, whether in Germany, in England or in France, the same conventions of sophisticated delicacy were shared well before the year 1300.

The full maturity of High Gothic in the North and the first intimations of a Renaissance in Italy coincided in late-thirteenth-century Europe. It was the naturalism of High Gothic which inspired imitation in the South. Italian sculptors like Nicola Pisano and Giovanni, his son, were influenced in turn by the models of Rheims and of Strasbourg, while Gothic, classical and Byzantine strands came together in the work of such late-thirteenth-century fresco-painters as the Isaac Master of Assisi, as in the frescoes and mosaics of the Roman Pietro Cavallini. It was from these last especially that the art of Giotto sprang, to be the real beginning of the Early Renaissance in the South.

Spain
Arab art was much affected by the progress of the Christian *Reconquista*, often reflecting the conflict in battlefield scenes.

Scene from chronicle of Alfonso X of Castile

Britain
Despite the evidence provided by the drawings of Matthew Paris for an indigenous English style, the Parisian court style is clearly visible—in manuscript illuminations, in a damaged retable in Westminster Abbey, and even in the minor art of tile-making.

Foliage capitals from Southwell Minster

David Harping, manuscript illumination from Oscott Psalter

Frontispiece of manuscript illuminated by Matthew Paris

St Peter, detail from Westminster Retable

Tiles from Chertsey Abbey

The Massacre of the Innocents, scene from the north cloister, Notre Dame, Paris

Figure from the west façade, Rheims Cathedral

Reliquary of St-Taurin, Evreux

Manuscript illumination by Maître Honoré

Figures from the north transept, Chartres Cathedral

South Rose window, Notre Dame, Paris

France
Architectural sculpture was all in the High Gothic style. The techniques of stained glass were perfected, especially apparent in the great rose windows. In the manuscript illuminations of Maître Honoré—which epitomized the Parisian court style—there was the first intimation of a new Italian influence.

Jesse asleep,
ceiling-painting from
St Michael's, Hildesheim

Foliage capital
from Naumburg
Cathedral

Germany
German Gothic was still based
on the formality of the Byzantine
style. Drapery in both sculpture
and painting was angular,
rather than elegantly soft like its
French equivalent. The
naturalistic foliage capital
made an appearance at
Naumburg Cathedral.

Synagoga figure
from the
south transept,
Strasbourg Cathedral

Disputing Prophets,
choir screen from
Bamberg Cathedral

Apocalyptic Christ,
detail of a pulpit
in Siena Cathedral
by Nicola Pisano

Tomb of
Cardinal de Braye
by Arnolfo di Cambio

baptistery at Pisa
by Nicola Pisano

Italy
Although classical and Byzantine
influences continued to prevail in
Italian art, Gothic made some
impact. The result was a new
naturalism, and an attempt at
realistic portraiture on sepulchral
effigies. The fusion of these
various styles in certain frescoes of
the period anticipates the Early
Renaissance.

Isaac and Esau,
fresco by the Isaac Master,
in S. Francesco, Assisi

Detail from Last Judgment
by Pietro Cavallini,
fresco in S. Cecilia
in Trastevere, Rome

	Events and developments	People	Technology
Western Europe	France most powerful, advanced state. John of England's *Magna Carta* (1215). Decline of Holy Roman Empire; concession of power in Germany to princes. Christian reconquest of Spain complete. Commercial dominance of north Italian city-states. Formation of Hanseatic League, commercial and political alliance of Germanic towns. Erosion of feudalism.	Frederick II, Holy Roman Emperor 1215-50. Louis IX, French King 1226-70. St Thomas Aquinas, medieval philosopher (d. 1274). Roger Bacon, English scientist (1214-94). Marco Polo, Italian traveller (?1254-1324).	Introduction of cog (type of cargo vessel). Development of English longbow. Invention of wheelbarrow. Spectacles, spinning wheel in common use. Refinement of distilling techniques. Minting of gold coins in Italy. Coal-mining at Liège.
Far East	Proclamation of Genghis Khan as "Universal Ruler" at assembly of Mongol chieftains (1206). Conquest of China by Mongols under Kublai Khan (1279). Yüan dynasty founded by Kublai Khan in China. Unsuccessful attempts by Kublai Khan to conquer Japan (1274 and 1281) and Java (1293).	Genghis Khan, founder of Mongol Empire 1206-27. Kublai Khan, grandson of Genghis Khan 1260-94.	Halt brought to advances in both medicine and mathematics in China as a result of Mongol conquest.
South-East Asia	Cambodia, Java and Burma dominant. Capture of South Vietnam by Cambodia (1203). Destruction of Pagan by Mongols (1287). Arrival in Burma, Siam, and Cambodia of Thais from South China. By 1300, distinct hierarchical societies known to be established on most Polynesian islands.		
India	Founding of dynasty of Slave Kings of Delhi by Aybak (1206). Raids on North-west India by Mongols (1299) but no permanent conquests. Division of former empire of Cholas in south between Pandyas and Hoysalas.	Aybak, Muslim ruler of north-west India 1206-10.	
Near East	4th Crusade: sack of Constantinople (1204); re-conquest of city for Orthodoxy (1261). Capture of Bukhara, Samarkand and Baghdad by Mongols; advance into Syria and Palestine checked by Mamelukes at Ain Jalut (1260). End of Christian presence in Holy Land, with sack of Acre, Crusader port, (1291).	Michael VIII Palaeologus, Emperor of Constantinople 1258-82. Osman I, founder of Ottoman Empire c. 1281-1326. Baybars I, Mameluke Sultan 1261-77.	Introduction to Persia, via Mongol Khanate, of Chinese techniques in painting and ceramics.
Eastern Europe	Mongol conquest of Russia, Poland and Hungary (1237-41); sack of Kiev (1240); establishment of Khanate of Golden Horde. Victory of Russian Alexander Nevski (of Novgorod) over Swedes (1240), Teutonic Knights (1242). Gradual rise of Moscow.	Wenceslas I, King of Bohemia 1230-53. Alexander Nevski, Prince of Novgorod (and later Vladimir) 1236-63. Batu Khan, Mongol ruler of Eastern Europe (d. 1255).	
Africa	Destruction of Kumbi, former capital of ancient Ghana, by Sun Diata (1240). Exploitation of east coast of Africa by Arab traders; prosperity of Muslim coastal cities of Mogadishu and Kilwa.	Sun Diata, powerful King of Mande of West Africa.	
The Americas	Continuation of Peruvian Chimu Empire. First signs of Inca culture, Cuzco Valley, Peru. Drought in American south-west, probably causing evacuation of some Anasazi "apartment-house" towns.		Era of Mayan metalwork: gold, copper, silver.

Religion	Architecture	Art and music	Literature and learning
Authority of popes confirmed by 4th Lateran Council (1215). Inquisition (*c.* 1233) into heresy of French Albigenses: declaration of Albigensian Crusade by Pope Innocent III. Flowering of Catholic Scholastic theology under Albertus Magnus and Thomas Aquinas. Last phase of Crusades in Holy Land.	Rheims, Amiens Cathedrals; churches of Notre Dame and Sainte Chapelle, Paris. Florence, Siena Cathedrals; Castel del Monte. Leon, Toledo Cathedrals. Wells, Salisbury Cathedrals. Welsh castles. Cologne Cathedral.	Nicola Pisano's pulpits at Pisa and Siena. Sculptures at Chartres, Rheims, Strasbourg. Chertsey tiles. *Carmina Burana*, collection of German and Latin songs. *Sumer is icumen in*, English song.	De Lorris' and de Meung's *Roman de la Rose*. Von Strassburg's *Tristan and Isolde*. Chronicles of Matthew Paris. *Liber Abaci*, account in Latin of Arabic numerals. Universities founded at Cambridge and Padua.
Toleration of Buddhists, Muslims and Christians by Mongol rulers.	Miao-ying-ssu pagoda, Peking, China. Engakuji relic hall, Kamakura, Japan. Zen architecture in Japan influenced by Southern Sung buildings.	In China, Lung-ch'üan celadons, Kuan ware; landscape paintings of Ma-Hsia School; Mu-ch'i's *Six Persimmons*, Zen painting, Hangchow. In Japan, *Burning of Sanjo Palace*, narrative scroll; Kosho's wood figure of Kuya.	Sung Tz'u's *Instructions to Coroners*. First known treatise on landscape gardening by Fujiwara Nagatsune (1206).
Singhalese Buddhism in Burma, Siam, Cambodia and Laos.	Mahabodhi Temple and Mingalazedi stupa, Pagan, Burma. Wat Chet Yot, Siam. Revival of temple-building in Java. Coral trilithon on island of Tonga.	Sculpture at Wat Chet Yot. Earliest colossal stone statuary of Easter Island. Rock-art in Maori New Zealand.	
Toleration of Hinduism by early Muslim rulers.	Kesava Temple, Somnathpur, southern India. Jain temple of Tejpala, Mount Abu, Rajputana, central India. Surya Temple, Konarak, central India.	Erotic sculptures at Surya Temple, Konarak.	
Final Islamic reconquest of Holy Land. Assault on Islam by Mongols. Preaching of Francis of Assisi in Egypt (1223).	Sircali Medrese, Konia; Sultan Han caravanserai, Turkey. Mausoleum of Mustafa Pasha, Cairo, Egypt. Little Metropole, Athens; Church of Parigoritissa, Arta, Epirus, Greece.	Mosul metalwork, Persian painted pottery. Byzantine wall-paintings at Sopocani and Trebizond.	Nicetas Acominatos' *History of Constantinople*.
Suppression of Orthodoxy in Russia by the Mongols.	Suzdal Cathedral; Church of St George, Yuriev-Polsky. Pjatnica Church, Chernigov, Russia.	Relief sculptures at Suzdal Cathedral and Church of St George, Yuriev-Polsky.	
	Great Mosque, Kilwa. Lalibela Church, Ethiopia.	Importation of Chinese porcelains to Kilwa by Arab traders.	
	Decline of Toltec capital at Chichén Itzá, replaced by lesser one at Mayapán. Cahokia temple mound, Mississippi Valley. Ball-courts of Greater Antilles.	Peruvian Chimu goldwork in Calima and Quimbaya styles. Vigorous Mesoamerican pottery and sculptural tradition.	

The Fourteenth Century

PREVIOUS PAGE

The Lion Court of the Alhambra, Granada, Spain
The Alhambra was built by the Sultans of Muslim Granada in the two centuries before its fall to Spanish crusaders in 1492. It is a fortified citadel which once contained both the Sultan's palace and his court, built around a series of open quadrangles, of which the Lion Court is among the most beautiful.

The Black Death in Europe
Originating in the steppes of Central Asia, the Black Death travelled the trade routes opened up by the Mongols, reaching Constantinople in 1347. By the end of the following year it had spread through Italy, France, Spain, and Portugal, and had appeared in southern England. The infection was then carried north, through Scotland and Germany, reaching the Baltic in 1350. A few sparsely populated areas were spared, but overall perhaps a third of the population of Europe perished in the first epidemic of 1347-50.

Historical Context

With Kublai Khan, last of the "Great Khans", Mongol expansion reached its uttermost limit. Before the end of the thirteenth century, the peoples of the world had either succeeded in deflecting the Mongols or had learnt to live alongside them. But great though the scourge of the Mongols had been, it was as nothing before their ultimate legacy. There is no means of telling with any precision what part the Mongols themselves may have played in the propagation of *Pasteurella pestis*, the bacillus of bubonic plague, and many independent factors undoubtedly contributed to its spread. Nevertheless, the opening-up of the Central Asian trade routes, for which the Mongol Empire at its largest extent was certainly chiefly responsible, had facilitated the movement of peoples and infections across precisely those great open spaces which, in earlier times, had served as effective barriers. The well-organized Mongol caravan routes which had brought, for example, the secrets of Chinese glazed earthenwares to the Persians, transmitted with equal and terrifying speed the deadliest plague bacillus. Just as Columbus' bridging of the Atlantic in the late fifteenth century brought smallpox to the Americas, so the removal of the "fire-break" of Central Asia opened the West to a new infection against which neither immunities nor existing medical knowledge could offer any promise of protection. They called it then "The Great Dying". We know it, still more sombrely, as the Black Death.

The many epidemiological speculations on the source and transmission of bubonic plague have not as yet been reduced to a single acceptable solution. However, it is important to remember that *Pasteurella pestis* thrives most particularly in dense populations, and that its success in passing from one population nucleus to another depends on rapid transmission. In early-fourteenth-century Europe, brimming with population and fed by a very brisk

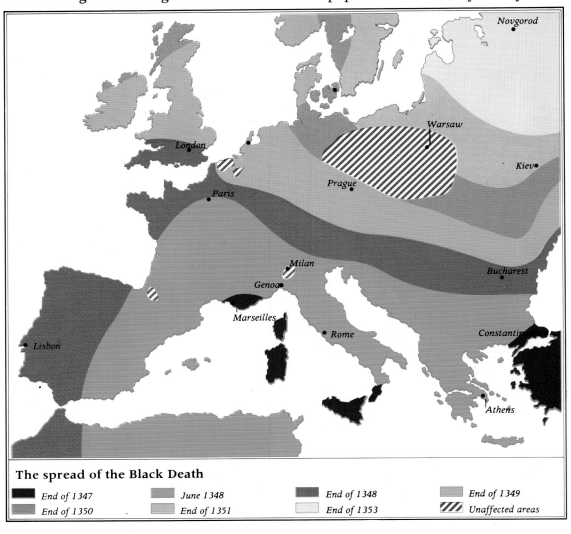

The spread of the Black Death

■ *End of 1347*	■ *June 1348*	■ *End of 1348*	■ *End of 1349*
■ *End of 1350*	▦ *End of 1351*	▨ *End of 1353*	▨ *Unaffected areas*

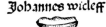

John Wycliffe
*John Wycliffe (1329-84)
was an anti-clerical
English church reformer
and bible-translator, whose
denial of the doctrine of
transubstantiation,
shared by his "Lollard"
followers, led to his
condemnation as a heretic
in 1381.*

international trade, exactly these conditions were present. When the plague first touched the West in 1347, there was literally nothing to stop it.

Although probably dislodged from its original Himalayan-foothill homeland as early as the mid-thirteenth century, to build from there a chain of infection across the Central Asian steppes, the plague bacillus did not emerge historically as a major killer until its documented devastation, in 1331, of the province of Hopei in northern China. To be sure, there is nothing to establish that the Chinese epidemic of 1331 was in fact an outbreak of the Black Death. But contemporary opinion at least had it that the plague reached Islam by way of India and China. And indeed it seems likely that the first more westerly outbreaks of bubonic plague, in Georgia and in the Crimea by 1346, were the consequence of transmission along the caravan routes—the geographical chain of the caravanserais passing along its length the biological chain of black rat, flea and human, the bacillus' natural hosts. By 1347 "The Great Dying" had reached Constantinople and was invading the Italian coastal cities, spreading into southern France. It had moved through Italy and through most of central and northern France by the middle of 1348, along with the eastern third of Spain. Before the end of the year, it had taken in the rest of Spain with Portugal, and was known through southern Central Europe, north-west France, and in the more southerly counties of England.

This stage-by-stage movement of the Black Death expanded steadily north and east as it absorbed northern England and Scotland, central and northern Germany, Scandinavia, and finally, in 1351-3, the Christian principalities of North Russia. It left inexplicable islands of immunity, first at Milan and then in southern Aquitaine, central Flanders, Poland and eastern Germany. But in general the only areas untouched by the mortality were those of especially dispersed population, most notably the Balkans and southern Russia. Elsewhere the toll is now usually estimated to have been as much as a third of the pre-plague population, scything down all ages and social classes from the humble to the great and the good. Neither was this the end of it. In 1361-2 and again in 1368-9, there were further major outbreaks of bubonic plague. Through the

rest of the Middle Ages, pestilence was the constant companion of every man, woman and child in the West.

Another presence in late-fourteenth-century Europe was the spectre of social unrest. Alongside the disasters of plague, and in part a consequence of them, protest movements swept Europe in the fourteenth century. They shook the foundations of the established regimes, even if unable in the final event to dislodge them. And indeed there was much to cause dissension—not least a widespread failure of leadership. The papacy itself, in opulent exile under French domination at Avignon from 1309, discovered new enemies in every opponent of France. Then, from 1378, it became the victim of a still greater scandal, the dual headship known as the Great Schism, with a French-backed pope remaining at Avignon, and another pope, enjoying German, English and Neapolitan support, re-installed once again in Rome. By the time the Schism was healed at the Council of Constance in 1417, heresies had begun to be discussed openly in the works of theologians like John Wycliffe (c. 1320-83); the Friars Minor (Franciscans) were at war with each other as the left- and right-wing branches of the order (the Spirituals and the Conventuals) squabbled over their right to hold property; and the dangerous implications to Church and State of permitting such heretical discussions were shown quite explicitly in the peasant rebellions, frequently supported by the lesser clergy, common throughout Europe in the late 1370s and 1380s. Meanwhile, in Germany the Emperor Charles IV's so-called "Golden Bull" of 1356 formally conceded power everywhere beyond his own personal dominions to a college of seven German electors, thus perpetuating the divisions of the Empire. In Spain, the Christian *Reconquista* failed to push the Muslims finally out of Granada, following the triumphs, in the previous century, of St Ferdinand and of Alfonso the Wise. Flanders, since the late thirteenth century, had been the scene of successful artisan risings. And both France and England, from 1337, revived their old antagonisms in a long-lasting struggle, the Hundred Years War, from which both were to emerge, in the final event, almost equally weakened and exhausted.

Towards the end of the century, the popular rebellions which broke out simultaneously in Germany, France, England,

English architecture

By the 14th century, the leadership in architecture in the Christian West had passed from the French to the English. This was particularly true of ecclesiastical building, where it showed, for example, in the sophisticated vaulting of the cloisters at Gloucester. But it was also the case in secular architecture, finding its most perfect expression in the remarkable roof carpentry of the period. The crowning glory of English roof carpentry is the great hammer-beam roof of London's Westminster Hall, constructed to span this much earlier building during the last decade of the 14th century. However, another fine survival is the octagonal timber-built lantern over the crossing of the cathedral-priory church at Ely, successfully mastering one of the most difficult of architectural challenges.

LEFT *The hammer-beam roof of Westminster Hall, London, by master-carpenter Hugh Herland*

ABOVE *Ightham Mote, a moated manor-house in Kent*

ABOVE *A misericord in the choir stalls of Southwell Minster, Nottinghamshire*

LEFT *The octagonal lantern tower of Ely Cathedral, Cambridgeshire*

FACING PAGE *Fan-vaulting in the cloisters at Gloucester Cathedral, Gloucestershire*

Italy, and the Netherlands, made the years between 1378 and 1382 one of Europe's earliest periods of revolution. Moreover, in England certainly and probably elsewhere as well, the most significant characteristic of the protest movements was that they proceeded not from wretchedness, as they might have done a century before, but from affluence. In the continuing shortage of labour throughout Western Europe, wages were rising and expectations too had climbed. As the prices of what they could produce on their estates failed to keep up with the costs they had to meet in wage bills, the great landowners withdrew from direct cultivation, preferring the role of *rentiers*. In their place, the smaller men—the franklin (freeholder) and the yeoman farmer—established themselves on the land, increasingly prosperous and ever more resentful of the social conventions that continued to depress their status.

For better or for worse—and there were obviously those who came out very well from the plague—the great pandemic of 1347-50 and its almost equally devastating successors turned the world upside down. In politics also, the plague took its toll. The heavy mortalities of the thickly settled West were not matched in the less densely populated kingdoms of Eastern Europe; indeed, the immunity of these kingdoms from the worst ravages of the plague became an important factor in their revival. Certainly, Charles the Great's promotion of Bohemia in the third quarter of the fourteenth century owed a great deal to his own election as Holy Roman Emperor. But Bohemia, too, was one of the regions comparatively little touched by the Black Death. Through most of Central Europe, from Poland in the north to the Balkans in the south, the elements of a new emergence were already visible, even before the devastations of the plague in Byzantium and in the West had given them an additional advantage. Casimir the Great of Poland (1333-70), Lewis the Great of Hungary (1342-82), and Olgierd Prince of Lithuania (1341-77) all took their part in the expansion and modernization of their territories, while under them or their successors formidable new alliances were forged. Under Lewis the Great, in 1370-82, the states of Hungary and Poland were brought temporarily together. This union was succeeded from 1386 by the still more powerful partnership of Lithuania and Poland, on the coronation of Jagiello of Lithuania as Vladislav II of Poland (d. 1434), himself victor over the Teutonic Knights at Tannenberg (1410). Much earlier than this, a great Balkan empire had been assembled around Serbia under Milutin (1282-1321) and then consolidated under Stephen Dusan (1331-55), self-proclaimed "Emperor of the Serbs and the Greeks".

It was on this world, and especially on its southern flank in the Balkans, that the Ottoman Turks, from their base in Anatolia, burst in the mid-fourteenth century, at first as the mercenaries of an enfeebled Byzantium, then as its rivals and finally its conquerors. They brought down all but the city of Constantinople itself and a handful of associated territories. Exposed to the Ottomans, the Serbs suffered their first serious defeat at Crnomen in 1371, followed by the submission of Prince Lazar (1371-89) in 1386 and his defeat and death at Kossovo three years later, in a battle that signalled the total disintegration of his empire. By the end of the century, Ottoman expansion had taken in the whole of the Balkans, bringing Islam into a new confrontation with Catholic Christendom on the borders of a now seriously threatened Hungary. In the many generations of warfare that ensued, one major interlude occurred

Political realignments in Eastern Europe
Less devastated by plague than the West, the kingdoms of Eastern Europe flourished in the 14th century. Poland under Casimir the Great annexed Ruthenia and Galicia, and was itself united in 1386 with Lithuania, a vast kingdom that already stretched deep into European Russia. Hungary, after a brief union with Poland in the early 1380s, found itself confronted to the south by the vigorously expanding Ottoman power in the Balkans, which had destroyed the recently created Serbian empire.

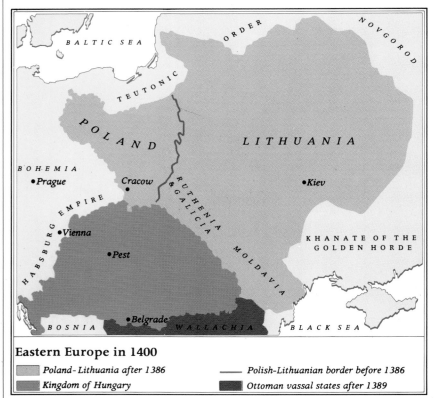

Eastern Europe in 1400

- Poland-Lithuania after 1386
- Kingdom of Hungary
- Polish-Lithuanian border before 1386
- Ottoman vassal states after 1389

Tamerlane

Timur, or Tamerlane (above), became king of Samarkand in 1369. In twenty years of uninterrupted war he seized, and ultimately destroyed, the Chagatai Khanate and the Khanate of the Golden Horde. In 1400 he destroyed the Mameluke army at Aleppo; and in 1402 the Ottomans at Ankara. He also struck south-east into India where he sacked Delhi in 1398, and was on his way to China when he died at Otrar in 1405.

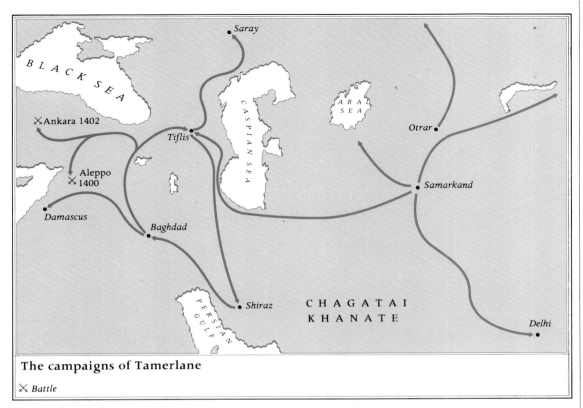

The campaigns of Tamerlane

✕ *Battle*

quite soon on the defeat of the Ottomans themselves in 1402 by Timur of Samarkand, better known as Tamerlane. For a full half-century the Ottoman advance was halted, only beginning again in the 1450s with the conquest of what was left of the Byzantine state.

The collapse of Byzantium had long been anticipated, laying a blight of its own on the entire Orthodox Christian world. For centuries, Byzantium had been under serious threat—from the Seljuks and Latin Christendom in the eleventh and twelfth centuries, from the Mongols (if only indirectly) in the thirteenth century, and now, in the fourteenth, from the Ottomans. The resulting erosion of their territories had left the Byzantine emperors unable to exert any effective leadership even within regions traditionally their own. Stephen Dusan's short-lived Serbian empire, tragically cut-down by the Ottoman Turks, was a natural response among Orthodox Balkan peoples to the failure of contemporary Byzantium. Meanwhile, those principalities of East Russia which had survived the thirteenth-century assault of the Mongols were turning increasingly towards Muscovy, thus rewarded for its military leadership against the Tartars of the Golden Horde. The transformation of the princes of Moscow into tsars of all Russia had to wait until

towards the end of the fifteenth century. But Moscow's leadership from the fourteenth century was founded on successful territorial encroachments throughout these years, building up a power in central Russia only rivalled by Novgorod in the North. To Moscow, certainly, the collapse of Byzantium, paving the way as it did for a transfer of moral leadership in Orthodoxy, brought another important accession of strength.

The fourteenth century before its end saw major political re-alignments in Central Europe, in Russia, and in the regions, Byzantine and Ottoman, of the north-east Mediterranean. Yet there were other areas of the world that were simultaneously experiencing an unprecedented degree of prosperity. One of these was Africa.

Even if still little known to the European West, Africa had already become, well before this date, the principal source of western gold. Exploiting the trade, the empire of Mali and its successor Songhai straddled the routes to that part of West Africa which, under the Europeans, would come to be labelled as the Gold Coast. In the south-east of the continent, the African regime at Zimbabwe flourished, feeding its gold through the port of Sofala northwards along a chain of Islamic trading cities of which the most important was probably Kilwa.

Giotto

Giotto di Bondone, the Florentine painter, was already middle-aged when he came to paint his masterly frescoes at the Arena Chapel, in Padua. But even while this work proceeded from its start in 1304, Giotto showed that his innovatory genius, which has caused him to be described as the true father of the Early Renaissance in Italy, was still in the course of developing. As he worked down the walls of the chapel he was decorating, his command of perspective and richness of detail improved, he exhibited greater boldness in his use of foreshortening, and the drapery on his figures fell more subtly. Indeed, at his best Giotto shows a mastery of fresco-painting for which there were no real precedents and few equals, even in Byzantium. In the clear intelligence of his compositions, he set an entirely new standard for the developing art of the South.

LEFT *Arena Chapel, Padua*
BELOW The Marriage at Cana, *Arena Chapel, Padua*

ABOVE Presentation of the Virgin, *Arena Chapel, Padua*

ABOVE *Detail of fresco attributed to Giotto, in S. Francesco, Assisi*

BELOW *Panel from life of St Francis, attributed to Giotto, in S. Francesco, Assisi*

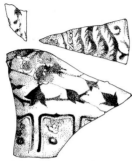

Chinese pottery in Kilwa
These fragments of a blue and white Kuan jar from Kilwa illustrate the growing trade in Chinese porcelains that led, by the 14th century, to the predominance of Chinese over Islamic wares on the Kilwa market.

India in the 14th century
Under Muhammad bin Tughlug the Delhi Sultanate reached its greatest extent, stretching from the Himalayan foothills south almost to the tip of the peninsula. But in the 1340s the empire was already beginning to fragment, and after 1398, when Tamerlane sacked Delhi and added the Punjab to his empire, the sultan's power was limited to a small area. India, however, remained at the centre of a Muslim trading network, established by the Delhi Sultanate, leading east to South-East Asia and the Spice Islands, and west to Persia, Arabia and East Africa.

Kilwa itself was only one element in a comprehensive Islamic trading system that by now took in the whole of the Indian Ocean, and was encroaching more and more on those parts of South-East Asia that controlled the rich trade to the Far East—in particular Malacca, at the tip of the Malay Peninsula, and the islands of Sumatra and Java. It was during the second quarter of the fourteenth century that Islam in India, under Muhammad bin Tughlug, sultan of Delhi (1325-51), extended its frontiers to the limit. And although this, in the event, was to prove too ambitious even before the end of Muhammad's reign, the return of central and southern India to its Hindu rulers was nevertheless far from being the end of the Delhi Sultanate or of the trades it had been instrumental in promoting.

In the sixteenth century, the Delhi Sultanate would be transformed into the Mughal Empire, bringing almost all the regions of India back under Muslim leadership once again. And, broadly speaking, the religious dispositions of the fourteenth century were preserved, both in India and in South-East Asia, through to modern times. In India itself, the Muslim aristocracy never contrived, nor perhaps even wished, to impose its religion on the Hindu minority it controlled. But in South-East Asia, the continuing demand in the Mediterranean, Near

Eastern, and Northern European civilizations for the spices, silks and porcelains of the East, led to the establishment throughout the region of a chain of Muslim trading centres, later developed into individual empires expanding under the banner of Islam. In this way Muslim Malacca, developing from what had started as no more than a commercial base, mopped up what was left of the ancient Shrivijaya island empire, taking in the more accessible parts of Java and Sumatra, in addition to the Malay peninsula itself. Another Muslim kingdom, at Arakan on the west coast of Burma, preserved its independence from Burma itself through the fourteenth and fifteenth centuries. Contemporaneously, the beliefs of Islam were also being carried further East, to become permanently established in the Moluccas, also known as the Spice Islands, and on Mindanao in the southern Philippines as well.

It was in these regions that Muslim traders built up the close contacts with China that became so important as the collapse of the Central Asian Mongol trading systems over the traditional land routes forced increasing dependence on the sea. Inevitably, in such a setting, Cheng Ho, the great Chinese admiral of the early fifteenth century, owed a good part of the success of his extraordinary voyages to the fact that he happened to be a Muslim.

Under the Mongols, Islam built up a following even in China itself. But it was never significant in an ancient culture deeply committed to the quite contrary values of Mahayana Buddhism, and where Confucianism and Taoism were also strong. Buffeted first by the Mongols in the thirteenth century and then by plagues and civil wars in the fourteenth, Chinese civilization had reached what was certainly one of its lowest ebbs by the mid-fourteenth century. Yet one consequence of the confusions was to push to the fore a number of potentially national leaders. Chu Yüan-chang, the most notable of these, successfully ended Mongol Yüan dominance and established his own Ming dynasty at Nanking in 1368. Although it took him another twenty years to get rid of the Mongols altogether, a new era for China had begun.

After so many disasters, with the population reduced by almost a half from the level it had reached under the Sung, the

Map:

• Lahore
Delhi
• Karachi
MALWA
Calcutta
ORISSA
• Bombay
BAY OF BENGAL
HOYSALAS
ARABIAN SEA
Madras
To Far East
To Africa
PANDYAS
CEYLON
INDIAN OCEAN

Muslim India in 1335
▨ Empire of Muhammad bin Tughlug
▨ Independent areas
→ Trade routes

recovery of China inevitably took some time. Consequently the major achievements of the new Ming dynasty very clearly belong to the fifteenth and sixteenth centuries, being no more than anticipated in the fourteenth. Nevertheless, Chu Yüan-chang, retitled Hungwu (1368-98) initiated during his long reign a number of important agricultural and re-settlement programmes. And if the economy of China experienced a renewal after the neglect of the Mongol Yüan, its culture, even through the worst of that period, had remained exceptionally soundly based. Through all the divisions and hardships of more than a century of Mongol rule, the leadership of China over the entire Far East had been preserved essentially unchallenged.

The Mongols had not struck at China alone. Their conquest of Korea in 1258 had been followed by a century of colonial rule during which the surviving Koryo kings had inevitably become aligned with their Mongol suzerains in China. The collapse of Mongol power in Korea brought down the Koryo dynasty, and five hundred years of Koryo supremacy gave place to the equally long-lasting dynasty of the Yi. The first Yi ruler, Yi Song-gye, from the time of his military coup in 1388 and his subsequent usurpation of the throne just four years later, was committed to supporting Ming China,

The Ming takeover of Mongol China
A series of local rebellions against the Mongol Yüan dynasty led slowly to its defeat: the native Ming dynasty which replaced it established a capital at Nanking in 1368, and twenty years later the reconquest of China was complete. The Ming consolidated their hold over south-west China, but left Tibet and the Mongolian heartland outside their empire.

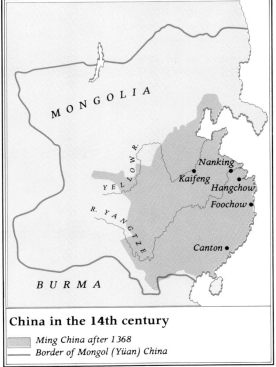

China in the 14th century

▨ *Ming China after 1368*
── *Border of Mongol (Yüan) China*

with which tributary relations were at once successfully established. Korea under the Yi, in almost every way, was thus made a dependency of the Ming and their successors.

In Japan, the Mongol threat, though averted in the event, had seriously weakened the Kamakura shogunate. The Ashikaga shoguns, who succeeded the Kamakura in 1338, were unable to restore central control over an aristocracy which, once freed from the grip of the Kamakura warrior clan, preferred to set off on a path of its own. This path in the end led to the further feudalization of sixteenth-century Japan. Meanwhile, Japan as a whole fell deeper even under the influence of its powerful Chinese neighbour than it had done already with the Kamakura.

Understandably enough, Ming China saw itself as the centre of a unique world order to which every civilization owed its existence and, accordingly, ought to give tribute. Chinese geographers knew of the West, and in the early fifteenth century if not before, Chinese shipping was to penetrate as far as East Africa. But the Chinese were as ignorant as the Arabs and the Europeans about the Americas. Lost behind its ocean barriers, the American continent in the fourteenth century was as remote, as isolated, and as unchanging as it had ever been.

The continuity of American life was scarcely broken in the nomad cultures of the northern continent and in the more settled civilizations of the Mississippi valley and of the North American Southwest. These experienced few dramatic changes, so far as is known, of more than local importance until the period of European contact. But while the same could be said for Central and South America too over the best part of the fourteenth century, the first intimations of the rise of new empires were present already before the end of it. The Aztecs of Tenochtitlán (now Mexico City) and the Peruvian Incas of Cuzco were both settled peoples in the fourteenth century, establishing in each case an individual culture which, during their period of major expansion in the fifteenth century, they would carry far and wide. Of these, the Aztecs at any rate began their programme of conquest some decades before 1400. For such neighbouring civilizations as the Maya of Yucatán, victims first of the Aztecs and then of the Spaniards, the future was black indeed.

The court style in Italy and France

The qualities most admired in the Parisian court style of the decades on either side of 1300 were its naturalism, its delicacy, and its refinement. It was these that influenced contemporary Italian painters like the Sienese Duccio di Buoninsegna (d. 1318) and his equally talented fellow-citizen and apprentice, Simone Martini (d. 1344), giving to their art an exactness and a clarity for which there were no local precedents. Simultaneously, French painters in the court tradition, like Maître Honoré in the late 13th century and Jean Pucelle in the early 14th, learned some of their techniques from the Italians, most especially in the use of light and shade to give an illusion of depth in their paintings. Jean Pucelle was a follower of Duccio; Simone Martini, under papal patronage in Avignon, spent the last years of his life in France.

ABOVE The Annunciation, *page from the* Book of Hours of Jeanne de Savoie, *by Jean Pucelle*

ABOVE LEFT *Front face of the* Maesta, *altarpiece by Duccio*

LEFT The Agony in the Garden *(one panel from rear face of the* Maesta), *by Duccio*

RIGHT Guidoriccio da Fogliano, *fresco by Simone Martini*

ABOVE The Annunciation, *altarpiece by Simone Martini*

Material Culture

Western Europe

The heavy mortalities of the fourteenth-century plagues had one clear consequence: they united the survivors, of all ranks and conditions, in a common fellowship of death. Inevitably, the terrible experiences of the plague-ridden West resulted, throughout the Later Middle Ages and for as long as the plague persisted, in a morbid preoccupation with mortality. And it is not to be wondered at that some of the greatest masterpieces of late-medieval European art should have come to belong to this cult of the dead, reaching its peak in the death-obsessed societies of fifteenth-century Rhineland, Burgundy and Flanders, but evident already much earlier.

The popular arts of the sepulchral effigy, the moralizing wall-painting and the stained-glass window each returned continually to the forbidding themes of judgment, evil conscience, and death. It was from early in the fifteenth century that the grisly fable of the Dance of Death first gripped the popular imagination. But its readily-understood message of the rotting cadaver, that takes no account of differences in wealth or social class among the men it leads off in the dance, had a

"The Three Living and the Three Dead"
The 14th-century preoccupation with death is illustrated in this wall-painting at Peakirk Church in England, representing the popular fable of the Three Living and the Three Dead, which contrasts the splendours of the living with the inevitable corruption of their death. Here two corpses are surrounded by worms, slugs and insects, symbolic of decay.

long ancestry before this in the older legend, popular in the fourteenth century, of "The Three Living and the Three Dead". In many renderings of the fable, the Three Living are shown as princes or bishops who, while hunting or in the course of a journey, meet the Three Dead at a cross-roads (see page 212). It is the rank of those taking part in the encounter that gives it particular emphasis.

Social grievances and death together left their mark on contemporary society. Yet art, for all their pressures, would develop on more than these, and already, in early-fourteenth-century Italy, it had taken a new turn in direction. Northern Italy's situation at a meeting-point of trades had brought it unparalleled wealth, and while its patrons were richer than they had ever been before, they were also more open to new influences. Italian bankers and merchants were familiar figures in the trading-fairs north of the Alps; they were known in Spain, were not unwelcome in Byzantium, and found their markets throughout the Near East. Such men brought home an appreciation of cultures widely different in assumptions from their own. They were ready to welcome innovation in art where others, less sophisticated, might have spurned it.

The key figures in Italy of this first half-century of what we have come to call the Renaissance were Dante Alighieri, the poet, Giovanni Pisano, the sculptor and architect, and the painters Giotto, Duccio, and Simone Martini. They all reflected the creative interaction, especially obvious in their period, between the drama and mystery of the Gothic North and the traditional restraint of the classical world, still present in the cultural milieu of northern Italy. Dante's *Divina Commedia* is timeless in its portrayal of the human predicament. Yet it contains, too, a strong element of mystery and faith very much of the poet's period. What gave body to the infant Renaissance of *trecento* Italy was the classical culture of the Antique World where Dante, for example, could find his companion in Virgil. In the expressive realism of the north European Gothic masters, that same art found its soul.

In no one artist was this convergence of influences more obvious than in the work of Giovanni Pisano, the son of Nicola Pisano whose carved pulpits at Pisa and Siena in the 1260s had shown the strength of these cross-currents already. Giovanni

Dante
Dante Alighieri (1265-1321) was a Florentine, exiled from his native city from 1301 until his death. During this period he wrote the Divina Commedia, *the first great work of Italian vernacular literature.*

Pulpit, Pisa Cathedral, Italy
Giovanni Pisano's cathedral pulpit at Pisa, carved between 1302 and 1310, shows the northern European influences that were so strong in his father Nicola Pisano's work.

Pisano's own Pistoia pulpit of 1301 was carved in styles which might almost have been those of two different artists, the vivid and comparatively crudely-carved expressionism of the *Massacre of the Innocents* panel contrasting most strongly with the tranquil, meticulously-finished *Nativity*. This was not the sort of expressionism that Giovanni's contemporary, the painter Giotto, himself borrowed from the North. However, Giotto's naturalism and the plasticity of his figures were ultimately derived from the High Gothic masterpieces of such northern sculptors as the Joseph Master of Rheims. Giotto's individual contribution to the painting of his time was to introduce that high seriousness, intelligence and order which we associate with the Early Renaissance in Italy, together with the development of such painterly techniques as the first convincing perspective (see pages 150-1).

Time and again, the representation of Gothic architectural detail in a fresco by Giotto will remind us of the mainsprings of his art. Yet Italian fresco-painting,

promoted by such massive building programmes as the construction and decoration of the basilica of St Francis at Assisi, had moved far in advance of its equivalent in the North. A more direct link with the highly decorative court styles of Gothic Paris and Westminster can be found in the work of the Sienese panel-painter Duccio di Buoninsegna whose great altarpiece (the *Maesta*) for Siena Cathedral was painted between 1308 and 1311 (see page 154). Although much was still Byzantine in Duccio's figure painting, continuing probably the strongest tradition in thirteenth-century Italian art, the association in style with the best work of the manuscript illuminators and miniaturists of the northern courts was also very close. In its delicacy and refinement especially, the art of Duccio picked up a tradition of the Parisian court style which had no obvious equivalent in the South. Maître Honoré, in late-thirteenth-century Paris, had already shown in his use of light and shade the dependence of one form of art on another, learning the technique from Italy. And whether directly or not, the Parisian miniatures of Maître Honoré and his fellow court painters inspired the work of the Sienese Duccio, with these influences reflected again in the miniatures of the French royal painter Jean Pucelle (see page 154), a follower and contemporary of Duccio.

Indeed, the exchange of ideas, in art particularly but also in military expertise and technology, is known to have been especially lively during this period over Europe as a whole. Duccio's Sienese apprentice, the remarkable Simone Martini, ended his days as a painter at the papal court at Avignon. However, before making this move he had been instrumental already in introducing his countrymen, more extensively than Duccio, to the delicate mannerisms and refined posturing of the contemporary Parisian court style. For the first time, too, Simone Martini's work brought to Italian painting the emotional range of the High Gothic sculptors, which he combined with portraiture and an interest in heraldry to open up many new avenues. One of Simone Martini's most memorable works, and certainly his most original, was his equestrian portrait of the Sienese general Guidoriccio da Fogliano, a fresco commissioned for the Palazzo Pubblico in 1328 in recognition of Guidoriccio's victories

Chivalry in Europe

Heraldry and the panoply of war inevitably preoccupied the ageing aristocracy of Europe. Old-established families recorded their ancestry in the common rolls- or books-of-arms of the period, and even a king, like Richard II of England, might call on the heralds to confirm his royal dignity with display. Richard II's *Wilton Diptych* is a fine devotional work, one of the great masterpieces of International Gothic painting; but it is also a political document, emphasizing by its repetition of the white hart livery-badge the loyalty of Richard's personal army of retainers. The literature of chivalry, with its fanciful record of heroic deeds and unlikely courtesies between knights, was often finely illustrated with miniature views of battles, sieges, and tournaments, in almost all of which the first stress was placed on the splendour of the profession of arms.

LEFT *Detail from* Falconry, *one of four Devonshire Hunting tapestries, c. 1430*

BELOW *The* Wilton Diptych, *14th century*

ABOVE LEFT *Knight in a 14th-century window at Tewkesbury Abbey, England*
ABOVE RIGHT *Kneeling knight in a panel from a 14th-century German window*

ABOVE *A herald, from a French treatise on heraldry, c. 1450*

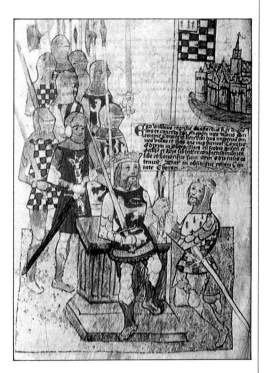

RIGHT *Surcoats of William the Conqueror and other knights, from a 15th-century manuscript*

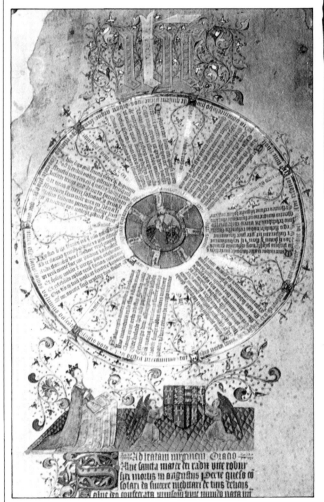

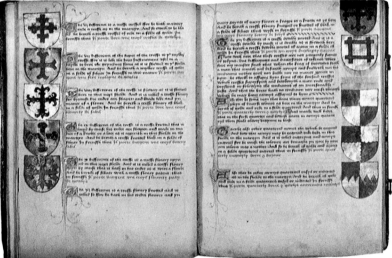

ABOVE *Shields charged with crosses from* Tractatus de Armis, *an English 15th-century book of arms by Johannes de Bado Aureo*

LEFT *The arms of Margaret of Anjou, showing prayers and a hymn to the Virgin, from a 15th-century roll-of-arms*

RIGHT *An unidentified battle scene from the Froissart Chronicles, 15th century*

The Golden Bull
The Golden Bull of 1356 gave the government of the Holy Roman Empire largely to the electors: this copy, executed about 1390 in Prague for the Emperor Wenceslas, is in the Bohemian court style of illumination developed in his reign, highly decorated with feathery acanthus foliage, armorial bearings, monsters and other features.

over the Florentines (see pages 154-5). In its naturalistic military details, Simone Martini's fresco borrowed from the art of the North. Yet its composition, isolating the general in a barren and unpeopled landscape, was both most effective and completely unprecedented, utterly unlike the more conventional altarpieces for which Simone Martini was also in his time well known (see page 155).

Simone Martini's departure for Avignon in about 1340, towards the end of his life, is a good demonstration of the tendency of art, throughout the ages, to cluster at great centres of patronage. Avignon quite recently had become such a centre, following on the exile or "captivity" of the popes in southern France and the intensifying Schism in the papacy. Another was Charles of Bohemia's imperial capital at Prague. The elevation of Charles to the kingship of the Romans in 1346 had followed a decade of regency in Bohemia. And what brought Prague to cultural prominence was the continued presence and personal interest of its ruler and principal patron. Charles' bargain with the pope in 1346, giving him his first Roman title, included the promise to abandon, once and for ever, German political ambitions in Italy. And when, in 1355, he took the next step in securing the imperial crown itself, he followed it almost immediately with another characteristic compromise, giving Germany over to the government of its electors, while retaining for himself, as the Emperor

Charles IV, a personal centre of power in Bohemia. From the promulgation at Metz in 1356 of Charles' "Golden Bull", the bulk of Germany was left divided, exposed for centuries to the destructive rivalries of its princes and deprived of all but the fiction of a head. Yet for the Holy Roman Empire there were obvious advantages in a reorganization that had cut it down at last to size and that had given it an identifiable centre. Like Avignon, like Paris, or like London, Prague had become a cultural focus, remaining that way for another half-century, or as long as the emperor chose to reside there.

An imperial capital could scarcely be untouched by the main currents of international Gothic. Bohemian painting certainly showed the influence of the Sienese panel-painters, and perhaps especially of Simone Martini, while in the architectural detail of Prague Cathedral, under the direction of the German architect-mason Peter Parler from 1353 to 1399, there was both English and French inspiration. Nevertheless, there were peculiarities in the art of Prague which must have originated locally, especially obvious in the eccentric gem-studded decorations of Charles IV's Chapel of the Holy Cross at Karlstein Castle, but perhaps present also in the panel-paintings of that same chapel. A series of vigorous and earthy portraits of the saints, in the tradition but not the style of an icon, these panel-paintings were the work of an enigmatic individual genius now known as Master Theodoric.

Karlstein Castle, near Prague, Bohemia
The Chapel of the Holy Cross at Karlstein Castle is an extreme example of the decorative style developed in 14th-century Bohemia. The palace was built outside Prague by the Emperor Charles IV and completed c. 1365. Its lower walls are studded with large semi-precious stones, while the upper walls are lined with Master Theodoric's vigorous panel-paintings of the saints.

Prague Cathedral, Bohemia
Prague Cathedral was one of the most important churches built in the 14th century. Begun on conventionally French lines soon after Prague was made an Archbishopric in 1344, direction of the building was taken over in 1353 by Peter Parler, who introduced several specifically English features, such as the arrangement of the triforium, stepped back from the line of the lower walls.

Doge's Palace, Venice, Italy
Begun by Pietro Barseggio in 1343, the Doge's Palace is the epitome of the blend of Byzantine, Gothic and Islamic influences that characterized the proud civic architecture of Venice from the 14th century.

In manuscript illumination and in painting generally, Bohemian artists before the end of the fourteenth century evolved a style that without question was recognizably their own (see page 169). Yet they had arrived there originally by way of Sienese and Parisian models. When a similar search is made in architecture for the antecedents of Charles IV's imperial tomb-house at Prague Cathedral, they occur chiefly at this period in England.

The overall design of Prague Cathedral, as first conceived in 1344 by Mathias of Arras, the architect of Narbonne, was certainly conventionally French. But both in France and in the Empire, the exciting architectural initiatives of the twelfth and thirteenth centuries had died away almost without trace by the fourteenth century, not to be revived again until the fifteenth. Only in England was architecture still experiencing a period of innovatory growth during the fourteenth century. Some of these innovations may be attributable to contacts with the East, perhaps by way of embassies to the Persian Mongol khanate during the last decade of the thirteenth century. Certainly, the extraordinary north porch of the great church of St Mary Redcliffe, Bristol, with its characteristic orientalized ogee arches under the gables and the strangely Middle Eastern mouldings of its door, would be hard to explain in any other way. Furthermore, the ogee, blending convex and concave curves, and in use at Bristol in the 1320s, became one of the more familiar decorative motifs in the repertory of the English fourteenth-century architect. However, oriental influences, important though they were both in England and, for example, in the contemporary façades of the great public buildings of Venice, do not by themselves explain the growing individuality of English ecclesiastical architecture. What was plainly an indigenous English style was in the course of evolution: the restrained and perfectly-proportioned Perpendicular.

With such notable patrons as William of Wykeham, bishop of Winchester, and the artistically sensitive Richard II (1377-99), such architects as Henry Yevele and William Wynford, and such roof-carpenters as William Hurley (towards the beginning of the century) and Hugh Herland (just before its end), there can have been few periods in the history of architecture in England more open to experiment and change (see pages 146-7). The great monuments of the era included the choir and cloister at Gloucester Abbey, built on the proceeds of a popular cult at the tomb of the murdered Edward II. There was William Hurley's timber octagonal lantern over the crossing of the great church at Ely, Henry Yevele's Canterbury Cathedral nave, and William Wynford's Winchester nave, the last of which was erected to the order of William

of Wykeham, himself an experienced supervisor of works who had learnt his trade in the service of Edward III. Most remarkable of all, and surely one of the supreme architectural masterpieces of the entire medieval world, was the hammer-beam roof of Westminster Hall, in London, built to the order of Richard II between 1394 and 1400 by Hugh Herland, master-carpenter. It was the culminating achievement of a tradition in timber roof-construction which, in England at any rate, had begun its flowering no earlier than the thirteenth century.

Richard II's interest in building, and in the material comforts of the cultivated life in general, was very much in keeping with his period. Married first to a Bohemian princess and then to a daughter of France, Richard had kept his court in touch with the main currents of European culture and with the civilized aristocratic society of the times that saw virtue in conspicuous consumption. It was Richard's court that nurtured the talent of Geoffrey Chaucer, a poet of international standing. And it was for Richard again that one of the most celebrated devotional paintings of all time, the Wilton Diptych, was commissioned (see page 158). This Anglo-French work of the last years of the century represents the king himself, accompanied by his patron saints, kneeling before the Virgin and Child. The personal confrontation of king and Virgin had an obvious political significance, placing emphasis on Richard's luckless claim to a God-given authority in government. But the Wilton Diptych puts before us also many of the other preoccupations of Richard's period and class. The fine clothes and jewellery of the king and his two royal patrons, the Anglo-Saxon Saint Edmund and Saint Edward, were just those on which Richard himself and his relatives-by-marriage, the French royal dukes, typically lavished attention.

One of the most splendid figures of this complex and self-absorbed society was Jean de Berry, brother of Charles V of France and great-uncle of Richard's second queen. The individual work of art for which Jean de Berry is now best remembered is the magnificent book of hours known as the *Très Riches Heures du Duc de Berri*, begun by the brothers Limbourg in 1413 and left incomplete in 1416 on the death both of the duke and of the miniaturists. Yet Jean de Berry, as well as

supporting manuscript illumination in those Parisian workshops which were especially famous in his period, was also a builder on a munificent scale and a collector of discerning but eclectic taste. Two of his most extravagant castles, now either demolished or transformed, were those at Mehun-sur-Yèvre and Saumur, both of them illustrated in the remarkable miniatures of the Limbourgs' *Très Riches Heures* (see pages 164-5). Something of their splendour can still be seen in the hall of the duke's palace at Poitiers, dominated at one end by the great triple fireplace, crowned by Flamboyant open-work tracery, which was Jean de Berry's characteristic contribution to an earlier, more austere apartment (see page 164).

There is very little that is obviously military in the great castle-palaces of the French aristocracy in the late fourteenth and early fifteenth centuries. Certainly they were furnished with considerable splendour, their walls hung with the magnificent tapestries of Paris and Arras, very often individually commissioned. A splendid surviving series is the *Apocalypse* set at Angers, woven by Nicolas Bataille between 1373 and 1380 for the king's brother, Louis of Anjou, from a model in Charles V's personal library (see page 164). And no doubt the tapestry industry of late-medieval France would never have flourished as it did without the patronage of the king and his wealthy brothers. But to say that Charles V and the dukes of Anjou, Berry and Burgundy were discerning patrons of the best in art, and that they liked to live comfortably and well, is not to deny them a claim to an interest, similarly supported by their wealth, in the refinements of contemporary military technology. A favourite residence of Charles V was his castle at Vincennes, on the outskirts of Paris. Very largely re-modelled at the beginning of his reign, it was dominated by an impressive central tower-keep which provided an influential example for many less ambitious successors. And while Charles was putting up his *donjon* at Vincennes and others, like Sir John Delamare at Nunney in Somerset, were building tower-keeps of their own in emulation, the passion for gunpowder —almost the cult of the gun—was beginning to grip their contemporaries.

Europe in the fourteenth century, as in the thirteenth, was undergoing a period of technological advance so swift that it

Nunney Castle, Somerset, England
The fortifications of Nunney Castle were purely cosmetic, since Nunney was not equipped to house a single horse: it was a residential castle, built in emulation of the contemporary French fashion.

English cannon
The first known illustration of a cannon, from an English manuscript of 1327, shows it used against a castle: the 14th century saw the introduction of "missile weapons"—the crossbow and the cannon—that would change warfare fundamentally.

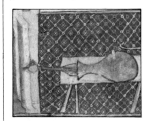

The castle of Saumur, in a scene from the Très Riches Heures du Duc de Berri *depicting the month of September*

The castle of Vincennes, shown in the background of a hunting scene from the Très Riches Heures du Duc de Berri

The late-medieval French castle

One of the shared characteristics of the highly sophisticated aristocracies of late-medieval Europe was an abiding passion for building. Especially active in this role were Charles V of France and his brothers, the dukes of Anjou, Berry and Burgundy; and it was some of their more extravagant creations that were recorded in the *Très Riches Heures du Duc de Berri*, a book of miniatures painted by the Limbourg brothers in the early years of the 15th century. In the surviving palace at Poitiers, with its huge triple fireplace at one end of the main hall, something of the magnificence of these 14th-century castles remains. Many great landowners were also successful soldiers, and they were interested, of course, in the very latest techniques of military architecture. However, they wanted their castles to be sumptuously furnished residences as well, their walls often hung with specially commissioned tapestries. But the competing purposes of these buildings could result in the most extraordinary architectural confections. Although aware, as soldiers, of the new potential of artillery, the greater part of the aristocracy still very obviously preferred to concentrate on such impressive features as the bulk of the keep and the number and height of the towers.

FACING PAGE
The castle of Mehun-sur-Yèvre, as depicted in a scene from the Très Riches Heures du Duc de Berri *ostensibly showing the Temptation of Christ*

Triple fireplace in the hall of Jean de Berry's palace at Poitiers

"Babylon was not forgotten", from the Apocalypse *tapestries at Angers, woven for Louis, Duke of Anjou by Nicolas Bataille*

ident gue mont sacoullent la uolee

Flemish post-mill
This Flemish manuscript illumination of about 1340 shows a post-mill: the whole body of the mill rotated to face the wind.

Western pottery
By the 14th century the potter's craft in Western Europe was extensively industrialized: the knight-jug could be found as far away as Flanders and Norway, often alongside the highly prized and richly decorated polychrome wine-jugs of Saintonge, a pottery centre north of Bordeaux.

English knight-jug

Saintonge wine-jug

left many, including the castle-builders, stranded on their own traditions. From early in the century, long after its first development in China, the secrets of gunpowder were made available to the West in the *Liber Ignium* of Marc the Greek and through the inventions of the German Franciscan Berthold Schwarz, attributed to 1313. In an English manuscript of 1327, the first known illustration of a cannon showed it already in use against the defences of a castle. And although it would take many years for the cannon and more portable firearms to replace the stone-throwing trebuchet and the bow, the general interest that the new inventions provoked was very much in character with a contemporary enthusiasm for advanced military technology. It was during the fourteenth century, alongside the gun, that the steel crossbow was first fully developed. Sophisticated plate armour, from the very beginning of the century, increasingly took the place of chain mail.

What was happening experimentally in military technology had its parallels in industry and science. Thirteenth-century innovations in the use of water-power were carried several stages further in the fourteenth century, especially in the operation of bellows and tilt-hammers in the iron industry, but also in the manufacture of paper and silk. Water was used in wire-drawing too, while its control was facilitated by the contemporary development of sluices, weirs and locks, with important consequences for the transport of goods by river. Before the end of the century, the tower-mill had come into use, its swivelling top being a major improvement on the earlier post-mill structure, the whole body of which

had had to be swung to face up into the wind. Other mechanical advances included the perfecting of new clock mechanisms and further progress in printing, among this the use of movable type. The pottery industry in Western Europe had never been more advanced, reaching a peak of extravagant decoration in the elaborate anthropomorphic vessels of the turn of the thirteenth and fourteenth centuries: the knight-jugs of the English North Midlands industries finding a place alongside the handsome painted vessels of the Saintonge potteries, north of Bordeaux. In food production, the agricultural treatises of Walter of Henley and of Pietro dei Crescenzi (d. 1307) were both well known and widely observed. The very important development of new salting and packing techniques in the herring industry enabled sea-fish to reach communities previously starved of such a diet.

Intellectually, in the wake of the High Scholasticism of the thirteenth century, this was a period of doubt. But even that has been seen as a necessary preparation —a clearing of the ground by criticism— for the true development of science. In the more practical sciences, certainly, time was not standing still. After the first numbing shock of the onset of the Black Death, the symptoms of which were nevertheless very precisely described, the physicians of the West applied themselves to the problems of the transmission of infection, already recommending in the later 1370s quarantine regulations which came to play an important part in the isolation and control of plague. In a similarly empirical vein, Pegolotti's commercial handbook, the *Practica della mercatura*, gave advice to travellers going as far afield as China, while the map-makers also made significant progress with such achievements as the *portolani* (navigational maps and directories) of Pietro Vesconte (1311) and Francesco Pizigano (1367), the Catalan Atlas of 1375 with its attempt to depict the whole world, and that unique road and waterway map, the so-called Gough Map of England.

Byzantium

For most of these cartographers the Mediterranean Sea remained the hub of the world as they knew it. And vital still to the trades of that sea was the ancient city of Constantinople, on the boundary of Europe and Asia and yet preserving a

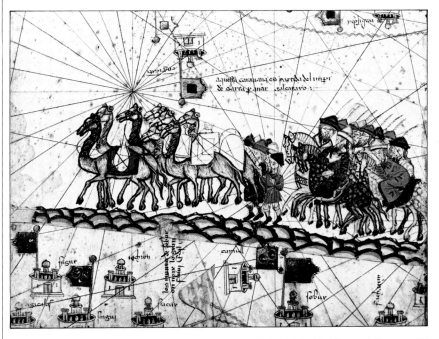

14th-century maps
*The map-makers of the
14th century began to
replace earlier illustrated
itineraries with ideas
more recognizable to the
modern eye. Abraham
Cresques, cartographer to
Peter III of Aragon, drew
his Catalan Atlas (detail
above) in 1375: it is based
on an intricate network of
compass bearings, and
although illustrative
features, like the caravan
here, still survive, the
towns have been reduced
to standardized symbols.
The mid-14th-century
Gough Map of England
(below, with detail right)
clearly illustrates the
major carting routes and
waterways, as well as
recording—highly
unreliable—distances
between important places.*

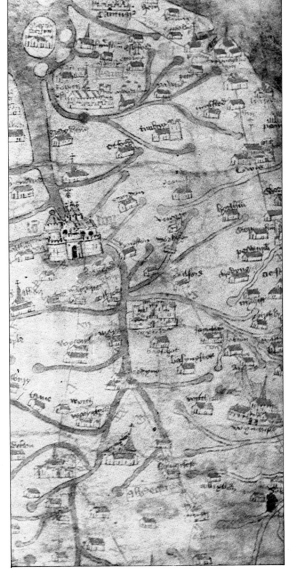

precarious independence from both. It is
easy enough from our present modern
perspective to see Byzantium in its final
years as a spectacle of melancholy decay.
With money in relatively short supply,
patronage in architecture had certainly
declined, the great days of Byzantine
building having gone beyond recall.
Nevertheless, in both fresco-painting and
in mosaics the art of the continuing
Palaeologue Revival reached new peaks
in the fourteenth century that set it on a
level with contemporary developments in
Italy. The architecturally undistinguished
monastic church of Christ of the Chora
(Kariye Camii) at Constantinople was restored and rebuilt between 1316 and 1321
for Theodore Metochites, a wealthy statesman and scholar. It is the home of mosaics
and frescoes of the highest quality (see
page 168) and of a talent fully equal to the
simultaneous genius of Giotto.

Both at the Kariye Camii and at the
contemporary memorial chapel of St Mary
Pammakaristos (Fetiye Camii), which was
built in about 1310 to a higher architectural standard, the characteristics of the
decorations combined a love of intimate
detail with a further extension of the
tenderness in portraiture (especially of
the Virgin) familiar in Byzantine art since
the days of the *Virgin of Vladimir* (c. 1125).
In panel-painting and in the remarkable
miniature mosaics of the period, detail
and tenderness again were the dominant
emphases, establishing a tradition that
remained influential through subsequent
centuries of Orthodox Christian art.

Certainly, the same characteristics were
recognizable in the cultural florescence
of late-medieval Serbia, which had been
brought back from Catholicism securely
into Byzantine Orthodoxy by the conquests of its victorious kings, Milutin
(1282-1321) and Stephen Dusan (1331-55).
Serbia's hegemony in the Balkans was
comparatively short-lived, threatened in
the mid-fourteenth century by Ottoman
expansion and lost in vassalage before
the end of that century to the Ottoman
Bayezid I, known as "the Thunderbolt".
Nevertheless, even in that short period a
distinctively Serbian culture, under the
patronage of vigorous and wealthy rulers,
had the opportunity to emerge. No longer
exposed to the dominating influence of
the Latin West, in particular as transmitted through Venice and its satellite
trading cities, Serbian architecture now

Byzantium, Serbia, and Bohemia

Byzantine art in the 14th century was still of very high quality. There were few spare resources at Constantinople itself for grandiose architectural projects, yet this was the time of the rebuilding (1316-21) of the monastic church of Christ of the Chora (Kariye Camii), redecorated at the expense of a wealthy scholar-statesman with some of the finest mosaics and wall-paintings of the so-called Palaeologue Revival. Byzantine traditions were influential too in contemporary Serbia, where the campaigns of conquest of Milutin (1282-1321) and Stephen Dusan (1331-55) were building an independent empire. Milutin's architectural patronage, in particular, brought into being a native Serbian school of painting, developing on Byzantine models to produce, at churches like Gracanica, wall-painting cycles of a characteristically expressive and powerful style. Later in the century, the evolution of a new native art in Charles IV's Bohemia has a similar political explanation, owing much to Charles' elevation in 1355 to the imperial throne. Bohemian painting, under the emperor's patronage, developed a characteristic softness of expression which was subsequently widely copied in Germany.

TOP LEFT *Woman with haemorrhage touching Christ's robe, mosaic, Kariye Camii, Constantinople*

LEFT *The Dormition of the Virgin, mosaic, Kariye Camii, Constantinople*

BELOW *Dome of Kariye Camii, Constantinople*

ABOVE *Wall-painting of the prophet Elias, Gracanica, Serbia*

RIGHT *Entombment of Christ, by the Master of Wittingau, Bohemia*

BELOW *Fresco of warrior-saint, Gracanica, Serbia*

BOTTOM RIGHT *The Annunciation, St Clement, Ochrid, Greece*

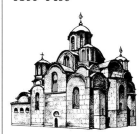

Gracanica Church, Serbia
The monastery church at Gracanica, built between 1318 and 1321, was the last foundation of King Milutin of Serbia. It is a departure from the more conventionally Byzantine style of his previous projects, with a doubled tier of cruciform barrel-vaults below the dome, and pointed arches in the upper tier.

discovered its inspiration in the best work of the Palaeologue Revival, with which it was brought into direct contact as territories formerly Byzantine were absorbed. And although there continued to be western Gothic survivals, in individual architectural details and in the plainly Italianate monastic church at Decani (1327-35), these were important chiefly as an ingredient in the characteristically Serbian stylistic blend, in which the dominant inspiration was Byzantium.

The most individual Serbian buildings were those built by Milutin, especially the Gracanica monastery church that was his final foundation during the last three years of his reign. The chief interest of the Gracanica church is that it abandoned the more usual Byzantine horizontal emphasis of such other Milutin buildings as the church of St George at Staro Nagoricino (1312-13), in favour of a verticality more closely paralleled in Russia. There is nothing to establish direct contacts with Russia, at least in this particular. But the Serbian taste for great height in buildings, vault being piled on vault to achieve just this effect, seems to have been shared by other Slavic peoples, taking its place in the Slavic revival which Milutin's Balkan successes briefly brought into being.

Stephen Dusan's reign, although politically even more glorious than Milutin's, was not characterized by architectural advance. However, the strikingly vertical emphasis· of the church at Gracanica reappeared in the works of Prince Lazar at Ravanica (c. 1375) and at Krusevac (c. 1377-8), where it was joined by a new extravagance in external decoration which might itself have been an expression of the taste of the Slavs, echoing Vladimir-Suzdal. Certainly, whether or not these racial instincts may truly be detected in buildings, there had clearly emerged a new Slav spirit in fourteenth-century Serbian painting, where not only was the character of the modelling different but Slavonic lettering quite frequently replaced the Greek. In the work of the painter Astrapas at the Church of the Virgin Ljeviska at Prizren, completed in 1306-7, and in the only slightly later fresco cycles at Gracanica and Decani, Serbian painting displayed a vigorous and expressive naturalism that was both powerful and very much its own (see page 169). Later in the same century, as the Ottomans

pushed the Serbs steadily northwards, local artists (as is so often the case) seem to have turned their backs on a political scene they no longer wished to contemplate, evolving a style that was as gentle, delicate, and refined as the earlier works had been forceful, bold, and impressionistic. This same gentleness, verging on effeminacy, had come to characterize the declining years of later Palaeologue Byzantium —not an inaccurate reflection of the inertia and disenchantment felt by a refined society already under siege by the Ottoman Turks and spared for another half-century not so much by any effort of its own as by the timely eruption of the central Asian Tamerlane (1336-1405), one of whose achievements, shortly before his death, was the destruction of the first Ottoman Empire.

Weak though the empire of Byzantium had become, years of tradition preserved it still as a centre of excellence in the arts. In its ancient spheres of influence—the Balkans and Russia—the Byzantine legacy was strong. It was natural enough that when each of these experienced a revival, the first resort of the painters of the renewal should have been to the fount of their earliest inspiration. Under Milutin and Stephen Dusan, and perhaps especially under the latter's ephemeral "Empire of the Serbs and the Greeks", proclaimed in 1345, Serbia underwent a deliberate Byzantinization which, while it gave scope for the fostering of a national culture, nevertheless kept the focus on Constantinople. Similarly, when the princes of Russia disentangled themselves from the grip of the Mongol Golden Horde, the dominant voice in their cultural renewal was predictably discovered in Byzantium.

Eastern Europe

For something like a century from the first arrival of the Mongols in 1236, patronage in Russia had dried up almost entirely under the crushing weight of Tartar taxation and the threat of further oppressions. It is true that in individual buildings like the Church of St Nicholas, on the Lipna near Novgorod, built in 1292, the characteristic gabled roofing system of North Russia was still in the course of development, yielding a style very much more appropriate to the heavy snow-falls of the North than the vaults of the original Byzantine model. However, the chief architectural achievements, even in the

Icon from Novgorod, Russia
This icon of the Nativity of the Virgin, painted in early-14th-century Novgorod, dates from the period when Novgorod's icon-painters were cut off from contact with Byzantium by the Tartars. While the effect of the icon is rich and impressive, the rather crude handling of perspective and detail show that the painter was working before the renewed contact with Greek artists of the second half of the century.

relatively Tartar-immune merchant community of Novgorod, belong mainly to the second half of the fourteenth century, as seen in the great Church of St Theodore Stratilates, built in the early 1360s, and in the Cathedral of the Transfiguration, not more than a decade later.

Both these buildings had the gabled roofs, the decorated façades, and the lofty central drum and dome of the mature

Frescoes at the Church of the Transfiguration, Novgorod, Russia

The Church of the Transfiguration (above), founded in 1374, is decorated with the only surviving frescoes of Theophanes the Greek. His impressionistic style (right) did much to shape the character of Novgorodian, and later Muscovite, painting.

Novgorod church-building tradition. In both, again, there was the characteristic emphasis on verticality which we have already seen in the contemporary Balkans as typical of the architecture of the Slavs. During the same century, these distinctively Russian styles found their fullest expression in the carpentry-based architecture of Novgorod's companion trading city of Pskov. Here the exotic piled-up profile of a building like the now-vanished Cathedral of the Trinity (1365-7), utterly traditional, later became highly influential in the nationalistic re-building of late-fifteenth-century Moscow. Yet the strikingly indigenous quality of Russian church architecture was much less evident in painting. At Novgorod, a local icon-painting style had certainly developed by the early fourteenth century, and it was not without its charm. The iconostasis, being a screen separating nave and sanctuary, on which to hang such paintings, was introduced at just this time, to reflect the devotion of the Novgorod citizen centering now on his icons. But the flat two-dimensional art of North Russia in the decades of Tartar dominance was very clearly a provincial development, a native growth away from the focus of Byzantium. In the later-fourteenth-century work of the immigrant Theophanes the Greek and his followers, a more sophisticated emphasis on plasticity and movement was at last restored.

In due course Theophanes left Novgorod, moving on again to Moscow early in the 1380s. However, in the meantime he had been present at Novgorod during the building of the Cathedral (or Church) of the Transfiguration, and it is only there that his frescoes have survived. They show us a confidently vigorous and impressionistic style totally different from the cruder and less certain native tradition, and evidently the product of the long experience Theophanes had enjoyed, before coming to Russia, of fresco-painting at Constantinople and in the surviving Byzantine provinces. Not surprisingly, Theophanes' work, at the Transfiguration and elsewhere, was much admired and imitated. At Moscow in the early fifteenth century, he was still exerting a major influence on the art of his authentically Russian continuator, Andrey Rublev (d. 1430), usually ranked in Russian art history as the greatest religious painter of them all.

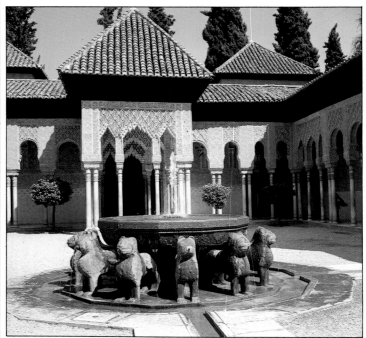

The Alhambra

In the Alhambra, at Granada, the decorative potential of Islamic abstract and calligraphic ornament was developed to an unusual extent. The Moorish occupation of Spain was nearing its end, and the frail plasterwork of the Alhambra seems to reflect the insecurity of a society constantly at risk, building for the present rather than for all time. In the event, the Alhambra's perfection appealed as much to its Spanish conquerors—Granada fell to Ferdinand and Isabella in 1492—as it had to the Moorish kings they dispossessed. It has been preserved as a monument to late-medieval Islamic civilization at its most cultivated and luxurious: a rare intact survival of palace architecture.

LEFT *The Lion Court*

BELOW *The Court of the Myrtles*

ABOVE *Detail of decorated plasterwork*

RIGHT *Fountains playing in the gardens of the palace*

BELOW *Mirador of the Baraxa Tower*

BOTTOM RIGHT *Base of arch decorated with tiles and painted plasterwork*

The Islamic Near East

Like Byzantium and the Balkan principalities, Muscovy benefited from the indiscriminate maraudings of Tamerlane of Samarkand whose armies, having come to the gates of Moscow itself, destroyed the forces of the Golden Horde a full decade before they laid low the Ottoman Empire in 1402. Ultimately, however, Tamerlane's vastly over-extended dominions came to a dissolution of their own. And the Ottomans, their fortunes reviving from quite early in the fifteenth century, were best placed to pick up the pieces.

Indeed, if it had not been for the intervention of Tamerlane, it is hard to see how Ottoman expansion, proceeding outwards in the fourteenth century from its base in Anatolia, could have been held in check. In Islamic society, certainly, the future lay with the Ottomans, on the move against Byzantium from the 1320s and laying siege already, if unsuccessfully, to Constantinople itself in 1391, having absorbed most of its empire. The contrast between Ottoman vigour in the Eastern Mediterranean and the luxurious decline of Muslim Granada in the West was one of those coincidences in the medieval world from which morals are most frequently drawn.

Initially, the preoccupation with conquest of the Ottoman sultans was not favourable to patronage of the arts. Fourteenth-century Ottoman buildings bore the unmistakable stamp of Seljuk inspiration, and it is generally acknowledged that a genuine climax in Ottoman architecture was not reached before the mid-sixteenth century. Nevertheless, there are buildings of importance at Isnik and Bursa, in Anatolia, dating back to the first Ottoman Empire. Moreover, they demonstrate the driving force of the Ottoman faithful very well in their concentration on those typically Islamic religious monuments, the mosque and the mausoleum.

At Bursa especially, devotional and commemorative functions were brought together in a succession of memorial mosques, built there in the tradition originated by the sultan Orkhan (1326-59), whose earliest achievement had been the capture of Bursa and who made it thereafter his capital. Orkhan buried his father Osman at Bursa, to be buried there later in his turn. And Orkhan's son, Murad I, and his grandson, Bayezid "the Thunderbolt", continued this memorial practice.

Bayezid's Great Mosque at Bursa, with its twenty domes, was not his only

The spread of the Ottomans
The Ottoman state in Anatolia expanded slowly throughout the 14th century—by 1359 all the Byzantine strongholds in Asia Minor had fallen, and the first conquests in Europe had been made. Subsequently Murad I and Bayezid pushed the frontiers outwards to include all of Asia Minor in the east, and Bulgaria in the west; Serbia and Wallachia were reduced to vassal states. Only the devastating defeat of the Ottoman army by Tamerlane at Ankara in 1402, and a subsequent period of disintegration, postponed the fall of Byzantium and further European conquests until the mid-15th century.

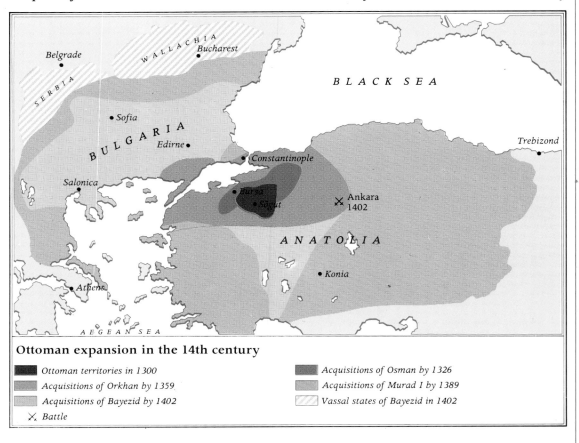

Ottoman expansion in the 14th century

■ *Ottoman territories in 1300*	*Acquisitions of Osman by 1326*
Acquisitions of Orkhan by 1359	*Acquisitions of Murad I by 1389*
Acquisitions of Bayezid by 1402	*Vassal states of Bayezid in 1402*
✕ *Battle*	

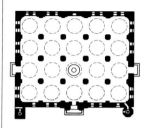

Great Mosque, Bursa, Turkey (plan)
Sultan Bayezid's Great Mosque at Bursa, the Ottoman capital after 1326, was still essentially Seljuk in style. In plan it is a magnificent pillared hall, crowned by 20 domes.

Hispano-Moresque pottery
In the area around Valencia, particularly at Manises, Mudejar Muslim potters under Christian rule produced wares that were prized throughout Europe. These colourful lustrewares were decorated to appeal to their different markets: Arabic calligraphy and designs (below) appear as well as heraldic motifs and Latin texts (bottom).

building enterprise there. Outside the city, he completed a complex of mosque, *medrese* and tomb which, while on a less magnificent scale than the Great Mosque, was architecturally of greater refinement. But what was most striking about these early Ottoman buildings, especially if set against the practice of contemporary Islamic Spain, was their comparative restraint and austerity. In Spain, the most remarkable monument of Muslim Granada was, of course, the incomparable Alhambra, the decorative extravagance of which constituted an absolute reversal of every principle followed, whether deliberately or not, by the Ottoman rulers of Bursa.

The Alhambra, after the fashion by then current in Islam, was a citadel—a large, fortified, exclusive enclosure cast in the same mould as the contemporary Russian *kremlin* or the much earlier "urban élite centres" of Jayavarman's Cambodia or the northern Peruvian Chimu. As well as the palace of the ruler, it included within its walls the mosques, schools and administrative buildings, with the gardens and apartments of the court. In the curious political truce of the late-medieval Spanish *Reconquista*, during which Arab and Christian lived uneasily side-by-side, Moorish Granada was still able to experience a period of great artistic brilliance, especially during the second half of the fourteenth century with the work of the poets Ibn Khatima (d. 1369) and Ibn Zamrak (d. 1393) and with the completion of that crowning glory of western Islamic domestic architecture, the superb palace of the Alhambra itself (see pages 172-3).

In the Alhambra, there was nothing of the weight and solid permanence of Seljuk and Ottoman monumental architecture. Few would have believed in the fourteenth century that Granada had been granted any more than a stay-of-execution. And something of this insecurity was surely reflected in the fragile plasterwork, the stucco ornament, and the light timber and brick structures of the Alhambra's manicured courts. The palace, like a modern exhibition pavilion which is here today and gone tomorrow, was built for the pleasures of the moment. It made full use, with its gardens, its fountains, its ornamental pools and shaded arcades, of the balmy southern climate. Its focus was on great open courts, the so-called Lion Court and Court of the Myrtles. And its

principal apartments, among them the Hall of the Ambassadors and the glorious Hall of Judgment, were themselves open to the courts they adjoined. The pleasure pavilion of a cultivated literary aristocracy, it was entirely appropriate that the walls of the Alhambra should have been decorated with the verses of Ibn Zamrak, including celebrations by the poet of its beauty. It was for this that Boabdil, dispossessed king of Granada in 1492, wept as he went into exile.

What he left has been carefully preserved by his Christian successors ever since. And indeed, respect for each other's artistic traditions had long been characteristic of late-medieval Spain, where the Christian architecture of reconquered Seville continued to show Moorish inspiration, and where the art of the Mudejar potters of Valencian Manises was so closely related to that of their brethren at Moorish Malaga that their products were often virtually indistinguishable. The Mudejars were the Moors who had remained behind, living as Muslims in a Christian kingdom with communities and privileges of their own. And their unusual status is reflected still in the hybrid designs on the Hispano-Moresque lustrewares for which they were famous and for which they found markets all over the Christian West. While decorating their wares with the traditional Kufic calligraphy which would have been meaningless in non-Arab societies, they also turned their hand to the heraldry so important by now to the decadent chivalry of the North. Jean de Berry, that great northern patron and connoisseur of the arts, is known to have employed potters from Manises in his palaces at Bourges and at Poitiers. Even in the comparatively humble society of England's south-coast ports, Spanish lustrewares were not at all uncommon in the pottery repertoire of the period, brought there as a by-product of a flourishing maritime trade which exchanged the wine, oil and fruits of Mediterranean Spain for the cloth and the pewterwares of England. One of the more common motifs in Manises lustre design of the later Middle Ages was the ship by which this trade was carried. Another was the jousting knight whose luxurious tastes and surplus wealth were what made such exchanges along the still perilous sea-routes ultimately so very worth while.

ABOVE *The Golden Pavilion (Kinkakuji) in Kyoto*

LEFT *Portrait of the monk Muso Soseki by Muto Shui*

Zen Buddhist influence on Japanese art

The Ashikaga shoguns, surrounded by Zen monks in their Muromachi suburb of Kyoto after 1336, became increasingly epicurean and devoted to culture as their hold on the country weakened. The Kinkakuji, or Golden Pavilion, erected in 1397 for the monastic retirement of the third shogun, combines a Chinese silhouette with a much lighter, more graceful, Japanese treatment of detail. Zen had a profound influence too on painting: Muto Shui's polychrome portrait of his master Muso Soseki exemplifies the typical Zen subject of the revered sage.

Sankore Mosque, Timbuktu, Africa
Built of mud-brick and rubble rendered with clay, and bristling with permanent wooden scaffolding, the Sankore Mosque centres upon a courtyard surrounded by arcaded galleries. It was probably founded by Mansa Musa, King of Mali (1312-37).

Africa

The court society of late-medieval Europe, with its tradition of conspicuous waste, was one of the chief elements in a growing demand for the more exotic luxuries and in an apparently insatiable quest for gold. In the thirteenth century, Arab traders had begun the exploitation of the gold reserves of southern Africa along their East African trade routes, and this was further developed in the fourteenth century, itself the period of maximum expansion for an east-coast port like Kilwa. Traditionally, however, gold had come mainly from West Africa, south of the Sahara, and from the legendary empires of Mali and Songhai. By the fourteenth century, after many generations of contact, Islam had touched Mali, at least in its ruling classes. It was commemorated in the mud-walled Sankore mosque at Timbuktu, probably built for *Mansa Musa* (1312-37), and was also the cause of that ruler's famous pilgrimage to Mecca by way of Egypt in 1324, accompanied allegedly by such lavish distributions of gold that the value of the metal in contemporary Cairo is said to have fallen by as much as 12 per cent.

We know something from North African writers of the period about the nature of the *Mansa*'s empire, which would seem to have been distinguished by good government. And although there is no equivalent historical record of the course of events in the forested areas to the south, it is abundantly clear from the archaeological evidence that the pursuit of gold, and of slaves as well, was the cause of an increase in the wealth of the region which then influenced its material culture. Of course, by the fourteenth century the sculptural tradition of Nigerian Ife was already old, being well into its "classical" period. For this reason, it is not certain that the remarkable collection of terracotta heads and other objects from Obalara's Land, in Ife, is as late as the securely dated early-fourteenth-century stone- and potsherd pavements in which they were set when found. Nevertheless, the pottery vessels from this group, which must surely be contemporary with the pavements, are themselves remarkable, being elaborately modelled and decorated in vivid high relief. They continued the exotic pottery tradition of the twelfth-century Lafogido site in the same Yoruba city, being no less significant in their own

cultural context than the more sophisticated contemporary lustrewares of the Mudejar potters of Manises.

On the other side of Africa, a change of dynasty at the end of the thirteenth century, being a further encouragement to trade, was simultaneously bringing great wealth to Kilwa. The new rulers, from a family originating in the Yemen, restored order at Kilwa after the troubles that had finally brought down the Shirazi founders of Kilwa's trading prominence. And like the Shirazi before them, they were merchants at least as much as they were sultans and dynasts. The great monument of their period was the building known as Husuni Kubwa, dated by its excavators to the first decades of the fourteenth century, and probably to be associated with the scholar-prince al-Hasan b. Sulaiman, also called "the father of gifts". Husuni Kubwa combined two functions. At the end of the spur on which it was situated, the residential complex was built around a series of courts—the palace court, the domestic court, the audience court and pool. However, immediately adjoining this and separated from it only by a triple range of rooms, there was also the great South Court, surrounded by storerooms and clearly intended for the commercial activities controlled by the sultan and in which he himself, very probably, engaged.

What generated this commerce was still the trade that had brought Arab merchants to the East African coast in the first place: the quest for ivory and for gold. Throughout the later Middle Ages, this exceptionally wealthy trade encouraged the foundation of many Arab commercial settlements along the same coastal strip, including Zanzibar, (flourishing especially in the fifteenth century) and Mombasa (at its peak rather later in the sixteenth). The trade had its effect too in the remoter regions of the interior, particularly at the source of the gold itself in what is now the Zimbabwe high veld. The spectacular stone walls of Great Zimbabwe are probably not medieval. But stone, the natural building material of the region, was certainly in use at Zimbabwe by the fourteenth century, as it was also in a whole series of related settlements nearby, suggesting a fair degree of commercial organization in that part of East Africa, opposite Madagascar, and a relatively sophisticated polity.

Head from Obalara's Land, Ife, Nigeria
Although possibly earlier in date than the 14th-century potsherd pavement near which it was found, this grotesque terracotta head is a fine example of Nigerian Ife sculpture in its "classical" period.

Religion in the islands of South-East Asia
While Theravada Buddhism took firm root on the South-East Asian mainland in the 14th century, Islam spread throughout the islands, propagated by the fast-expanding maritime empire of Malacca. Malaccan traders carried the faith to eastern Sumatra, northern Java, the Spice Islands and Mindanao. Among the islands, the older blend of Hinduism and Buddhism survived only in Western Sumatra and in southern Java.

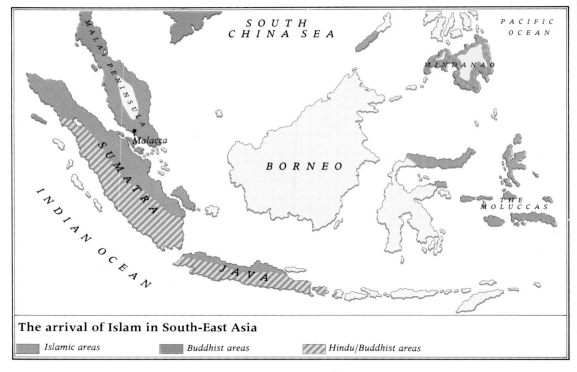

The arrival of Islam in South-East Asia

Islamic areas   Buddhist areas   Hindu/Buddhist areas

We cannot now measure the degree of this sophistication, and the ruins of Great Zimbabwe, remarkable as they are, remain one of the unsolved mysteries of our time. Nevertheless, what both they and the great Arab palace at Husuni Kubwa exemplify is the commercial initiative of the Arab trader and the continuing power of medieval Islam. By the fourteenth century, the greater part of northern and central India was under Muslim rule. The Islamic faith was taking a hold as far afield as the coastal plains of Java, and the Indian Ocean had become by this time little more than an Islamic lake. Something of this is plainly evident in the very common occurrence of Chinese porcelains in East Africa. They have been found even in the interior at Zimbabwe, and were such a familiar component of the pottery assemblage at fourteenth-century Kilwa that they came to outnumber the Islamic wares which, in the previous century, had constituted the dominant import. In this international trading society, Lung-ch'üan celadons, the mass-production of which had continued under the Mongol conquerors of South China, were in common use. But other more refined Chinese export wares have also been found at Kilwa, including the clear white, or *ch'ing-pai*, porcelain of Jao-chou, in northern Kiangsi, a bottle in this ware being a remarkable find from the palace court complex of early-fourteenth-century Husuni Kubwa.

South-East Asia

The export of fine porcelains had been deliberately promoted by the Chinese emperors since the days of the Southern Sung. And the traditional sea route by way of Malacca, on the Malaysian mainland opposite Sumatra, touching southern India and thence to the Persian Gulf and East Africa, became even more important in the later fourteenth century, as Mongol power in Central Asia disintegrated and the overland tracks became once again impassable. A good measure of this trade was carried in Muslim ships, engaged for the most part in the traffic in spices— pepper, nutmeg, cinnamon, mace, cloves, and many more—which were the product especially of southern India, Ceylon, and Indonesia (particularly the Moluccas), and which were as much in demand in late-medieval China as they were in the contemporary West. In the ports along the way, Chinese porcelains and silks found purchasers among the Arab and Indian traders who had come to South-East Asia for the spices, and it was cosmopolitan exchanges of this sort that made the pottery of remote Kiangsi more accessible to the sultans of Muslim Kilwa than the wares of their own Arab homeland.

Of course, trade on such a scale and of such permanence presented many opportunities for Muslim proselytization; it was trade, for example, which brought Islam to Java as early as the thirteenth

Siva Temple, Panataram, Java
The Siva temple at Panataram, completed in 1370, is part of a complex built to house the ashes of the Majapahit princes of East Java. The emphasis is on decorative sculpture rather than monumentality —the building is cubic, in traditionally Indian style; but the pyramidal tower, the grotesque masks over the doors, and the intricate relief carvings of the base are all characteristic of the final pre-Islamic period of Hindu patronage in Java.

Banteai Srei, Cambodia
At Banteai Srei, an elaborate Shaivite temple founded in 1304, and the last Khmer foundation, Khmer decorative sculpture reached its final, most florid form. The carved figures are set in intricate "rococo" niches and surrounded by highly elaborate floral panels.

century. But before Muslim iconoclasm could do for Javanese sculpture what it had already done so disastrously for Indian, there intervened a final phase of Hindu and Buddhist patronage in East Java, begun under the Singhasari rulers of the second half of the thirteenth century, and continued by the Majapahit dynasty in the fourteenth. Of this last flowering under the Majapahits, the principal surviving monuments are the ingenious and original Buddhist shrine of Candi Jabung (c.1354), its unique circular tower rising on the traditional rectangular terraced basement, and the burial complex of the Shaivite rulers of East Java at Panataram, begun earlier in the fourteenth century and completed before 1370.

The Panataram buildings are distinctively Javanese, and they illustrate further two tendencies already noticeable under the thirteenth-century Singhasari rulers —a movement away from the monumentality of the Indian-dominated temple architecture of eighth- and ninth-century Middle Java, and an emphasis, more extravagant than before, on the decorative qualities of sculpture. At Panataram, the sanctuaries built to hold the ashes of the Majapahit rulers are sited irregularly, without any evident order or plan. They were conceived on no more than a modest

scale, and are remarkable not so much for the architectural achievement of such earlier Indonesian monuments as the great Buddhist temple at Barabudur, but for the supreme competence of their decorative mouldings and for their characteristically Javanese sculpture. Prominent in these sculptures are the deliberately grotesque masks which seem to be derived from Javanese drama and the popular art of the folk. They had occurred before over the doorways, blind and real, of the thirteenth-century Singhasari temples, the Jago and the Kidal.

The compression of scale and delight in ornament of fourteenth-century Java were repeated throughout South-East Asia. They are evident, for example, in the elaborately-carved Shaivite sanctuary of Banteai Srei (c. 1304), one of the last monuments of Khmer Cambodia, as also in the originally derivative but increasingly individual architecture of the Thai peoples who had come to dominate both Siam and Cambodia itself. The new Thai capital at Sukhodaya was equipped in the fourteenth century with its own religious buildings, of which the Monastery of the Great Relic (Wat Mahadhatu) is one impressive and characteristic survival. Like others of its period and class, the shrine at the Wat Mahadhatu was approached through a majestic pillared hall, now roofless, which would have held a monumental effigy, or a series of effigies, of the Buddha. This characteristically Hinayana Buddhist emphasis on the power of the Buddha image, picked up from the now Thai-dominated Cambodians, was responsible for the most important development in Thai art of the period: the carving of Buddha heads. At first mainly of stone, they came to be translated increasingly into bronze, with the finest products of the new tradition dating from precisely these centuries of conquest.

In the development of an idealized portrait bust, Siamese art was exploiting a vein of its own. However, there were areas in which the local talent could not reasonably be expected to stand up for long against the pressure of outside competition, and this was particularly evident in pottery. Before the fourteenth century, many Siamese ceramics had been of very acceptable quality, equalling anything in the region. Yet under the flood of Chinese export wares released in South-East Asia during the fourteenth century, they too

Sukhodaya, Siam
*When the Thais
established a state in
Siam at the end of the
13th century, pushing out
the Khmers, they founded
the city of Sukhodaya as
their capital. During the
14th century it was
embellished with religious
foundations, the greatest
of which was Wat
Mahadhatu, the Monastery
of the Great Relic, the
slender, white-tipped
tower of which is visible
in the photograph (right).*

became submerged. Their only reappearance as quality wares in late-medieval Siam was as direct imitations of the better-known Chinese celadons which had captured the market as completely there as in trading economies as far apart as the Philippines, Indonesia, and East Africa.

Far East

Mass-production in the Chinese pottery industry had been common since the Southern Sung promotion of Lung-ch'üan celadons, primarily as a device for raising revenues. And these celadons, along with the white ware known as *ch'ing-pai*, headed the first intensive Chinese export drive in the thirteenth and early fourteenth centuries, encouraging local imitations in those regions, including Siam and South-East Asia in general, to which they most commonly penetrated. However, it was a ware in which the Chinese themselves were essentially the imitators that came ultimately to dominate all exports. The Chinese blue and white wares which are so often described generally as "Ming" had already made their first appearance some decades before the successful establishment of that dynasty by Chu Yüan-chang in 1367-8. And the origins of this now very familiar and characteristically Chinese underglaze painting in cobalt blue were to be found not in China itself but in Persia.

The cobalt pigment, deriving from an ore mined near Kashan in north-central Iran, was shipped to China along the Islamic trade route via India and the Straits of Malacca. In this way, Mongol-protected Persian merchants sought to marry the ancient decorative tradition of the Islamic Near East to the high-quality porcellanous fabrics long since developed in China, and the initial production of Chinese blue and white wares was clearly intended for the Near East market. In the earliest of these wares, that is, the models were Islamic, both in decoration and vessel form. Understandably, the comparative gaudiness of these export pieces, produced specifically for a market very unlike their own, excited the contempt and derision of the more traditional Chinese connoisseurs. But they too, in their time, were converted to the new style, with the not altogether happy result that decoration began to take priority over form. Well before the style's full acceptance in China, achieved by about 1400, the painted blue and white porcelains of the Late Mongol (Yüan) and Early Ming pottery industries had won admirers and purchasers in every market already open to the earliest celadons. A full mastery of the rich underglaze painting technique, at first delayed by the novelty of the imported colouring material, was the last great achievement of Chinese ceramic technology. Most particularly outside China, it won for itself instant acceptance and acclaim.

Within China, the reservations of the connoisseurs spoke well for the sureness of contemporary cultivated taste. To the conservative scholar-nobleman of Southern Sung China, the Mongol Yüan rulers remained unacceptably alien, being of a coarser fibre altogether than the dynasty they had eventually overthrown. The reaction of many of China's more refined spirits was thus not to come to terms with the Mongol conquerors, accommodating though they were, but to wait for better times in seclusion. The middle decades of

the fourteenth century, right up to the establishment of Ming rule, were torn by military upset and by plague. Serious rebellion against the Yüan had begun as early as 1315, continuing sporadically through later decades, and becoming especially threatening to the Mongol regime during the 1330s and 1340s as economic difficulties intensified. In 1331, China is thought to have experienced its first outbreak of the Black Death. Floods on the Yellow River devastated large areas of the richest agricultural land in China, and caused extensive and prolonged famines. More seriously, the Black Death returned again in 1353-4, with a death-toll which, in the contemporary estimate, rose to as much as two-thirds of the pre-plague population in the many provinces it touched.

Certainly, whether by this agency or another, the total population of China, from the great days of the Southern Sung to the ousting of the Mongol conquerors, had been effectively halved. Neither did the restoration of Chinese power under

Chu Yüan-chang, himself only the most successful of the many war-lords who carved out their personal domains in the 1350s, bring any immediate relief. Chu Yüan-chang, called Hung-wu ("Boundless Valour"), was a narrow-minded despot. In his own later years of obsessive tyranny, many of those who had helped him to power at the expense of the Mongols themselves experienced oblivion.

Political rivalries, plague and famine could scarcely have made this century a period of creativity and hope. Nevertheless, Yüan China, if it failed to measure up to the glories of the Sung, was far from barren artistically. Mongol lack of sympathy with the classical Chinese educational system, and with the literary language it promoted, was one of the reasons for the emergence of a more popular vernacular culture in drama, as also in the novel. At the same time, the deliberate withdrawal from Mongol court circles of the cultivated *literati* of Sung China developed in them a new sensitivity especially evident in their paintings. The so-called "literary man's" painting style in fourteenth-century China was a characteristic product of the gentleman-amateur who had washed his hands of the world and its endemic brutalities. Wang Meng, one of the greatest painters from the generation that spanned the take-over of the Yüan by the Ming, died in prison in 1385, a victim of Hung-wu's tyranny. In the dense and agitated brushwork of his landscapes, something of the violence of the period shows through. However, a more familiar reaction to the pressure of the times was that of Wang Meng's slightly older contemporaries, the Taoist gentlemen-painters Wu Chen (1280-1354) and Ni Tsan (1301-74), each of whom withdrew to a recluse-like seclusion, painting chiefly for the delectation of his fellow-religionists and friends. Both Wu Chen and Ni Tsan painted with the great exactness and realistic detail which had become part of the Chinese tradition, and Wu Chen especially was a noted connoisseur of bamboo-painting. Yet where in particular both found their individual expression was in the assured reduction of their landscapes to what they positively wanted to express, and no more. In the work of both painters there was the same sort of economy that characterized the decoration of the most refined Southern Sung celadons. To them, the crowded

Blue and white Yüan plate

Blue and white Ming vase

painted patterns of the contemporary blue and white wares, with their clearly alien inspiration, must have seemed like the ultimate betrayal.

Such an upheaval of values, commonly attributed (although not with complete justice) to the Mongols, provoked an inevitable reaction once the invaders were successfully expelled. The Yüan blue and white wares remained and were perfected, becoming identified in due course with the Ming. But architecturally, especially in the great Ming building period of the fifteenth-century reconstruction of Peking, the inclination was to revert to the earlier "classical" simplicities of the still much-admired T'ang style, with a characteristic emphasis on symmetry of layout and a rejection of such later Sung and Yüan frivolities as the extravagant curving of roofs. Yet it was exactly this unnecessary elaboration of detail, now gradually being abandoned in China, which had found its way with the Zen Buddhist missionaries over the Sea of Japan. An effete and debased Chinese architectural style, relatively short-lived in its country of origin, was thus sedulously preserved as an inalienable element of the first Zen heritage in Japan.

Zen Buddhism had come to Japan during the full vigour of the thirteenth-century Kamakura shogunate, and to a large degree it was the austerity of Zen that had appealed to the warrior rulers. Yet Zen's popularity among court circles in Southern Sung China had caused the early monasteries at Hangchow to be associated with a rich and elaborate culture, to the more extravagant architectural manifestations of which they were thereafter linked by tradition. The *Karayo*, or "Chinese", style in Japanese architecture had initially been a Zen-inspired import of the later thirteenth century. In the fourteenth century, it yielded such characteristically ornate structures as the Kaisando (1352), a memorial chapel at the Eihoji monastery, near Nagoya east of Kyoto, where the system of bracketing was taken to such lengths as to make it far more decorative than functional. But this was only one manifestation among many of the pervasive Chinese influences on the arts of Japan which the cultural sterility of the Mongol-threatened years had already done much to let in. And the political decay of the Kamakura shogunate later pushed these tendencies still further.

The Kamakura system in its better years had relied on the feudal loyalty, now difficult to sustain, of its original Minamoto retainers. Moreover, the prolonged prospect of a Mongol invasion had imposed intolerable strains on the military classes, increasingly released in private warfare as Kamakura leadership weakened and as the ambitions of the old imperial families at Kyoto were gradually allowed to revive. In the event, the attempt to restore imperial rule under Go-Daigo in the 1330s proved abortive. However, the rebellion begun in his name in 1331 led instead to the establishment in 1338 of the Ashikaga shogunate based at Kyoto, the imperial capital, again under the merely nominal suzerainty of a puppet emperor chosen from Go-Daigo's rivals.

Neither Takauji, the founder of the new shogunate, nor any of his Ashikaga successors were ever fully successful in imposing their rule on the whole feudal class of Japan. And one of the more obvious consequences of this political impotence was to turn the Ashikaga shogunate in upon itself, reducing the shoguns to that same decorative round of court ceremonial and pleasure to which they had consigned the emperors. Significantly enough, the period as a whole is usually called the Muromachi Period (lasting until 1573), taking its name from that quarter of Kyoto in which the Ashikaga built their luxurious palaces. Here, one of the most characteristic of the Muromachi monuments is the restored Golden Pavilion (Kinkakuji) on a lakeside in Kyoto, built for the personal delectation of Yoshimitsu, the third Ashikaga shogun and a notable aesthete in his own right, shortly after his retirement from the shogunate (see page 176).

The Golden Pavilion, erected in 1397, was a graceful three-storeyed building, combining the functions of villa and Zen chapel, in which both Chinese and Japanese architectural traditions were brought together with very evident good taste and harmony. Yoshimitsu became a Zen monk in his retirement, and his personal devotion to Zen principles was symptomatic of the effect on Japanese culture produced by the very general reception of Zen Buddhist teachings in shogunal and imperial circles at Kyoto. To be sure, the fullest development of the Japanese monochrome ink-painting style did not occur before the fifteenth century, in the works of such

Zen-inspired masters as Josetsu, Shubun, and Sesshu. Nevertheless, well before their time, the austerely immediate paintings of Mu-ch'i and other thirteenth-century Chinese masters had been much admired in Japan, and were beginning to inspire imitations. The shogun Yoshimitsu was himself a collector of Mu-ch'i's work. Among Japanese artists of the fourteenth century, Mokuan and Ryozen were successful painters in the Zen ink style, the former being often compared with Mu-ch'i. In a rather different medium, the realistic full-colour portrait of the Zen master Muso Soseki (d. 1351) by Muto Shui, his disciple, was both representative of a very common Zen practice and itself outstanding in quality (see page 176).

Certainly, the cultural aestheticism of Zen evoked a response in both Kamakura and Ashikaga Japan which cannot be explained in historical terms alone. The restraint, the tranquillity, and the sophisticated simplicity, already apparent in Heian art of the eleventh century and before, became, under the influence of Zen, the permanent ideals of Japanese culture and even, insofar as such generalizations can ever be true of a people as a whole, a part of the national temperament. In this, of course, the Japanese remain unique, to be much admired by those in the West who would strive to achieve the same.

The Americas

In political terms, both Central and South America in the fourteenth century were standing on the brink of change. The great Aztec civilization of Mexico and the Inca empire of Peru were just around the corner, the former's aggressive expansion from Tenochtitlán beginning already some decades before 1400. What was left of the Maya of Central America and even the better-organized Chimu of Peru were ultimately helpless against such pressures, yet both still experienced in the fourteenth century a final flowering of their cultures. In Central America, to the south of those areas later dominated by the Aztecs even at their greatest extent, there were the impressive walled cities and ceremonial complexes of Cahyup, Tulum, and Mayapán. In Peru, the more sophisticated enclosures of the Chimu capital at Chanchan are as likely to date from the fourteenth and early fifteenth centuries as they are from the thirteenth or earlier. In

all of these, the characteristically elaborate art of pre-Columbian America was continued in the manufacture of artefacts in stone, pottery, and precious metals which, because of their repetition of the traditional motifs, are often very difficult to date. Even in the remoter areas of the South American continent, for example at Santarém on the Lower Amazon, the decorative potential of modelled clay was exploited from about this period in the extraordinary modelling of bowls and jars which can only have been ceremonial in function. Unusual though they were, the position of these within the cultural context of southern Central America is definitively established by the accompanying figures, which had very clear Panamanian echoes.

This rich ceremonial life of the Americas, before the arrival of Christianity with the Spaniards, is just as plainly to be seen in the *pueblo*-style ruins and their accompanying artefacts in the North American Southwest. Mexican influence is very obvious in the platform mounds and ball courts of the Tardio Period (post-1300) at the impressive building complex at Casas Grandes. Yet there continued to be a uniformity of material culture over the whole Southwest region, taking in the Mogollon, the Hohokam, and the Anasazi, in which the dominant influences were clearly derived at least as much from the North as from the South. On the precise relationships of one culture with another the arguments are still continuing, the dating of their buildings and associated artefacts being as yet far from clear. Nevertheless, there is a plain family likeness between the delightful black-on-white painted vessels of the Mimbres style of the Mogollon Period 5 and the contemporary Anasazi pottery of the later Pueblo Periods. Moreover, both the Mogollon and the Anasazi wares were very close in design to the Tardio polychrome vessels of the Chihuahua site at Casas Grandes. And all three traditions, linked already by their distinctive apartment-house architecture, have yielded similar assemblages of stone tools, basketwork, and jewellery. With Pueblo IV of the Anasazi, with Mogollon 5, and with the Tardio Period at Casas Grandes, the often spectacular artistic tradition of the North American Southwest continued right through to the historic period of early-modern European contact.

American pottery
At Santarém on the lower Amazon, sophisticated modelled wares were produced in the 14th century, light tan or buff in colour, supported by a caryatid base. In the North American Southwest, Hohokam potters in the final phase of their culture produced red-on-buff wares decorated with graceful geometric and human designs.

Hohokam pot

Santarém bowl

World Architecture

Following the reversals and humiliations it had suffered under the Mongols, Islam's recovery in the fourteenth century was both swift and very comprehensive. In particular, it was characterized by the first Ottoman expansion through Asia Minor and up into the Balkans. But this was the period of the furthest extension of the Delhi Sultanate with the empire of Muhammad bin Tughlug, as it was of the most systematic settlement and exploitation of the Islamic East African coast. Consequential to this new self-confidence was a revival of religious building. In Delhi itself, the Tughlug period was commemorated in a fine series of monumental tombs, massive and almost fortress-like in their construction. While both at Delhi and at Bursa, the Ottoman capital in Anatolia, the monumentality of the sultans' mausolea was repeated again in their mosques.

In Africa, secular building in the fourteenth century has left impressive remains in the Islamic palace complex at Husuni Kubwa, with some of the earlier defences at the mysterious inland city of Zimbabwe being datable also to this century. The Peruvian city of the Chimu at Chanchan was similarly at just this time reaching the highest tide of its development. Nevertheless, it was in religious architecture, above all, that the century made its mark, whether this be seen in the Orthodox Christian cathedrals and monastery churches of Russian Novgorod and Pskov, in the Buddhist shrines of Siamese Sukhodaya, or in the platform mounds and ball courts of the Chihuahua settlement at Casas Grandes, on the borders of Mexico and the North American Southwest.

Undoubtedly the most sophisticated of the religious buildings of the period were those of Zen-influenced Japan. It is true that there is little functional purpose in the elaborate ''Chinese'' timber bracketing that supports the roof of the Kaisando memorial chapel at Eihoji. However, the same Zen ideals that had brought to Japan some of the more extravagant expressions of the Southern Sung architecture of Hangchow were also responsible for the much purer work of the Muromachi Period, as exemplified by the shogun Yoshimitsu's Golden Pavilion (Kinkakuji), built in 1397 as both chapel and villa for the third shogun in the Ashikaga line, by then a Zen monk in his retirement.

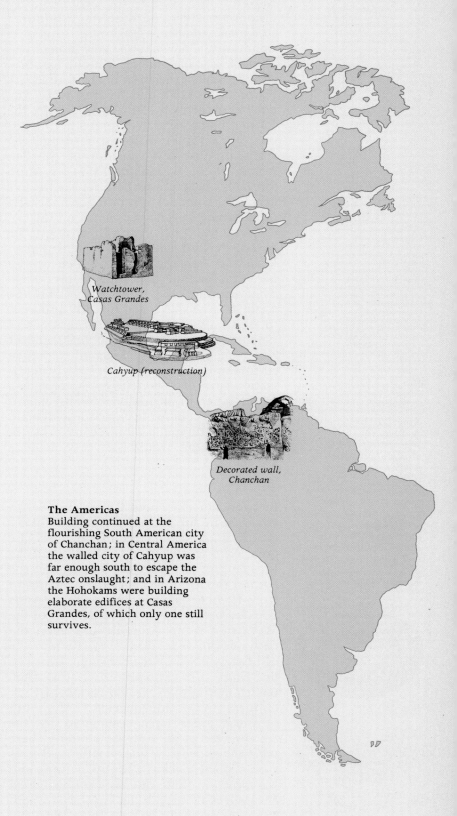

Watchtower, Casas Grandes

Cahyup (reconstruction)

Decorated wall, Chanchan

The Americas
Building continued at the flourishing South American city of Chanchan; in Central America the walled city of Cahyup was far enough south to escape the Aztec onslaught; and in Arizona the Hohokams were building elaborate edifices at Casas Grandes, of which only one still survives.

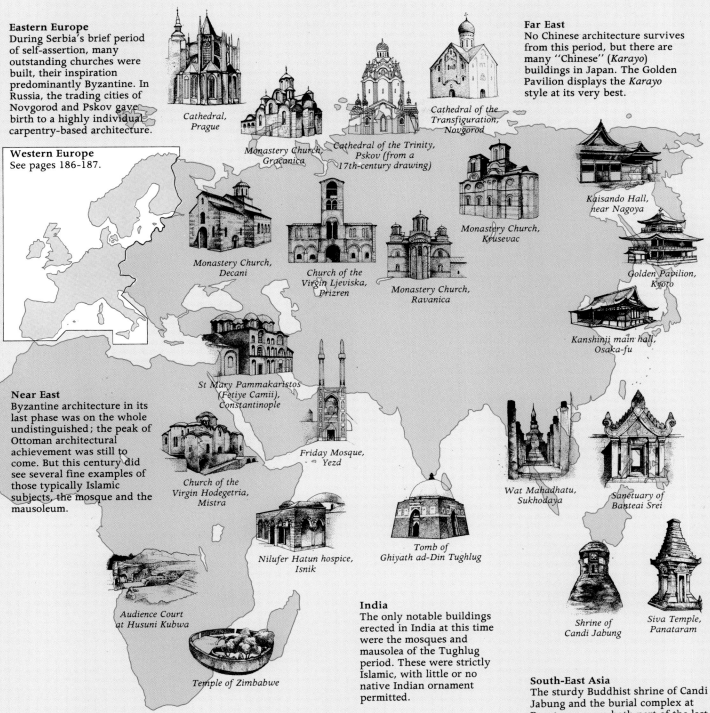

Eastern Europe
During Serbia's brief period of self-assertion, many outstanding churches were built, their inspiration predominantly Byzantine. In Russia, the trading cities of Novgorod and Pskov gave birth to a highly individual carpentry-based architecture.

Far East
No Chinese architecture survives from this period, but there are many "Chinese" (*Karayo*) buildings in Japan. The Golden Pavilion displays the *Karayo* style at its very best.

Cathedral, Prague

Monastery Church, Gracanica

Cathedral of the Trinity, Pskov (from a 17th-century drawing)

Cathedral of the Transfiguration, Novgorod

Kaisando Hall, near Nagoya

Western Europe
See pages 186-187.

Monastery Church, Decani

Church of the Virgin Ljeviska, Prizren

Monastery Church, Ravanica

Monastery Church, Krusevac

Golden Pavilion, Kyoto

Kanshinji main hall, Osaka-fu

Near East
Byzantine architecture in its last phase was on the whole undistinguished; the peak of Ottoman architectural achievement was still to come. But this century did see several fine examples of those typically Islamic subjects, the mosque and the mausoleum.

St Mary Pammakaristos (Fetiye Camii), Constantinople

Church of the Virgin Hodegetria, Mistra

Friday Mosque, Yezd

Nilufer Hatun hospice, Isnik

Tomb of Ghiyath ad-Din Tughlug

Wat Mahadhatu, Sukhodaya

Sanctuary of Banteai Srei

India
The only notable buildings erected in India at this time were the mosques and mausolea of the Tughlug period. These were strictly Islamic, with little or no native Indian ornament permitted.

Audience Court at Husuni Kubwa

Temple of Zimbabwe

Shrine of Candi Jabung

Siva Temple, Panataram

South-East Asia
The sturdy Buddhist shrine of Candi Jabung and the burial complex at Panataram were both part of the last Javanese flowering before the arrival of Islam. The relatively modest scale of these buildings is repeated at the Cambodian Banteai Srei, and at Wat Mahadhatu in the new Thai capital of Sukhodaya.

Africa
The east coast had been greatly enriched by Arab trade; this new wealth financed both the magnificent Arab palace of Husuni Kubwa and the native stone settlements of Zimbabwe.

Western European Architecture

Architectural development in fourteenth-century Europe was curiously uneven and dispersed. By a freak of geography and of conquest, it included the extraordinary palace of the Alhambra, the focal point of the surviving Muslim kingdom of Granada. Yet in Northern Europe, and in Italy too, architectural initiatives were at a standstill. The Black Death and economic recession were both especially damaging to what had been centres of wealth.

If there was progress at all in church-building in the fourteenth century, it came rather from England, where the native development of the Perpendicular style was still assisted by major building projects. One of these was on the choir and cloister of the abbey church at Gloucester, financed out of the profits from a lucrative cult of the remains of the murdered Edward II.

French patronage was contemporaneously diverted to the building of the lavish fortress-palaces of the Valois kings and royal dukes. Among these, Jean de Berry was outstanding, with major works to his credit at Poitiers and Saumur, as well as the now vanished fairy-tale Mehun-sur-Yèvre. But his elder brother, Charles V, was almost equally ambitious, completing John II's castle at Vincennes as only one of a programme of expensive works.

Spain
The palace of the Alhambra was the last and greatest achievement of the Muslims in Spain. Both fortified citadel and pleasure pavilion, the palace concentrated on open courts, and made much use of fountains, pools, gardens and shaded arcades.

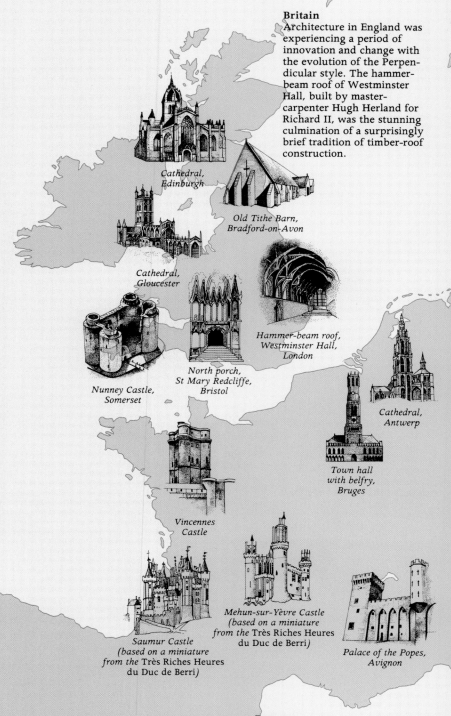

Britain
Architecture in England was experiencing a period of innovation and change with the evolution of the Perpendicular style. The hammer-beam roof of Westminster Hall, built by master-carpenter Hugh Herland for Richard II, was the stunning culmination of a surprisingly brief tradition of timber-roof construction.

Cathedral, Edinburgh

Old Tithe Barn, Bradford-on-Avon

Cathedral, Gloucester

Hammer-beam roof, Westminster Hall, London

North porch, St Mary Redcliffe, Bristol

Nunney Castle, Somerset

Cathedral, Antwerp

Town hall with belfry, Bruges

Vincennes Castle

Mehun-sur-Yèvre Castle (based on a miniature from the Très Riches Heures du Duc de Berri*)*

Saumur Castle (based on a miniature from the Très Riches Heures du Duc de Berri*)*

Palace of the Popes, Avignon

Court of the Myrtles in the Alhambra, Granada

France
The papacy, powerful in France during its period of residence at Avignon, was based in an austere and impenetrable palace, protected by the walls of a fortified town. This palace was in sharp contrast to the great castles of the French aristocracy, which were above all intended to be luxurious residences.

Low Countries
The largest cathedral in Belgium was begun at Antwerp, with its dominating tower (not completed until 1519) standing 400 feet high. The emphasis was again on height in many Flemish secular buildings, their huge and ornate belfries a distinctive feature of Flemish Gothic.

Italy
Italian buildings reflected diverse influences. Milan Cathedral and S. Maria della Spina have the feel of northern European churches, while oriental influence is clear in the façade of the Doge's Palace. The ambitious church of S. Petronio was never completed; it was built originally with the intention of outclassing Florence Cathedral (the campanile of which was designed by Giotto).

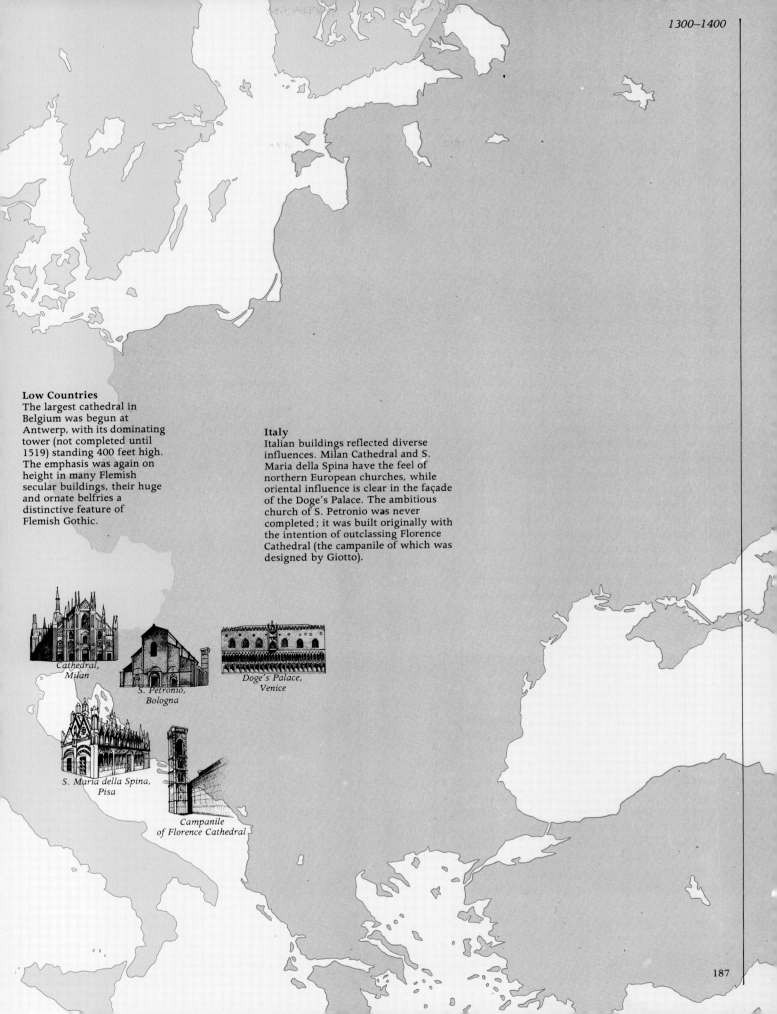

Cathedral, Milan

S. Petronio, Bologna

Doge's Palace, Venice

S. Maria della Spina, Pisa

Campanile of Florence Cathedral

World Art

There is the broadest of contrasts in fourteenth-century art between the disillusioned sophistication of the painters of Byzantium and China on the one hand, and the vigorous exuberance of the craftsmen-potters of Ife in Nigeria on the other. All belonged to an antique tradition, but whereas the potters very clearly worked within their own times, meeting the demand of an active local market, the painters just as obviously turned their backs on an age which could offer them little but disappointment. Byzantine art of the Palaeologue Revival is characterized by a sweet and melancholy tenderness which seems to reflect the escapism of a society watching still from the security of Constantinople the crumbling of a once great empire. In China, the "literary man's" painting was an introverted art— the art of the gentleman-recluse who painted principally for friends.

Of course, the Greek and the Chinese traditions in art were too strong to be merely backward-looking. It was a Byzantine artist, Theophanes the Greek, who brought new life to the Russian fresco-painters of late-fourteenth-century Novgorod and Moscow. And even while the more sophisticated spirits of fourteenth-century China rejected the barbarities of the Mongol capital at Peking, the opening of the trade routes across Central Asia to Mongol-controlled Persia had brought to potters of the Yüan and Ming periods a precious new infusion of technique. The Chinese blue and white wares, which would shortly become so much in demand in every export market to which they penetrated, were painted in a cobalt pigment that was mined near Kashan, in Persia. It had been under Mongol sponsorship that the traffic in cobalt had begun, with Chinese wares, painted in the colours already traditional in the Near East, making the return journey to these markets.

Other painted pottery of great vigour and distinction, although within an entirely separate tradition, was contemporaneously being produced in the North American Southwest, including the Mimbres wares of Mogollon Period 5 and the Tardio Period polychromes of Casas Grandes. Pottery of this kind was only one of a variety of equally active crafts, among them stone-working, jewellery-making, basketry, and weaving.

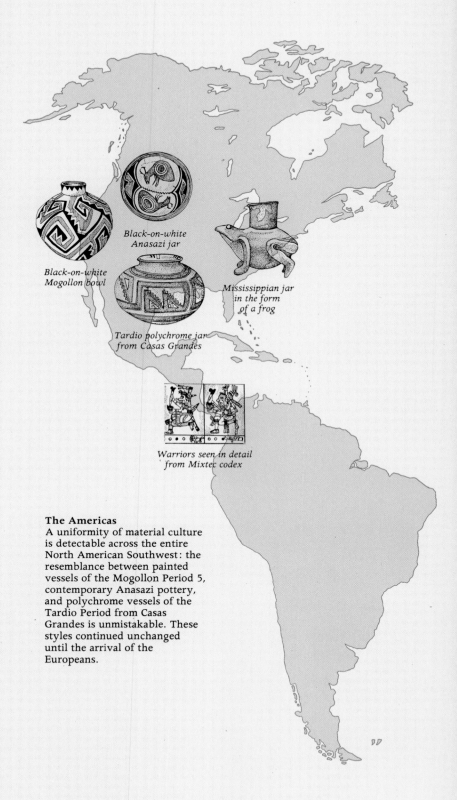

Black-on-white Anasazi jar

Black-on-white Mogollon bowl

Mississippian jar in the form of a frog

Tardio polychrome jar from Casas Grandes

Warriors seen in detail from Mixtec codex

The Americas
A uniformity of material culture is detectable across the entire North American Southwest: the resemblance between painted vessels of the Mogollon Period 5, contemporary Anasazi pottery, and polychrome vessels of the Tardio Period from Casas Grandes is unmistakable. These styles continued unchanged until the arrival of the Europeans.

Eastern Europe

The earthy portraiture of the Bohemian Master Theodoric stood out in a Prague much affected by Western Gothic. A similar native vigour existed in Serbian frescoes. In Russia itself the work of Theophanes the Greek made a long-term impact.

St Matthew, *panel-painting by Master Theodoric*

The Crucifixion, *wall-painting by Astrapas*

Fresco of the Virgin, *Gracanica*

Fresco by *Theophanes the Greek, Novgorod*

The Assembly of the Apostles, *Russian icon*

Icon of the Archangel Gabriel, *Decani*

Far East

The agitated landscapes of the Chinese painter Wang Meng were exceptional among his contemporaries. In Japan, the ink works of Mokuan and Ryozen reflected the strength of Zen Buddhism.

Porcelain *vessel*

Landscape painting *by Wang Meng, detail*

Painting *of heron by Ryozen*

Western Europe

See pages 190–191.

Mosaic, *Kariye Camii, Constantinople*

Syrian glass *mosque lamp*

Kashan *lustreware wall-tile*

Group of Ladies at a Spring Festival, *Ming painting*

Samurai *suit of armour*

Near East

The Ottoman preoccupation with conquest meant that their art differed little from that of the Seljuks 200 years earlier. It was Byzantium, despite its decline, whose art included mosaics and frescoes of the highest quality.

Mosaic in the dome of Fetiye Camii, *Constantinople*

Syrian glazed *earthenware jar*

Yüan *blue and white plate*

Hotei *by Mokuan*

Africa

The pottery vessels set into stone-and-potsherd pavements in Obalara's Land continued the exotic sculptural tradition of Nigerian Ife, well advanced by now into its "classical" period. On the east coast, Christian Ethiopian art was undergoing a late flowering.

Potsherd pavement, *Obalara's Land, Ife*

Terracotta head, *Obalara's Land, Ife*

Ethiopian *manuscript illumination*

Pottery vessel, *Obalara's Land, Ife*

Siamese *Buddha figure*

Carvings *from Banteai Srei*

Stone head of Kali *from Candi Jago*

South-East Asia

A widespread delight in ornament ranged across South-East Asia, from the Javanese shrine of Candi Jago to the elaborate carvings of the Cambodian sanctuary of Banteai Srei. Meanwhile Siamese art, like Cambodian art before it, laid stress on the power of the Buddha image.

Western European Art

The crossing and exchange of cultural influences in fourteenth-century European art resulted in a new kind of internationalism. Beyond this unity there were, of course, outsiders. The extraordinary art of Hispano-Moresque potters, even in reconquered Spain, had an obvious Arab derivation. Nevertheless, the major painters and sculptors of the European West were learning very swiftly from each other. Giotto, the great master of the Early Renaissance in Italy, was an experimentalist and an innovator in his own right. Yet even he must have owed a good part of the realism and plasticity of his painted figures to the model of the High Gothic sculptors of the North. In the contemporary work of Duccio and Simone Martini in Siena, or of Jean Pucelle, the French royal painter in Paris, the cross-currents are still more apparent.

The delicacy and refinement of Duccio and the French court painters, which were the most obvious characteristics of Gothic art, are repeated in the Wilton Diptych, an important Anglo-French work of much iconographic significance. But in both painting and sculpture, from 1400 and before, the idealization of the earlier court styles would yield increasingly to realism. High Gothic sentimentalism, for all its charm, was soon to be brushed aside.

Spain
Although only Granada was left of Muslim Spain, the influence and excellence of Arab art remained strong. Even under Christian rule, Muslim potters were producing ceramics for export all over Europe.

Britain
The Anglo-French court of Richard II was much preoccupied by costume, heraldry and status, all present in the Wilton Diptych. Paradoxically, the effects of the plague led to a simultaneous cult of death.

The Three Living and the Three Dead, wall-painting, Peakirk Church

Pottery knight-jug

Gothic embroidery (Opus Anglicanum)

Wilton Diptych

Royal seal of King Edward III

Syon Cope (Opus Anglicanum)

Brass figure of the Black Prince, from his tomb in Canterbury Cathedral

Silver-gilt statue of Virgin and Child, St-Denis

Ivory statue of Virgin and Child, Sainte Chapelle

Gold cup given to King Charles VI by Jean de Berry

Page of the Belleville Breviary by Jean Pucelle

Detail of an "Apocalypse" tapestry at Angers

Fireplace in the Great Hall of Poitiers Castle

Saintonge pottery wine-jug

Valencian drug-jar

Ornamental calligraphy from the Alhambra, Granada

Stucco ornament from the Alhambra, Granada

France
There was money to spare for art: costly Gothic sculptures were added to the treasures of St-Denis and Sainte Chapelle. Jean de Berry's triple fireplace at Poitiers and Louis of Anjou's *Apocalypse* tapestries at Angers were both products of the wealthy aristocracy's discerning patronage. The miniatures of the royal painter Jean Pucelle were directly influenced by the Italian Duccio.

*Detail of wooden
Haekendover Retable*

*Embroidery
of the
Crucifixion*

*Siege warfare depicted
in a Book of Hours
executed at Maastricht*

Low Countries
Sculptures, manuscript
illuminations and tapestries
were all showing Gothic
characteristics, the direct
result of the artists' close
contact with France.

*Detail of shrine
at Nuremberg*

*Wooden carving
of Christ
and St John*

*Detail from a copy of
the Golden Bull*

Germany
Wood-carvings and
manuscript illuminations
from this period were the
first to be part of a Gothic
rather than a Byzantine
tradition.

Italy
The Sienese painters Duccio and
Simone Martini were foremost in
establishing a cosmopolitan court
style closely linked with French
manuscript illumination. In Giotto a
new element is present: his aware-
ness of space, form and proportion
were crucial to the 15th-century
classical revival.

*The Nativity,
scene from the
Pisa pulpit of
Giovanni Pisano*

*The Marriage at Cana,
fresco by Giotto*

*Detail of saints
and angels from the
Maesta by Duccio*

Umbrian reliquary

*St Louis Altar
by Simone Martini*

*Silk and silver-gilt
patterned singlet*

	Events and developments	People	Technology
Western Europe	Devastation of Europe by Black Death (bubonic plague) from 1347. Start of 100 Years War between England and France (1337). Golden Bull of Charles IV (1356). Social unrest caused by agricultural depression; Peasants' Revolt, England (1381), also revolts in France, Flanders, Italy. Bankruptcy of 2 Florentine banking houses.	Dante Alighieri, Italian poet, (1265-1321). Giotto, Italian painter and architect, (d. 1337?). Charles IV, Holy Roman Emperor 1355-78. Geoffrey Chaucer, English poet, (?1340-1400).	Gunpowder in use (1313). Paper and silk mills; wind-driven tower mills. Sluices, locks and weirs. Introduction of steel crossbow. Use of artillery; introduction of plate armour.
Far East	Plague in northern China (1331). Overthrow of Mongol Yüan dynasty by national Ming dynasty (1368). Establishment of Nanking as Ming capital by Hung-wu. Civil war against Hojo regents in Japan; beginning of Ashikaga (Muromachi) era (1336).	Chu Yüan-chang, called Hung-wu, Chinese Emperor 1368-98.	Water-powered machinery used for the manufacture of iron and silk in China.
South-East Asia	Siamese invasion of Cambodia. Establishment of Muslim trading centres, based on trade in spices, at Malacca; the Moluccas (Spice Islands); Arakan (Burma); Mindanao (southern Philippines). Rise of Majapahit kingdom in Java: extensive commercial empire.		
India	Delhi Sultanate at greatest extent under Muhammad bin Tughlug; disintegration of Sultanate towards end of his reign. Tamerlane's invasion of northwest India, as far as Delhi (1398-99).		Department of agriculture set up, because of widespread famine.
Near East	Rise of Ottoman Turks in northwest Anatolia; establishment of Edirne (Adrianople) as their capital. Last Byzantine possessions in Asia Minor lost to Turks (1390). Conquest of Baghdad by Tamerlane.	Osman I, founder of Ottoman Empire 1290-1326. Tamerlane, also known as Timur, descendant of Genghis Khan, (d. 1405).	*Correction of the Optics*, including theory about the rainbow, by Arab writer Al-Farisi.
Eastern Europe	Defeat of Tartars by Dmitry IV of Moscow at Kulikovo (1380). Alliance of Poland and Lithuania under Jagiello (1386). Creation of Greater Serbia under Stephen Dusan. Loss of Serbia to Turks at battle of Kossovo (1389). End of 2nd Bulgarian Empire as a result of Ottoman attacks.	Casimir the Great, King of Poland 1333-70. Stephen Dusan, King of Serbia 1335-46. Ivan I, Grand Duke of Russia, (d. 1341). Grand Prince Jagiello, later King Vladislav II of Poland 1386-1434.	
Africa	Marinid dynasty of Morocco (1296-1470). Apogee of Mali Empire under Musa, after subjugation of Songhai Empire. Exploration of Sahara by Ibn Battuta, Arab traveller. Brilliant culture of Timbuktu.	Ibn Battuta of Tangier, traveller, (1304-77). *Mansa* Musa, ruler of Mali 1312-37. Ibn Khaldun, greatest Arab historian, (1332-1406).	
The Americas	Founding of Tenochtitlán by Aztecs (about 1325). Expansion of Maya trade. Last flowering of Chimu Empire. Origins of Inca power; establishment of Quechua as official language.	Acamapitzin elected first Aztec king (1352).	

Religion	Architecture	Art and music	Literature and learning
"Babylonian Captivity": exile of popes at Avignon (1309-77). Great Schism of the West: papacy split between Rome and Avignon, from 1378. Popes attacked as "Antichrists" by English reformer John Wycliffe. Growth of popular mystical movement in Germany, under influence of theologian Meister Eckehart.	Cloister, Gloucester Cathedral; hammer-beam roof, Westminster Hall. Doge's Palace, Venice; Campanile, Florence; Milan Cathedral. Papal Palace, Avignon. Saumur, Vincennes, Poitiers. The Alhambra, Granada.	Wilton Diptych. Giotto's frescoes, Arena Chapel, Padua; Giovanni Pisano's pulpit, Pisa Cathedral; Duccio's *Maesta* altarpiece, Siena Cathedral. Guillaume de Machaut's "ars nova" style Mass. "Apocalypse" tapestries, Angers.	Dante's *Divina Commedia*; Boccaccio's *Decameron*; Petrarch's *Rime sparse*. Chaucer's *Canterbury Tales*; *Piers Plowman*, attributed to William Langland. Wycliffe's English Bible. Gower's *Confessio Amantis*. Jean Froissart's *Chronicles*.
Zen Buddhism and Shinto in Japan.	Restoration of Great Wall of China. Kaisando memorial chapel, Eihoji monastery, near Nagoya; Golden Pavilion, Kyoto, Japan.	Chinese paintings of Wang Meng, Wu Chen and Ni Tsan; Japanese paintings of Muto Shui.	Drama in China: Li Hsing Tao's play *The Chalk Circle*. Development of Noh plays in Japan.
Islamic faith established on South-East Asian islands as result of Muslim trade.	Buddhist shrine of Candi Jabung; burial complex, Panataram, Cambodia. Monastery of the Great Relic (Wat Mahadhatu), Sukhodaya, Siam.		
Hinduism once more predominant through most of India after collapse of Muslim Delhi Sultanate.	Tughlug tombs, Delhi. Great Mosque, Gulbarga. Durbar hall, Hindola Mahall, Mandu.		
Hesychast Controversy in Greek Orthodox Church (1341-51); conflict between mystic teachings (from Mt Athos) and rationalism of clergy.	St Mary Pammakaristos (Fetiye Camii); Great Mosque, Bursa, Turkey.	Mosaics and frescoes, Kariye Camii, Constantinople.	Richness of Byzantine culture during Palaeologue revival; contributions to thought and learning of Planudes Maximus, monk and scholar, and Gemistus Pletho, Platonic philosopher. Persian poet Hafiz, chief work, *Divan*.
Lectures on theology at Prague University by the reformer Jan Hus (1398).	Church of St Theodore Stratilates; Cathedral of the Transfiguration, Novgorod, Russia. Gracanica monastery church, Serbia.	Icons and frescoes by Theophanes the Greek (Cathedral of the Transfiguration, Novgorod). Byzantine influence in Serbia, Bulgaria and Russia.	Universities of Prague and Cracow founded.
Musa's pilgrimage to Mecca (1324). Ethiopia: search initiated by Pope to find legendary Christian king, Prester John; carried out by 8 Dominicans, (1316).	Sankore mosque, Timbuktu, West Africa. Arab palace, Husuni Kubwa, East Africa.	"Classical" period of sculpture at Ife, Nigeria.	Accounts of Mali's civilization and scholarship by Ibn Khaldun and Ibn Battuta.

The Fifteenth Century

Map of the world
This map was executed in 1500 by Juan de la Cosa, a Spaniard who took part in the first two voyages of Columbus. The map is believed to be the first on which the lands discovered by Columbus were considered part of a New World. On the left of the map Columbus himself can be made out in the guise of St Christopher, holding a staff.

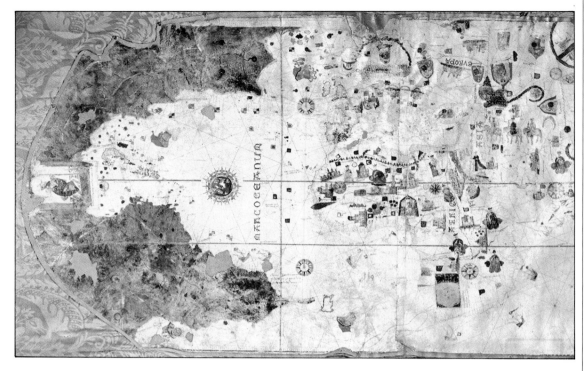

Pizarro and Cortes
In 1519 Hernan Cortes (1485-1547) landed in Mexico with 500 men and conquered the Aztec empire of Montezuma in two years. Francisco Pizarro (1475-1541) invaded Peru in 1531, with 180 men, and destroyed the Inca empire.

Hernan Cortes

Francisco Pizarro

PREVIOUS PAGE
Machu Picchu
The Inca city of Machu Picchu, high in the Andes, was never found by the Spaniards and remained unseen by Europeans until 1912.

Historical Context

Few of those who survived the plagues and depression of the late fourteenth century can have looked forward with any confidence to the fifteenth. Nevertheless, before the end of it, the Renaissance had flowered in the Italian cities and had begun to penetrate the North; technology had taken a leap forward of its own; and Columbus had discovered the Americas.

The new world revealed by Columbus' voyages had a long ancestry of its own. Yet one of the most significant characteristics of the great civilizations that astonished the Spanish adventurers Cortes and Pizarro was that they were themselves comparatively young.

Although the Aztecs had arrived in the Valley of Mexico as early as the mid-thirteenth century, they had then lived for over a century in obscurity and subjection before fleeing to an island refuge on Lake Texcoco, subsequently developed by them into their capital city of Tenochtitlán (Mexico City). Similarly, the Peruvian Incas of Cuzco, highly organized and aggressive though they already were in the fourteenth century, were still not powerful enough to embark on a systematic campaign of conquest of their neighbours until the very end of that century. Both the Aztecs of Mexico and the Incas of Peru built their great empires in somewhat less than a hundred years.

What distinguished the Incas was sophistication of government to a quite unusual degree, and this enabled them to construct a dominion unequalled in extent throughout the whole known history of the pre-Columbian civilizations of America. It was not the Incas who converted the Andean peoples to urban living; fortified towns, many of stone and some of a considerable size, had become a characteristic of the region well before the period of Inca expansion. Nevertheless, it was the Inca road and communication system which kept their great empire together. And something of the quality of their extraordinary organization, through territories generally hostile to any such centralized rule, can be appreciated if it is recalled that the Spaniards never reached the Inca mountain-top city of Machu Picchu, discovered only in 1911, after a full four centuries of Spanish colonial rule.

The driving force behind the Aztecs, however, was both different and altogether more terrible. The practice of human sacrifice was central to the Aztec belief in the annual refreshment and renewal of their gods, claiming victims in numbers that became so large that they could only be gathered in by conquest. Just before the collapse of the Aztec tyranny, this sacrificial toll, without which the light of the sun would go out and the harvest wither on the stem, had risen, some claim, to as many as 50,000.

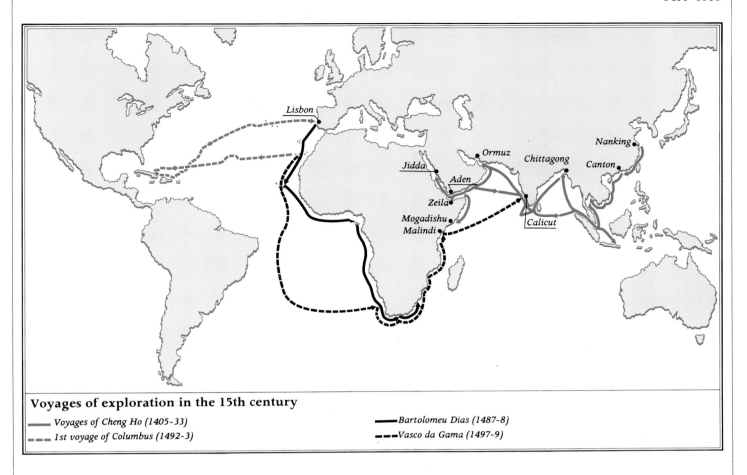

Voyages of exploration in the 15th century

―――― *Voyages of Cheng Ho (1405-33)*
- - - - *1st voyage of Columbus (1492-3)*

━━━━ *Bartolomeu Dias (1487-8)*
▬ ▬ ▬*Vasco da Gama (1497-9)*

15th-century explorers
In the 15th century the sea routes of the world began to be opened up. Cheng Ho, the Ming admiral, reached East Africa and the Red Sea from China in the early part of the century. Looking for a south-western route to China in 1492, Christopher Columbus discovered the West Indies for Spain. Sailing south-east from Portugal, Bartolomeu Dias reached the Indian Ocean round the Cape of Good Hope on his voyage of 1487-88, and a decade later his compatriot Vasco da Gama reached India by the same route.

These empires were not brought down by the Spaniards alone. Expansion in each case had been too rapid. Government was over-extended, while enemies had been made whose hostility to the empires was even greater than their fear of the incoming Spaniards. Over the centuries, too, population on the continent had risen to such a degree that the more favoured regions—in Mexico especially and in coastal Chile and Peru—were now significantly overcrowded. Dense populations like these were harvested by the Aztecs for their victims. But their very density also exposed them to the ravages of imported disease. Cortes and Pizarro both consolidated their conquests on the wings of an epidemic of smallpox, to which they, as Europeans, could be counted relatively immune. Other epidemic diseases, many of which, like mumps and measles, meant little in their European homelands, helped to cut the Amerindians down.

Just a century after the fall of Tenochtitlán to the Spaniards in 1521, the population of what had been a mighty empire in Mexico, something like thirty million strong, had been reduced to just over a million and a half.

The demographic catastrophe of the Americas, more extreme than any other known to history, is undoubtedly the principal explanation for Spain's profound cultural impact on the newly-discovered continent. And, indeed, something of the same effect was also achieved, if with slightly less drastic consequences, in those other areas of the little-known world to which Europeans were beginning to penetrate from quite early in the fifteenth century. Portuguese voyages of exploration down the west coast of Africa followed shortly after the capture of Ceuta in 1415 had established a bridgehead for Christendom on what had long been the exclusive territory of Islam. But Ceuta was also a gold port: one of the principal Mediterranean outlets of the trans-Sahara trade. And what started as an incident in the Christian *Reconquista* of Iberia ended with the promotion of a Portuguese interest in the hitherto Muslim-controlled trades of Africa, which had permanent political consequences. By the 1480s, the Portuguese were establishing permanent bases of their own along the Gold Coast, trading with those kingdoms of inland Africa which the Arabs had

The art of the Aztecs

The principal inspiration of Aztec art was a religious emphasis on themes of warfare, human sacrifice, and the renewal of the gods by blood. According to Aztec belief, the ritual of human sacrifice was necessary to replenish the gods, without whose goodwill natural disasters could not be averted. Aztec warriors collected the victims for the annual rites of sacrifice of their priests, and these are the scenes familiarly depicted on the remarkable painted codices of the post-conquest period, prepared by native Mesoamerican artists to accompany Spanish historical texts. The recurring theme of these codices is the one of pain and sacrifice. The gods, however, rewarded successful sacrifice by granting the birth of a new time-period. This difficult idea could be expressed quite simply in Aztec sculpture: the parturition figure (far right) is expressive, but full also of symbolic meaning.

FACING PAGE
Wooden mask with mosaic decoration and shell teeth, possibly depicting the god Quetzalcoatl

BELOW *Aztec human sacrifice, scene from the Codex Magliabechiano*

ABOVE *Jade figure of the Aztec god Xolotl*

ABOVE *Figure of the goddess Tlazolteotl giving birth to the maize god*

Vasco da Gama
*Da Gama (1462-1524)
was the discoverer of the
sea route to India by the
Cape of Good Hope on his
great voyage of 1497-99.
His second voyage, in
1502, secured Portuguese
power in the Indian Ocean.*

known about for several centuries already but which they had never attempted to colonize. In 1488 Bartolomeu Dias rounded the tip of southern Africa, subsequently known as the Cape of Good Hope. Ten years later, Vasco da Gama opened the sea route to India.

By the mid-sixteenth century, Portuguese commercial enterprise had taken European seaborne trade as far east as Macao, in China, and there was little of the habitable world still unknown to the West. Yet there was one area certainly, in Oceania, remote enough from the main trade routes to preserve its identity intact. In the many island chains of the Pacific Ocean, a common culture had become established over two millennia which, unsurprisingly in such conditions of dispersal, exhibited many signs of individualism. Easter Island in particular, being especially remote, developed a distinct civilization, characterized by monumental sculpture, which was clearly hierarchical in its social structure and was probably priest-ridden as well.

Similarly hierarchical societies, although with distinguishing characteristics of their own, had emerged also in central Polynesia, as in New Zealand (to the south) and Hawaii (a long way to the north). And while these resulted in improved agricultural organization and in the higher crop yields that led to an overall population expansion in Oceania, they also encouraged aggressive rivalries throughout a society now girded for war. Fortifications, sometimes on a considerable scale, became familiar in Polynesian societies from the beginning of the fifteenth century. They point the contrast with the more sophisticated civilizations of the northern Pacific, just then returning to conditions of good government and public order.

In embattled China, much ravaged by conquest and by plague, a population recovery had at last begun with the establishment (from 1368) of the Ming. China's new rulers were not as concerned as either the Sung or the Mongol Yüan had been to encourage overseas trade, even the early-fifteenth-century journeys of the admiral Cheng Ho being less commercial than diplomatic in their purpose. Instead the Ming placed emphasis on a reformed agricultural policy which brought the necessary surpluses to feed the mouths of China and which in

consequence promoted both a rural and an urban renewal. Following the shock of the Mongol oppressions, Ming society remained introverted, suspicious of all foreigners, and culturally less advanced than the Sung. But for almost two centuries from the reign of Hung-wu (1368-98), right up to the return of Mongol pressure in the later 1550s, China was substantially at peace. For all their limitations, what the Ming restored was the precious guarantee of security.

One of the agencies that by the sixteenth century had come seriously to threaten China's security was piracy, conducted aggressively from Japan. And this piracy itself had its origins in a serious century-long breakdown of order in the Japanese homeland, beginning most obviously with the decade of civil conflict known as the Onin War (1467-77). In practice, the Ashikaga shogunate (in whose decline this war played a crucial role) had never re-established the grip over Japan enjoyed in their best years by the earlier Kamakura shoguns. Yet from their coming to power in 1338, the Ashikaga had at least advanced Kyoto to its old position of cultural pre-eminence: the ancient capital of Japan, it was now their own headquarters. And indeed, it is for their contribution to the persisting civilization of Japan that the Ashikaga are chiefly remembered. Like their Chinese contemporaries the Ming, by whom they were deeply influenced, the greatest of the Ashikaga shoguns, Yoshimitsu (1368-94) and Yoshimasa (1443-73), deliberately turned back to the culture of earlier years and of a more stable, pre-Mongol society. This new feeling for the past was probably responsible for the revival of the native Shinto faith in fifteenth-century Japan. But it also helped the further reception and dissemination of Zen Buddhist rituals which had first come to Japan in the golden days of the Kamakura military dictatorship. The tea ceremony, still practised in Japan today, was fully developed under Yoshimasa and his immediate successors, its spread throughout Japanese society in the later fifteenth and sixteenth centuries being one of the happier consequences of the political decentralization that accompanied the collapse of the Ashikaga shogunate.

Buddhism had had another recent triumph in the continuing expansion of a devoutly religious Siam, brought together in the mid-fourteenth century by Ramdhi-pati I (1350-69), generally thought of as the first king of Siam and founder of the new capital city of Ayut'ia. It was some time before Siam was fully united, the older northern kingdom of Sukhot'ai descending to provincial status only in 1438. But the aggressive Siamese, initially encouraged by their Chinese and Mongol northern neighbours, had become a major factor in the politics of South-East Asia well before this date. In the second half of the fifteenth century, under the great law-giver Trailok (1448-88), Siam emerged as a sophisticated and now fully centralized kingdom, with an administrative structure and defined social system that survived into the nineteenth century.

Essentially, Siam had owed its growth to the weakness of China, especially under its later Mongol Yüan emperors. It is doubtful, certainly, that a stronger China would have permitted the gathering together of such a powerful kingdom in a region traditionally its own. But Burma's collapse before the Mongols in the late thirteenth century, combined with the retreat of the Shrivijayan Empire and the steady descent of a once-powerful Cambodia, had left the door open in South-East Asia for other influences as well. For a time, it must have looked as if the Buddhists of Ayut'ia and the Muslims of Malacca, Arakan and northern Sumatra

and Java, would partition the whole area between them. In the event, this never occurred. Malacca went down in 1511 to the Portuguese in a new wave of European expansion, while the curbing of the Delhi Sultanate in late-fourteenth-century India had already served, well before this time, to limit the ambitions of Islam.

A major reason for the weakness of the Delhi sultans was the assault they suffered in 1398 from their co-religionist Tamerlane, whose invading army reached Delhi itself that year. Tamerlane's empire was not long-lasting, scarcely outliving the conqueror himself. But his sacking of Delhi and ravaging of northern India the following year permanently damaged the Delhi Sultanate, and the full recovery of Islam on the Indian subcontinent had to wait the sixteenth-century Mughal ascendancy. Elsewhere, Tamerlane's swift and savage campaigns took him from Samarkand, which he ruled from 1369, to the conquest of Mameluke Syria by 1400. He was engaged, through the 1380s and 1390s, in a long war with the Golden Horde in southern Russia which disrupted and then destroyed its economy. In Asia Minor, at a great battle near Ankara in 1402, he succeeded in overthrowing the Ottoman sultan Bayezid.

Tamerlane's achievement, although sufficiently astounding at the time, is now chiefly remembered for the unintended consequences of his campaigns. The capture of Bayezid "the Thunderbolt" in 1402, and his subsequent humiliation and death, brought to an end the first phase of Ottoman expansion through Anatolia and the Balkans, delaying the Turkish conquest of what was left of Byzantium by another full half-century. Constantinople had been under attack by the Ottomans in 1391. It was besieged by them again in 1422, but was not finally taken for Islam until 1453 and the storming of the city by Mehemmed II (1451-81).

Similarly, the elevation of the princes of Moscow to tsars of all Russia had a great deal to do with Tamerlane's campaigning and with his defeat of their enemies, the Tartars. Moscow had begun its expansion in the fourteenth century, taking in, among others, the adjoining principality of Vladimir-Suzdal. However, its most significant growth occurred rather later. As Moscow ceased to feel the threat of the Tartar khanate to the south, it was able to concentrate on a northward movement

Muscovy's rise to power
In 1300 Muscovy was still a small principality. During the 14th century it gained strength through managing to escape invasion by the Tartars, and proceeded to absorb various neighbouring states, including Vladimir-Suzdal. The 15th century saw a massive expansion, initially northwards into the territories of Novgorod and Pskov; this was largely a result of the relaxation of Tartar pressure in the south, and of Moscow's rise to primacy in Orthodox Christianity after the fall of Constantinople in 1453. By the death of Ivan III, in 1505, the Grand Duchy, which had been an isolated, land-locked state in 1462, had expanded westwards to include large areas of Lithuania, and eastwards beyond the Urals.

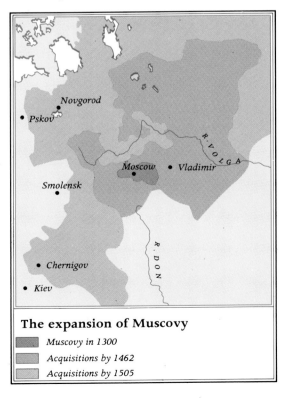

The expansion of Muscovy

▨ *Muscovy in 1300*

▨ *Acquisitions by 1462*

▨ *Acquisitions by 1505*

Russian icons

Icon-painting in 15th-century Russia reached a new perfection in the work of Andrey Rublev (c. 1370-1430), a former monk and pupil of Theophanes the Greek. It was Rublev's contribution to introduce a compassionate spirituality to icon-painting, which raised his Muscovite school above all its contemporary competitors. And certainly the icons of Rublev and his followers are very unlike the charming, but considerably less subtle, work of the 15th-century historical painters of Novgorod. Moscow's growing dominance in the politics of Russia inspired in Novgorod, as it lost its independence, a mood of patriotic retrospection. The *Battle between Novgorod and Suzdal* was painted in the third quarter of the 15th century, shortly before the subjugation of Novgorod to Moscow in 1478; in this and similar icons, both the painter and his audience sought to re-live one of the more inspiring moments in the remote history of their threatened city.

ABOVE The Archangel Michael, *in the Cathedral of St Michael the Archangel, Moscow*

LEFT The Annunciation *by Andrey Rublev, in the Cathedral of the Annunciation, Moscow*

ABOVE St George and the Dragon,
Novgorod School

RIGHT St Ephrem the Syrian, *of
unknown origin*

CENTRE *Four-part icon from St George's
Church, Novgorod*

FAR RIGHT Battle between Novgorod
and Suzdal, *from a church in the village
of Kuretsa, Novgorod*

203

Ivan the Great
The Grand Duke Ivan III (1462-1505) was responsible for the expansion of Muscovy into Novgorod, Lithuania, and east to the Urals: by the early 16th century Muscovy ranked as one of the four great powers of Europe.

The unification of France
During the 15th century the French crown asserted its real control over much of France, expelling the English by 1453 and adding the reconquered territories to the royal domain. In the second half of the century a series of confiscations from magnates added Burgundy, Artois and Picardy (1477), Anjou and Provence (1481), and Brittany (1491); Orléanais and Blois came to the crown in 1498. By 1500 the king directly controlled virtually all of France except for a few independent lands, most of which would pass to the crown in the next century.

that, before 1500, had absorbed the territories of both Novgorod and Pskov. Remote from the threat of Ottoman imperialism which was troubling south-eastern Europe and the Near East, Moscow became the beneficiary of Mehemmed the Conqueror's triumph over Constantinople in 1453, assuming the leadership of Orthodox Christianity at just the time when its princes could profit most, politically, from such a role. Within a short space of years, Ivan III, grand duke of Moscow (1462–1505), was able to convert his isolated principality into an empire that, by early in the sixteenth century, had come to rank as one of the four great powers in the West. As others in his position have since tried to do, he made an attempt to modernize the state he had inherited and then rebuilt, although with similarly limited success.

The three remaining powers in the late-fifteenth-century West were the Ottomans, a threatening presence on the southern border of Hungary, the Habsburg emperors, just beginning their phenomenal expansion out of Austria, and the reconstituted kingdom of France. The last of these, after two centuries of dominance in Western Europe, had lately come into exceptionally hard times, the prey of English marauders and occupation armies, as well as of its own civil conflicts between the Armagnacs and their enemies, the rival Burgundians. Yet the quarrels had been patched up and the English defeated, with the French kings emerging

France in 1500

▢ *Lands of French crown*

▨ *Independent possessions*

Map labels: ARTOIS, PICARDY, Calais, BRITTANY, Paris, ORLEANAIS, ANJOU, BLOIS, BURGUNDY, BOURBON, AUVERGNE, Lyons, Bordeaux, BEARN, PROVENCE

in the final decades of the fifteenth century as a monarchy better organized now and more openly absolute than it had ever been before.

Over Europe as a whole, the unremitting wars of the fifteenth century, many of them little more than dynastic squabbles, promoted a mood of profound disillusion, hostile to the preservation of civic liberties. In Italy, most obviously, the avaricious Visconti and then the Sforza of Milan, the Medici of Florence, the Gonzaga of Mantua, and the Este of Ferrara—all built their tyrannies on contemporary distaste for the still greater evils of disorder. However, the collapse of popular rule was as true of northern Europe, where the young rulers of the sixteenth-century Renaissance in the North owed their wealth and self-confidence to a sudden accretion of power. By professionalizing their armies and perfecting the machinery of royal law, they at last brought their turbulent and disruptive aristocracies under more effective control. The new monarchs of early-modern Europe included three who were young and optimistic together, each of them a great patron of the arts. Henry VIII of England (1509-47), Francis I of France (1515-47), and the Emperor Charles V (1519-56), all experienced the support, at least initially, of the majority of their more influential subjects. They used it, very much to their personal advantage, to re-draw the map of the world.

Of course, they could not have got as far as they did had the way not been thoroughly prepared. Economic growth began again in Western Europe during the last decades of the fifteenth century. A population recovery, although very slow at first, had followed the retreat of plague, while a new mood of technological experimentalism suggested fresh avenues of expansion. With the development of printing, ideas could spread quickly, reaching a far wider audience than ever before. The technology of the gun revolutionized warfare, especially in the design of fortifications. In shipping, the introduction (with the carrack) of more sophisticated rigging was to open, from before the mid-century, an adventurous and innovative era.

It is one of the ironies of history that those who laid the groundwork for expansion in the late fifteenth and the sixteenth centuries were not generally the

The Habsburg Empire by 1556

Habsburg lands

Siege-gun from ''Bellifortis''
Cannons were becoming increasingly common throughout the 15th century. This siege-gun is an illustration from Conrad Kyeser's Bellifortis, *an exuberant and somewhat fanciful manual of military technology dating from about 1405.*

The Habsburg Empire under Charles V
The vast Habsburg Empire of Charles V (1519-56) was made up of four separate dynastic inheritances: from his mother's side came Castile, with its empire in the New World, and its holdings in North Africa; this was complemented by Aragon and its Mediterranean empire in Italy and the islands of the western Mediterranean; through his father came the Burgundian inheritance of the Netherlands, and the Habsburg patrimony of Austria, Alsace, Styria and the Tyrol.

European carrack
The vessel of European overseas expansion was the carrack, developed from the Hanseatic cog: it had three masts, the fore- and mainmast square-rigged, and the mizzen-mast lateen-rigged.

ones who got most profit from it. The extensive late-medieval commercial empire of the Hansa, an association of north German cities known collectively as the Hanseatic League, made a substantial contribution before 1500 to the economic recovery of the West. Its trade routes radiated west to London, north to Bergen and Trondheim, east to Novgorod and Kiev, and south to those especially valuable markets of northern Italy from which access was obtained to the Mediterranean. In a close partnership with the major Italian cities, renewed regularly at the fairs of Lyons or at the so-called ''Assemblies'' at Bruges, the Hansa had refined mechanisms of international exchange that were a vital encouragement to new trade. At the same time, North European seafaring expertise, developed in the sturdy but unbeautiful Hanseatic cog, combined with the experience of Mediterranean shipbuilders to produce the fully-rigged carrack. Yet the commercial and technological brilliance of these enterprising merchants was overtaken in the sixteenth century by forces they themselves had been responsible for unleashing. Charles V's mighty Habsburg Empire, which eventually absorbed Spain and Flanders, extending from its Central European base in Austria and Bohemia to take in the kingdoms of Naples and Sicily, with Tunis, Sardinia and Milan, could

scarcely have got under way without the financial backing of the Fugger merchant family of Augsburg, in South Germany. Nor could Spanish Habsburg carracks have reached their objectives overseas had it not been for the skill of the navigational instrument-makers of Augsburg and of other south German towns. However, for the Fuggers, their association with Spanish imperialism brought them bankruptcy in 1575, when Philip II repudiated his debts. As for the Hanseatic League, the religious wars of the sixteenth century, with the expansion of Sweden in the North under Gustavus Vasa (1523-60) and the growing competition of Spanish and Portuguese merchants in the South, brought about a steady and irreversible decline.

For Europe and the Americas, for Africa and the East, the opening years of the sixteenth century held the promise of accelerating change. As late as 1492, in the same year that Columbus set sail for the Americas, a corner of the old world, in Moorish Granada, had at last changed its allegiance. Ferdinand and Isabella, whose victory over the Muslim Boabdil brought to completion the Christian reconquest that had been a lasting preoccupation of medieval Spain, were also those whose support of Columbus assisted, perhaps more than anything else would do, the birth of an entirely new era.

Stained glass

Glass-painting in 15th-century Europe had become a sophisticated and specialized art. While it had lost some of the monumentality and the richness of colour of Romanesque stained glass, it had gained a naturalism and complexity of invention perfectly suited to the great windows of the Late Gothic churches. Like many of the buildings themselves, the purpose of the glass was frequently commemorative by this period; the donors were shown at prayer, and their status in society was recorded by the prominent display of heraldry.

FACING PAGE
The Annunciation window, Bourges Cathedral, France

North Rose window with Labours of the Months in the outer roundels (see July *detail, above), Angers Cathedral, France*

ABOVE The Nativity *(detail), by Uccello, one of seven Occhio windows in the dome, Florence Cathedral, Italy*

BELOW *Eight figures of famous men, south transept, Toledo Cathedral, Spain*

ABOVE The Youthful Knight, *Strasbourg, Germany*

RIGHT *Bird quarry window, Yarnton, near Oxford, England*

Material Culture

The Americas

In contrast with much of the rest of the world, during the fourteenth century and still in the fifteenth, the isolation of the American continent kept its populations remarkably free from disease. Yet the American peoples had suffered from harvest failures and famines, the more terrible as the land became more crowded. And it followed at least in part as a response to these that the sacrificial beliefs of the Aztec priesthood took a firm hold over the territories ruled by Montezuma (1502-20) and by his predecessors in Mexico. In the Aztec canon, natural disasters could be expected to result from a failure to replenish the gods, nor could this replenishment be achieved in any better way than by practising the ritual of human sacrifice.

In practice, there is very little in the art of fifteenth-century Mexico that can be explained without reference to these rituals. Neither the architecture nor the pottery of the Aztecs were especially remarkable, both simply continuing the existing traditions of the region. Indeed, the most striking Aztec architectural monument was undoubtedly the massed conurbation of Tenochtitlán itself, now underlying and permanently concealed by the streets of Mexico City. Nevertheless, the Aztec genius found individual expression in the mediums of painting and sculpture, and here especially the dominant inspiration was the theme of pain and of sacrifice.

Most of what we know of Aztec painting comes from the sixteenth-century manuscripts—the so-called *codices*—of the early-colonial period, where a Spanish historical or ethnographic text is accompanied by native Mesoamerican illustrations. But authentic fifteenth-century sculptures, in stone, in pottery, and occasionally in wood, are not at all uncommon, and they show the development after the mid-century of a distinctive Aztec tradition in carving which, although clearly the result of a number of inspirations absorbed during the period of conquest, had an expressiveness all of its own. Aztec sculptures were often very complex. Characterized by their free use of symbolism, they were intended to be read for their meaning at least as much as to be admired for their form. But a quite complicated idea like the birth of a new time-period, the reward of successful sacrifice, could also be expressed very simply, as in that remarkable parturition figure which is one of the best known surviving examples of Aztec art (see page 199), being as expressive within its own tradition as the finest portrait sculptures of High Gothic realism. In another work of rare distinction, skilfully carved in crystal, the subject (typically Aztec) is a skull.

For all the great extent of the area throughout which the Aztecs gathered their tribute, Aztec supremacy in Mesoamerica never equalled the more southerly dominions of the Incas. In the ancient Maya territories of south-east Mexico and Guatemala, the breakdown of central government and the fall of Mayapán were the result essentially of internal rivalries for which the Maya themselves were to blame. And even within those areas normally assigned to the Aztecs, the rich and ancient civilization of the Mixtecs of Oaxaca was never totally suppressed, Mixtec influence being especially visible

The Spanish discovery of the Aztec and Inca Empires
When the Spaniards reached America in the early 16th century, they found two great and flourishing civilizations: the Aztec Empire in Mexico, and the Inca Empire which covered Peru, Ecuador, Bolivia, northern Argentina and northern Chile. The Aztec Empire had been unified under a single ruler only at the end of the 14th century: when it fell to Cortes it was still vigorous, and expanding eastwards into Maya territories. The Incas had been in Peru since about the 12th century, but, like the Aztecs, their imperial period was in the 15th: more than four-fifths of the empire that Pizarro found in 1531 had been conquered since 1460.

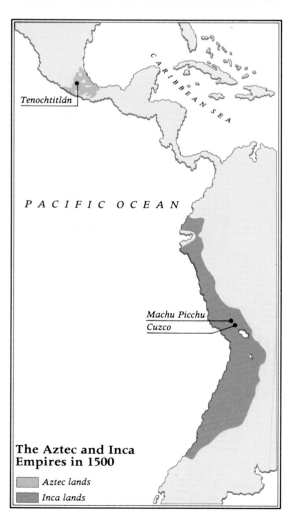

Tenochtitlán

CARIBBEAN SEA

PACIFIC OCEAN

Machu Picchu
Cuzco

The Aztec and Inca Empires in 1500

Aztec lands
Inca lands

Chinese porcelains

The restoration of a strong centralized government under China's Ming emperors led to a revival of the pottery industry, encouraged by bulk orders from the court at Peking. For the blue and white wares first introduced under the Mongols, the emperor Hsüan-te (1426–35) favoured a naturalistic painting style more in accord with refined Chinese taste than the earlier Persian-inspired designs. Later, during the reign of Ch'eng-hua (1465–87), a new overglaze enamelling technique was perfected, making possible the practice of polychrome painting, especially in the court-favoured *tou-ts'ai* ("contrasted colour") style. A further important innovation towards the end of the fifteenth century was the introduction of a form of cloisonné enamelling, in the so-called *fa-hua* style, where threads of trailed slip, outlining the designs, prevented the thick-painted enamels from running.

ABOVE *Polychrome enamel dish from the reign of Ch'eng-hua*

Cloisonné enamel jar in the fa-hua *style*

Cloisonné enamel two-handled bowl in the fa-hua *style*

Tou-ts'ai *polychrome jar from the reign of Ch'eng-hua*

Blue and white Ming bowl from the reign of Hsüan-te

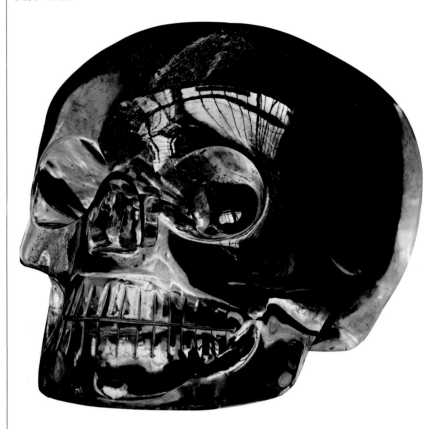

Aztec crystal skull
The skull, symbol of the death god Mictlantecuhtli, was preserved after human sacrifice—the Spanish explorer Bernal Diaz saw a rack containing thousands at Tenochtitlán —and is a common theme in Aztec art. This example is carved from extremely hard rock crystal, a technical feat which almost surpasses the superb realism of the skull itself.

Votive llama figure
This statuette of a llama from the southern highlands of Peru has a hollow cut in its back for votive offerings of fat: a common model, it was carved in about 1500.

in Aztec manuscript paintings. Divisions such as these, continuing throughout the period of Aztec ascendancy in Mesoamerica, were what let the Spaniards in. But it was as much the grouping together of the Central and South American tribes under one identifiable lordship, the direct product of Aztec and of Inca imperialism, that enabled Cortes and Pizarro in each case to locate their victims and to topple the existing structures of government.

Pizarro himself never got there, but one of the most impressive surviving monuments of Inca government is the mountain-top city of Machu Picchu, not very far from Cuzco. Machu Picchu, like Cuzco, was an élite centre, grouping the buildings of religion and government in an aristocratic complex supported by the labours of a peasantry resident elsewhere. In Cuzco itself, one palace enclosure was added to another as ruler succeeded ruler, the total effect being not unlike the courtyard development of Chimu Chanchan from which, very probably, the Incas would have borrowed at least some of their architectural ideas. Inca expansion had of course been exceptionally rapid, and the cultural eclecticism this induced in Inca art showed itself in a number of different ways. In pottery, as

in architecture, Chimu influence was important. The Incas are known to have brought Chimu potters from the conquered coastal lands to work at their capital at Cuzco, and it may well have been their influence which led to a recognizably new style there in the mid-fifteenth century, being the so-called Cuzco Polychrome. These Cuzco ceramics are brightly painted, with a technical perfection showing most clearly in the characteristic "aryballoid" jar, pointed at base and long of neck, which is present in so many Imperial Inca pottery assemblages. However, the exact repetition of shapes and mechanically geometric decoration of these vessels are symptoms nevertheless of that poverty of imagination in Inca art which is equally detectable in sculpture.

The monumental cult figures of the Inca religion fell a victim, for the most part, to the colonial-period Spanish missionaries. But smaller figurines, both animal and human, have survived in quantity, and what they show is the sacrifice of individual characteristics in favour of a generalized representation of form, often reproduced geometrically. Inca sculptors rejected the more fanciful expressions of Andean art, replacing imagination with purpose and myth with something nearer reality. Very typical of their work is the votive llama figure which, with its stylized geometrical shaping and obvious utility, is surprisingly modern in conception.

The Incas, of course, are remembered especially as engineers: the builders of highways with their accompanying bridges, lodging-houses and stores, and the patrons of temple- and palace-building enterprises distinguished as much by their symmetry as by their scale. Most particularly, too, they developed a building style in which the fitting of one stone against another was achieved with a wholly distinctive precision. This could take the form of well-cut rectangular blocks, resting snugly against each other with scarcely a crack in the masonry. However, it is a craft seen at its most impressive in the "polygonal" masonry of many Inca walls, where the extraordinary skill of the builders in the selection and shaping of the boulders is given additional aesthetic effect in the completed wall by a deliberate shadowing of the joints, each boulder being finished with a convex outer face.

Oceania

Inca masonry has its parallel, wholly coincidental, in the rusticated façades just then coming into fashion in fifteenth-century Italy. But a more real connection has long been observed with the cyclopean masonry of Easter Island in the South Pacific, inducing the dispute which still continues on the sources of Easter Island's art. What is repeated on Easter Island is the rectangular rather than the polygonal technique of Peru. Nevertheless, so exactly is the craft of Inca masonry matched by that at the *ahu* (or ceremonial platform site) at Vinapu on Easter Island that even the most severe critics of the thesis of American origins (most recently elaborated by the Norwegian explorer Thor Heyerdahl) have had to admit contact of some kind. One site, however, does not make a culture, and it is much more difficult to establish any other characteristic of Easter Island art which could not have had its origins in the indigenous Polynesian tradition. In fact, the isolation of the Easter Islanders from the rest of the Polynesian community seems to have been complete from the date of initial settlement in 400-500 AD. In these unusual circumstances, they developed an art, characterized by the *ahu* and the monumental figure, which has remained mysterious.

There is no easy way of dating the colossal stone heads and torsos for which Easter Island is especially well known. The *ahu*, it is thought, may date in its earliest manifestations from the so-called Early Period (before 1100), and the statues were certainly being carved and erected during the Middle Period which ended with the civil war between the "long-ear" and the "short-ear" islanders in 1680, or thereabouts. Their source was the quarries at Rano Raraku, an extinct volcano, and from there they were taken in an almost finished state to the platforms (the *ahu*) for which they were intended.

From this same Middle Period, during which both building and artistic activity may well have peaked as late as the fifteenth and sixteenth centuries, are the boat-shaped houses of Easter Island, with the village of Orongo having nearly fifty of these, radiocarbon-dated to *c.* 1500.

Some Easter Island rituals, still observed in the mid-nineteenth century and recorded by European settlers, may have originated in the rich ceremonial life of the Middle Period. But there is reason to suppose that this particular priestly society went into a decline before 1600. And whether then or shortly afterwards, Easter Islanders were certainly exposed in their turn to the civil wars which had long troubled the other communities of Polynesia. In the Tongan Islands, the ceremonial centre of the Tui Tonga dynasty at Mu'a, on Tongatapu, was being fortified in about 1400, while Polynesian societies with a less strongly developed centralized government than the Tongans were showing the strain still more clearly. In New Zealand, the Classic Maori cultural phase, which thereafter lasted until the period of European contact, began abruptly in about 1350 with the building of prominent earthwork fortifications in the North Island and with a change in the characteristic weapon and tool assemblages which may itself have been the result of increased warfare. Accompanying these innovations, and perhaps their cause, was a pronounced deterioration of climate, signalled in the North Island by a sudden increase in the practice of pit-storage of the sweet potato, and probably responsible in the longer term for a population slump in the South. The concentration of Maori population in the North Island of New Zealand, where subsistence was still relatively easy, undoubtedly led to a competition for resources which was resolvable only by violence. Maori society, as described by European explorers of the second half of the eighteenth century, was both warlike and highly artistic. Most of this art is still hard to date, being without a context in the archaeological sequence and having been collected primarily by the ethnographers. Nevertheless, it has been established that the Maori of the Classic Period were building their fortified settlements, or *pa*, from the late fourteenth century, and that these *pa* were already numbered in their thousands before the arrival of the first Europeans.

Statue on ''ahu''
The colossal statues of Easter Island have not yet been dated exactly, but this example, re-erected on an ahu *in modern times, shows the effect of a complete head and torso with the separate red topknot.*

ilex quoniam ex
audict dns voem
orationis mee

The cult of death

The Black Death, in the mid-14th century, had been the first visitation of bubonic plague, but it was certainly not the last. In the circumstances, an obsession with death in the religion and art of the 15th century is no more than one might expect. It inspired such great masterpieces as the anonymous *Triumph of Death*, painted for a Sicilian hospital, while explaining also the contemporary preference for extravagantly realistic sepulchral sculpture. Another consequence of the plague mortalities was a rising tide of social protest, likewise reflected in art. Popular moral tales of the times like the *Dance of Death* and the story of *The Three Living and the Three Dead* stressed the rank of the men and women led off to perdition.

FACING PAGE
The Three Living and the Three Dead, *scene from a French Book of Hours*

ABOVE Dance of Death *in the Church of St Andrew, Norwich, England*
BELOW *Detail of the* Last Judgment *in Freiburg Münster, Germany*

ABOVE *The tomb of Philippe Pot, attributed to Antoine le Moiturier*

BELOW *The* Triumph of Death, *by an anonymous Sicilian artist*

T'ai-ho Men, Peking, China
The T'ai-ho Men is the ornate gateway to the Forbidden City, which was the palace enclosure of the emperor Yung-lo.

T'ai-miao hall, Peking, China
Although subject to a great deal of restoration at different times, the huge T'ai-miao hall in the palace precinct of the Forbidden City still looks much as it did when first constructed in the 15th century.

Far East

As with Easter Island, one of the most interesting features of the material culture of Maori New Zealand is that it developed in almost complete isolation. It has been claimed that the Chinese admiral Cheng Ho, standard-bearer and tribute-collector for the great Ming emperor Yung-lo (1403-24), touched Australia on one of his extraordinary voyages. However, it is more likely that Cheng Ho contented himself with the more profitable objective of Eastern Java, still under its Majapahit kings. And certainly there has never been any question of him sailing any further through Melanesia to islands like New Zealand in which the Chinese had no traditional trading concern. Cheng Ho's voyages, in any event, were only incidentally commercial, following known routes and opening up little that was new. Indeed, the Ming tribute system in the first decades of the fifteenth century was a political institution, not a commercial one. When Cheng Ho's fleet returned to China for the last time in 1433, the lack of official interest in further overseas involvement killed Chinese commercial imperialism at its source.

Back in the late fourteenth century, an essential part of the Ming restoration and the destruction of Mongol power had been a return to that traditional view of a world order, established and then dominated by China, which is sometimes described as "Confucian". According to this belief, the Chinese emperor ("Son of Heaven") stood between mankind and heaven itself, and it followed that all those with whom the Chinese had dealings must pay, as a part of the price for such contact, at least a measure of formal homage to the Ming emperor. This world view enabled the first Ming emperor, Hung-wu (1367-98), to call the Japanese rulers "stupid eastern barbarians . . . haughty and disloyal", which brought him the perfectly justified reply—"The world is the world's world; it does not belong to a single person." And although the Chinese concept of the role of their emperor was never more than grudgingly accepted anywhere beyond the boundaries of China itself, it promoted at home a deliberate glorification of the Son of Heaven which found expression most obviously in building programmes of ever-increasing magnitude.

Hung-wu himself had developed his imperial capital at Nanking on a scale that was certainly unprecedented. However, we know more of the works of Yung-lo ("Perpetual Happiness"), who was responsible in 1421 for the re-siting of the Ming capital at Peking. As it exists now, Peking is the work of successive Ming emperors, later extended and embellished by the Ch'ing. Furthermore, it overlies the great capital city of Kublai Khan, some of the marks of which are still to be seen in its plan. Nevertheless, it was Yung-lo's interest, from the beginning of his reign in 1403, that established Peking for the first time in what has remained its final form. His promotion of Peking from auxiliary capital to chief city of the empire, before his death in 1424, was a necessary guarantee of its permanence.

Peking is not an entirely symmetrical city, and in this it escapes from the more rigid conventions of the earlier Chinese and Mongol tradition. Yet there is a strong element of regularity in the city's overall planning, and this becomes symmetry of the purest kind in the centrally-placed Forbidden City, which was Yung-lo's palace enclosure. So much remodelling has taken place at Peking that genuine fifteenth-century work is hard to identify in its buildings. Even the great T'ai-miao hall in the palace precinct, which certainly belongs to this period, has been subject to successive restorations. However, the Son of Heaven's original grand design has undoubtedly been preserved in Yung-lo's capital. The outer city, or southern suburb, is an extension of the sixteenth century. But the concentric defences of inner city, imperial city (now wall-less), and palace enclosure are Yung-lo's, as is the main north-south axial line from the great south gate of the inner city to the slopes of Coal Hill, an artificial mound immediately north of the Forbidden City, created during the digging-out of ornamental lakes for the Mongol Kublai Khan. It was this axial line, very precisely, which determined the layout of the palace, imposing on any visiting dignitary the chilling experience of a multi-layered approach—through formal gateways, courtyards, and intervening buildings—to the sacred presence of the emperor.

There is no doubt at all of the impact of Yung-lo's civic architecture both at home and upon China's neighbours. Among those directly influenced were the Koreans, whose contemporary gateways and city walls in the Ming manner were one part of a more general cultural revival under the new Yi dynasty, first established in place of the decadent Koryo in 1392. Yi Song-gye, the founder of the dynasty, had come to power as a direct consequence of his recognition of the futility of further resistance to the Ming, and he lost no time in entering into tributary relations with China. In the fifteenth century and thereafter, the Koreans both gained and lost by the association. Symptomatic of the revived intellectual vigour and originality of the Early Yi Period in Korea was the invention of an alphabetic script, called *han'gul*, ideally suited to the Korean language for which it is still used today. Another consequence of the new scholarship was that it promoted experiments in printing, resulting in the use of movable type on a scale not previously attempted. Yet such was the influence of China at this time that neither invention was developed to the point at which Korean culture could have taken off in a direction of its own. The *han'gul* phonetic system, although adopted officially in 1446, continued to be used only for business and personal correspondence, having no status in Korean literature or scholarship, where the Chinese ideographic script was retained. As for scholarship itself, the intellectual flowering of the Yi dynasty, particularly remarkable during the fifteenth century, yielded many great works of the encyclopedic kind favoured in China at that time. One of the best known of these, the *Koryo sa*, was an official compilation in the Chinese manner on the history of the Koryo dynasty. The most noteworthy quality of another, the *Hunmin chongum* (Proper Phonetics for Instruction of the People), was that it was written in *han'gul*.

Chinese dominance in East Asia is perhaps most easily explained in terms of the great scale of many Ming enterprises. The Ming emperor Yung-lo, who dispatched Cheng Ho's fleets on diplomatic missions throughout the known world and who initiated the rebuilding of Peking, was also the sponsor of a grand encyclopedic work. Called the *Yung-lo Ta-tien*, this work ran to many thousands of volumes on which some two thousand scholars were engaged between 1403 and 1407, assembling the totality of Chinese knowledge. Likewise it was the sheer scale of official court requisitions that encouraged the Ming pottery industry, one order of

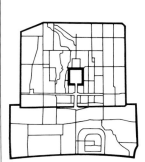

Peking, China (plan)
The Emperor Yung-lo returned to the old Mongol capital of Peking, and made it the capital of Ming China in 1421. The Forbidden City in the centre, and the axial Processional Way that leads to it, were designed and built by Yung-lo, as were the walls of the inner city.

1433 running to almost half a million pieces. In this case the order was directed to the kilns of Jao-chou, the home of the new blue and white porcelains. And what similar requisitions help to document is an important shift in Chinese imperial taste away from the traditional Lung-ch'üan celadons, towards the Mongol-inspired blue-painted porcelains of Jao-chou. As a result of this shift the celadons themselves, losing favour at court, deteriorated noticeably in quality, while the blue and white wares, no longer intended for export alone, dropped much of their Middle Eastern emphasis (see page 209).

During the short reign of Hsüan-te (1426-35), famous also for its bronze work, the Jao-chou porcelains reached a particular perfection. Hsüan-te himself was a painter of distinction, and it was enlightened patronage of his sort (which included the order of 1433) that encouraged the development at Jao-chou of a naturalistic painting style unequalled since in quality. But there was yet another peak in porcelain production before the end of the century during the reign of the Ch'eng-hua emperor (1465-87), directed not so much towards an improvement in painting skills as to a popularization of the new overglaze enamelling technique. This involved two firings: one of the underglaze blue painting of the first application, the other of the polychrome over-painting then added to it. And inevitably the process was not easy, especially in the case of the better quality *tou-ts'ai* polychromes particularly favoured at Ch'eng-hua's court (see page 209). What it shows is a mastery of pottery technology that could not have been achieved without generous and yet discriminating patronage, these being exactly the qualities most likely to emerge in the wealthy and aristocratic society of the Ming.

Indeed, the relative security of fifteenth-century Ming rule, after successive generations of brutal invasions and civil wars, brought into being a unique society of *literati*, connoisseurs, and collectors to which we owe the survival of many fine specimens of China's earlier art. Some of these scholars lived and worked at court, there being fine paintings in the basically conservative Ming court style from the brush of painters like the late-fifteenth-century Lü Chi. Paintings of this school were boldly decorative, intended for a wide non-specialized audience, and they

The Flemish masters

Flemish painting in the 15th century owed much to the Gothic miniaturists and manuscript illuminators, and it was from these that it derived its clarity and the naturalistic exactness of its detail. But the best of the Flemish masters of the first half of the century—among them, Jan van Eyck, Rogier van der Weyden, and the anonymous Master of Flémalle—were also innovators in their own right, making use of a new painting medium in oils to develop a realism and a quality of light which has been greatly admired ever since. So incredible was the perfection of Jan van Eyck's *Ghent Altarpiece* (1432), that a later painter, Hugo van der Goes (d. 1482), is said to have been driven mad by contemplation of its unattainable mastery. Yet Hugo van der Goes himself was a talented and influential painter, certainly the best of his day in Flanders and known in the South for works like the *Portinari Altarpiece* (1475), ideas from which were borrowed quite freely by the Italians.

FACING PAGE
Double Portrait of Giovanni Arnolfini and his Wife *by Jan van Eyck*

Shrine of St Ursula *by Hans Memlinc*

ABOVE LEFT John the Baptist *by the Master of Flémalle*
ABOVE RIGHT *Right wing of the* Portinari Altarpiece *by Hugo van der Goes*

Descent from the Cross *by Rogier van der Weyden*

Central panel of the Ghent Altarpiece *by Hubert and Jan van Eyck*

Chinese painting
Chinese painting in the 15th century flourished mainly in the hands of scholar-painters away from the imperial court. Tai Chin (1388-1462), whose most famous work is the Fisherman Scroll, was the founder of the Che school, looking to 13th-century painters like Hsia Kuei and Ma Yüan for inspiration. Shen Chou (1427-1509) founded the Wu school, finding the models for his paintings in the Four Great Yüan Masters of the 14th century, particularly Wu Chen: like them, Shen Chou emphasized Zen impressionism rather than making any attempt at the picturesque.

Fisherman Scroll *by Tai Chin*

River Landscape *by Shen Chou*

had their own considerable merits. But they were very unlike the more subtle introverted style of the scholar-aesthetes of the period, and it is certainly true that the best work in Ming painting was not done in the turmoil of court life at Peking but in the isolation of the gentleman's country retreat.

Rather as they had done under the Mongol Yüan a century earlier, many of the more refined spirits of fifteenth-century China withdrew from the official responsibilities of their class, in order to develop their connoisseurship in an almost monastic seclusion, no doubt influenced by the principles of Zen. Tai Chin, one of the more notable artists of the first half of the fifteenth century and the founder of the Che School of painting, began his career at court only to reject the intrigues of eunuch-dominated palace society in favour of a quieter existence at home in the

province of his birth. In the same way, Shen Chou, the founding genius of the slightly later Wu School, spent most of his life in a country haven, where he could share his preoccupations, both artistic and literary, with a group of like-minded friends. It was a part of the tradition of such scholar-painters as these that their work should be modelled on that of great artists of the past, an important influence on the style of Shen Chou being the abbreviated landscapes and naturalistic bamboo paintings of the Yüan gentleman-painter Wu Chen (d. 1354). The objectives the scholar-painters shared with their masters, and later developed themselves, were the freshness and spontaneity, resulting in a form of impressionism, so much admired within their own circle of self-consciously cultivated *cognoscenti*. It is the same capture of the fleeting moment that had been pioneered so very effectively two centuries earlier by the Zen monk-painter Mu-ch'i.

In Japan too, where Zen Buddhism had found much favour since the thirteenth century, the works of Mu-ch'i and his many Zen imitators continued to be deeply influential. Throughout the fifteenth century, the fine arts (though less obviously the crafts) of Japan were dominated by Chinese models. These were not the models of contemporary Ming China nor even of the immediately preceding Yüan, but went back much further to the fount of Chinese Zen Buddhism at the Southern Sung capital of Hangchow. In effect, Japanese painters of the fifteenth century were carrying on the traditions of Southern Sung China as if little or nothing had intervened. It was on this base that they began building a structure that was perceptibly their own.

Characteristically, Zen influence in fifteenth-century Japan stripped art down to its essentials. In its earliest thirteenth-century manifestations, Zen piety had preserved the debased and over-elaborate architecture of Southern Sung China introduced by the original missionaries. Yet the essential austerity of Zen was beginning to assert itself more obviously during the full flowering of the Muromachi Period, finding expression in such varied arts as landscape gardening, the tea ceremony, and architecture. The so-called Silver Pavilion (Ginkakuji) at Kyoto, built for the retirement of Yoshimasa, the eighth Ashikaga shogun, was a two-storeyed building, noticeably more austere than its companion structure, the Golden Pavilion, which was nearly a century older. It had in addition another hall, the Togudo, part of the function of which was to provide accommodation for the tea ceremony, of which Yoshimasa's tea-master, Shuko, was one of the chief pioneers in Japan.

The tea ceremony, then as now, was distinguished by its extreme simplicity — in equipment, in furnishings, and in setting. And a point of focus in the traditional chamber set aside for the ceremony was the niche or recess (*toko-no-ma*) in which a single art object was displayed for the purpose of contemplation and discussion. The idea of such concentration of the mind is certainly Zen-inspired, the architectural device of the *toko-no-ma* being developed in Zen monasteries of the early fifteenth century as a deliberate practical aid to meditation. Inevitably, it had its effect on the shape of the art objects presented in it. The vertical hanging scroll, with a poem at the top and a landscape at the base, very much in the Chinese manner, became common in fifteenth-century Japan, not replacing entirely the more traditional horizontal narrative scroll but meeting a new need.

Many of these influences were visible in the work of a notable line of Zen priest-painters, from Josetsu through Shubun to Sesshu. Each passed on to the other the Zen technique of monochrome ink-painting which went back to the Chinese master Mu-ch'i. And although there is little that is certainly from the brush of Josetsu surviving in present-day Japan, it is clear that each of the three painters practised an art in which the Zen ideal of vigorous immediacy was among the principal objectives. Sesshu, in particular, was a painter of generous talent and very wide range, as adept in the impressionistic ink sketch so characteristic of Zen painting as in the more carefully filled-in landscape. Whereas Josetsu and Shubun both played their parts in the reception and assimilation of the Chinese Southern Sung style in Japan, it was Sesshu, building on the work of his acknowledged masters, who gave this style a twist of his own which, at last, was distinctively Japanese.

In later-fifteenth-century Japan, a new freedom from Zen symbolism began to show in the popular and very influential court art of the Kano school at Kyoto. But the principal innovations of the Kano painters belong to a later period. And what is most striking about the culture of

Silver Pavilion, Kyoto, Japan
The Ginkakuji, or Silver Pavilion, was built in 1483 by the eighth Ashikaga shogun for his retirement. It closely resembles the 14th-century Golden Pavilion which stands nearby, but it is more austere, and stands a storey lower than the earlier building.

Renaissance Italy

Complete mastery of perspective, first achieved in the work of Masaccio (1401–28), a young Florentine painter, was the outstanding characteristic of Italian painting during the 15th-century Renaissance. For Masaccio, the chief inspiration was classical antiquity. And it was classicism again that informed the work of a later fresco-painter like Piero della Francesca (d. 1492). But there were other influences at work as well in contemporary Italy. Fra Filippo Lippi (d. 1469), the pupil of Masaccio, plainly owed less in his more mature work to his original master than to the still-surviving highly decorative lyricism of International Gothic. In portraiture, the outstanding paintings of Giovanni Bellini, the Venetian, and Antonello da Messina, the Sicilian, were directly influenced by the Flemish masters, both in their realism and in the quality of their light. Even Piero della Francesca, late in his life, felt the pull of the Flanders oil-painting style, his *Nativity* owing much to the example of the *Portinari Altarpiece* by the Fleming, Hugo van der Goes.

ABOVE The Worship of the Golden Calf *by Fra Filippo Lippi*

FACING PAGE
The Nativity
by Piero della Francesca

BELOW Madonna and Child with St Anna *by Masaccio*

ABOVE The Annunciation *by Antonello da Messina*

BELOW Portrait of a Young Senator *by Giovanni Bellini*

Japanese painting
*Japanese painting
continued in the 15th
century to be influenced by
China through Zen
Buddhism: Josetsu was the
first of the great priestly
exponents of the
monochrome ink-style. His
Three Teachers is a
typically Zen subject,
portraying Buddha,
Confucius and Lao-Tzu,
and suggesting the unity of
truth behind diversity of
doctrine. Later in the
century Kano Masanobu
(1434-1530), the first of a
family line that would
dominate Japanese art for
seven generations,
developed a truly Japanese
handling of Sung Chinese
models: shown here is his
portrayal of a favourite
Zen subject, the fat and
jolly Hotei, rich in spirit
through intuitive
understanding.*

Three Teachers *by Josetsu*

Hotei *by Kano Masanobu*

fifteenth-century Japan is the long continuance of the so-called "Chinese Renaissance" and the abiding influence of Zen. The one, of course, sprang from the other. Indeed, Japan's experience of the dominant role of religion in art, although having a flavour unquestionably its own, was shared by every nation in the Orient.

South-East Asia

In South-East Asia, both Burma and Cambodia, after their periods of greatness in the twelfth and thirteenth centuries, were now in irremediable decline. However, Siam's growth at the expense of its neighbours had resulted in the development of a new capital at Ayut'ia from the mid-fourteenth century, with a late flowering of Buddhist art in its many brick-and-stucco stupas, said to have totalled more than five hundred by the time of its destruction in 1767 and subsequent abanddonment for Bangkok. Certainly, other areas, whether absorbed by Islam or merely touched by its more puritanical principles, were less lucky artistically than those that remained faithful to the Buddha, it being in the fifteenth century that the spread of Islam through Java, for example, finally cut off the Majapahit cultural revival.

India

Although it is true that there had been a retreat well before this time of the power of the Delhi Sultanate in India, those regions again under independent rule were unable, for all that, to recover their earlier cultural initiative. Wealth, clearly, was not lacking in fifteenth-century Bengal, its prosperity and active trading life being enough to impress even the sophisticated Chinese who called there in 1421 and again a decade later. But the high architectural standards of the pre-Islamic years were not regained in any part of India before the great achievements of Mughal patronage, beginning in the sixteenth century. And what remains chiefly memorable in Indian architecture of the fourteenth and the fifteenth centuries is the introduction of the Muslim traditions of the mosque and the mausoleum, both of them—in defiance of every local decorative instinct—distinguished by a relentless austerity.

In an Indian context, total austerity must always have been difficult to achieve. The Qutb Minar at Delhi, built at the end of the twelfth century as the first major monument of the new faith, had already carried decorative stone-carving of native Indian workmanship (see page 74), and in the many mosques and tombs of later years a distinctive hybrid Indo-Muslim style had ample opportunities to emerge. Nevertheless, what the Muslim architect excelled at above all—at least before such

Friday Mosque, Ahmadabad, India

In the sultanate of Gujerat on India's west coast, Muslim architecture absorbed the Jain building style of earlier generations to produce fine mosques in the Indo-Muslim tradition. At the Friday Mosque at Ahmadabad, built by Ahmad Shah (1411-42), many of the carved details, and particularly the superb windows, one of which is illustrated above, exemplify this highly individual style.

masterpieces of the Mughal period as the mid-seventeenth-century Taj Mahal—was monumentality rather than grace. The colossal tombs of the Tughlug and Lodi dynasties in fourteenth- and fifteenth-century Delhi had the qualities less of burial chambers than of fortresses. And indeed the same monumentality characterized the Indo-Muslim mosque—the religious citadel of an alien and still insecure aristocracy. In the very remarkable fifteenth-century mosques of the Sharqui dynasty of Jaunpur in north-east India, a recurring feature was a massive false façade, rising several storeys above the main body of the building to screen the central dome. On the other side of India, in Gujerat on the west coast, the capitals of Ahmad Shah (1411-42) and Mahmud Beghara (1459-1511), at Ahmadabad and Champanir respectively, each provided an opportunity for building on a staggeringly munificent scale. There, indeed, the Friday Mosque (Jami-Masjid) at Ahmadabad (1411) and its equivalent at Champanir (1485) have come to represent the apogee of mosque-building as practised in western India.

Gujerat, in a very favourable position to take an active part in the flourishing Indian Ocean trade, had long enjoyed an exceptional wealth. In earlier generations, this had supported the building of Jain shrines at sites such as Mount Abu. Inevitably, the indigenous Jain style continued to be particularly influential in this part of India, where the new tradition of Indo-Muslim architecture, as evidenced for example in the very Indian design of the columns at the Gujerat Friday Mosques, experienced an obvious flowering. Certainly, conditions had never been more propitious for such patronage, nor for the dissemination of the highly individual style that it fostered. The Indian Ocean trade, always important, had been much increased by the collapse of the Central Asian overland routes as Mongol power foundered. And these conditions meant a still greater tightening of Muslim control over trading exchanges already the traditional concern of Islam. One of the reasons why the Chinese fleets in the early fifteenth century were permitted free use of the trade routes was that their admiral, Cheng Ho, was a Muslim. And at the end of a journey that took Cheng Ho from Ormuz (on the Persian Gulf), to Dhufar (in Oman), Aden (in the South Yemen), and Zeila (in northern Somalia), was the East African port of Mogadishu (see page 197).

FACING PAGE
King's College chapel, Cambridge, England
Built between 1446 and 1515, King's College chapel is divided simply into chapel and ante-chapel, flanked by rows of low chantry-chapels. The Flemish stained glass occupies much of the wall-area, admitting a great deal of light; the sculptural ornament is exclusively heraldic and secular, commissioned by Henry VIII. John Wastell's fan-vaults were a late improvement on the original plans, and are highly effective, with their rings of ornament and transverse four-pointed arches (made necessary by the width of the nave).

Portuguese discovery of the West African coast

Prince Henry the Navigator (1394-1460, above) was the moving force behind early Portuguese exploration of the West African coast: his ships sailed as far south as Sierra Leone. In 1469, after Henry's death, Fernao Gomes, a Portuguese merchant, was granted an exclusive contract by the Portuguese monarchy for further exploration, and reached the River Congo in 1475.

Africa

No doubt, Cheng Ho's visit brought more of the Chinese porcelains which had already bulked large in the ceramic assemblages of fourteenth-century East Africa. Yet it was only an episode in the much larger pattern of the traditional trade in ivory, gold and slaves, flowing north from Africa to meet the cottons, silks and spices of India and the Far East. In coastal East Africa during the fifteenth century, the source of the architecture of the more than thirty stone-built towns engaged in this trade was as likely to be found in Muslim India as in the original Arabian homelands—just another indication of the strength of a trading system still as strong in the decades immediately preceding European maritime expansion as it had been for centuries already.

It was this trade which revitalized Kilwa towards the middle of the fifteenth century after some decades of stagnation or decline. Sulaiman b. Muhammad's rebuilding of the Great Mosque at Kilwa was completed before the mid-century, and there are other buildings like the Jangwani Mosque and the so-called Small Domed Mosque in the same city which very probably date from this period. Nothing of this domed and vaulted architectural tradition of the Muslim coastline penetrated the East African interior.

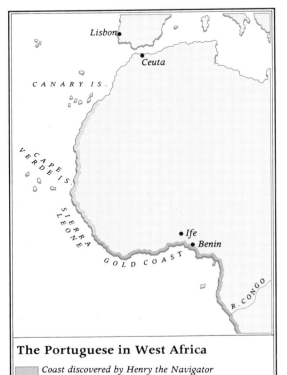

The Portuguese in West Africa

☐ *Coast discovered by Henry the Navigator*
☐ *Coast discovered by Fernao Gomes*

Indeed, it is the complete absence of any mortar and concrete mixtures in the great stone buildings of Zimbabwe and its associated towns, or cult centres, that is the most convincing evidence of the development there of an independent indigenous culture. Almost certainly, the earliest buildings at Zimbabwe would have been of mud, and it is surely significant that when, by the fifteenth century, the first free-standing stone walls were erected, they should have been butted against each other, as mud walls are, without any evidence of keying.

In Zimbabweland, the trade in gold and copper generated wealth on such a scale as to support a priest-king and his entourage, encouraging their architectural ambitions. Similarly, in West Africa the long-established Saharan overland trade continued to reinforce the authority of the Gold Coast rulers, bringing to prominence such kings as Ewuare, traditionally the builder of the central ditch and rampart at Benin. At Ife, too, and at Old Oyo, there are rampart defences on a comparable scale, which, although in great part later than the fifteenth century, certainly originated before the period of European contact and the first explorations from Portugal. The famous Benin brasses are difficult to date, and some see them only as sixteenth-century and later, following the importation of European bronze. Yet the tradition of brass-working at Benin is unquestionably much earlier, and there are even brass heads which, according to a recent typology, may be assigned to the fifteenth century.

Naturalistic representations of Portuguese soldiers, dating from the early-modern period, are not uncommon at Benin. And it is certainly true that the establishment of Portuguese trading stations on the Cape Verde Islands in the 1440s and at Elmina (São Jorge da Mina) on the Gold Coast after 1482 brought great changes to West Africa. However, the interest of the exploratory expeditions organized from Portugal by Henry the Navigator (1394-1460) and his successors lies at least as much in the role they played in the *Reconquista* and in the perennial struggle with Islam. Portugal's capture of Ceuta, on the North African coast, brought it from 1415 into a confrontation with Muslim Africa which not only excited Portuguese interest in the gold trade of the Moors but also provoked

225

Bronzes of Benin, West Africa
Benin, a kingdom of the Edo people, emerged into prominence to the west of the Niger delta in the 15th century. It produced very fine examples of the plastic arts, of which the "Benin Bronzes" are the most famous: this plaque shows an oba (king) of Benin between two of his warriors.

military revival under the next sultan, Murad II (1421-51). It was Murad's successor, Mehemmed II (1451-81), known as "The Conqueror", who finally breached the defences of Constantinople in 1453, making it thereafter his capital, and his absorption of what was left of the Christian Balkans during the next three years, although halted at Belgrade in 1456, took Islam to the banks of the Danube and to the Hungarian frontier of Latin Christianity in the West.

It was in the sixteenth century especially, under Selim (1512-20) and Suleiman "the Magnificent" (1520-66), that the Ottomans would experience their apogee. And, appropriately enough, it was in the middle years of that century that Ottoman building achieved a new sublimity in the work of Suleiman's great architect, Sinan. Nevertheless, the best period of Ottoman art was already beginning as far back as the sultanate of Mehemmed I, at least some of the characteristics of this early florescence being owed to the influence of Timurid buildings, put up for the Ottomans' recent conqueror. In particular, the decorative brilliance of the faience-enriched buildings of Samarkand, and perhaps especially the tomb of Tamerlane himself, was directly influential in introducing the new richness of ceramic tiling first seen at Bursa in Mehemmed I's Green Mosque and its accompanying Green Tomb. With Murad II's astonishing "Three-balconied Mosque", begun in 1438 at Edirne (Adrianople), these were the outstanding monuments of the first major phase of Ottoman architecture before the establishment of a permanent capital at the former Byzantine city of Constantinople.

With that, of course, a new era undoubtedly began, appropriately symbolized by the immediate conversion of the ancient Christian basilica of St Sophia into an Islamic mosque. Mehemmed the Conqueror's decision to make Istanbul his new capital was the signal for a programme of conversion and new building such as the city had not seen for some centuries. Mehemmed was himself something of a connoisseur. Indeed, the famous portrait of him sniffing a rose suggests that he was an aesthete as well. And something of this may surely be recognized in that exquisite garden pavilion, the so-called Tiled Kiosk, built in 1472 as an element of the Conqueror's great palace on Seraglio Point,

an ultimately frustrated ambition to discover Christian allies beyond them. The target was increasingly a desirable one. Great profits were to be made by Portuguese entrepreneurs in Africa from as early as the mid-fifteenth century, and these were an end in themselves. But at just this time, too, the thunder-clouds of an Islamic revival were gathering in the East, encouraging new initiatives among all Christian peoples to find the resources to disperse them.

Near East
After its humiliating defeat of 1402 at the hands of the Samarkand conqueror Tamerlane, the Ottoman Empire underwent a period of reconstruction under Mehemmed I (1413-21), closely followed by a

Isnik pottery
At Isnik in western Anatolia, Ottoman potters developed new techniques: limited at this time to a cobalt blue underglaze, their wares anticipated the high achievements of the 16th century, when the range of possible colours was extended.

Pantanassa Monastery, Mistra, Greece
Mistra, in the Peloponnese, was an important Byzantine centre in the 15th century: the last emperor was crowned there. The Monastery of the Pantanassa, founded in 1428, successfully combines Byzantine and Western styles.

Mehemmed the Conqueror
This 15th-century miniature by Sinan Bey shows Mehemmed II (1451-81), who in 1453 captured Constantinople, making it his capital. Although renowned as an aesthete and connoisseur of art, his reign was one of continuous, and successful, warfare, in the Balkans, Eastern Europe and Anatolia.

and one of the very few authentic survivors of the major building programme of his reign.

So rapid and so complete was the recovery of Ottoman fortunes that it is not surprising that it should have taken some time for the new empire to evolve a style that was entirely its own. The same Timurid influence visible earlier in the Green Tomb and Green Mosque at Bursa was still detectable at Istanbul in Mehemmed the Conqueror's Tiled Kiosk. In miniature-painting, the sources were both Timurid and Chinese, while in ceramics the fifteenth-century Ottoman potter still relied on his Chinese and Persian models. And yet, although Chinese subjects became steadily more important in Persian painted pottery under the sixteenth-century Safavids, the contrary was true of the Ottoman potters of Isnik (Nicaea), in western Anatolia, who even before the end of the fifteenth century were developing new techniques of their own. For the time being, Isnik wares were painted cobalt-blue on white, without the application of the reds, purples and greens which would later further enliven them. But the range of pot-shapes was already large, and the quality of the product very high. It was a promising beginning for a pottery industry that continued throughout the sixteenth and early seventeenth centuries to manufacture a good number of the world's most remarkable ceramics.

Mehemmed the Conqueror took his connoisseurship even to the point where he invited Western artists to his court. He borrowed the styles of Timurid Persia and Samarkand, and felt the attraction of Ming China both in painting and in those finer porcelains of which his successor, Bayezid II (1481-1512), built up a notable personal collection. Yet Constantinople, that once great centre of Byzantine civilization, had very little to give to the Ottomans, this being some indication of the desperate poverty into which the city had fallen before its conquest. In architecture, certainly, the leadership of the capital had long since passed to the provinces. One such example of continuing architectural initiatives, away from Constantinople, may be found in the surviving buildings at Mistra, in the former Byzantine principality of the Morea, south-west of Athens. The interesting characteristic of Morean architecture is that, because of the western connections of the princes of Mistra (both political and by marriage), Frankish and Byzantine elements were brought together in their city in a highly individual harmony. The palace at Mistra, completed between 1400 and 1460, although now no more than a roofless ruin, has a Venetian look, more obviously at home in the Venice-dominated Adriatic than in the still Byzantine territories of the Peloponnese. Similarly, the monastery of the Pantanassa at Mistra, founded in 1428, was very much a hybrid building. Essentially modelled on the earlier church of the Virgin Hodegetria (*c.* 1310), which was itself of Byzantine inspiration, the Pantanassa yet displayed a clear western influence in its Gothicized architectural details.

Eastern Europe

In the northern Balkans—in Serbia, Wallachia, and Moldavia—the cultural dominance which Byzantium had still been able to maintain in the fourteenth century, while political interests were shared, was swamped by the Ottoman tide. Independently, Serbia enjoyed a last cultural florescence under Stephen Lazarevic (1389-1427), continuing the earlier traditions of Milutin, Stephen Dusan and Prince Lazar to create the extraordinary Church of the Virgin (1413-17) at Kalenic, a building in which the decorative inclinations of Lazar's architects have been taken to exceptional lengths. But Serbian art soon afterwards became a victim of the Ottoman ascendancy, and it was only in the more autonomous vassal states of the

Church of the Virgin, Kalenic, Serbia
Built by Stephen Lazarevic between 1413 and 1417, this church follows the trefoil plan typical of late Serbian churches. The extensive and intricate carving is entirely secular in character, and possibly of Russian inspiration.

Voronet Church, Moldavia
Moldavia remained sufficiently independent of the Ottomans to develop its own architectural style in the 15th century: Voronet Church shows the articulated roof and tower-like dome typical of the tradition. The external wall-paintings are of the 16th century.

north-east Balkans, in present-day Rumania, that the architectural traditions of the Late Middle Ages were allowed to survive and develop. The most considerable achievements of the Moldavian architects would belong to the sixteenth and early seventeenth centuries. However, there was already a distinctive Moldavian flavour in such a building as Stephen the Great's monastery church at Voronet, dating from the late fifteenth century, and it is certainly true that the principal characteristics of later Moldavian architecture (as developed, for example, in the sixteenth-century cathedral of St George, Suceava) were all to be found in this reign.

Apart from the natural wealth of the Rumanian principalities, strung out along the rich Danube plain, an important element in the continuing prominence of the Orthodox Church in Rumania was the failure in leadership of Constantinople. The Moldavians and the Wallachians, on winning their freedom from Latin Hungary, had been received into the Orthodox community comparatively recently, no earlier than the mid-fourteenth century. Yet from 1453 they found themselves patrons and protectors of the ancient and now destitute Constantinople patriarchate, sharing this role for several centuries with the princes of Orthodox Russia.

For Russia, indeed, the collapse of Byzantium had many similarly important consequences. Political consolidation on Moscow continued through the fifteenth century, drawing in even the fiercely independent Novgorod before the end of it. But now there was added the unanticipated role of successor to the Greeks in Orthodox leadership, making Moscow not merely the new capital of a united people but also nothing less than "the third Rome". The old Byzantine belief in "renewal", which had kept up a forlorn faith in the resurrection of the empire long after all success had deserted it, was now transferred to Russia, where Orthodoxy triumphed, intact and independent still. At Moscow the symbol of this, appropriately enough, was that multi-churched fortress, the Kremlin, completely remodelled by Italian architects and engineers in the last quarter of the fifteenth century for Ivan III (1440-1505), Great Prince of Moscow, whose tsarina, Zoë, was a Greek princess, brought up in Rome and niece of the luckless Constantine XI, the last of the Byzantine emperors.

Again in this century Russia was torn by the familiar conflict between traditional and imported values. In painting, the work of Theophanes the Greek, at first at Novgorod and then later at Moscow, had reintroduced a level of expertise, learnt in Byzantium, which the local artists had lost. Yet Theophanes' own pupil, Andrey Rublev (c. 1370-1430), was able to show his independence from the obvious Byzantine models in the development of a highly influential Russian style, the primary quality of which was a compassionate spirituality in tune with the Russian instinct and unmatched at Constantinople (see page 202). Rublev's icon of the *Old Testament Trinity*, painted for the Trinity-Sergius Monastery at Zagorsk where he had served as a monk, shares with the much earlier *Virgin of Vladimir* (c. 1125) the very highest rank in traditional Russian affections, both paintings undoubtedly touching a chord that was deeply and unashamedly sentimental.

Another characteristic of fifteenth-century Russia—its intense patriotism—became evident (in rather melancholy fashion) in the historical themes increasingly familiar in Novgorod painting during the course of the century. Novgorod, after a history of independence stretching back into the immemorial past, was on the verge of collapse before Moscow. But it clearly suited the beleaguered citizens to recall a past in which there had been many much brighter experiences. One of these had been the defeat of the Suzdalians, besiegers of Novgorod in 1169 and allegedly driven off with the aid of the Virgin. The well-known *Battle between Novgorod and Suzdal*, of which at least three approximately contemporary versions are known to exist, was a work of the mid-fifteenth century (see page 203). Although falling within the existing Novgorod tradition of narrative painting on religious themes, these *Battle* icons were the earliest known attempt to represent in paint some part of the national story.

With the first major defeats of the Tartars in the late fourteenth century, the story of Russia had shown signs of a new awakening through what was essentially a Muscovite period. But the process of unification under Muscovite leadership was a slow one and, even in the case of the Tartars, it was not until 1480 that Ivan III (called "the Great") felt strong enough to refuse their traditional tribute payments.

Walls of the Kremlin, Moscow, Russia
The rebuilding of the Kremlin walls between 1485 and 1495 by Rodolfo Fioravanti, a pupil of Alberti, was a visible expression of the growing power of Moscow's ruler, Ivan III, "the Great", who, having adopted the title of Tsar, conquered Novgorod and stopped the payment of tribute to the Tartars, thus demonstrating his power and independence.

Moscow cathedrals
Church-building in 15th-century Moscow drew upon the Novgorodian tradition—masters from Pskov built the Cathedral of the Annunciation (1484-89)—but also on more cosmopolitan sources: the Bolognese Rodolfo Fioravanti was brought to Moscow to rebuild the Cathedral of the Dormition, completed in 1479, in which Italianate tendencies are visible.

Cathedral of the Annunciation, Moscow, Russia

Cathedral of the Dormition, Moscow, Russia

It was at just about this time too, initiated only a few years before, that the rebuilding of Moscow had begun. And here again tradition and innovation were at war.

There is no doubt at all that the roots of Russian architecture, as shown in the development of its own distinctive late-medieval character, lay in the stone churches of Vladimir-Suzdal and in the essentially timber tradition of the roof-carpenters of Novgorod and, more particularly, Pskov. In a characteristic Muscovite mixture of the two, the Cathedral of the Annunciation, re-using existing earlier foundations, was rebuilt in the Kremlin between 1484 and 1489. And it was imported masters from Pskov again who put up the exactly contemporary diminutive Kremlin church known as the Cathedral of the Ordination. Yet the tendencies of Ivan the Great, and perhaps even more of his tsarina Zoë, were towards a style more international in character, calculated to enhance the prestige of their emergent principality and to set it apart from its defeated provincial rivals. In the 1470s, the Great Prince's emissaries found him an Italian architect in the Bolognese Rodolfo Fioravanti, willing to serve in Moscow. The completion of the new Cathedral of the Dormition (1479) was Fioravanti's first commission.

In the event, although it might have looked as if the Renaissance had come to stay in late-fifteenth-century Russia, the forces of traditionalism ultimately proved too strong. The extraordinary votive churches of sixteenth-century Moscow

and its environs, culminating in Ivan the Terrible's bizarre Cathedral of St Basil the Blessed (1555-60), now the principal ornament of Red Square, show a self-conscious reversion to an exclusive national tradition. And even the Italians, faced with the strength of Russian Orthodoxy, were restricted from the beginning in what they could set out to achieve. Fioravanti's brief, on his arrival at Moscow, was to improve on, but essentially to repeat, a model taken from the Cathedral of the Dormition at Vladimir. And if the architect's Italian background was recognizably reflected in the geometrical symmetry of both plan and elevations at the Moscow Dormition, the building retained an overall character which was nevertheless wholly Russian. In just the same way, the more obviously Renaissance Cathedral of St Michael the Archangel, projected in 1505 just before Ivan the Great's death and completed in 1509, despite its flamboyant scallop-shell decoration in the contemporary Italian manner, was in fact a reversion to the traditional Russian plan, with the nave wider than its adjoining aisles and without Fioravanti's individual paired apses. Influential though the St Michael Cathedral would certainly be, especially in its introduction to Russia of some of the more familiar Renaissance decorative motifs, it had neither the structural merits of an Italian building nor the traditional appeal of a Russian one. In the nationalistic posturings of the succeeding reigns, it was quickly (and rightly) forgotten.

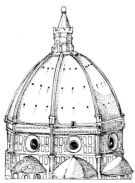

Dome of Florence Cathedral, Italy
Filippo Brunelleschi's dome for the Gothic cathedral at Florence was probably the greatest engineering feat of the 15th century. A double-shelled dome with light brick infilling, it derives its shape from the requirements of the existing cathedral, which prevented it from being a more purely classical form.

Western Europe

Fioravanti and his associates were military engineers as much as they were civil and ecclesiastical architects, and it was they, between 1485 and 1495, who equipped the Kremlin with the towers and walls which, still today, make it one of the world's most impressive fortified enclosures. As early examples of artillery fortifications, these walls take us back down a chain of technological innovation and experiment which included Leonardo da Vinci and Leon Battista Alberti (Fioravanti's master) along its length, and which may properly be said to have begun its course with the work of a brilliant Florentine engineer-architect, the great Filippo Brunelleschi (1377-1446).

To all of these, the practice of fortification, the application of mechanics in engineering projects, and the building of bridges, locks and canals, were of as much concern as the arts of the painter, the sculptor and the architect. And although few, perhaps, brought all together with the same enthusiasm and effortless panache as Leonardo, between them they established a traditional catholicity of interest which was the essential inspiration of the Renaissance. Exposed to this for the first time towards the end of the fifteenth century, the Russians nicknamed Fioravanti "Aristotle" in recognition of the breadth of his knowledge. And among the things that Fioravanti taught them, along

S. Spirito, Florence, Italy
Not completed until after his death, S. Spirito was conceived by Brunelleschi as the purest fulfilment of his theories on architectural proportion. Totally symmetrical, the church is constructed only in the ratios of 1:1 and 1:2.

with the full range of Italian constructional devices and techniques, was the use of a thin brick in vaulting, which had been one of the innovations adopted by Brunelleschi to lighten the dome of the cathedral he thus completed at Florence.

Brunelleschi's dome of Florence Cathedral, all but finished before his death in 1446, was a remarkable technical achievement, celebrated in every work on architectural history from that day through to the present. But its purpose was to crown an existing Gothicized building from which, inevitably, it had to take some of its form. And the restoration of purely classical principles of design, which was Brunelleschi's individual contribution to the architecture of his day, is certainly easier to see in other building projects on which he was also engaged. Brunelleschi had learnt from the masters of Antiquity the importance of proportion in architecture, to be established with mathematical precision. Symmetry was the outstanding characteristic of his celebrated façade, with loggìa, of the Foundling Hospital (1419-24) at Florence. However, the Foundling Hospital was one of his earlier works, with echoes still, in the slender columns of the loggia arcade, of an earlier Romanesque tradition. A still more influential building, in which Brunelleschi's mathematical theories were rather later to be fully developed, was the church of S. Spirito in the same city, hardly more than begun at Brunelleschi's death in 1446, but seen by the master himself as the complete expression of his views on architectural proportion. S. Spirito, indeed, was something of a mathematical exercise. Completely symmetrical in plan, with a characteristically assured use of Roman architectural detail, S. Spirito exhibited a harmony of proportions which made it the model for many parish churches in Renaissance Italy of similar basilican type. The nave arcade and its over-riding clerestory were precisely equal in height, while the width of the nave was exactly half the total height of arcade and clerestory together. Similarly, the bays of the aisles were twice as high as they were wide, being half as high and half as wide as the bays of the nave itself. Such meticulous adherence to the ratios 1:1 and 1:2 may seem to us a little unimaginative. And later, in the High Renaissance of sixteenth-century Italy, they provoked an extravagant reaction in that style we have come

Frederico da Montefeltro
Painted here by Piero della Francesca, Frederico da Montefeltro, Duke of Urbino, was one of the greatest soldiers of his age, and patron of an unparalleled artistic and cultural centre at his court.

Sketches of Leonardo da Vinci
Leonardo da Vinci (1442-1519) worked on almost every area of study available to a man of his time. Even in architecture his influence was far-reaching: one of his sketches inspired Bramante and, later, Michelangelo in the building of St Peter's, Rome.

to describe as "Mannerist". Nevertheless, to contemporaries the confidence of Brunelleschi's architectural mathematics opened a new world in which little or nothing was impossible. It was his "science of space", above all, which Alberti admired and which led him to place Brunelleschi first in the company of the painter Masaccio and the sculptors Ghiberti, Luca della Robbia, and Donatello. Among these, his contemporaries, Alberti claimed "there was talent for every noble thing not to be ranked below any who was ancient and famous in these arts."

Alberti's treatise *Della Pittura* (On Painting) was completed in 1435. But a more ambitious work, his *De re aedificatoria*, more usually known as the *Ten Books of Architecture*, although available in a first version as early as the mid-century, preoccupied him for the rest of his life. In essence, Alberti saw it as his role to reinterpret for his own times the principles of the classical architect Vitruvius. He developed, in doing so, an architectural archaeology which placed much emphasis on the recovery of classical detail and on the analysis of the laws governing the five orders, or styles, of the classical tradition—Doric, Ionic, Corinthian, Tuscan, and Composite. Alberti practised as an architect himself, with such achievements to his name as the Tempio Malatestiano at Rimini and the façade of S. Maria Novella at Florence, begun in 1446 and 1458 respectively. However, he is now remembered chiefly for his work as a theoretician, and for the contribution he made, more in writing than in practice, to such Renaissance masterpieces as Luciano Laurana's arcaded courtyard at the Palazzo Ducale, Urbino, completed in the 1460s for Frederico da Montefeltro, that great soldier and patron, and known especially for the harmony of its proportions.

The palace society of Frederico's Urbino welcomed such visitors as the architect Alberti and the painters Mantegna and Piero della Francesca, while Urbino itself, small town though it was, is known to have been the cradle of two outstanding masters of the High Renaissance in Italy—Bramante (d. 1514) and Raphael (d. 1520). Typical, moreover, of the constant intellectual stimulus of the Renaissance was Bramante's own contact, while working in Milan in the 1480s, with the engineer and painter, Leonardo da Vinci (1452-1519), himself deeply influenced by the work of his fellow Florentine, Filippo Brunelleschi, still new and exciting in his day. Although well acquainted with the architectural theorizing of Alberti, Leonardo himself built nothing, and some of his more complex architectural inventions could never, in fact, have been erected. But there is no question of his influence, in architecture as in so much else, on the intellectual climate of Italy at the turn of the fifteenth and the sixteenth centuries. Bramante's original design for St Peter's, Rome, is thought to have been modelled on one of Leonardo's sketches. Moreover, Michelangelo in his turn, when commissioned to complete in the mid-sixteenth century the still unfinished basilica, remained wedded to the principles of central planning which had fired the imagination of Leonardo.

The outstanding characteristic of Leonardo da Vinci was unquestionably his fertility of invention. One of his objectives, never completed, was to compile a scientific encyclopedia for his own times. And there is no doubt that the fifteenth century, back along the length of which he could now look, saw some impressive advances in all fields. Not least of these had been what was close to a revolution in the arts, associated above all with the name of a young Florentine painter, Masaccio (1401-28), whose contribution to painting, almost from nowhere, was a mathematically flawless perspective (see page 220). After Masaccio, no artist who saw his work could fail to be inspired by his mastery of every painterly technique—his lighting, his modelling, and his grasp of perspective, learnt at the knee of Brunelleschi. However, Masaccio died too young to found a clear school of his own, only Fra Filippo Lippi (1406-69) being thought to have been his pupil. And his harsh realism was too powerful and sombre to recommend itself for long to patrons brought up in the superficially more light-hearted world of International Gothic. It is likely that Masaccio was influenced originally by the robust and heroic vision of the sculptor Donatello (1386-1466), friend of Brunelleschi and a Florentine like Masaccio himself. Yet Donatello in his later years explored an emotionalism in expression which took him away from the monumental tradition he had shared with the young Masaccio. And Filippo Lippi's more mature work, at least from the 1440s, exhibited a lyricism

Bronze of "David" by Donatello, in Florence, Italy
Donatello achieved, through his own studies of antiquity, a mastery of depth, perspective and relief, that was enormously influential. His David is an urbane, self-confident youth, a splendid treatment of this Florentine theme.

Second Baptistery Doors by Ghiberti, at Florence, Italy
In this panel, the Story of Joseph, from his Second Baptistery Doors at Florence, Lorenzo Ghiberti showed a new mastery of graded relief and mathematical perspective, learned from Donatello, that was absent from his earlier work.

which associates him less with the vigorous classicism of his master Masaccio than with the rich and delicately decorative International Gothic of Masaccio's older contemporary, the Umbrian painter Gentile da Fabriano (*c.* 1360-1427).

This mixture of Northern and Mediterranean traditions was entirely characteristic of a society with many obvious links with the troubled world north of the Alps. The *rayonnant* Gothic of the new cathedral in Milan, begun as late as 1387, stood side-by-side with the classical severity of a building like Brunelleschi's Florentine church of S. Spirito. And while Filippo Lippi's later paintings showed the continuing attraction of Gothic art even to one brought up at the centre of a classical revival, the rather earlier sculptures of Lorenzo Ghiberti (1378-1455), contemporary and rival of the great Donatello, took exactly the opposite direction. In the story of West European sculpture, one of the best-known contrasts is between Ghiberti's sculptural style on his First Baptistery Doors, completed by 1424, and the technique he adopted for the Second Baptistery Doors, again at Florence and begun the following year. In the one, the scenes on the panels were enclosed in a Gothicized frame, and their execution, although certainly skilful enough to win the admiration of contemporaries, was flat and entirely conventional. Yet by the time Ghiberti came to work on his Second Baptistery Doors (1425-52), he had learnt so much from Donatello and the classical revival that his entire technique had changed. What he could now achieve was a refined perspective, mathematically governed as it had been with Masaccio and further improved upon by the device, borrowed from Donatello, of modelling the foreground figures in a deeper relief than those set behind them on the panel. Ghiberti's conversion is significant. It demonstrates the power of the individual example (in this case that of Donatello) to shape the whole culture of his times.

Ghiberti sought, on his Second Baptistery Doors, to "observe every measure of proportion". And this pursuit of a perfect perspective became something of an obsession among his contemporaries. It can be seen again, for example, in the architectural paintings of the Tuscan artist Piero della Francesca (*c.* 1410-92), and it would, perhaps, have led to a confining aridity in painting had it not been for the arrival of some altogether new ideas from a North European source. Piero della Francesca was a master of fresco-painting, one of the greatest artists in this medium that the world has ever seen. Yet in the last years of his life he was also being influenced by the oil-painting tradition of contemporary Flanders, and it is clear that the arrival in Florence in about 1475 of Hugo van der Goes' *Portinari Altarpiece*, commissioned by a Florentine family, had had an impact already of unexpected proportions (see page 217). Piero della Francesca's *Nativity*, one of his last works (see page 221), took its inspiration quite unmistakably from the Flemish altarpiece of Hugo van der Goes. He was not the only Italian artist to feel the draw of this particular northern painting, nor was he the first to be influenced by Flanders.

The Flemish masters had their limitations, being unable as yet to achieve the control of perspective which to the Italian artist of the *Quattrocento* was by now part of his essential equipment. Nevertheless, what they did offer was a new intensity of light and fresh perfection of detail, owing a good deal to their novel oil medium, and unmatched in the more traditional South. Furthermore, the increasingly exact realism of International Gothic had been preserved and extended in fifteenth-century Flanders at just that time when, in contemporary Italy, the emphasis was shifting to the representation of a classical ideal. In portraiture, especially, the Flemish example was important. Still, in the third quarter of the fifteenth century, one of the few successful southern imitators of the Flemish portrait style was the Sicilian artist Antonello da Messina (*c.* 1430-79). He had grown up in the relative isolation of Southern Italy where, at the ports of Messina, Palermo and Naples, the work of Jan van Eyck (d. 1441) and Rogier van der Weyden (d. 1464) was at least as well known as that of their contemporary Masaccio. In Antonello's portraits, the most appealing of which are probably his three *Annunciations*, the identifiable qualities he shares with the Flemings are their realism, their use of intense colour, and the extraordinary clarity of their light (see page 220). It was these, in due course, that he brought to Venice in 1475, to influence the work of that prolific and long-lived master Giovanni Bellini (*c.* 1430-1516), founder of the High Renaissance Venetian School renowned especially for the painters Giorgione, Veronese, and Titian, all of the sixteenth century.

Bellini's technique, which he learnt from Antonello, was to flood his paintings with light in the Flemish manner, illuminating every detail within them (see page 220). Moreover, the brilliance and clarity to be found in his work go back a full century to the work of the best Gothic miniaturists. Early in the fifteenth century, the Limbourg brothers stood at the peak of this ancient and still far from exhausted tradition. Their *Très Riches Heures*, painted for Jean de Berry and left incomplete on the death of both patron and artists in 1416, was never afterwards excelled. But extravagant court patronage was being brought to an end in France at just about that time by the English invasions under Henry V and by an intensification of the civil war between Armagnacs and Burgundians. And one major consequence of the extinction of Paris as a centre of the arts was the re-establishment of patronage in the still wealthy cities of fifteenth-century Flanders, with a base no longer aristocratic but bourgeois.

After the civil wars and demographic catastrophes of the previous century, Flemish society had re-established itself in close partnership, among others, with the Italians. Jan van Eyck's *Double Portrait of Giovanni Arnolfini and his Wife* (1434) was one of the more celebrated works of the Early Renaissance in the north (see page 216). Significantly, here the patron was a merchant of Lucca, resident in Bruges and engaged in the rich trade between Flanders and Northern Italy which had made the western sea route up the coasts of Europe perhaps the major commercial artery of the known world. The *Double Portrait* was a sophisticated work, loaded with complex symbolism. But on a more obvious level it exhibited all those qualities which recommended Flemish art to the Italians: the lighting was brilliant and clear, the portraiture was realistic, every detail of costume and furnishings, even to the reflection of the scene in a mirror, was represented with an astonishing virtuosity.

It is no longer maintained that Jan van Eyck himself was the founder of the so-called Flemish School; this honour is probably due to the anonymous Master of Flémalle whose *Mérode Altarpiece*, over a decade earlier than the van Eyck *Double Portrait*, shares many of its characteristics.

Yet the acknowledged masters of this first phase of the Northern Renaissance were undoubtedly the contemporaries Jan van Eyck and Rogier van de Weyden, with Hugo van der Goes (d. 1482) as their later-fifteenth-century successor. Already, in the *Ghent Altarpiece* of Hubert and Jan van Eyck, completed in 1432 (see page 217), the Flemish School had reached a high perfection—so high, indeed, that Hugo van der Goes, by a contemporary account, is said to have been driven insane by the sense of his own inadequacy before it.

Jan van Eyck started his career as a miniaturist: the illuminator of expensive books of hours in the tradition of the brothers Limbourg. And much of the exact quality of his work, together with some of its serenity, may be explained by his early training. In contrast, the panel painters, Rogier van der Weyden and Hugo van der Goes, strove to achieve a new dramatic urgency in their art, given power by the total composition. Rogier was acquainted with the work of his contemporaries in Italy. He had Italian patrons, visited Italy himself in 1450, and employed an Italian apprentice. And while he remained throughout his life very much within the developing tradition of the North, quite early on, in his *Descent from the Cross* (c. 1438) he had already shown a mastery of the deployment of figures to highlight a central theme that was more Italian than Flemish in origin (see page 217). It was both a strength and a weakness in the art of the Flemish School that the individual portrait was frequently so vivid and exact that it might actually benefit by its removal from the general context of the painting. The contrary virtue in Italian painting was the subordination of the parts to the whole. And it is not without significance that one of the largest and most unified of the Flemish works—Hugo van der Goes' *Portinari Altarpiece*—was also the most influential ambassador of the North.

In many ways the *Portinari Altarpiece* was an eccentric work, making dramatic use of that ancient device by which a figure is accorded the size it deserves by its importance. But in its very selection of individual points of emphasis, it broke from that confining tradition of the Flemish School, which gave equal weight to every component of the picture, threatening to develop the craft element in painting at the expense of the creative imagination. Italy itself would experience a violent reaction in the sixteenth century away from the classical certainties of its *quattrocento* Renaissance. Nevertheless this very classicism did much in its period to discipline the arts which, in the North, were permitted to develop a competitive (and ultimately destructively extravagant) exuberance.

One of the ways in which this exuberance manifested itself was in the elaboration of architectural sculpture. The great wealth of the Flemish trading and manufacturing cities of the Late Middle Ages enabled them to engage in a succession of frankly competitive municipal building enterprises. Contemporary London had its own equivalent in the early-fifteenth-century Guildhall which still remains the principal late-medieval monument of that city. But despite its great size, the London Guildhall was a building of comparative austerity, in keeping with the more restrained architectural style that is known in England as "Perpendicular". In contrast, the early- to mid-fifteenth-century town halls of Brussels and of Louvain, following the precedent established only a few decades before by Bruges (1376-87), were buildings of astounding and increasing elaboration, in which civic pride and the joy of craftsmanship were given uninhibited expression.

Mourner at the tomb of Philip the Bold
Claus Sluter designed the arcade of mourners around the base of the tomb of Philip the Bold, Duke of Burgundy: highly realistic, and swathed in robes, each mourner seems to process through the delicate Gothic arcade, a lasting symbol of grief.

"Eve" by Tilman Riemenschneider
One of a pair of carved wooden figures by Riemenschneider, this carving of Eve displays the emotional intensity typical of late Gothic sculpture.

Later in the fifteenth century, the so-called "Flamboyant" Gothic style reached its peak in the work of Martin Chambiges at the French cathedral of Sens. And a good example of the flame-like traceries after which the style was named may be found at Bruges itself in the façade of the Chapelle du Saint Sang. Nevertheless, what clearly appealed to contemporary bourgeois taste was less the grace of Chambiges' rose window on the south transeptal façade at Sens (1490) than the technical virtuosity of the pinnacled and turreted Hôtel de Ville at Louvain (1448-63). Neatly combining the luminous art of the Flemish School with the unrestrained sculptural vigour of fifteenth-century Flanders, Hans Memlinc's *Shrine of St Ursula* (1489) set portraits of characteristic tranquillity in a casket frame of restless flamboyant Gothic. Memlinc's *Shrine*, painted for the Hospital of St John at Bruges, can be counted among the masterpieces of this prolific and very professional painter, and it is certainly his best-known work (see page 217). However, the sheer technical skill of Memlinc as a painter was at least one reason why his *oeuvre* as a whole suffered from a distinct poverty of imagination.

In just the same way, the wood- and stone-carvers of the South Netherlands and Germany were to be handicapped by their own virtuosity. Netherlands architectural altarpieces in the late fifteenth century were in demand throughout the West. But one of the consequences of this widespread interest was an inevitable switch to mass-production. Even in a relatively early work of Jan Borman the Elder, his very remarkable *Altar of St George* (1493), the complexity of the carving and its technical brilliance somehow dissipate the emotional impact of the whole. And to appreciate the genuine artistry of Borman, we must look for it rather in the single portrait sculpture or effigy, among the finest of which is the bronze effigy of Mary of Burgundy, cast in the 1490s by Renier van Thienen from Borman's original wood model.

Late Gothic sculptors were undoubtedly capable of achieving in their work a high level of emotional intensity. Indeed, in the carvings, both stone and wood, of the Würzburg artist Tilman Riemenschneider (c. 1460-1531), this quality was developed with a remarkable sureness of touch. Nor were there anywhere better opportunities for the representation of emotion than in the sepulchral effigy. Since the coming of bubonic plague in the mid-fourteenth century, the cult of death in its many manifestations had continued to hold its grisly grip on the popular culture of the day. In painting, a full century after the Black Death, it had inspired that magnificent Sicilian masterpiece *The Triumph of Death* (c. 1450) (see page 213). And in sculpture it gave limitless opportunities in the adornment of the tombs for the inventiveness of the artist. Some of the finest work in this specialized tradition was done in Burgundy, where the funereal effigies of a brilliant aristocracy were given a special flavour of melancholy realism by their company of attendant mourners in conventional poses of grief. In a succession of royal and magnate tombs, including those of the Burgundian dukes Philip the Bold and John the Fearless, the themes of mourning were elaborated, to issue in one of the most moving sepulchral monuments of all time, the effigy supported by eight hooded figures of Philippe Pot (d. 1493), Grand Seneschal of Burgundy (see page 213).

Philippe Pot was himself a notable patron of the arts, and the monument he commissioned for erection in the abbey church at Cîteaux was carved, probably by Antoine le Moiturier, over a decade before his death. It was Antoine, in the late 1460s, who completed the tomb of John the Fearless, begun by the Spanish sculptor Juan de la Huerta. And this blending of Avignonese and Spanish talent should remind us that Gothic art, through its final manifestations, was just as international in the late fifteenth century as it had been in 1400. Juan de la Huerta's work was characterized by precise realism in the manner of contemporary Flemish sculpture. Moreover, this imported Netherlands realistic tradition was developed further in Spain itself, to the point at which it improved on the art of its homeland. Spanish tomb sculpture in the last decades of the century had a truly Renaissance flavour, while in such major commissions as the high altar at Toledo Cathedral, carved between 1498 and 1504, the individual talents of Flemish and German, Spanish and Burgundian woodcarvers were brought together in a single cooperative enterprise.

Another elaborate altarpiece, that in Seville Cathedral, was conceived by the Netherlands sculptor Pieter Dancart (d.

Detail of the high altar, Seville Cathedral, Spain
Designed by the Flemish sculptor Pieter Dancart, the altarpiece at Seville is the largest in Spain, consisting of 45 scenes positioned in a complex architectural framework.

Beverley Minster, England
The west front of Beverley Minster, completed early in the 15th century to one consistent design, is perhaps the best example of a Perpendicular west front in England. Very tall in proportion to its width, and built on the continental two-towered model, it has a fine unity of composition, enhanced by the decorative features.

1489) and continued by a fellow country-man. In contrast, the distinct austerity of the cathedral interior at Seville is reminiscent of English Perpendicular. Seville Cathedral, on which work continued throughout the fifteenth century, was by deliberate purpose the largest Gothic cathedral yet (or ever) built, being conceived by its patrons to be "so great and of such a kind that those who see it finished shall think that we were mad". Furthermore, it was only one of the many ambitious architectural enterprises, throughout the European West, that distinguished the fifteenth century. While, that is, the Italian architects Brunelleschi, Alberti, Luciano Laurana and Donato Bramante were shaping their classical revival, the last monuments of Gothic civilization were attaining a new perfection of their own. To this period in England belong the supreme achievements of the Beverley west front at the beginning of the fifteenth century and King's College Chapel, Cambridge, started in 1446 as one of the major works of piety of that architectural connoisseur Henry VI, but not completed until early in the next century (see page 224). In France, there were the *style flamboyant* façades at the cathedrals of Sens and at Beauvais. In Germany and in Austria, the sophisticated openwork tracery of Strasbourg Cathedral was successfully re-used in such major buildings as the spectacular Stephansdom, Vienna.

Architectural ambitions, at the end of the Gothic period, not infrequently exceeded the technical competence of the architects called upon to live up to them. At Seville, as later and more disastrously at Beauvais, the tower over the crossing collapsed. Yet these ambitions also belonged to a mood of increasing technological self-confidence which, already in the fifteenth century, pointed the way forward to centuries of industrial and intellectual dominance in the West, promoted by colonial expansion. The foundations for this had, of course, been laid by earlier generations. But the mathematics and mechanics of the *Quattrocento* in Italy, empirical as yet rather than theoretical, were the direct product of progressive patronage in architecture both civil and military. It was on the experimental ingenuity of Brunelleschi and Leonardo, as well as, for example, on the innovatory skills of the Nuremberg instrument-makers, that the revival of western science was based.

Initially, this revival was deliberate and self-conscious. It was contrived in Florence in the first years of the fifteenth century as an assertion of a profoundly-felt civic identity, threatened just then by the expansion of the Visconti principate of Milan. Florence, under its humanist chancellors Collucio Salutati and Leonardo Bruni, saw its own salvation in a return to the virtues, as much cultural as political, of republican Rome. This was the occasion for a massive (and deeply influential) programme of investment in public works. And although Florence itself lost its leadership when the republic went down before the Medici, to the city's later cultural impoverishment, the intellectual momentum, once generated at Florence, was not thereafter to be lost. Much of Leonardo da Vinci's best work, including his great *Last Supper* (c. 1497), was completed at the court of Lodovici il Moro at Milan. The rebuilding of Rome, which began soon after the healing of the Great Schism at the Council of Constance in 1417, provided in due course a sensational arena for the talents of Bramante, Raphael, and Michelangelo, dependent on papal patronage.

Continuity in the revival was above all secured by a technological revolution in the dissemination of knowledge: the refinement of printing under Johann Gensfleisch (Gutenberg) at Mainz. Gutenberg's development of movable metal type for

Mainz Bible
The Mainz Bible was the first printed work from the press of Johann Gutenberg, produced in the early 1450s.

The first voyage of Columbus
Christopher Columbus (1451-1506), a Genoese in the service of the crown of Castile, sailed to the West Indies in 1492 on the first of four voyages to the New World. The Santa Maria was the largest of the three ships he took in 1492: about thirty metres long, it almost certainly carried two square-rigged and one lateen-rigged mast, and a crew of forty.

Christopher Columbus

Conjectural model of the Santa Maria

printing on a commercial scale should not be seen in isolation. It had a very exact equivalent in contemporary printing practice in Korea, while in the West block-printing had been known since the late thirteenth century and cast metal type had been in use in Limoges from not more than a century later. Important also to the impact of Gutenberg's revolution had been earlier improvements in paper-making, as water-power was employed to drive pulping-mills, with the more recent development of an oil-bound ink (perhaps derived from the experiments with oil-based paints of the early-fifteenth-century Flemish masters), and such related advances as a new understanding of the principles of optics and the consequent invention of spectacles. All of these, even before Gutenberg's successful experiments with type-making at Mainz, had contributed already to an opening up of the world of the book. Nevertheless, what Gutenberg and his partner, Johann Fust, developed for themselves were commercially viable techniques for striking and casting metal type that permitted for the first time a massive expansion of book production. The implications of their work were enormous.

Between the printing of the Mainz bible in the early 1450s and the end of the fifteenth century, many thousands of influential works, hitherto reserved for a small readership, became very widely accessible. In 1465, an Italian press began printing at Subiaco, and not much later, in the early 1470s and the 1480s, presses were operating in France, in Hungary, and in England. Yet, important though it was, this achievement in printing was only a part of a more general revolution in mechanics. Gutenberg himself was a goldsmith by trade, and it was fellow metal-workers, the instrument-makers of Nuremberg and Augsburg, who played a role at least as vital as that of the theoreticians in the development of fifteenth-century science. The so-called 'Nuremberg egg'', a portable spring-driven clock, was only one of their many inventions. Alongside the navigational and astronomical instruments of the same skilled craftsmen, it was a major symptom of a technological coming-of-age in the West.

In part, this new technology was directed to peaceful purposes: to canal-building and the improvement of locks, and to other advances in contemporary hydraulics such as the development of better wind-mills for pumping. In the fish industry, new techniques of curing and packing greatly widened the potential market for sea-fish, while in agriculture one result of better irrigation and drainage in the north Italian river valleys was the introduction for the first time of rice. But the most powerful encouragements of technological progress, in the fifteenth century as still today, were warfare and the more aggressive manifestations of trade. Two early works of military technology were the *Bellifortis* (c. 1405) of Conrad Kyeser (see page 205) and the anonymous *Feuerwerk-buch* (c. 1420), a manual on cannon and explosives. They were well-informed and sometimes fanciful compilations: characteristic products of the cult of the gun.

Of course, it was the hand-gun, from the early sixteenth century, that came to be a principal instrument of European expansion overseas. However, the voyages of discovery which took Portuguese and Spanish seamen first down the coast of Africa, and then across the Atlantic to the Americas, were more directly the consequence of significant improvements in transport. The North European cog and the Mediterranean galley had been adequate enough in the fourteenth century for a coast-hugging seasonal trade. But the cog, with its single square-sail, lacked manoeuvrability, and it was the introduction of the fully-rigged carrack in the mid-fifteenth century, developing out of both the cog and the Portuguese caravel of Henry the Navigator's expeditions, that opened the way to the Indies.

Almost half a millennium had passed since the voyage of Leif Ericsson, in 1003, had alerted Europe to the existence of a trans-Atlantic continent. Yet that continent had been left to develop in isolation for want of a method of getting there. When Christopher Columbus set sail from Palos on 3 August 1492, he had little real concept of where he was going and, to our minds, was pathetically ill-equipped. But his ships were rigged in the new fifteenth-century manner with square-sails, lateen-sails and jibs, and they carried their complement of guns. Two years later, in 1494, we hear for the first time of a "New World", as applied to Columbus' discoveries. The words are important, for they imply both the recognition of an "Old World", and the consciousness of the dawning of an age.

World Architecture

It was the engineer, in the fifteenth-century world, who frequently took over from the architect. Undoubtedly, the greatest single engineering achievement of the age was Yung-lo's re-planning of Peking, with its triple fortified circuit. But this was also the century of Rodolfo Fioravanti's rebuilding of the Moscow Kremlin for Ivan the Great, first effective tsar of all the Russias. While across the ocean, in Inca Peru, civil engineering was perhaps the principal preoccupation of the state.

Fioravanti started his career at Bologna, and it was entirely characteristic of his generation of Italian architect-engineers that he was able to turn his hand as readily to the building of a new cathedral as to the design of the defences that protected it. The Cathedral of the Dormition at Moscow, which is Fioravanti's work, is still very much a Russian building, in line with its 12th-century model at Vladimir. Yet the overall symmetry of the cathedral's design and the structural refinements it embodies could only have been learnt in Italy, betraying the touch of a skilled engineer more at home with Brunelleschi, the Florentine master, or with Fioravanti's own contemporary, Leonardo.

Other opportunities for ambitious re-buildings accompanied the resurrection of the Ottoman Empire. Ottoman building in Anatolia, before the capture of Constantinople in 1453, included Mehemmed I's Green Mosque and Tomb at Bursa and the great "Three-balconied Mosque" of Murad II at Edirne. However, the principal stimulus to Ottoman patronage was the re-siting of the Turkish capital at Constantinople (Istanbul). Mehemmed's Tiled Kiosk is an exquisite reminder of the very considerable sophistication of palace life on the Seraglio Point.

Something of the same conflict of values characterized contemporary Japan. The declining years of the Ashikaga shogunate were violent and torn by civil wars. Nevertheless, it was under the shogun Yoshimasa that the tea ceremony, a relaxing and sophisticated Zen Buddhist ritual, came to be disseminated throughout Japan. The architecture of the tea pavilion, austere but perfect, with the focus it provides on the single art object in its niche, is as complete a statement of human achievement as any architecture before or since.

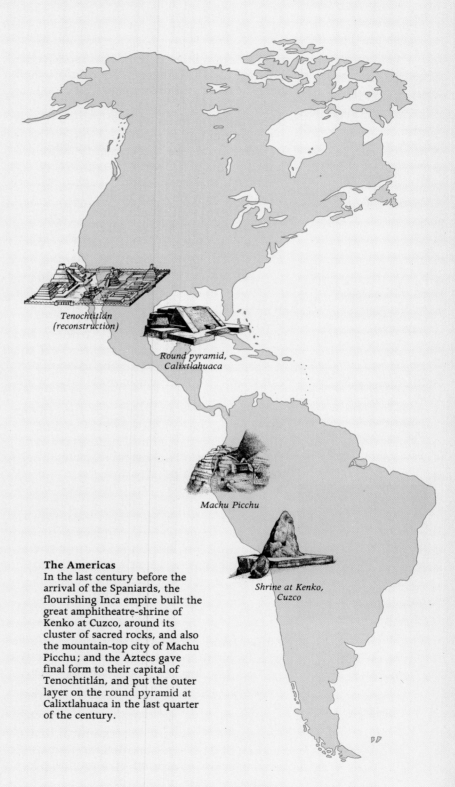

*Tenochtitlán
(reconstruction)*

*Round pyramid,
Calixtlahuaca*

Machu Picchu

*Shrine at Kenko,
Cuzco*

The Americas
In the last century before the arrival of the Spaniards, the flourishing Inca empire built the great amphitheatre-shrine of Kenko at Cuzco, around its cluster of sacred rocks, and also the mountain-top city of Machu Picchu; and the Aztecs gave final form to their capital of Tenochtitlán, and put the outer layer on the round pyramid at Calixtlahuaca in the last quarter of the century.

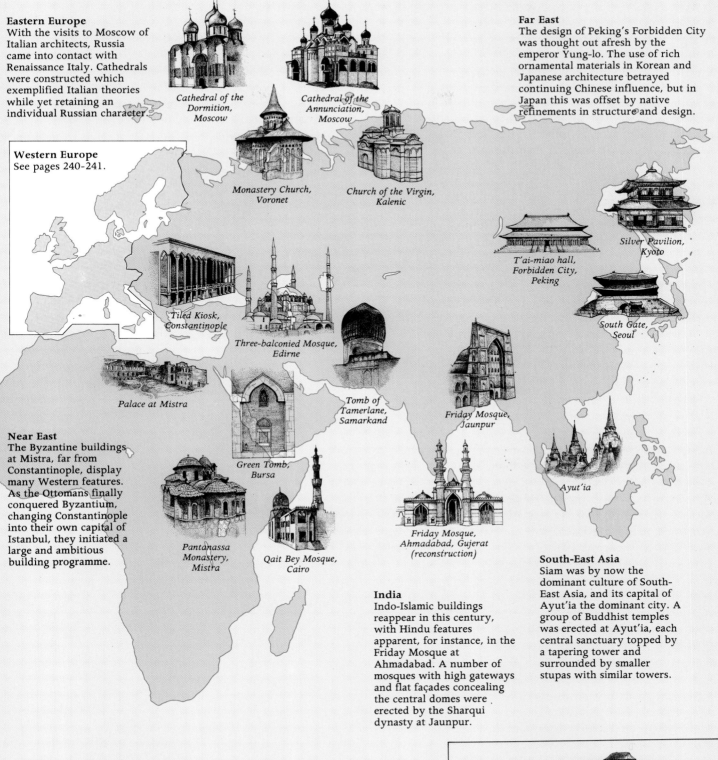

Eastern Europe
With the visits to Moscow of Italian architects, Russia came into contact with Renaissance Italy. Cathedrals were constructed which exemplified Italian theories while yet retaining an individual Russian character.

Cathedral of the Dormition, Moscow

Cathedral of the Annunciation, Moscow

Monastery Church, Voronet

Church of the Virgin, Kalenic

Western Europe
See pages 240–241.

Tiled Kiosk, Constantinople

Three-balconied Mosque, Edirne

Far East
The design of Peking's Forbidden City was thought out afresh by the emperor Yung-lo. The use of rich ornamental materials in Korean and Japanese architecture betrayed continuing Chinese influence, but in Japan this was offset by native refinements in structure and design.

Silver Pavilion, Kyoto

T'ai-miao hall, Forbidden City, Peking

South Gate, Seoul

Palace at Mistra

Green Tomb, Bursa

Tomb of Tamerlane, Samarkand

Friday Mosque, Jaunpur

Near East
The Byzantine buildings at Mistra, far from Constantinople, display many Western features. As the Ottomans finally conquered Byzantium, changing Constantinople into their own capital of Istanbul, they initiated a large and ambitious building programme.

Pantanassa Monastery, Mistra

Qait Bey Mosque, Cairo

Friday Mosque, Ahmadabad, Gujerat (reconstruction)

Ayut'ia

India
Indo-Islamic buildings reappear in this century, with Hindu features apparent, for instance, in the Friday Mosque at Ahmadabad. A number of mosques with high gateways and flat façades concealing the central domes were erected by the Sharqui dynasty at Jaunpur.

South-East Asia
Siam was by now the dominant culture of South-East Asia, and its capital of Ayut'ia the dominant city. A group of Buddhist temples was erected at Ayut'ia, each central sanctuary topped by a tapering tower and surrounded by smaller stupas with similar towers.

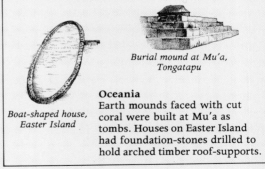

Burial mound at Mu'a, Tongatapu

Boat-shaped house, Easter Island

Oceania
Earth mounds faced with cut coral were built at Mu'a as tombs. Houses on Easter Island had foundation-stones drilled to hold arched timber roof-supports.

Western European Architecture

The architecture of Europe throughout the fifteenth century is characterized by its overweening ambition. Seville Cathedral, designedly, was the largest Gothic cathedral ever built. In Northern France and in Flanders, the extravagant complexity of "Flamboyant" Gothic, although far from the most perfect of Gothic traditions, undoubtedly ranked as the most expensive.

The final florescence of medieval architecture in the North was not everywhere marred by such tasteless extravagance as distinguished the Flemish town halls. The English "Perpendicular" King's College chapel at Cambridge, started in 1446 for Henry VI and completed only in 1515, has a structural unity that marks it out still as one of the most satisfying architectural achievements of the Middle Ages.

In Italy, the classical revival began in earnest with the practice and teachings of the great Brunelleschi, architect-engineer. In his church of S. Spirito in Florence, designed in 1436, he achieved complete command of the formal principles of building in the Vitruvian manner, a full decade before his death. It was these principles that took hold in Italy, routing what was left of Gothic. The future lay in the perfectly-controlled proportions of Luciano Laurana's celebrated Great Courtyard of the Palazzo Ducale at Urbino.

Spain

The building of Seville Cathedral, the largest Gothic cathedral ever to be completed, brought with it the culmination of Spanish Gothic.

Britain

The central tower at Canterbury and the west front at Beverley are gratifying examples of the Perpendicular style, and the harmonious unity of the exterior of King's College chapel is surpassed only by its fan-vaulted ceiling. Gothic in Scotland was much more after the French style.

Melrose Abbey

Minster, Beverley

King's College chapel, Cambridge

Raglan Castle

Guildhall, London

Central tower of Canterbury Cathedral

Southease Church, Sussex

Palais de Justice, Rouen

Town hall, Brussels

Town hall, Louvain

Château, Amboise (reconstruction from drawing)

House of Jacques Coeur, Bourges

Cathedral, Seville

France

The Gothic castles of the period were the last of their type, and most were later converted into Renaissance residences. The house of the merchant and financier Jacques Coeur is a fine example of Late Gothic domestic architecture.

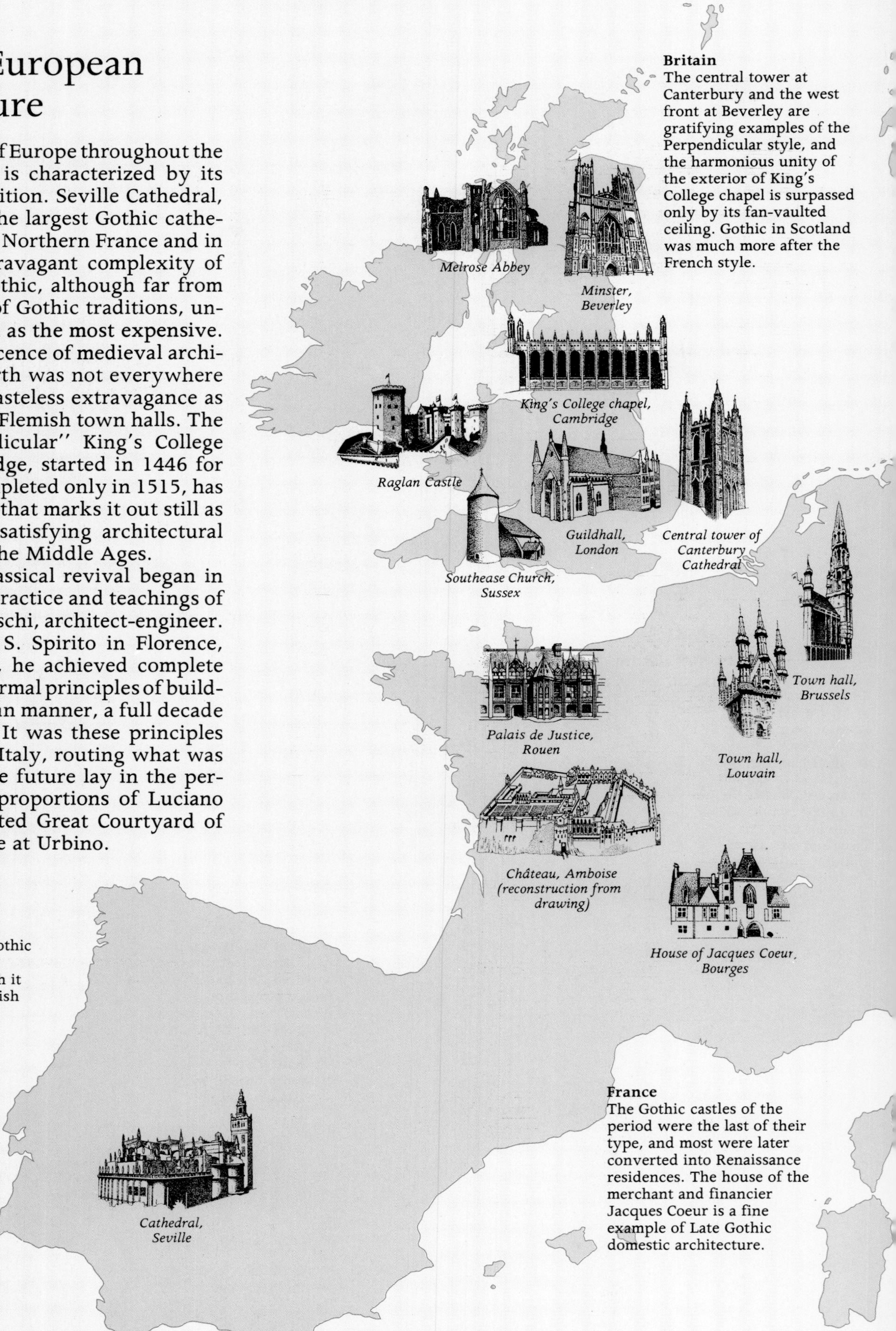

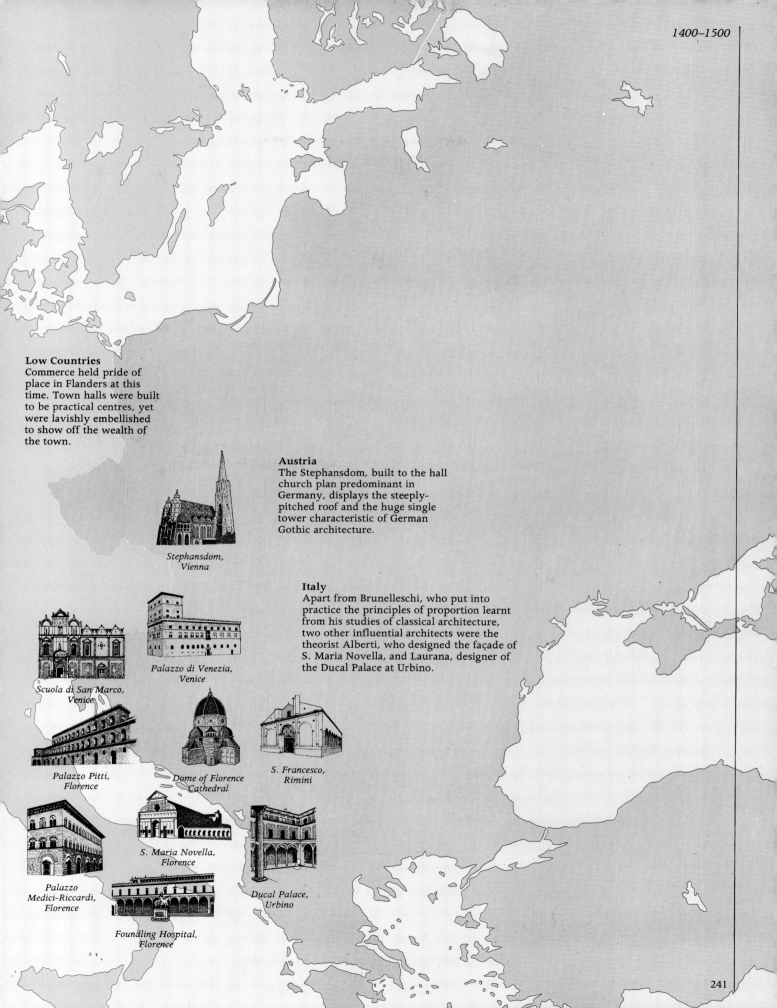

Low Countries
Commerce held pride of
place in Flanders at this
time. Town halls were built
to be practical centres, yet
were lavishly embellished
to show off the wealth of
the town.

Austria
The Stephansdom, built to the hall
church plan predominant in
Germany, displays the steeply-
pitched roof and the huge single
tower characteristic of German
Gothic architecture.

*Stephansdom,
Vienna*

Italy
Apart from Brunelleschi, who put into
practice the principles of proportion learnt
from his studies of classical architecture,
two other influential architects were the
theorist Alberti, who designed the façade of
S. Maria Novella, and Laurana, designer of
the Ducal Palace at Urbino.

*Palazzo di Venezia,
Venice*

*Scuola di San Marco,
Venice*

*Palazzo Pitti,
Florence*

*Dome of Florence
Cathedral*

*S. Francesco,
Rimini*

*Palazzo
Medici-Riccardi,
Florence*

*S. Maria Novella,
Florence*

*Ducal Palace,
Urbino*

*Foundling Hospital,
Florence*

World Art

The short-lived empires of the Incas and the Aztecs had little opportunity to generate a great art of their own. Nevertheless, they were to place a mark on the ancient cultures of Peru and Mexico which reflected very exactly their philosophies. The characteristically geometric art of Inca Peru, with its emphasis on functional utility, precisely corresponds with the manifest values of a society of architects and engineers. In Aztec Mexico, those themes of death and of re-birth which, throughout the fifteenth century, recur in the sculptures and painted codices of the period, merely repeat in another form the driving forces of a religious belief that was itself the inspiration of Aztec imperialism.

Contemporaneously, on isolated Easter Island in the South Pacific, another society ruled by priests was requiring the carving of the colossal stone heads which still remain as one of the most remarkable expressions of a lost culture. Like the heads of Benin, in Nigeria, just then beginning to be made alongside the more familiar terracotta sculptures of the region, they belonged to a religion which placed much emphasis on the stylized portrait bust, yet otherwise is little understood.

Both in China and in Japan, the art of the fifteenth century is traditional and essentially backward-looking. However, at its best it cultivated a spontaneity which, although itself based on the now long-established canons of Zen Buddhism, still had a freshness of its own. There is a confident economy in the landscapes of the Chinese painters Tai Chin and Shen Chou which captures the sensation of the moment. In just the same way, the inspired ink sketches of the Japanese Zen painter Sesshu are designedly impressionistic in their manner.

In Russia, too, spontaneity of expression had been one of the lessons taught by Theophanes the Greek to the Russians who worked alongside him. Yet the principal appeal of the work of his greatest pupil, Andrey Rublev, lay rather in a compassionate spirituality—a sentimental and often melancholy emotionalism—which stirred the heart of contemporary Russia. To this day, Rublev's icon of the *Old Testament Trinity*, now at the Tretyakov Gallery in Moscow, is ranked at the very peak of its tradition.

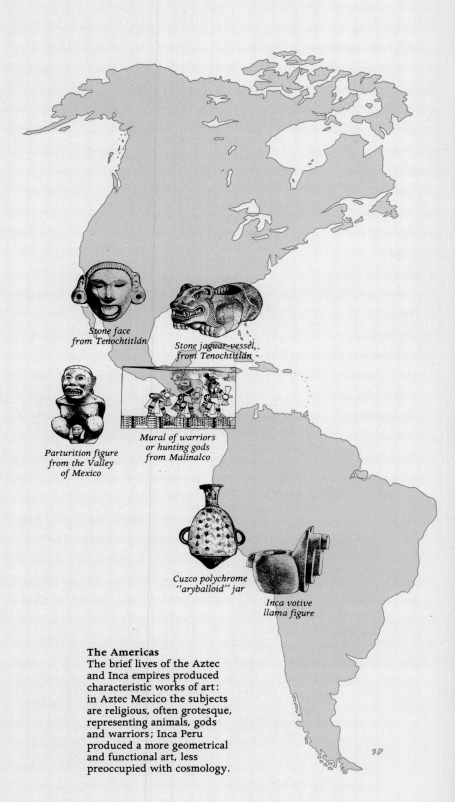

Stone face from Tenochtitlán

Stone jaguar-vessel from Tenochtitlán

Parturition figure from the Valley of Mexico

Mural of warriors or hunting gods from Malinalco

Cuzco polychrome "aryballoid" jar

Inca votive llama figure

The Americas
The brief lives of the Aztec and Inca empires produced characteristic works of art: in Aztec Mexico the subjects are religious, often grotesque, representing animals, gods and warriors; Inca Peru produced a more geometrical and functional art, less preoccupied with cosmology.

Eastern Europe
Drawing on the renewed Greek influences of the 14th century, Russian icon-painting reached a peak in the work of Andrey Rublev, who moved the centre of Russian art to Moscow from the flourishing School of Novgorod.

Western Europe
See pages 244-245.

Near East
In the Ottoman Near East, the potters of Isnik experimented with the blue and white wares which would lead to the supreme polychromes of later times, while in Timurid Persia an exquisite miniature-painting tradition flourished.

Far East
In both China and Japan, painting combined Zen inspiration with a close attention to the masters of the past. Zen Buddhism lay too behind the growth of the Japanese Noh theatre.

Battle between Novgorod and Suzdal, icon

Old Testament Trinity, detail of icon by Andrey Rublev

Manuscript illumination of historical scene

Blue and white Ming vase

Tou-t'sai Ming jar

Life on the River by Tai Chin

Winter Landscape by Sesshu

Studio of the Three Worthies by Shubun

Poet on a Mountain by Shen Chou

The Three Teachers by Josetsu

Japanese Noh mask

Geese beside a Snowy Bank by Lu Chi

Persian manuscript illumination

Isnik mosque lamp

Stone screen of window, from the mosque of Sidi Sa'id at Ahmadabad, Gujerat

India
Muslim influences combined with indigenous Jain and Hindu traditions, particularly in Gujerat, to create a delicate style of architectural decoration, in the aftermath of the Delhi Sultanate.

Head of Buddha from Ayut'ia

Majapahit figure in volcanic stone

Ivory mask from Benin

Terracotta male torso from Igbo' Laga

South-East Asia
The rise of the Thai kingdom in Siam was expressed in the decoration of Ayut'ia, its capital; elsewhere the spread of Islam was detrimental to Hindu and Buddhist art.

Africa
Benin, in modern Nigeria, was the seat of a high culture responsible for extraordinary sculptural work in ivory and cast bronze, as well as for fine pottery.

Polynesian statue re-erected with topknot

Oceania
Many of the 600 colossal statues produced on Easter Island are thought to date from this century. Raised on *ahus* (stone platforms) across the island they are highly stylized, and of unknown devotional significance.

Western European Art

In European art of the fifteenth century, the great divide between North and South showed as yet few signs of closing. In Flanders, painting continued within the broad tradition of the miniaturists and manuscript illuminators of Valois France, while the sculptors of Germany, well into the sixteenth century, were recognizably the successors, in their intense emotionalism, of the thirteenth-century masters of the Rhineland. Meanwhile, the classical revival in late-medieval Italy had become a full-blown Renaissance. From very early in the fifteenth century, the paintings of Masaccio and the sculptures of Ghiberti and Donatello opened the door to a new form of art characterized by its mathematically flawless perspectives and perfectly in tune with the contemporary classicizing architecture of Brunelleschi, Alberti, and their followers.

The art of Flanders came to full maturity in the work of Rogier van der Weyden, the contemporary of Jan van Eyck, and their successor Hugo van der Goes. These painters, taking instruction in total composition from the Italians, infused their art with a dramatic urgency which gave new life to the altogether too perfect realism of their contemporaries in the Flemish School.

Britain
Although architecture and architectural decoration were at a peak, in other fields only the minor arts were much in evidence. Alabaster carvings were being made in the Nottingham area, for the mass-market as well as for export.

The Dunstable
swan jewel

Painted
English alabaster
of St Michael

Alabaster head of
St John the Baptist

Low Countries
Flemish painting, closely related to French manuscript illumination, flourished in the Burgundian lands.

Descent from the Cross
by Rogier van der Weyden

Right wing of the
Mérode Altarpiece
by the Master
of Flémalle

Ghent Altarpiece
by Hubert and
Jan van Eyck

Giovanni Arnolfini
and his Wife
by Jan van Eyck

Shrine of St Ursula
by Hans Memlinc

Detail of the
Portinari Altarpiece
by Hugo van der Goes

Detail of calendar miniature
(July) from the
Très Riches Heures
du Duc de Berri

Tomb of Philippe Pot,
probably by Antoine
le Moiturier

Burgundian
tomb carving
by Juan de la Huerta

South Rose window,
Sens Cathedral

Mourner from
the tomb of
Philip the Bold

Spain
Altarpieces were the most sumptuous features of most Spanish church interiors, with artists from all over Europe coming to work in Spain: the altarpiece at Seville was designed by a Netherlands sculptor, Pieter Dancart.

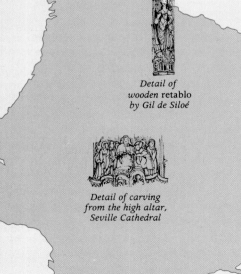
Detail of
wooden retablo
by Gil de Siloé

Detail of carving
from the high altar,
Seville Cathedral

France
France developed a panel-painting tradition of its own, though its miniature-painting and tomb-sculpture were largely shared with Burgundy. The stained glass integral to the "Flamboyant" style, like the great rose window at Sens, gave scope for the work of the Gothic glass-artists.

*Head of the
Mourning Virgin
by Tilman Riemenschneider*

*Goblet in the shape
of a miniature
walled city*

*Wooden sculpture of
St George and the dragon
by Jörg Syrlin*

*Bust of Pythagoras
from Ulm Minster
by Jörg Syrlin*

Germany
Germany's Late Gothic
sculpture is marked by
technical virtuosity and by
the emphatic emotionalism of
artists like Riemenschneider.
Metalwork flourished,
especially in the South,
alongside wood- and stone-
carving.

*The Last Supper
by Leonardo da Vinci*

*Remains of altarpiece
by Antonello da Messina*

Italy
The classical revival, with its
emphasis on mathematical
relationships, led to a mastery
of perspective in painting, and
in sculpture to the sophisticated
relief-work of Donatello and
Ghiberti—the opening stages of
a new, Renaissance art.

*Portrait of an Old Man
by Fra Filippo Lippi*

*Panel from the
First Baptistery Doors
by Ghiberti*

*Heraldic lion
of Florence
by Donatello*

*Enamelled
terracotta roundel
by Luca della Robbia*

*Raphael's house
designed by Bramante*

*The Resurrection
by Piero della Francesca*

*The Triumph of Death,
artist unknown*

	Events and developments	People	Technology
Western Europe	End of *Reconquista* with capture of Granada (1492). End of 100 Years War between England and France (1453). Wars of the Roses, England (1455-85). Birth of Renaissance in Italy. Start of European expansion; da Gama's sea-route via Cape to India, voyages of Columbus and Cabot to Americas. Rise of national monarchies.	Leonardo da Vinci, Florentine artist (1452-1519). Lorenzo de' Medici, Florentine ruler 1469-92. Michelangelo Buonarroti, Italian artist (1475-1564). Prince Henry the Navigator, Portuguese maritime explorer (1394-1460).	Development of military technology: Conrad Kyeser's *Bellifortis*. Development of navigational techniques and vessels. Movable type applied by Gutenburg at Mainz (1447). Efficient clocks common by 1500.
Far East	Resurgence of China during period of relative security under Ming: renewed population growth. Expeditions (up to 1433) of great fleets under Cheng Ho, to India and Persian Gulf. Cultural brilliance in Japan under Yoshimasa; establishment of tea ceremony. Decline of Ashikaga shogunate; Onin War (1467-77).	Yung-lo, Chinese Emperor 1403-24. Hsüan-te, Chinese Emperor 1426-35. Yoshimasa, 8th Ashikaga shogun 1443-73. Ch'eng-hua, Chinese Emperor 1465-87.	Experiments in printing in Korea: use of movable type. Introduction of new overglaze enamelling technique under Ch'eng-hua: high peak of pottery technology.
South-East Asia	Burma and Cambodia in decline: expansion of Siam. Check of Majapahit revival in Java by spread of Islam.	Trailok, Siamese ruler 1448-88.	
India	Division of India into numerous dynasties. Rise of Lodis at Delhi. Independence of Malwa (1392-1531) and Jaunpur (1394-1479). Prosperity of Gujerat under Muslim Rajput dynasty (1396-1572). Ahmadabad developed as capital by Ahmad Shah, Champanir by Mahmud Beghara. Decline of Hindu empire of Vijayanagar.	Ibrahim, King of Jaunpur 1400-40. Hushang Shah, King of Malwa 1406-35. Ahmad Shah, King of Gujerat 1459-1511. Bahlol Lodi, King of Delhi 1451-89.	
Near East	Damascus and Baghdad conquered by Tamerlane (1401); reconstruction of Ottoman Empire under Mehemmed I. Conquest of Greece, Crimea, Albania, Trebizond, together with capture of Constantinople by Mehemmed II (1453). End of Byzantine Empire. 1st Turco-Venetian war (1463-79); 2nd war (1499-1503).	Constantine XI, last Byzantine Emperor 1448-53. Mehemmed II, greatest ruler of Ottoman Empire 1451-81.	
Eastern Europe	End of 250 years of Mongol domination in Russia. All Russian lands ruled by Muscovy. Hungary dominant power in central Europe under Corvinus. Victory of Poles over Teutonic Knights at Tannenberg (1410). Conquest of Serbia by Ottoman Turks (1459).	Sigismund, Holy Roman Emperor 1433-37. Janos Hunyadi, Hungarian leader against Turks (d. 1456). Matthias Corvinus, King of Hungary 1458-90. Ivan III (the Great), Russian Grand Duke 1462-1505.	
Africa	Beginning of European enterprise and exploration in Africa. Capture of Ceuta, Morocco, by Portuguese (1415); discovery of Congo estuary (1482). Da Gama's voyage up East African coast to India and back to Portugal (1497-9). Arrival at Mogadishu of Chinese admiral Cheng Ho.	Sonni Ali, Songhai leader ?1464-92. Askia Muhammad, Ali's successor 1493-1528.	
The Americas	Rapid expansion of Aztec and Inca empires, based on conquest. Destruction of Mayapán (1451), abandonment of Chichén Itzá and Uxmal. Decimation of population due to hurricane (1467) and yellow fever (1482). Discovery of South American mainland by Columbus (1498); discovery of North America by Cabot (1497).	Montezuma I, Aztec ruler ?1436-64. Huayna Capac, greatest Inca conqueror 1487-1525.	High degree of development of engineering and architectural skills among Aztecs, Mayas, and Incas. Era of Inca road-building.

Religion	Architecture	Art and music	Literature and learning
Great Schism healed; unity restored to Western Christendom at Council of Constance (1414-18). Trial of Savonarola, Italian reformer, for sedition and heresy; hanged (1498). Inquisition in Spain; organized by Torquemada, Grand Inquisitor. *The Imitation of Christ*, religious treatise, ascribed to mystic Thomas à Kempis.	S. Maria Novella; Foundling Hospital; Palazzo Pitti, Florence. Brussels town hall. Seville Cathedral. King's College chapel, Cambridge; Guildhall, London; St George's chapel, Windsor.	Botticelli's *Primavera*; da Vinci's *Last Supper*; Michelangelo's *Pieta*; Durer's *Apocalypse* woodcuts; Van Eyck's Ghent Altarpiece. Development of counterpoint by Dunstable, English composer.	Lyric poems by Villon. Malory's *Morte d'Arthur*. Spread of humanism through writings of Erasmus. Printing of Gutenberg Bible. Foundation of Aldine press by Manutius, Italian scholar. Translations by Caxton, first English printer.
Revival in Japan of native Shinto faith; further spread of Zen Buddhism. Return to traditional Confucian outlook in China, with belief in emperor as "Son of Heaven", mediating between heaven and mankind.	China: rebuilding of Peking by Yung-lo—the Forbidden City, with its palace enclosure. Japan: Silver Pavilion (Ginkakuji), Kyoto.	Jao-chou porcelains and bronze work under Hsüan-te. Development of naturalistic painting style. Scholar-painters in China, such as Tai Chin and Shen Chou. Tradition of Zen priest-painters in Japan, such as Sesshu (1419-1506).	Cultural flowering of Yi dynasty, Korea. Invention of alphabetic script (*han'gul*). *Koryo sa*, history of Korea's Koryo dynasty. Sponsorship of Chinese encyclopedic work in many volumes, *Yung-lo Ta-tien*, by Yung-lo (1403-1407).
Continuing strength of Buddhism in Siam. Spread of Islam, notably in Malay archipelago.	Many brick-and-stucco stupas at Siam's capital, Ayut'ia.		
Destruction of Hindu temples and conversions to Islam forced by King of Kashmir in 1416.	Mosques of Sharqui dynasty, Jaunpur. Friday Mosque, Ahmadabad; Great Mosque, Champanir, Gujerat.		
After fall of Constantinople, conversion of St Sophia Basilica into mosque by Turks. Declaration of crusades against Turks by Western Church.	Mausoleum of Tamerlane, Samarkand; Mehemmed I's Green Mosque, Bursa; Murad II's "Three-balconied Mosque", Edirne; Mehemmed II's "Tiled Kiosk" garden pavilion, Istanbul. Palace at Mistra.	Byzantine schools of painting at Constantinople, Macedonia, Crete.	Cultural revival in Byzantium despite decline of Byzantine Empire: outstanding scholars, theologians, historians, such as Bessarion and Phrantzes. Mistra in Peloponnese centre of thought and learning.
Moscow ("Third Rome") successor in Orthodox leadership after fall of Constantinople to Turks (1453). Movement of reform in Bohemia under Jan Hus, a follower of Wycliffe's doctrines. Trial of Hus for heresy, burnt (1415): cause of war between Bohemian Hussites and Holy Roman Empire (1419-36).	Kremlin, Moscow, rebuilt with assistance of Italian architects; completion of new Cathedral of the Dormition (1479), Moscow, Russia. Church of the Virgin, Kalenic; Voronet Monastery Church, Rumania.	Novgorod narrative painting: *Battle between Novgorod and Suzdal*. Icons of Andrey Rublev (c. 1370-1430), notably the *Old Testament Trinity*. Veit Stoss' carved altar, St Mary's, Cracow.	Corvinus patron of Renaissance learning in Hungary: his *Bibliotheca Corvina* among finest libraries in Europe. University of Buda founded (c. 1475).
Expansion of Christian Ethiopia at expense of pagan south. Dominance of Islam in West and East Africa.	Conical tower and girdle-wall, Great Zimbabwe. Rebuilding of Great Mosque, Kilwa; Jangwani Mosque, Kilwa. Portuguese fort, Elmina, Gold Coast: first of series of coastal forts.		
Aztecs' extensive system of human sacrifice, based on worship of god of war, Huitzilopochtli.	Inca city of Machu Picchu. Great temple to Aztec god of war, Huitzilopochtli.	Production of Chimu-influenced Inca ceramics at Cuzco ("Cuzco Polychrome"). Paintings and sculptures of Aztecs.	Aztecs and Mayas, and to lesser extent Incas, accomplished in mathematics and astronomy. Evolution of picture writing by Aztecs. Development of accurate calendar by Mayas.

Index

Photographic Sources & Acknowledgments

(B = Bottom; C = Centre; L = Left; R = Right; T = Top.)
Front cover: Sonia Halliday and Laura Lushington
Back cover: Michael Holford

Hallam Ashley:
213 CL
Asian Art Museum of San Francisco, The Avery Brundage Collection, Gift of the deYoung Museum Society:
121
Bibliothèque Nationale, Paris:
76 TL (Weidenfeld and Nicolson archives); 76 TR (Cooper-Bridgeman); 76 CL (Weidenfeld and Nicolson archives); 76 B (Cooper-Bridgeman); 100 (Weidenfeld and Nicolson archives); 101 CR; 102 T; 102 B.
Bibliothèque Publique de Dijon:
57 B (photo Minirel Creation)
Bildarchiv Foto Marburg:
4 (Hamlyn Group); 235 B.
Bildarchiv Preussicher Kulturbesitz/Staatliche Museen, Berlin:
105 BL
Bodleian Library, Oxford:
9BR; 16; 56CL; 71T; 114T; 117 C; 159 TCR; 159 TR; 159 BL; 159 CR; 159 BR; 166 T; 167 BR; 212.
Erwin Böhm, Mainz:
122T; 122B.
Boston Museum of Fine Arts:
128 T (Werner Forman Archives)
Boudot-Lamotte:
113 C (Hamlyn Group)
By courtesy of trustees of British Library:
116 TL
By courtesy of trustees of British Museum:
58 T (Werner Forman Archives); 105 BR; 106 B; 210 T (Hamlyn Group).
John Bulmer:
11 BL
Bury Peerless:
18; 19 T; 19 BL; 34 B; 60; 74 B; 120 T.
Caisse Nationale des Monuments Historiques (SPADEM), Paris:
40 B; 63 TR.
Camera Press Ltd:
124 T; 146 TR; 223.
Christchurch, Oxford:
163 B
Cooper-Bridgeman:
97 T; 97BR; 175 T; 175 B; 198; 209 BR; 224.
Crown Copyright reproduced with permission of the Controller of Her Majesty's Stationery Office:
146 TL
Douglas Dickins:
78 B
Dunbarton Oaks:
199 TR (Hamlyn Group)
Foto Ritter:
73 BR
Giraudon:
1; 65; 68 BL; 73 TR; 73 C; 73 BL; 78 TR (Hamlyn Group); 101 LT; 104; 108 BL (Hamlyn Group); 160; 164 BL; 164 BL; 165; 167 T; 213 T; 217 T; 217 CR; 217 BL; 217 BR; 220 BL; 232 T.
Susan Griggs:
11 BR (photo Marcus Brook); 94-5 (photo Adam Woolfit).
Sonia Halliday and Laura Lushington:
7 B; 10-1 (photo Jane Taylor); 19 BC; 21 TL; 23 BR; 62 B; 68 T; 68 C; 68 BC; 101 B; 111; 112; 159 TL; 159 TCL; 164 BR; 168 (all); 172 TL (photo F. H. C. Birch); 206-7 (all); 213 BL; 227 B.
Hamlyn Group:
78 TL; 126 TL; 154 T; 181; 222 T.
Robert Harding Associates:
36 T; 67; 75 R; 107; 109; 162 B (photo John G. Ross); 179 B; 180; 173 TR.
Hirmer Fotoarchiv:
23 T; 105 T; 113 R; 169 BR (Hamlyn Group).
Michael Holford:
9 BL; 26-7 B; 64 BL (photo Jerry Clyde); 76 CR; 77; 108 CR; 113 L; 131 TR; 131 BL; 131 CL; 131 CR; 131 BR; 131 BC; 142-3; 146 BL; 147; 164 TR; 173 TL (photo Ann Mowlem); 217 CL; 226.
Holle Verlag:
23 BL
Angelo Hornak:
8-9; 13 BL; 54-5; 232 B.

A. F. Kersting:
12-3; 14-5; 41 T; 114 BR; 156; 162 T; 229 T.
Landesmuseum, Stuttgart:
199 TL (Hamlyn Group)
Larousse:
81 R (Hamlyn Group)
The Macquitty International Collection:
219
Mansell Collection:
25 C; 56 TL; 56 BL; 59 T; 97 BL; 103; 117 B; 145; 149 TL; 157 T; 196 C; 196 B; 200; 204 T; 225 L; 231 T; 237 T; 237 C.
Collection of Marquis Kurada:
126 TR (Hamlyn Group)
MAS, Barcelona:
196 T; 236 T.
John Massey-Stewart:
203 BL (Hamlyn Group)
Musée de Dijon:
235 T
Musées Royaux, Brussels:
73 TL
National Gallery, London:
158 B; 216; 220 T; 221.
National Gallery, Prague:
169 TR
National Museum, Tokyo:
127 (Hamlyn Group)
Collection of the National Palace Museum, Taipei, Taiwan, Republic of China:
30 T; 31; 98 T; 98 B.
Nelson-Atkins Gallery Museum, Kansas City (Nelson Fund):
126 CL
Novosti Press Agency:
24 T; 38 T; 69; 110 T; 171 T; 171 B; 202 L; 202 R; 203 T; 203 CL; 203 BR.
Orion Press, Japan:
176 R (Hamlyn Group)
Osterreichische Nationalbibliothek, Vienna:
2; 161.
Percival David Foundation:
209 T; 209 CR.
Photoresources:
26 T; 27 TR; 27 CT; 27 CB; 40 T; 146 BR.
Picturepoint Ltd:
105 C; 173 BL; 173 BR.
Pierpont Morgan Library, New York:
234 T
Public Record Office:
25 B
Sakamoto Photo Research Lab., Tokyo:
32 B (Hamlyn Group); 80 BL; 82 B (Hamlyn Group); 126 B; 129; 176 L; 222 B.
Scala, Florence:
22 (Hamlyn Group); 37 BL; 68 BR (Hamlyn Group); 101 CL; 105 CL; 115 T; 115 B; 116 TR; 116 B; 150 T; 150-1 B; 151 TL; 151 BR (Hamlyn Group); 154 CL; 154 BL; 155 T; 154-5 B; 157 B; 199 B; 213 BR; 220 CL; 220 BR; 230 B; 231 B (Weidenfeld and Nicolson archives).
Ronald Sheridan:
6-7; 151 TR; 169 TL; 169 BL; 172 B.
Courtesy of the Smithsonian Institution, Freer Gallery of Art, Washington DC:
108 TR; 218 T; 218 B.
Snark International:
21 TR; 96.
Wim Swaan:
33 T (Hamlyn Group)
Tokugawa Museum, Nagoya:
80 T (Hamlyn Group)
Victoria and Albert Museum, London:
72 T (Michael Holford); 72 B (Cooper-Bridgeman); 108 C; 108 BR (Cooper-Bridgeman); 158 T; 209 BL; 209 CL.
Weidenfeld and Nicolson Archives:
101 TR
Werner Forman Archives:
13 BR; 19 BR; 42 T; 43 B; 79 B; 80 BR; 108 TL; 131 TL.
Yan, Toulouse:
70 B
ZEFA, London:
194-5

Dorling Kindersley would like to thank the following for their special assistance: Janis Beavon; Michael Burman of F. E. Burman; Jackie Douglas; Lesley Gilbert; Caroline Lucas; Phil Baskerville, John Foster and Mike Snaith of MS Filmsetting; Negs Photographic Services Ltd.; Frederick Ford and Michael Pilley of Radius; Martin Rose; Shirley Willis; Adolf Wood.

Picture Researcher
Caroline Lucas

Artists
David Ashby
David Baird
Linda Broad
Nigel Fradgely
Vana Haggerty
Nicholas Hall
Richard Jacobs
Sally Launder
George Thompson
Shirley Willis

Cartography
Arka Graphics
Eugene Fleury

Calligraphy
Thomas Perkins